TO THE GATES OF ATLANTA

MERCER
UNIVERSITY PRESS

Endowed by
TOM WATSON BROWN
and
THE WATSON-BROWN FOUNDATION, INC.

TO GATES OF ATLANTA

From Kennesaw Mountain to Peach Tree Creek

July 1–July 19, 1864

Robert D. Jenkins, Sr.

MERCER UNIVERSITY PRESS
MACON, GEORGIA

MUP/ H902

© 2015 by Mercer University Press
Published by Mercer University Press
1400 Coleman Avenue
Macon, Georgia 31207

9 8 7 6 5 4 3 2

Books published by Mercer University Press are printed on acid-free paper that
meets the requirements of the American National Standard for Information
Sciences—Permanence of Paper for Printed Library Materials.

ISBN978-0-88146-527-3
Cataloging-in-Publication Data is available from the Library of Congress

To my mother, Joy Jenkins. All my love and adoration.

CONTENTS

ACKNOWLEDGMENTS

I am indebted to a number of people who graciously provided invaluable information to me for this work. I am sure that in my desire to name them all I will inevitably miss someone, but I do thank and appreciate each and every person whom I have met during this project for their kind and generous contributions to this work. Thank you to the late Franklin W. Garrett, Wilbur G. Kurtz, Allen P. Jullian, and William R. Scaife who blazed the trail for future students of the Georgia Campaign. While these men have passed on, they each gave over a half-century of their lives to research, writing, touring and teaching on the Civil War in Georgia.

To Charlie Crawford of the Georgia Battlefields Association and Gordon Jones of the Atlanta History Center, thank you. Your leadership and direction for your groups are matched only by your passion and knowledge of Atlanta's rich history. Thank you for giving so freely of your time, wisdom, and critique to me and for continuing to light the path for future generations of Civil War students. Thank you to Steve Davis and Richard McMurry for daring to question established thought on Georgia's Civil War history and for kindly sharing your knowledge and findings with me.

To Chief Historian James Ogden of the Chickamauga-Chattanooga National Parks, Dr. William Blackman, of Dalton, Ga., the late Bob Lurate from Lexington, Va. and Dr. Timothy Smith and Greg Biggs of Tennessee, thank you for encouraging me. To Grady Howell and the staff at the Mississippi Department of Archives and History, thank you for helping me find the most obscure records and resources. Nobody does it better than you folks. To The Atlanta History Center, Kenan Research Center, Mercer University, Georgia Southern University, the University of Georgia, Ole Miss. (a/k/a The University of Mississippi), Mississippi State University, The University of Southern Mississippi, The University of North Carolina at Chapel Hill, Emory University, The University of Wisconsin, and Louisiana State University, and to the National Archives, and the Archives of Alabama, Georgia, Mississippi, Tennessee, Wisconsin, and every county, city and local library and museum along the way, and the staffs, libraries and special collections departments, thank you.

To Joan and Murray Scripture of Greenville, South Carolina, who have tirelessly edited my poor English skills into a polished work, thank you. It is a blessing to have friends who read, re-read and re-re-read just to make sure that it is the best work that it can be. So, thank you to Joan for editing my grammar, and Murray for editing the content, to make my rambling thoughts and nonsense into some kind of sense. Any errors in grammar or content which remain are strictly my own.

To my mother and late father, Joy and Bob Jenkins, and to my extended family of Grandparents, Aunts and Uncles, many of whom have passed on, thank you for giving me such a rich and loving upbringing with all the support that a child and young adult could ever hope for, and with the encouragement to inspire me to fulfill any dream, thank you. Thank you, also, for teaching me the importance of history and for allowing me to explore it. Mom, I dedicate this book to you. To my children, Katie Beth and Robby, who have endured countless hours of Civil War trips and talks, thank you for your love, patience and support. God has blessed me with two wonderful children and I am truly grateful for each of you.

To my friend Dave Helton of Dalton, Ga., who turns my poor sketches into beautiful maps that can be easily followed by viewers wishing to retrace the movements of units in the action depicted in the book, thank you. Thank you, Dave, for putting your incredible computer and design skills to use in my books, and thank you for your friendship.

To Shari Halliburton who burned the midnight oil to assist me with last minute revisions and edits to ensure that this book would make it to the press on time and as accurately and errorless as possible, thank you.

Finally, to Marc Jolley, director of Mercer University Press, and to Marsha Luttrell and all of the fine folks of Mercer University Press, thank you for your love, support, and encouragement. Thank you, Marc, for your timeless efforts in making this work as detailed and effective as hopefully it will prove to be for the reader. The shelves of our nation's rich history continue to be blessed by the constant devotion that you and everyone at the press give, and we are all blessed and enriched by your dedication and commitment to preserving and spreading our history.

"The Transfer" by Wilbur G. Kurtz
Courtesy of the Atlanta History Center

Williams Kentucky Brigade at Nancy Creek, July 18, 1864
Painting by Wilbur G. Kurtz

General John (Cerro Gordo) Williams

Henry Irby's Store and Tavern at Buckhead
Sketch by Wilbur G. Kurtz

Buckhead Tavern
Sketch by Wilbur G. Kurtz

Howell's Mill

Moore's Mill

Federals crossing the Chattahoochee near Roswell.
Courtesy Library of Congress

William Brownlow's naked Troopers crossing the Chattahoochee River.

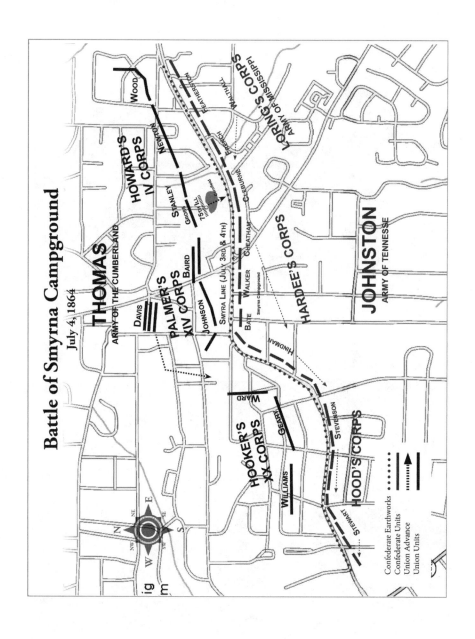

Battle of Smyrna Campground
July 4, 1864

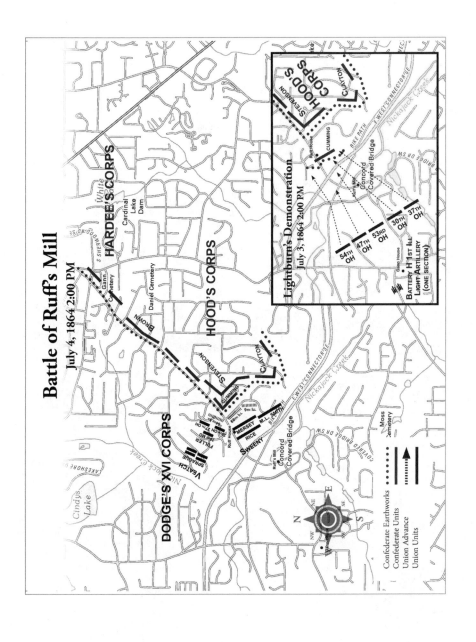

Battle of Ruff's Mill
July 4, 1864 2:00 PM

HARDEE'S CORPS

HOOD'S CORPS

DODGE'S XVI CORPS

White

Cardinal
Lake
Dam

Gann
Cemetery

Daniel Cemetery

BROWN

STEVENSON

CUMMING

CLAYTON

SPRAGUE
FULLER
VEATCH

MERSEY
RICE
M.L. SMITH
SWEENY

Ruff's Mill
Concord
Covered Bridge

Nickajack Creek

E. WEST CONNECTOR SE

S. SHERWOOD RD SE

Cindys
Lake

LAKESHORE DR

Moss
Cemetery

COVERED BRIDGE DR SW

Confederate Earthworks
Confederate Units
Union Advance
Union Units

N NW NE W E SW SE S

Lightburn's Demonstration
July 3, 1864 2:00 PM

HOOD'S CORPS

STEVENSON

CLAYTON

CUMMING

Ruff House

BIKE PATH

E. WEST CONNECTOR SE

Nickajack Creek

Concord
Covered Bridge

Ruff Mill

BRIDGE DR SW

Gann House

54TH
OH

47TH
OH

53RD
OH

30TH
OH

37TH
OH

BATTERY H 1ST ILL
LIGHT ARTILLERY
(ONE SECTION)

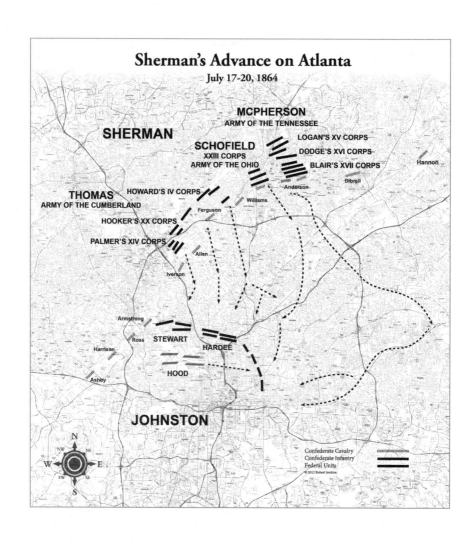

Sherman's Advance on Atlanta
July 17-20, 1864

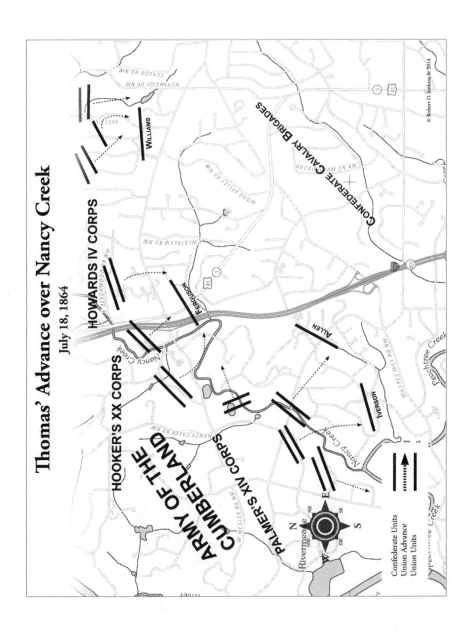

Thomas' Advance over Nancy Creek
July 18, 1864

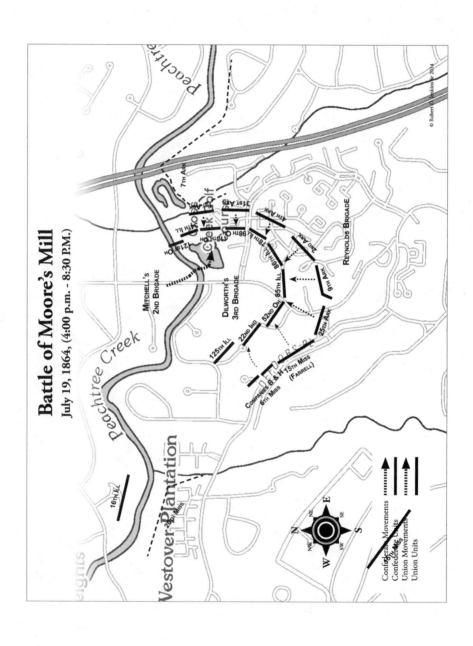

Battle of Moore's Mill
July 19, 1864, (4:00 p.m. - 8:30 P.M.)

Peachtree Creek

Peachtree Creek

Vestover Plantation

16TH ILL.

29TH MISS.

MITCHELL'S 2ND BRIGADE

DILWORTH'S 3RD BRIGADE

125TH ILL.

22ND IND.

COMPANIES B & H
6TH MISS

15TH MISS (FARRELL)

52ND OHIO

85TH ILL.

25TH ARK.

9TH ARK.

2ND ARK.

86TH ILL.

110TH ILL.

98TH OH.

4TH ARK.

REYNOLDS BRIGADE

31ST ARK.

7TH ARK.

1ST ARK.

34TH ILL.

121ST OH.

113TH ILL.

N NE NNE
W E
S SE SW

Confederate Movements
Confederate Units
Union Movements
Union Units

© Robert D. Jenkins 2014

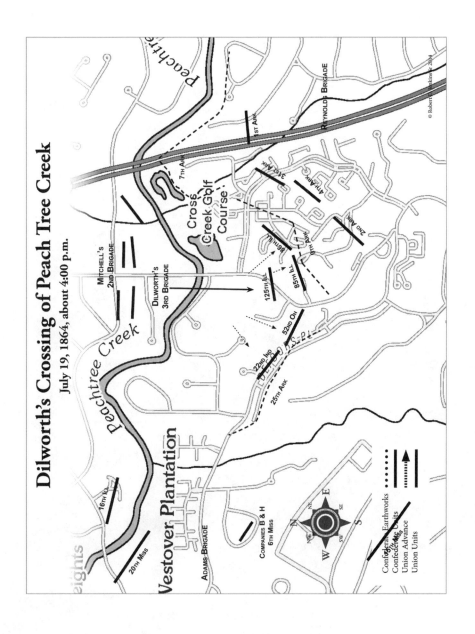

Dilworth's Crossing of Peach Tree Creek
July 19, 1864, about 4:00 p.m.

Peachtre

1ST ARK

REYNOLDS' BRIGADE

© Robert Jenkins, 2004

7TH ARK

3RD ARK

4TH ARK

Cross Creek Golf Course

2ND ARK

86TH ILL

9TH ARK

MITCHELL'S 2ND BRIGADE

85TH ILL

DILWORTH'S 3RD BRIGADE

125TH ILL

Peachtree Creek

52ND OH

DILWORTH'S PL.

22ND IND

25TH ARK

16TH ILL

Vestover Plantation

20TH MISS

ADAMS' BRIGADE

COMPANIES B & H
6TH MISS

N
NE
NW
E
W
SE
SW
S

Confederate Earthworks
Confederate Units
Union Advance
Union Units

eights

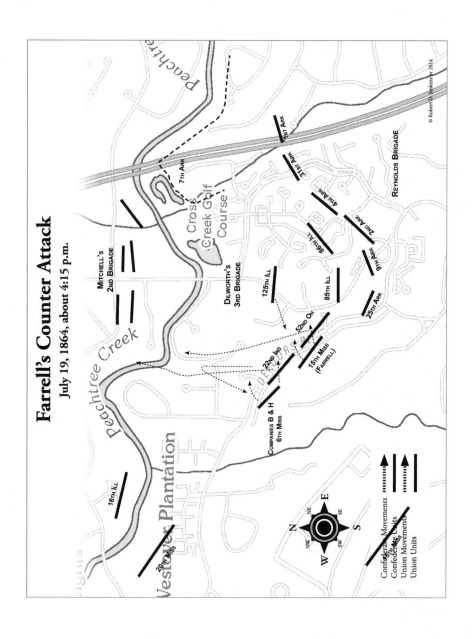

Farrell's Counter Attack

July 19, 1864, about 4:15 p.m.

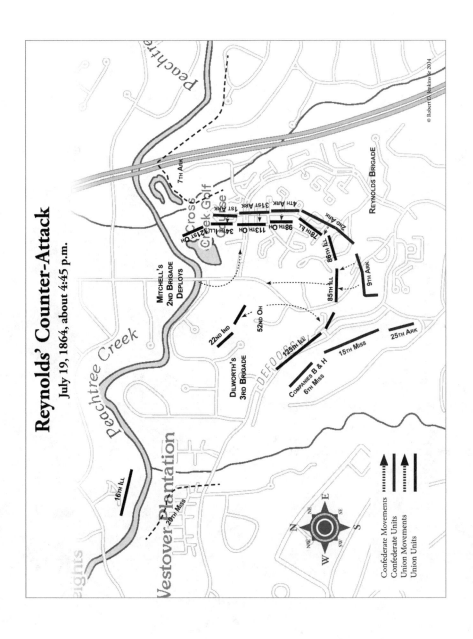

Reynolds' Counter-Attack
July 19, 1864, about 4:45 p.m.

Peachtree

Peachtree Creek

Heights

Westover Plantation

16TH ILL

20TH MISS

MITCHELL'S
2ND BRIGADE
DEPLOYS

Cyclos G

Creek Golf
House

7TH ARK

34TH ILL / 121ST OH

113TH OH

98TH OH

78TH ILL

1ST ARK

31ST ARK

4TH ARK

2ND ARK

REYNOLDS BRIGADE

86TH IL

85TH ILL

9TH ARK

22ND IND

52ND OH

DILWORTH'S
3RD BRIGADE

D E F O O G

125TH ILL

COMPANIES B & H
6TH MISS

15TH MISS

25TH ARK

Confederate Movements
Confederate Units
Union Movements
Union Units

N   NE
NW   E
W   SE
SW   S

© Robert D. Jenkins Sr. 2014

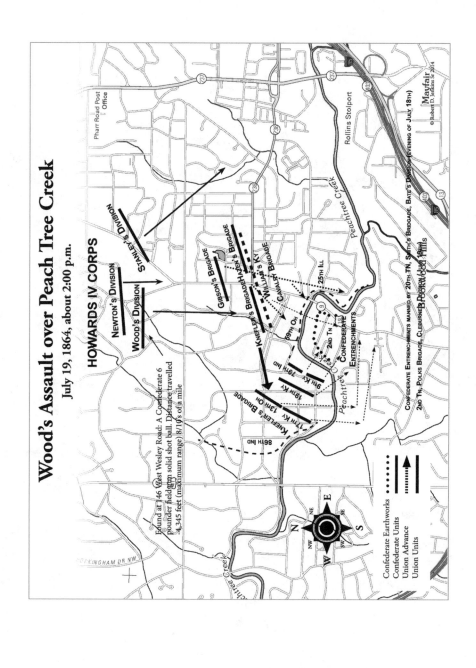

Wood's Assault over Peach Tree Creek

July 19, 1864, about 2:00 p.m.

HOWARDS IV CORPS

STANLEY'S DIVISION

NEWTON'S DIVISION

WOOD'S DIVISION

GIBSON'S BRIGADE

KNEFLER'S BRIGADE

HAZEN'S BRIGADE

WILLIM'S KY

CAVALRY BRIGADE

25TH ILL

59TH OH

79TH IND

19TH KY

2ND TN

9TH KY

KNEFLER'S BRIGADE

17TH KY

13TH OH

84TH IND

CONFEDERATE ENTRENCHMENTS

Peachtree Creek

Peachtree Creek

Phar Road Post Office

Rollins Stolport

Mayfair

©Robert D. Jenkins Sr 2014

CONFEDERATE ENTRENCHMENTS MANNED BY 20TH TN., SMITH'S BRIGADE, BATE'S DIVISION (EVENING OF JULY 18TH)

2ND TN. POLKS BRIGADE, CLEBURNE'S DIVISION (JULY 19TH)

BUCKINGHAM DR NW

HOPKINGHAM DR NW

Found at 146 West Wesley Road: A Confederate 6 pounder field gun solid shot ball. Distance travelled 4,345 feet (maximum range) 8/110's of a mile

Confederate Earthworks

Confederate Units

Union Advance Units

Union Units

N NE
NW
W   E
SW   SE
S

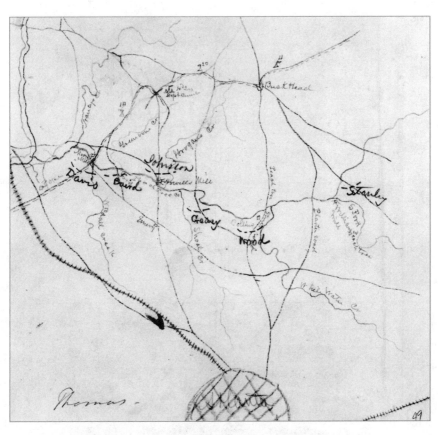

Sketch prepared by General Thomas on evening of July 19, 1864,
to show Sherman his troop positions.
Courtesy of Official Atlas.

85th Illinois National Flag captured at Moore's Mill, July 19, 1864

85th Illinois Regimental Flag captured at Moore's Mill, July 19, 1864

INTRODUCTION

The fourth summer of the war brought destruction and despair to the doorsteps of the citizens of Georgia as the nation's great struggle reached deep into her lands. For three years, most Georgians remained insulated from the war's ravages. With a false sense of security the people of the "Empire State of the South" continued to work their fields, factories, and mills producing large quantities of war materials, clothing, and food. No one in Georgia believed that the Federal army could penetrate the Rebel defenses of North Georgia, sustain a supply line of hundreds of miles back to Nashville, Tennessee, and survive in the extreme heat of the Deep South while attempting to press an offensive into the heart of the Confederacy.

Richmond was, of course, the capital of the Confederacy, but the bustling little city of Atlanta had rapidly become an important center of transportation, industry, and commerce. After the losses of New Orleans, Vicksburg, and the cities of Tennessee (other than Richmond), Atlanta became the most important city in the South. Atlanta was a vital transportation center as rail lines tied the city to every region of the South. Without possession of Atlanta, any Confederate movement of men and material, or communication via telegraph, would become difficult if not impossible. Without Atlanta, entire regions of the Southern nation would be cut off from the rest of the country.

In July 1864 General William Tecumseh Sherman's legions drew within sight of the "Gate City," a fitting nickname to the young city. Falling back in the wake of Sherman's advances was a tired but proud army under the direction of General Joseph E. Johnston. Not willing to risk a battle that could destroy his outnumbered force, Old Joe Johnston, as he was called, fell back from one defensive position after another. Johnston continued to withdraw rather than risk a decisive battle to prevent Sherman from getting behind him and cutting off his supply line via the Western & Atlantic Railroad, which linked his army with Atlanta. With a force of between 55,000 and 60,000 men, Johnston reasoned that he could not win a battle against a Federal force that averaged between 90,000 and 108,000 men. Instead, he would try to position his force to fight to advantage, either by striking a flank of Sherman's lines so a larger portion of his army could strike a blow against a smaller part of the Federal army, or by enticing Sherman to attack him while his army enjoyed the security of prepared defensive earthworks.

While Johnston's conservative strategy drew the praise of his men, who appreciated their commander's caution with their lives, many Georgians grew anxious that Old Joe never would strike a blow to preserve the Confederacy and protect their farms and their homes. Anxiety was widespread in Richmond where Confederate president Jefferson Davis became increasingly alarmed that Atlanta might be given up without a fight. This was a loss that Davis was unwilling to take, but forcing battle for the fate of Atlanta was a risk Johnston was apparently not willing to make.

The Campaign for Atlanta had begun at Dalton, a small rail junction located in northwest Georgia just three months earlier. Ninety days and ninety miles later, the focus of the campaign was along the banks of the Chattahoochee River as Sherman's men probed for a place to make a crossing over the last natural barrier between them and Atlanta. For Sherman, who had for the most part skillfully maneuvered Johnston out of the mountains of northwest Georgia without forcing a full-scale attack that would have yielded large casualties, Atlanta was a prize worth taking. With it, he could split the heart of the Confederacy and take a vital, war material-producing city from the South. He would also cut off Richmond and the Atlantic coastal states from the Gulf South. Communication between Virginia and Alabama, Mississippi, and Louisiana would be severed. If Atlanta were lost, the resources, war materials, and supplies from the Gulf states and the produce from the rich farm lands and plantations would be denied to Lee's Army of Northern Virginia and all of the Confederate garrisons along the east coast. Moreover, Johnston's army would have a choice: to make a desperate attempt to save Atlanta by coming out of its trenches to fight Sherman's forces in the open, or retreat to avoid encirclement and capture. If Johnston's force fell back, then it would have to move either east toward Augusta, south toward Macon, or southwest toward Columbus. Whichever direction they went, they would be giving up vast territories to the Yankee invaders.

Sherman was not without obstacles, however. His force had been depleted by the combination of almost daily skirmishing and partial battles as portions of the two armies clashed without respite since the opening day of the campaign on 7 May. Sickness and disease had also claimed a number of his men while still more units were mustered out as their terms of enlistment expired. Fortunately for the Sherman, he received reinforcements from units returning to from furloughs and from individuals recovering from wounds and illness. These reinforcements bolstered his numbers throughout the campaign almost in the amount of his losses. Johnston was also losing men to daily fighting and illness, but there were few reinforcements available except for the Georgia militia, a rag-tag outfit of old men and boys. Nicknamed "Joe Brown's Pets" after Georgia governor Joe Brown, who did not permit the unit to fight outside of the state, the Georgia militia would eventually muster some 5,000 men during Atlanta's defense. While this unit could perform guard duty and serve in the trenches around Atlanta, they were of little use in an offensive operation and were no match against Sherman's veterans.

Sherman was also aware of the political climate in the North during summer 1864. War weariness was reaching its height as General Ulysses S. Grant's Army of the Potomac had stalled before Richmond and Petersburg where General Robert E. Lee's Army of Northern Virginia had wrestled Grant's force to a standstill. Each day brought news of more casualties from the war with no appreciable results. It was an election year, and the Democratic Party was planning to mount a campaign on the platform of peace, a platform that resonated in many homes and hearts across the North. To many, continuing to wage war and lose more men to death and disability for the sake of freeing the slaves or maintaining a single nation just wasn't worth it. The Democratic Party promised to end the war and then talk to the Southern states about retaining their slaves and returning to the Union. Many in the North agreed with this strategy.

United States president Abraham Lincoln needed victories. With Grant bogged down in the East, Confederate general Nathan Bedford Forest running loose in Mississippi and west Tennessee, and Southern general Kirby Smith and his forces controlling everything west of the Mississippi River, Lincoln turned to Georgia and Sherman. Perhaps Uncle Billy Sherman, as his boys called him, could provide the news of military success so desperately needed. Perhaps in Georgia the Federal armies could show that the war can be won. Perhaps the taking of Atlanta could be the impetus needed to galvanize support to see the war through and save the Union.

At the Confederate capital of Richmond, Confederate president Jefferson Davis also knew the importance of the 1864 election in the North and the opportunity that it brought him and his fledgling nation. If his armies could only hold out long enough without losing an important city or region or without losing a substantial battle, perhaps the North would give up trying to impose its will on the South. Perhaps Johnston could arrest Sherman's offensive into Georgia by striking a blow somewhere in North Georgia. Perhaps Johnston could carry the war back into Tennessee, which would cause further despair in the North and prove that the Yankees were not able to suppress the South. Perhaps some external event such as foreign recognition by a European power or a Democratic victory in the North's November elections would lead to Independence.

But now, as the shores of the Chattahoochee River came into view of both armies, it became clear to President Davis that time was running out. Davis knew that should Atlanta fall, the Confederacy would fall as well. As long as Johnston continued to fight in the mountains of North Georgia, Atlanta remained secure, but once Sherman was within sight of Atlanta's church spires, the reality that Atlanta was at risk of capture and destruction set in.

The Confederacy could not lose this most important city, reasoned President Davis. The South could not lose this most important army, which held Sherman's superior army in check, reasoned General Johnston. The two leaders had clashed throughout the war because neither Davis nor Johnston trusted the other. The two had also clashed during the first three years of the war because their strategies were incompatible. Now, their conflict would come to a head. Incredulous that Sherman had been allowed to reach this far into the interior of Georgia without committing a battle, Davis knew the Chattahoochee River was the last straw. It would be his general's last stand.

Author's note: I have included quotes from many of the soldiers and civilians. Some of the material quoted contains grammatical and spelling errors. I have included them as originally written.

HOT ENOUGH

Our marches have nearly all been made in the night and many times in the rain and mud, when the darkness was so intense nothing could be seen. Still, the army would drag its slow length along passing over four or five miles during the night. The morning light would reveal the most haggard and hungry looking set of wretches you ever saw, dragging themselves along through mud half a leg deep and numbers of them bare footed, the mud being so adhesive as to pull a shoe to pieces, but on they would go being sure "Old Joe" was taking them to the right place.[1]

After three years of marching and shooting, drilling and digging, and freezing and sweating, the hardened survivors of the Western armies had come to Georgia. They had buried their own at Fort Henry, Fort Donelson, Shiloh, Murfreesboro, and Chattanooga in Tennessee; in Corinth, Grenada, Vicksburg, Holly Springs, Oxford, Coffeeville, Canton, the Delta, Jackson, Lauderdale Springs, and Meridian, in Mississippi; Baton Rouge, Camp Moore, and Greenwell Springs, in Louisiana; Demopolis, and Montevallo, in Alabama; and Chickamauga, Dalton, Resaca, New Hope, Lost Mountain, Noon Day Creek, and Kennesaw, in Georgia. It wasn't hard to follow their trail of graves, which had now led them to the outskirts of Atlanta, to the banks of a river named Chattahoochee where it was downright hot.

On the morning of 2 July, as the Federal army withdrew from the trenches below Kennesaw Mountain where it had clung to and fought from for two weeks before continuing its march toward Atlanta, the heat was already unbearable. One member of the 53rd Indiana noticed that the thermometer read 110 degrees. Yankee soldiers endured the long hot days of

---

[1]Walter A. Rorer to Cousin Susan, 9 June 1864, vertical files, 20th Mississippi Infantry, Carter House Library and Archives, Franklin TN, courtesy T. Glover Roberts, Historian.

the Georgia summer. The heat did not let up that month; a Federal soldier simply recorded in his diary entry for 20 July, "hot enough."[2]

The veterans of both armies were used to summer heat in Georgia, but it wasn't easy to bear. Many built arbors of brush to shelter themselves from the sun.[3] Aside from a few afternoon showers, which provided a brief respite from the high humidity and oppressive sun, it had hardly rained since the steady rains of the month before. It had rained so much in June that Confederate major general Samuel G. French wrote in his diary that "It rained forty days and it rained forty nights, And the ark it rested on the Kennesaw heights."[4]

The rain that had fallen in June had caused real inconveniences for the armies of both sides while they marched toward Atlanta. Trenches turned into muddy streams and roads became quagmires, but by July, the roads and trenches of Georgia had turned dusty and dry.[5] One violent lighting storm, however, cleared the Georgia air in its brief appearance. On the evening of 10 July, "a sudden and terrific thunderstorm broke over the camp." According to one Federal soldier from the 85th Illinois in the XIV Corps, "The lightning played most vividly and several trees were struck in the immediate vicinity, two men being killed by a single bolt in a regiment nearby." As the soldier explained, "the men were badly used up and glad when it was over."[6]

Three months of daily fighting in the red clay ditches of Georgia had not settled the contest. Many of the soldiers of both sides had concluded that it would be better to decide the issue in one grand battle rather than live

---

[2]Garland A. Haas, *To the Mountain of Fire and Beyond: The Fifty-Third Indiana Regiment from Corinth to Glory* (Carmel IN: Guild Press of Indiana, 1997) 145; Geo. H Cutter (3rd Wisconsin), diary, Hargrett Library Special Collections, University of Georgia, 90.

[3]Nathaniel Cheairs Hughes, Jr., *The Pride of the Confederate Artillery: The Washington Artillery in the Army of Tennessee* (Baton Rouge: Louisiana State University Press, 1997) 194.

[4]Samuel G. French, *Two Wars: An Autobiography of Gen. Samuel G. French* (Nashville TN: Confederate Veteran, 1901) 202.

[5]Chuck Brown, *Weather Conditions during the Atlanta Campaign* (Poster sold at the Pickett's Mill State Historic Park, 2000).

[6]Henry J. Aten, *History of the Eighty-Fifth Regiment, Illinois Volunteer Infantry* (Hiawatha KS: Regimental Association, 1901) 196.

under the daily trench-style warfare replete with its own privations. Lack of shelter and clean clothes had taken its toll. One Alabama soldier, in a letter to his wife, confessed, "I am so dirty that I am ashamed to be seen."[7] For most of the men from Stewart's Corps, the crossing of and subsequent time spent on picket duty around the Chattahoochee River was the first time they had taken a bath or washed their clothes since boarding the trains in Rome in early May.[8]

Moreover, the lack of variety and vegetables in the food provisions were causing sickness and malnutrition. Many officers and men of the Confederate army lost their appetite. According to Major Thomas J. Burnett of the 17th Alabama, the men were served a daily diet of coarse beef and "coarse cold corn bread & bacon [which] absolutely sickens me to look at, for we have had it so long without variation."[9]

After ninety days of constant fighting in the red clay ditches of northern Georgia, the Confederate soldiers looked more like ragged ditch diggers than soldiers, but there was an air of confidence among them. According to Lt. Col. Walter A. Rorer of the 20th Mississippi Infantry in Adams's Brigade of Loring's Division,

> Our marches have nearly all been made in the night and many times in the rain and mud, when the darkness was so intense nothing could be seen. Still, the army would drag its slow length along passing over four or five miles during the night. The morning light would reveal the most haggard and hungry looking set of wretches you ever saw, dragging themselves along through mud half a leg deep and numbers of them bare footed, the mud being so adhesive as to pull a shoe to pieces, but on they would go being sure "Old Joe" was taking them to the right place.[10]

---

[7]John Crittenden, [34th Alabama] to Bettie Crittenden, 7 July 1864, file Q491, Center for American History, University of Texas at Austin.

[8]H. Grady Howell, Jr., *To Live and Die in Dixie* (Jackson MS: Chickasaw Bayou Press, 1991) 292.

[9]Major Thomas J. Burnett, mailed from Georgia to wife Ann, Pearce Civil War Collection, Navarro College, Corsicana TX; Illene D. Thompson and Wilbur E. Thompson, *The Seventeenth Alabama Infantry: A Regimental History and Roster* (Berwyn Heights MD: Heritage Books, Inc., 2003) 84.

[10]Walter A. Rorer to Cousin Susan, 9 June 1864, Carter House Library and Archives.

The common soldiers during the Civil War had a way of reducing titles and accolades of one another into simple terms. For officers, the men found pet names characteristic of some quality they believed described the officer or reminded the men of him. The Army of Mississippi was no exception. Lieutenant General Leonidas Polk, the Episcopal bishop of Louisiana who was fifty-five years old when the war broke out, was called "The Bishop," "The Reverend," or simply "Father Polk." Major General William Wing Loring, the feisty one-armed division commander from Florida who had a reputation for cursing profusely, was known as "Old Blizzards" for he once commanded his artillerists to "Give them the blizzards, boys!" in the Mississippi Delta during the Vicksburg Campaign. Brigadier General William Scott Featherston was known by his Mississippi brigade as "Old Sweat," or "Big Sweat" because his big, bald and wrinkled forehead was constantly wet from perspiration. For the men, simplifying names and titles made it easier.[11]

Nicknames were not just limited to the generals. Southerners took pride in their prodding of each other, and quite often, what may have begun as a derisive name-calling spell turned into a term of affection. Texans were known as "Chubs," which means a low-class Mexican, while Mississippians called Arkansans "Joshes." No one knows where the Arkansan "Josh" label came from, but the name stuck, and an Arkansan soldier was called Josh, no matter what his mama may have named him.[12]

Mississippians were not as lucky. Those who hailed from the Magnolia State were dubbed "Mud heads." Colonel Henry G. Bunn, commander of the 4th Arkansas Infantry, who later commanded Reynolds's Brigade at Bentonville, North Carolina, at the end of the war, described the Mississippians' unfortunate sobriquet: "The Mississippians were called 'Mud heads;' why, I never knew, for it is a most villainous name for such gallant gentlemen to bear as were those same Mississippians."[13]

---

[11]Shelby Foote, *Fort Sumter to Perryville*, vol. 1 of the *Civil War, A Narrative* (New York: Vintage Books, 1986) 46–54; Thomas B. Buell, *The Warrior Generals: Combat Leadership in the Civil War* (New York: Three Rivers Press, 1998) 116–18; Bell Irvin Wiley, *Embattled Confederates* (New York: Harper & Row, 1964) 65–67.

[12]Mark L. Bradley, ed., "Two Confederate Views of Bentonville: The Official Report of Maj. Gen. Henry D. Clayton and a Reminiscence of Col. Henry G. Bunn," *Regiments: A Journal of the American Civil War* 6/1 (1998): 102.

[13]Bradley, 102. See Bessie Willis Hoyt, *Come When the Timber Turns* (Banner

Yankees were not immune from name calling, either, as they often gave their generals terms of endearment for those they admired, or prejudicial, if not well-suited, labels for those they abhorred. General William Tecumseh Sherman was called "Uncle Billy" by his soldiers and "Cump" by his friends and family. General George Thomas had many nicknames, including "Old Tom," "Old Pap," "Old Slow Trot," and "The Rock of Chickamauga" for his leadership in saving the Federal army from destruction in that battle. He would later be known as "The Sledge of Nashville" for his direction of the devastating assault by his forces on a battered and weary Confederate army that dared to oppose him.[14]

Other northern leaders who did not hold the esteem of their men were given less than complimentary nicknames, but these names weren't used to their faces. General William Ward, a division commander from the XX Corps, had lost the respect of many of his men. Reputed to be a drunk, he reputedly sought victory in battle by leading his men to the front without regard for their lives and safety. Ward, a lawyer from Kentucky, had fought in the Mexican War as major of the 4th Kentucky Infantry Regiment. A member of the old Whig party, Ward served first in the Kentucky legislature and then in Congress. When the Whig party folded, he became a Republican, saw eye to eye with President Lincoln politically speaking, and found favor with the president. Lincoln commissioned him to the rank of brigadier general in the United States Army, but he had done nothing on a battlefield to earn the position. Nicknamed "Old Falstaff" by one of his sergeants, Ward had taken the place of Major General Daniel Butterfield,

---

Elk NC: Pudding Stone Press, 1983) 119, in which Hoyt writes, "Mudhead was a name given to the religious followers of Thomas and Alexander Campbell, called Campbellites, whose belief in total immersion was so strong that when they were baptized in creeks they came up with mud on their heads." See also C. Robert Wetzel, "From the President—Mudheads," *Envoy* (April 1999): 3, where Wetzel comments on the term "mudheads" and its use in Hoyt's book. Perhaps Mississippi soldiers received this label because of the large number of Baptists who settled there, or maybe the term referred to the number of muddy creeks and streams found within her borders, including the father of all waters, the mighty Mississippi River.

[14]Freeman Cleaves, *The Rock of Chickamauga: The Life of General George H. Thomas* (Norman: University of Oklahoma Press, 1948) 6–7; Christopher J. Einolf, *George Thomas: Virginian for the Union* (Norman: University of Oklahoma Press, 2007) 22–25; Einolf, "Forgotten Heroism," *North & South—The Official Magazine of the Civil War Society* 11/2 (December 2008): 90.

who had been a popular leader. According to Sergeant George F. Cram of the 105th Illinois, Ward "hungered for the heat of battle" to get his name in the papers at the sacrifice of his men. Cram once exclaimed in a letter home to his mother that "Ward [is] a regular old Falstaff whose sheer delight is to swill whiskey, etc." "Falstaff" was a reference to the Shakespearean character who was described as drunken, swaggering, and unscrupulous.[15]

* * *

For three months Sherman skillfully directed his larger force across northwest Georgia and forced General Joe Johnston and his army to give up strongly entrenched positions without engaging in an all out assault. Thus, Sherman denied the Confederates the advantage of fighting from behind defensive works. After moving far into the interior of Georgia without catching Johnston's army in an exposed position where Sherman could destroy it, and after a month of incessant rainfall that turned the roads into quagmires and prevented further flanking maneuvers around the Rebels, Uncle Billy had grown impatient.

Sherman knew that things were not going well in Virginia as Lee had forced Grant into what appeared to be a stalemate, and the Lincoln administration needed a sign that the war was progressing and could be won. The South appeared to be winning or holding off Yankee parries in other theaters, but Sherman's advance far into Georgia offered the only positive news for the nation. Weary from the daily grind of the campaign and feeling the pressure of an anxious and tired country, Sherman decided to gamble in the hopes that his men could overwhelm the embattled Rebels, who were surely just as tired as his men and who could be vulnerable to a determined assault. On 27 June, Sherman ordered his army to attack the Confederate forces, who were entrenched on and around Kennesaw Mountain, the most formidable line that Johnston held during the entire Georgia Campaign (save his fortifications around Dalton that Johnston's men prepared during their winter encampment). Sherman's dream of a quick and decisive victory was not to be. The result was predictable.

---

[15]George F. Cram, *Soldiering with Sherman: The Civil War Letters of George F. Cram*, ed. Jennifer Cain Bornstedt (DeKalb IL: Northern Illinois University Press, 2000, letter to Mother, 23 April 1864, 76, 89, 190.

Johnston and his veteran army tore great holes into the onrushing Federals as they approached the Confederate lines.

Confidence ran high in the Confederate army after the victory at Kennesaw Mountain. The Northern soldiers suffered staggering losses in men and morale as they charged across open fields and were mowed down by the experienced Southern riflemen and gunners who waited for them. Kennesaw Mountain was more like a massacre than a battle, and it would prove to be Sherman's greatest blunder of the campaign. At Kennesaw, Sherman's forces lost some 3,000 men while Johnston's Confederates sustained just 600 to 700 casualties.[16]

Newspaper reports in Atlanta that Sherman's army had been defeated at Kennesaw Mountain brought "joy and revived hope" to her inhabitants. The Atlanta *Appeal* exclaimed that Sherman "has been successfully halted in his mad career" and bragged that Johnston had said to the Yankees, "Thus far shall thou come, and no farther." Meanwhile, in the *Intelligencer*, it was reported that Sherman "seems now to be in the condition of a wounded snake that spitefully turns and bites itself when it no longer can drag its slow length along." The news calmed most of Atlanta's citizens, including Mrs. Mary Mallard who, feeling no "immediate danger," wrote her mother in on the Georgia coast to come to Atlanta saying, "I want you to come while we are enjoying our vegetables."[17]

The Rebel euphoria along Kennesaw's defensive works after the Federal defeat was short lived. By 1 July, it was evident that Sherman was contemplating another flanking move, and on the evening of 2 July, Johnston withdrew his men from the "Confederate Gibraltar," as Kennesaw Mountain has been called by some Federals. What had been a blistering defeat and a demoralizing blow to Sherman's men was soon forgotten; on the morning of 3 July elements of Sherman's army soon occupied Kennesaw's heights and watched the unfurling of a large Union flag atop Kennesaw Mountain against the backdrop of a beautiful blue sky. Nixon

---

[16]Richard A. Baumgartner and Larry M. Strayer, *Kennesaw Mountain: June 1864* (Huntington WV: Blue Acorn Press, 1998) 160; Albert Castel, *Decision in the West* (Lawrence: University Press of Kansas, 1992) 319–20.

[17]Castel, *Decision in the West*, 327; *Atlanta Appeal*, 1 July 1864, 1; *Intelligencer*, 2 July 1864, 1; Robert Manson Myers, ed., *The Children of Pride* (New York: Popular Library, 1972) 1188.

Stewart of the 52nd Ohio remembered, "Our band played 'Old Hundred,' while we sang 'Praise God from whom all blessings flow.' It was joy to our boys as we had scarcely looked up for six days from our dangerous position. Marietta was ours, and our forces were pushing Johnston toward Atlanta."[18]

---

[18]Nixon B. Stewart, *Dan McCook's Regiment, 52nd O.V.I.: A History of the Regiment, Its Campaigns and Battles from 1862 to 1865* (1900; repr., Huntington WV: Blue Acorn Press, 1999) 129; Baumgartner and Strayer, *Kennesaw Mountain: June 1864*, 181; Castel, *Decision in the West*, 329–30.

2

THE BATTLE OF RUFF'S MILL

If you have ever worked in your life, work at daybreak on that flank crossing Nickajack [Creek] somehow, and the moment you discover confusion pour in your fire. You know what a retreating mass across pontoon bridges means, press the enemy all the time in flank till he is across the Chattahoochee.[1]

On 1 July, General Sherman wrote to his superior in Washington that he was mobilizing his force for another flanking movement, around Kennesaw Mountain and the Rebel defenses. As usual, he trusted the move to General James B. McPherson and the Army of the Tennessee, while he used the Army of the Cumberland led by General George H. Thomas and the small Army of the Ohio under General John M. Schofield to occupy the attention of the Confederates. "By this movement I think I can force Johnston to move his army down from Kenesaw, to defend his railroad crossing and the Chattahoochee, when I will, by the left flank, reach the railroad below Marietta; but I cut loose from the railroad with ten days' supplies in wagons," explained Sherman. "Johnston may come out of his intrenchments and attack General Thomas, which is what I want, for General Thomas is well intrenched, parallel with the enemy, south of Kenesaw.... The movement is substantially down the Sandtown road, straight for Atlanta."[2]

McPherson moved his army down the Sandtown Road on 2 July at 9:00 PM with Major General Francis P. Blair and his XVII Corps in the van, followed by Major General Grenville M. Dodge and the XVI Corps with the XV Corps led by Major General John A. Logan in the rear. Each regiment was to be accompanied by one wagon filled with ammunition with only one Battery of artillery to follow each division. Sherman's plan was for the movement to be made rapidly in the hopes of catching Johnston off-

---

[1]*OR*, vol. 38, series V, ser. no. 76, 30–31, 36–37.

[2]Richard A. Baumgartner and Larry M. Strayer, *Kennesaw Mountain: June 1864* (Huntington WV: Blue Acorn Press, 1998) 177; *The War of the Rebellion: A Compilation of the Official Records of the Union and Confederate Armies* (4 series, 70 vols. in 128 vols., Washington: Government Printing Office, 1880–1901), series IV, vol. 38, ser. no. 76, 3. Hereafter referred to as *OR*.

guard and bagging large portions of his army before they could retreat to the southern shores of the Chattahoochee River.[3]

Colonel William W. Belknap of the 15th Iowa remembered that during the evening of 2 July, the artillerists muffled the wheels of their guns in blankets "to prevent noise" as they "were brought down from the hills, while at the same time the skirmish line continued a furious fire." Belknap explained that at 8:30 PM, the XVII Corps moved from their positions in front of Kennesaw Mountain in the center of the line "under cover of darkness, and marched during the night in rear of the lines held by other corps formerly forming the centre of the army…and by 2:00 o'clock AM of July 3rd they had gained the Sandtown road, heading due south towards the Chattahoochie River," and making the XVII Corps "the extreme right of the army." By 3:00 PM, leading elements of Gresham's Division in the van of the XVII Corps reached within 2.5 miles of the Widow Mitchell's farm. There, across a small creek, they found a familiar sight. Across the creek on the high sloping ground beyond was a line of entrenchments containing a body of Confederate troops of unknown strength. In front of the enemy works was a line of Rebel skirmishers nearer to the creek.[4] Johnston had blocked Sherman once again.

The Georgia heat punished the Yankees as they marched toward the Chattahoochee River. General Gresham wrote his wife, Matilda, on Independence Day: "We had such a terrible march yesterday. The weather is hot beyond description. Several men fell dead from sunstroke." One of the soldier's in Blair's XVII Corps remembered 2 July as one of the hottest mornings of the summer with the thermometer reading 110 degrees that day. Noting that his orders were to continue to march his division toward the river in the hopes of trapping a portion of Johnston's retreating army, Gresham recorded that he was "only two miles from the Chattahoochee River and eight miles from Atlanta." Expecting to "cross the river soon," Gresham added that he was "on the extreme right of" the northern armies

---

[3]*OR*, vol. 38, series V, ser. no. 76, 28–29.

[4]William W. Belknap, *History of the Fifteenth Regiment, Iowa Veteran Volunteer Infantry, from October, 1861, to August, 1865, when disbanded at the end of the war* (Keokuk IO: R. B. Odgen & Son, Printers, 1887) 320.

where his brigades had driven the Confederates from their works at a loss of five men.[5]

The night of 2 July and pre-dawn hours of 3 July were some of the darkest of the war. With a new moon on the evening of 3 July, and with a cover of some of the clouds left from the two thunderstorms that had struck the previous afternoon, no stars were visible to light the path of the soldiers as they trudged through the roads made muddy and slippery by the rain. Fenwick Hedley of the 32nd Illinois remembered that it was so dark that an observer along the side of the road might feel the passing of the Yankee column, but that it would not be seen: "The army literally walked by faith, each man following in the steps of one he believed to be in advance of him. The ground, sodden with heavy rains, gave no sound of foot or hoof, and feet and wheels rapidly converted the roadway into a sea of mud."[6]

The Illinois soldier wrote of the miserable night march, which made an amusing impression on him:

> Now the troops "string out" in the darkness until they reach over three times their ordinary ground, even in marching order. The ranks are not compact and well dressed; each man goes as he pleases. The head of column halts on account of some obstacle, and those in rear, not knowing what has occurred, "close up" on their comrades in front, and collide in the darkness. Then is heard angry dialogue, the men being forgetful of all injunctions to silence. "Why the hell don't you keep up?" "What the hell are you running over me for?" "Hold up your damn gun, and keep it out of my eye!" "Damn your eye!" and so on, with countless variations. Then one finds himself anchored to the ground by the depth and consistency of the mud; and, while endeavoring to extricate himself, those hurrying on from behind stumble

---

[5]Matilda McGrain Gresham, *Life of Walter Quintin Gresham 1832–1895*, vol. 1 (Chicago: Rand, McNally & Co., 1919) 298–99; Garland A. Haas, *To the Mountain of Fire and Beyond: The Fifty-Third Indiana Regiment from Corinth to Glory* (Carmel IN: Guild Press of Indiana, 1997) 142–45.

[6]"Phases of the Moon," US Naval Observatory Astronomical Applications Department, http://aa.usno.navy.mil/cgi-bin/aa_moonphases.pl?year=1864&ZZZ =END (accessed 4 July 2014); Chuck Brown, The Atlanta Campaign, May 7 Through September 3, 1864, Map and Time Line, Pickett's Mill Visitor's Center, Dallas GA; Fenwick Y. Hedley, *Marching through Georgia* (Chicago: R. R. Donnelly & Sons, 1887) 132; Haas, *To the Mountain of Fire and Beyond*, 142–45.

over him in the darkness, until a score or more of men are piled on top of one another, before the words "ease up" can be passed back.

Oh! the profanity of that night march! The objurgatory division of the mother-tongue stood revealed in all its elaborateness and comprehensiveness; and yet, reinforced as it was by copious selections from foreign languages, it proved utterly inadequate for such an emergency. Oaths of the most intricate construction and far-reaching meaning were thrown upon the midnight air, with a vehemence that left no doubt as to the sincerity of the swearer. He damned all things, visible and invisible, known, unknown and unknowable. The United States and the "Confederacy" were alike relegated, side by side, to the grim sulphurous shades of the forever cursed; then the swearer wished that Sherman and Johnston were both in hadean regions "to fight it out themselves;" and further expressed the conviction that it would be comparative bliss to be there himself. Nor was the swearing spasmodic and occasional, but persistent and unanimous.[7]

On the Southern side, the pitch-black night was also creating problems. Along Cheatham's Division front, Lieutenant Thomas Maney with a detail of twelve men from the 1st and 27th Tennessee was ordered to keep a vigil along the "Dead Angle," one of the most hotly-contested portions of the Kennesaw Battlefield along Cheatham Hill. Maney described the "great risk" he and his men faced as they had to crawl out of the protection of their works and into no-man's land between the lines, saying "that if we shook a bush or made the least noise we would hear the unwelcome 'siz' of a minie ball."[8] Ordered not to return fire under any circumstances, the detail nervously moved forward. "It was our province to watch and listen, and if crowded to jump and run," explained Maney. "The men were placed in a zigzag line, I having to crawl out in the dark and post each one. It was the officer's duty to go along the line and ascertain if all were doing their duty—lying down and keeping awake. Not much trouble to keep awake that night!" remembered Maney. The total darkness caused him to crawl off-course in one of his excursions.

---

[7]Hedley, *Marching through Georgia*, 132–33.

[8]Thomas H. Maney, "Battle of Dead Angle on Kennesaw Line," *Confederate Veteran* 11/4 (April 1903): 159–60; Baumgartner and Strayer, *Kennesaw Mountain: June 1864*, 179.

On one of the tours of inspection I got a little off the line, and, it being crooked, I went clear outside and became so confused that I could not tell whether I was going to my own men or not. Creeping along in this frame of mind, I felt the muzzle of a musket right against my bosom, and then heard the click, click of the cocked hammer. Well, the past life of the writer came up before him. All the mean things I ever did were passed in review in a few seconds, for the ordeal was of short duration. I was afraid to catch the gun, for it would make the man at the other end of it pull the trigger. So I asked: "Who is that?" No answer. Then I said: "If you are Federals, I'm your meat." Still no answer. "If you are Rebs, I am your officer." No answer yet. The sweat was pouring down my face about that time.

The soldier took me for a Federal soldier, as my clothes were dark and my hat black, but he lowered his gun. The gun was down and I was down, lying prone on the ground by the soldier. When I realized that it was a man in our regiment who was considered unstable about the head, my scare came on good, for he had no more sense than to shoot. The reaction came to my nervous system and I was as weak as water. If the enemy had come on us then, it would have been impossible for me to rise from the ground. The poor fellow was frightened too, when he saw how near he came to sending me to my long home. At a given signal, about twelve o'clock, we moved back to the works and then on in quick time to catch up with the rear guard.[9]

Nearby, in Walker's Division, Colonel Charles H. Olmstead, commander of the 1st Georgia Volunteers, remembered as his men prepared to evacuate: "The order for this movement came to me about eleven o'clock at night when the whole command was in the profound slumber that blessed our eyes in these days. In a few minutes the Regiment was formed and we filed out onto the road to take our place in the Brigade column." Olmstead recalled that, "The night was dark and the little country road narrow, so progress was exceedingly slow because of the thousand and one obstructions to a march of troops under such conditions." He took "cat naps" on his horse during the night as his regiment was halted countless times. Later, when his men passed the Georgia Military Institute where he had studied to become a soldier before the war, the veteran officer reflected on the building's destruction that would surely come the next day when Sherman's legions reached it. Olmstead wrote, "It was the school in which I had spent four

---

[9]Ibid.

happy years. Many had been my dreams of the future while there but never had there been forecast of such an event as marching with an army corps at midnight through this beloved spot." He lamented, "Every inch of its soil, every brick of its buildings was dear to me and it saddened my soul to believe that its destruction was near. It had furnished too many officers to the Confederate Army to be spared and Sherman ordered it to be burned on the following day."[10]

General Arthur M. Manigault, commanding a Confederate brigade in Hood's Corps, also recalled the night of 2 July as being "a very dark one, and part of our line running thro a thick wood, it was impossible to get to work before daylight." His brigade arrived near Smyrna Campground about 1:00 AM of 3 July. "The men threw themselves on the ground in rear of their stack of arms, and slept until daybreak. As soon as it was light enough to see, the ground was laid out, and the labor of constructing breastworks and batteries was commenced," explained Manigault. He continued, "In a few hours the lines were in a condition to resist an attack, and by midday the enemy were upon us."[11]

Meanwhile, back on the Sandtown Road as the two divisions of Blair's XVII Corps rested from their overnight march, General Giles Smith's Brigade of General Morgan L. Smith's 2nd Division from the XV Corps deployed and made an attempt "to dislodge the enemy from its position," according to Colonel Belknap. The XV Corps, led by Major General John A. "Blackjack" Logan had followed the other two corps of the Army of the Tennessee from Kennesaw Mountain while the XVI Corps under Major General Greenville M. Dodge fanned to the east to look for a place to ford Nickajack Creek and threaten the flank and rear of Johnston's army.

Arriving at Marietta before the Federal cavalry, which had been ordered to take it, Logan's fast-moving XVI Corps captured some two hundred prisoners on the march. Logan's men remained at Marietta until the morning of 4 July when they were ordered to march via the Sandtown Road to the right of the Federal line in support of Blair's XVII Corps.

---

[10]Charles H. Olmstead (1st Georgia Volunteers), "The Memoirs of Charles H. Olmstead," *Georgia Historical Quarterly* 44/4 (December 1960): 430–31.

[11]R. Lockwood Tower, ed., *A Carolinian Goes to War: The Civil War Narrative of Arthur Middleton Manigault, Brigadier General, C. S. A.* (Columbia: University of South Carolina Press, Charleston Library Society, 1983) 194.

Leaving the 25th Iowa under Colonel Stone at Marietta to serve as a provost guard, Logan's force marched out of the town to the southeast and passed the Cheney House.[12]

Other Federal troops passed through the pretty square of Marietta on their way southward. One of the units, Eli Lilly's 18th Indiana Light Artillery Battery, remembered seeing palmetto trees on their march into town and noted that they must be getting pretty well south. Henry Campbell of Lilly's Battery said that Marietta reminded him of Murfreesboro after the Battle of Stones River "because nearly all the inhabitants had left town and the houses were filled with wounded Rebels." Claiming to have found 1,600 wounded Confederates in one hospital, Campbell said that "Just South of town are two fine looking buildings called the Georgia State Military Institute, now nursing the very offspring it taught the art of war." Campbell explained that "Business Houses are mostly brick 2 and 3 stories in hight. The R.R. runs through the center of town, with the track beautifully shaded with long rows of shade trees extending the entire length thro town."[13]

General Walter Q. Gresham's Division of Blair's XVII Corps reached Mrs. Marble's Plantation by 6:00 PM where, "after heavy skirmishing," it bivouacked for the night. Gresham described the heavy skirmishing in a letter to his wife, Tillie: "We left Kenesaw and marched around the rear of our army...until we passed on their extreme right. I was in advance and we soon struck the enemy and, as the boys say, 'went in.'" The general continued, "That day we marched twelve miles, and from 6 PM till dark drove four brigades of Rebel cavalry well supplied with artillery two miles. We are now five and a half miles from where we first struck the enemy on his flank, and we have fought for every inch of the ground." Wounded in this fighting was Private John G. Starr of the 2nd Georgia Cavalry in Iverson's Brigade.[14]

---

[12]*OR*, vol. 38, series I, ser. no. 74, 100.

[13]John W. Rowell, *Yankee Artillerymen: Through the Civil War with Eli Lilly's Indiana Battery* (Knoxville: University of Tennessee Press, 1975) 208.

[14]Gresham, *Life of Walter Quintin Gresham*, 299–300; Haas, *To the Mountain of Fire and Beyond*, 143; John Randolph Poole, *Cracker Cavaliers: The 2nd Georgia Cavalry under Wheeler and Forrest* (Macon GA: Mercer University Press 2000) 127.

The 15th Iowa's commanding officer, Colonel Belknap, recorded the regiment's activity for 3 July: "Met and fought the enemy four miles this side of the river." By 3:00 PM on 3 July, the 3rd Brigade of Gresham's 4th Division was within two and a half miles of the Widow Mitchell's farm. While the two divisions of the XVII Corps rested for two hours, Giles A. Smith's brigade of the XV Corps "tried to dislodge the enemy from its position," according to Belknap. He wrote, "Failing in this, however, at 7 o'clock PM the Iowa brigade of the 4th division was ordered to the front; the 11th and 13th in advance, supported by the 15th and 16th Iowa, soon crossed the creek, and after a lively fire from both sides, forced the enemy from his position, slowly but steadily, driving him for a mile, when night intervening, the movement was stopped by order of General Blair."[15]

Johnston had anticipated Sherman's flanking maneuver as he had done throughout the Georgia Campaign: "The reports of outposts, and observation from the top of Kenesaw on the 1st and 2nd of July, showed that General Sherman was transferring strong bodies of troops to his right," wrote Johnston, who noted that Sherman's forces were "already nearer to Atlanta than the Confederate left." Thus, Old Joe ordered his forces to fall back from the strong defenses he had held for twenty-six days along the Kennesaw Mountain line. "The Confederate army was therefore moved to the position prepared for it by Colonel Prestman, which it reached early on the 3rd, and occupied in two lines crossing the road to Atlanta almost at right angles," explained Johnston. He withdrew his men toward a position that he had allowed his engineers to create covering the last strategic position on the north side of Chattahoochee River, a series of high ridges covering Turner Ferry and the railroad bridge over the river.[16]

Cavalryman James Drury Flowers of the 2nd Alabama Cavalry remembered the withdrawal from Kennesaw Mountain vividly. "I shall never forget the night we fell back from Kennesaw Mountain. I being on picket duty was among the last to leave. Marietta was at the foot of the

---

[15]Supplement to *OR*, part II, vol. 20, ser. no. 32, 237; Belknap, *History of the Fifteenth Regiment*, 320–21.

[16]Baumgartner and Strayer, *Kennesaw Mountain: June 1864*, 177; Joseph E. Johnston, *Narrative of Military Operations* (New York: D. Appleton & Company, 1874) 345; William R. Scaife, *The Campaign for Atlanta* (Atlanta: self-published, 1993) 73–75, 82-A.

mountains and the rear guard crossed through the town just as day was breaking and such weeping and crying of the women and children I have never heard."[17]

As he fell back, Johnston formed his men along a temporary line formed roughly along today's Concord Road between Rottenwood Creek to the east and Nickajack Creek to the west. There, he disposed his forces thus, "Loring's corps on the right and Hardee's on the left of the [Atlanta] road, Hood's on the left of Hardee's, Wheeler's on the right of Loring's corps, and Jackson's supported by General Smith, on the left of Hood's." There, he hoped to stall Sherman and force him to attack another line of defensive works where the flanks of his smaller army were covered between two fairly large creeks. Unfortunately, his men did not have sufficient time to reconnoiter and prepare their new lines properly before Sherman's legions were on them, so some of his forward lines to be without proper support.[18]

Moreover, McPherson, his left flank screened by the creek, was able to march his troops practically unopposed along the Sandtown Road west of Nickajack Creek all the way to the Chattahoochee River. The only Rebel infantry opposing him was the newly arrived Georgia militia under Major General Gustavus W. Smith, who was either unwilling or unable to slow McPherson's veterans. Thus, Johnston's hope of funneling Sherman's force between the two creeks and into the teeth of his defenses along the Concord Road was thwarted. For the same reason, his stronger line along the ridges covering the river crossings (known as the Chattahoochee River Line, which he would occupy from July 5 to July 9) would also become untenable. With his superior number of men, Sherman would be able to find crossings over the river miles away from the Confederate defenses and thus flank Johnston once again out of a naturally strong position.[19]

Sensing Johnston's need to buy time for the evacuation of his wagon train, Sherman pushed his lieutenants on the evening of 3 July to move with

---

[17]Southern Style: A Downhome Perspective on All Things Southern, Southeast Alabama Heritage Association, http://www.southern-style.com/ http://www.southern-style.com/Inspiration/A%20Tribute%20to%20William%20Hampton%20Flowers.htm (19 September 2010).

[18]Johnston, *Narrative of Military Operations*, 345.

[19]Ibid., 345–46; William R. Scaife and William Harris Bragg, *Joe Brown's Pets: The Georgia militia 1861–1865* (Macon GA: Mercer University Press, 2004) 30–31.

all haste. Writing first to McPherson at 6:15 PM, Sherman lamented, "had the pursuit been vigorous we would have secured 3,000 or 4,000 prisoners and many wagons. Now the halt [by Johnston] is, of course, to save time." He commanded, "If you have ever worked in your life, work at daybreak tomorrow on that flank, crossing Nickajack [Creek] somehow and the moment you discover confusion pour in your fire. You know what a retreating mass across pontoon bridges means and press the enemy all the time in flank till he is across the Chattahoochee." Next, Sherman wrote Thomas at 6:45 PM expressing the same need to push Johnston with all dispatch.[20]

Blair's XVII Corps moved steadily down the Sandtown Road throughout 3 July, reaching the Marble House and very nearly to the Widow Mitchell House by dark. Offering token resistance, the Georgia militia dared the Federals to go further south toward the ferries over the Chattahoochee River. The militia's leader, Major General Smith, would later write that he "did not believe the small available force of raw militia, acting as a support to the cavalry, could stop Sherman's advance if he choose to move in force-around Johnston's left flank." While fending off the Yankee parries toward Mason and Turner's Ferry, nervous militiamen held to their posts along the Turner's Ferry Road (today's Bankhead Highway). Many were "powerful bad Sceared," but they covered Johnston's back door, affording him time to withdraw from the Smyrna Line.[21]

Bragging on the service of the militia, Johnston wrote to Georgia governor Joseph Brown explaining that they had effected good service: "While the army was near Marietta they were employed to support the cavalry on the extreme left and occupied a position quite distinct from any other infantry of ours. According to all accounts their conduct in the presence of the enemy was firm and creditable." While such accolades may have helped mollify the ego of the Georgia governor toward his "pets," as many termed the Georgia militia, the real credit should have gone to McPherson and Blair for failing to exploit the inexperienced Confederates.[22]

---

[20]*OR*, vol. 38, series V, ser. no. 76, 30–31, 36–37.

[21]Scaife and Bragg, *Joe Brown's Pets*, 32–34; Johnston, *Narrative of Military Operations*, 346; Earl J. Hess, "Civilians at War: The Georgia militia in the Atlanta Campaign," *Georgia Historical Quarterly* 66 (Fall 1982): 343.

[22]Scaife and Bragg, *Joe Brown's Pets*, 30–33.

Meanwhile, McPherson's Army of the Tennessee moved closer. Ordered to probe the Rebel defenses and push back any resistance, General Fuller moved his brigade across Nickajack Creek just after daybreak on 4 July. It would be a busy Independence Day for Fuller and his men. The 39th Ohio and the 64th Illinois formed in a line of battle along a hill east of Nickajack Creek, while the 18th Missouri remained "in column of companies in rear of the 39th Ohio." General Fuller had received orders to attack from generals Dodge and Veatch, his corps and division commanders, but Fuller remained cautious, unsure of the Confederate strength in his front. Fuller therefore instructed his regimental leaders to merely probe the Confederate lines after his advance had chased the Rebel pickets back to their main line. Meanwhile, the balance of Veatch's Division came up in support of Fuller and began to erect rifle pits and earthworks, and a Battery was brought up to begin a barrage on the Confederates.[23]

By noon Dodge ordered Veatch to attack the Confederate lines, so Fuller sent his 2nd Ohio regiments to advance. The Ohioans moved quietly and quickly toward the Rebel lines, which were manned by Stevenson's Division of Hood's Corps. Rushing the final hundred yards to the Rebel lines, the Ohioans managed to reach the enemy lines and deliver a blow to the surprised and unprepared Confederates. Bragging about the charge, Fuller later recorded that the Rebels "abandoned his entrenchments and retired. It is doubtful whether so small a force…ever emptied a longer line of works." In the 18th Missouri, two German immigrants were wounded, Lieutenant Partenheimer was shot in the right leg, and John Baptiste Priester, a thirty-five-year-old farmer was wounded in the left hip.[24]

For Confederate pioneer Hiram Smith Williams of the 40th Alabama in Clayton's Division, 4 July would be a day of toil and fear. Listening to the roar of federal cannon fire and bursting of shells while his pioneers (the engineers of the day) busily worked on a bridge across a stream, Williams's men stopped to cook dinner. They had worked on a redoubt the day before until dark where Baker's Brigade occupied the extreme left of the Confederate line in Hood's defense of Nickajack Creek at Ruff's Mill. "We ate dinner and was returning when we met the cavalry coming in,"

---

[23]Leslie Anders, *The Eighteenth Missouri* (Indianapolis: The Bobbs-Merrill Company, Inc., 1968) 227.

[24]Ibid., 228.

remembered Williams. "The cavalry reported that the enemy had turned our left flank and were coming on rapidly. We hurried on down to the bridge and found our company all confusion as the enemy were in sight not over a half-a-mile off, hurring on and firing rapidly, while the balls fell think and fast around us." Soon, the crisis was averted and the Rebel line was on the move again in their next evacuation. Exasperated, the veteran soldier added, "Will this falling back never come to an end?"[25]

While Dodge's XVI Corps pressed Hood's Corps at Ruff's Mill, Blair's XVII Corps continued to push down the Sandtown Road to the south. In the van of Blair's Corps was the 3rd Brigade of Gresham's Division. When they reached the Widow Mitchell's farm, Colonel Belknap led the 15th and 16th Iowa and the 1st Minnesota Battery commanded by Lieutenant Harker to the east, pressing the Georgia militia back toward Turner's Ferry. Covering the Federal right flank, General George Stoneman and his cavalry division continued south down the Sandtown Road toward Green and Howell's Ferry. Opposing Stoneman was Brigadier General Lawrence "Sul" Ross and his veteran Texas troopers, the 1st, 3rd, 6th and 9th Texas Legions. Colonel Belknap of the 15th Iowa wrote, "The 15th Iowa (with the16th Iowa) deployed as skirmishers ahead of the column. Kept gaining ground charging and taking the first line of Rebel works."[26]

Meanwhile, as darkness fell on the woodlands of Cobb County where Hood's Corps overlooked the valley of Nickajack Creek, despondency began to set in among many veterans who had celebrated victory at Kennesaw Mountain just one week before. Captain Thomas B. Hampton of the 63rd Virginia Infantry, writing to his wife, Jestin, explained, "there are a great many running away from our Brigade & I am sorry to say among the balence some of our county boys there has several went from Co. C which mortifies Capt. Waugh verry much...." The 63rd Virginia had lost eighty men during the fighting of 22 June at Kolbs's farm, while Reynolds's North Carolina and Virginia Brigade, of which it was a part, lost 250 men killed, wounded and captured, according to Hampton. Clearly, the losses sustained as well as the constant fall backs induced by the Confederates' failure to

[25]Hiram Smith Williams, *This War So Horrible: The Civil War Diary of Hiram Smith Williams*, ed. Lewis N. Wynne and Robert A. Taylor (Tuscaloosa: University of Alabama Press 1993) 100–101.

[26]Supplement to *OR*, part 2, vol. 20, serial no. 32, 237.

arrest the advance of Sherman's legions had taken its toll on the Virginians.[27]

The Battle of Turner's Ferry
July 5, 1864

Vastly outnumbered, Ross's Texans were compelled to fall back before Stoneman's Federal cavalry along Howell's Ferry Road. With only about a thousand men in Ross's four regiments that came to Georgia in May, after constant fighting from New Hope Church to Kennesaw Mountain, Ross's Brigade had an effective strength of fewer than six hundred men. They could not stop the horde of Stoneman's Cavalry, some 2,500 of them. Three times before noon, Ross's Cavalry took up positions along Howell's Ferry Road, but each time they were thrown back by Yankee cavalrymen. Finally, at 2:30 PM, they "moved back under a most galling fire from a rifled Battery." At this point, the men mounted their horses and galloped across a pontoon bridge over the Chattahoochee River "in a shower of shells." The tired Rebel cavalrymen continued to ride a couple of miles until they found their supply trains where they ate and rested a few hours for the first time in three days.[28]

Meanwhile, along the Turner's Ferry Road, Blair's XVII Corps continued to push the Georgia militia until it withdrew to the east of Nickajack Creek and Johnston's River Line along the north bank of the Chattahoochee River. (The remnants of this line are located just south of I-285 and are in danger of being destroyed by the expansion of the interstate and private construction.) Colonel Belknap, commander of the 15th Iowa,

---

[27]Thomas B. Hampton [captain, Co. B, 63rd Virginia Infantry, killed at Battle of Bentonville NC], to Jestin C. Hampton, 26 June 1864 and 4 July 1864, file 2R30, The Southern History Collection, Dolph Briscoe Center for American History, University of Texas at Austin.

[28]S. B. Barron, *The Lone Star Defenders: A Chronicle of the Third Texas Cavalry, Ross' Brigade* (New York: Neale Publishing Company, 1908) 197–98; A. W. Sparks, *The War between the States As I Saw It: Reminiscences, Historical and Personal* (Tyler TX: Lee and Burnett, Printers, 1901) 100; George L. Griscom, *Fighting with Ross' Texas Cavalry Brigade, C. S. A.: The Diary of George L. Griscom*, ed. Homer L. Kerr (Hillsboro TX: Hillsboro Junior College Press, 1976) 153–55; Martha L. Crabb, *All Afire To Fight: The Untold Story of the Ninth Texas Cavalry* (New York: Avon Books, 2000) 224–25.

remembered the regiment again skirmished the Confederates who were "driven below the Nickajack Creek, where the Corps took position one mile from the Rebel fort and main line on the Turner's Ferry (distance marched 18 miles)." Blair's Corps, with its two divisions—Gresham's, which proceeded down the Turner's Ferry Road, and Leggett's, which advanced down the Lickskillet (Gordon) Road to the south— reached Nickajack Creek at its juncture with the Chattahoochee River and deployed.[29]

Logan's XV Corps, which had followed Blair's Corps from Ruff's Mill, filed to the left off of Turner's Ferry Road and, forming at the Dodd Farm, linked up with the right of Hooker's XX Corps and advanced to Nickajack Creek just outside of the Confederate works. There, the Yankees brought up artillery and proceeded to pound the Southerners across the creek into submission. While the artillery of Logan's Corps was still far in the rear, Blair put the 10th Ohio Light Battery from his corps into Logan's line behind Harrow's Division. Next, Blair deployed from right to left from his link to the Chattahoochee River, Battery D of the 1st Illinois, Battery H of the 1st Michigan, the 3rd Ohio Battery, the 1st Minnesota Battery, and the 15th Ohio Battery. Thus, Blair placed twenty-four guns, including four twenty-four-pound Parrott rifles, into position to fire on the extreme left portion of the Rebel works. After advancing a heavy skirmish line across Nickajack Creek and pushing them to within seventy yards of the Confederate entrenchments, Blair ordered his artillery batteries to fire. Throughout the afternoon and well into the night, the Federals kept firing. Additional batteries from Blair's and Logan's corps would be brought up to continue the barrage through the night.[30]

Opposing Blair's artillerists were the three divisions of Hood's Corps who were not having a good time. First, when they arrived at the Chattahoochee River line, which had been built by slaves brought up from Atlanta for that purpose, the veteran Southerners did not like what they saw. The works were not the typical trenches they had been used to for the past three months; instead they were a series of small, arrow-shaped forts

---

[29]Supplement to *OR*, part 2, vol. 20, ser. no. 32, 237; David Seibert, "Georgia militia on Turner's Ferry Road," ed. Craig Swain, The Historical Marker Database, http://www.hmdb.org/marker.asp?marker=17022 (accessed 6 July 2014).

[30]*OR*, vol. 38, series III, ser. no. 74, 552–53; Scaife, *Campaign for Atlanta*, 82–84.

that could fit only about a hundred men. The forts were connected by lines of timbers that covered the intervening gaps between the little forts. The works were a product of the imagination of General Francis A. Shoup. General Johnston had given Shoup permission to build the experimental works, but both the soldiers and officers who saw them pronounced them a failure without giving them a chance. John Crittenden of the 34th Alabama from Brown's Division (General John C. Brown had replaced General Thomas C. Hindman after he suffered an eye injury on 3 July) thought that the works "were such that almost any set of boys might have built that had never seen a ditch." Crittenden explained, "We were put in the front lines at once. Tools issued and now we have good works [a better trench or fort]."[31]

As Crittenden and his fellow Alabamians worked on strengthening their lines, they could see the Yankees approaching from across Nickajack Creek to the west. Then, after allowing the Yankees time to get into position, "a fort on our left oppened on the enemy" against which the Union troops "commenced a heavy fire of artillery on a fort a little to our left." Crittenden and his comrades became "down in the mouth very much" when the Rebel Battery fell silent. The Confederate artillerists were under strict orders to conserve ammunition.[32]

Crittenden continued, "For some reason we were ordered to the rear as a reserve. We fell back under a hill and remained there until about one hour by the sun. the enemy in the meantime shelling furiously as if they would tear up the whole country." The Alabamians then prepared to move back to the front. "About this time the enemy made a demonstration in front as if they would bring on a general engagement. Our Brigade [Manigault's] was ordered to the left to support Tucker's Brigade. To get there we had to pass over a ridge that the enemy had been shelling all of the evening." This ridge is located along today's Oakdale Road.[33] Crittenden wrote,

---

[31]Scaife, *Campaign for Atlanta*, 75–78; John Crittenden [34th Alabama] to Bettie Crittenden, 7 July 1864, file Q491, The Southern History Collection, Dolph Briscoe Center for American History, University of Texas at Austin.

[32]John Crittenden [34th Alabama] to brother William, 9 July 1864, file Q491, The Southern History Collection, Dolph Briscoe Center for American History, University of Texas at Austin.

[33]Ibid., Crittenden to Bettie, Southern History Collection.

It seemed as if every shell that they fired passed over that place tearing up the earth in a frightful manner. But it was necessary for us to go. The Regt. was got into line and ordered forward. Just as we started Whit Hardy was struck down by a piece of shell and I thought that for time that he was killed, but he was wounded in the leg. We had to go up a hollow about one hundred yards, then to cross the Ridge. As soon as we began to ascend the ridge we had to double quick in order to get out of danger as soon as possible.

We were not very long in getting over the hill. Though the enemy poured a perfect shower of shell upon it Capt. Smith was the only man hurt in our Regt. He had his collar bone broken. Nothing but merciful Providence could have saved us from death. That night we were put in the front line again where we have been ever since. Yesterday, they shelled us all day. Taylor Gullahorn was shot through the calf of the leg by a piece of shell. Last night a young man was shot through the liver. This morning Lt. McCullough was shot below through the knee while asleep.[34]

According to General Blair, there was a "pontoon bridge over which…[the Confederates were] continually crossing troops, artillery, and wagons. Here the fire of our batteries was reported to have been very destructive, rendering the bridge almost entirely useless."[35] "News came down the line that our fort was going to try them again," remembered Crittenden.

"All of a sudden seven pieces—three 20 pound Parrot Guns and 4 of a smaller caliber—tore loose one after the other in rapid succession to the great satisfaction of the boys who sent up cheer after cheer. Each discharge was greeted in the same manner until they had fired 10 shots to the gun when they ceased." The Southern Battery then fell silent as their gunners had spent their allotment for the fight. In a letter to his brother, Crittenden wrote, "The enemy in the meantime were not idle. They oppened upon our little fort with three or four [actually six] batteries. It seemed as if they were determined to batter it down. But it still stands before them with its two flags flying as defiantly as ever." Crittenden and his comrades counted 706 Federal shells that were fired at them before sundown, and he guessed that another three or four hundred were fired after dark. "It was a pretty sight to see their shells flying through the air with the fuse burning. I say pretty but

---

[34]Ibid.
[35]*OR*, vol. 38, series III, ser. no. 74, 553.

it would have been more so if they had been going in some other direction." The Rebel gunners and infantrymen in the fort "kept up a continual cheering all of the time," despite not being able to return the fire. Crittenden remembered that "Only one man was hurt that I heard of and that only slightly." Shoup's "fort" had held firm and successfully passed its first test under fire. During the fighting, Private James Wright of the 2nd Georgia Cavalry of Iverson's Brigade was wounded.[36]

---

[36]John Crittenden [34th Alabama] to brother William, 9 July 1864, file Q491, Southern History Collection; Poole, *Cracker Cavaliers*, 127.

3

THE BATTLE OF SMYRNA CAMPGROUND

The Rebs artillery was giving us an ovation in shape of shell and cannister shot. We quit and laid now on the ground—their shells plowing up the dirt too close for comfort-in the open field with no shade, the heat about 100 degree F. shelled until you have buried yourself in the ground to some depth with only your bayonet and paws, half choked by thirst, sometimes wishing it was somebody else. We enjoyed our 4th.[1]

3 July 1864

While McPherson's Army of the Tennessee marched down the Sandtown Road toward the Chattahoochee River, General Thomas's Army of the Cumberland pivoted around the south base of Kennesaw Mountain and closely followed Johnston's retreating Confederates. Schofield's Army of the Ohio followed McPherson's force and guarded his rear in the event of a Rebel counterattack. Known as the Smyrna Line, Johnston's defensive position was not a naturally strong one. He needed to use it, however, for about twenty-four hours to give his supply wagons time to evacuate to the south side of the Chattahoochee River.[2]

Meanwhile, Newton's Division from the IV Corps reached Marietta. As Bradley's Brigade passed through the square of Marietta, Corporal Lyman Root of the 125th Ohio noticed a large signboard with a drawing of a Yankee soldier and "also a rebel soldier at a charged bayonet, with the point of the bayonet entering the seat of the Yank's trousers, with this

---

[1]Glenn W. Sunderland, *Five Days to Glory* (Cranbury NJ: A. S. Barnes & Co., 1970) 151–52.

[2]Joseph E. Johnston, *Narrative of Military Operations* (New York: D. Appleton & Company, 1874) 344–46; William R. Scaife, *The Campaign for Atlanta* (Atlanta: self-published, 1993) 73–5; William R. Scaife and William Harris Bragg, *Joe Brown's Pets: The Georgia militia 1861–1865* (Macon GA: Mercer University Press, 2004) 30.

inscription written under it: 'Gen'l. Sherman fleeing to the rear!' We laughed some over this, but the 'flea' was on the other fellow's leg."[3]

Other Federals enjoyed some of the many letters that Southerners had left for them as they traveled through Marietta with their Union flags flying. Maurice Marcoot, a German immigrant from St. Louis who served in the 15th Missouri, picked up one letter. It read, "Goodbye Yankees, the next time we will fight you nine miles on the other side of Atlanta and if you flank us out there, the next place will be on the other side of hell, where we are strongly fortified."[4]

A number of Confederates, who had "played out" of the war for one reason or another, were picked up by the advancing Yankees as they reached Marietta. "Played out" was a term for soldiers who were either no longer willing or able to continue to fight. Scores of sick or wounded Southerners were found in many of the buildings and homes throughout the city, and squads of Rebels simply gave up and walked into the Federal lines to surrender. One Georgia unit, the 1st Georgia Reserves, made up a particularly large number of the prisoners because they seemed to surrender en masse, according to Lieutenant Andrew J. Gleason of the 15th Ohio. Occasionally, the rattle of skirmish fire would erupt from the side of the road as the Yankees continued their march, and the bodies of two dead Rebels that were in plain sight of their southward path were clear evidence that not all Johnnies had given up. During the sporadic fire, Corporal Thomas C. Bethel of the 15th Ohio in Wood's Division of the IV Corps was mistaken for a Rebel soldier by someone in the XIV Corps who shot and killed him.[5]

In Palmer's XIV Corps, the Regular US Army Brigade, commanded by Colonel William L. Stoughton, took a brief respite when they reached Marietta. Arthur Carpenter, one of the brigade's soldiers, remembered

---

[3]Lyman Root (125th Ohio), "Kenesaw Mountain," *National Tribune* (magazine), 26 February 1891; Richard A. Baumgartner and Larry M. Strayer, *Kennesaw Mountain: June 1864* (Huntington WV: Blue Acorn Press, 1998) 181.

[4]Maurice Marcoot, *Five Years in the Sunny South: Reminiscences of Maurice Marcoot* (St. Louis: self published, c. 1890) 67.

[5]Theodore W. Blackburn, *Letters from the Front: A Union "Preacher" Regiment (74th Ohio) in the Civil War* (Dayton OH: Press of Morningside Bookshop, 1981) 203–204; Alexis Cope, *The 15th Ohio Volunteers and Its Campaigns: War of 1861–5* (Columbus OH: published by the author, 1916) 515.

Marietta as "a very pleasant little place. There are some grand estates in the suburbs, but all is deserted."[6] The 15th Ohio of Wood's Division in the IV Corps stopped west of the town near a large tannery by the railroad where they rested and ate lunch. After resting only an hour or two, Colonel Stoughton and his brigade led the Federal advance south of Marietta toward Smyrna and the Confederate lines.

General Sherman, believing that Johnston's force was beating a hasty retreat across the Chattahoochee River, recklessly rode forward with a lone staff officer, the eager general performing what a lieutenant or scout was perfectly capable of handling. Colonel Stoughton and his brigade followed. They had not marched long before skirmishers from the 1st and 15th US Regiment who were in the van "heard the thundering sound of multiple horsemen approaching. Captain [Albert B.] Dod, quickly deployed his battalion from column into line and waited. Two Federal officers, one obviously a general, came galloping around a bend in the road" toward them, "with a group of Southern horsemen in hot pursuit. The Confederates pealed off and headed back upon seeing a line of blue-clad infantry ahead." Relieved, Sherman and his aide "slowed to a canter upon approaching Dod's line...." One veteran from the 15th Regiment remembered, "Sherman looked confused...and we just smiled as he rode by."[7]

Realizing that the Confederates had dug in along a low ridge just south of Ruff's (or Neal Dow Station) Station, General Thomas and his three corps commanders, Palmer, Hooker and Howard, ordered their men to halt and dig in. This move infuriated Sherman, who still believed that Johnston was merely buying time to enable his supply train and artillery wagons to withdraw to the south side of the Chattahoochee River before Sherman's forces could trap them north of the river. The Federal commander relayed to Thomas, "The more I reflect the more I know Johnston's halt is to save time to cross his material and men. No general such as he, would invite battle with the Chattahoochee behind him.... I know you appreciate the situation." Sherman advised the commanders of the importance of pressing "with vehemence" Johnston's forces with all due haste.[8]

---

[6]Mark W. Johnson, *That Body of Brave Men: The U.S. Regular Infantry and the Civil War in the West* (Cambridge MA: Da Capo Press, 2003) 509.

[7]Johnson, *That Body of Brave Men*, 509–510.

[8]Albert Castel, *Decision in the West* (Lawrence: University Press of Kansas,

While the lead divisions of Palmer's XIV Corps and Howard's IV Corps stopped and began to entrench, Ward's Division of Hooker's Corps kept marching steadily on toward the Rebel lines. The political appointee, William Ward, who secured his generalship by virtue of his Republican party status and not because of any military genius, was an habitual drinker. This day would be no exception. Riding at the head of his column, Ward was in a drunken stupor. From time to time, he would awake to yell, "Forward there!" to his men as they plodded along. "Old Falstaff" as some of his men called him, was indifferent to his surroundings when, noticing the danger, General Hooker quickly galloped up to overtake Ward and his marching column. "What ails you? Are you drunk, or are you crazy, or are you a fool?" demanded Hooker. Ward could only muster a brief stare with "his drunken, half shut eyes." Hooker then relieved Ward and placed Colonel John Coburn in command. Ward's Division ended the day's march a mile ahead of the balance of Thomas's lines, a position that resulted in some unfortunate crossfire between two Federal forces the next day. Old Falstaff would sober up enough to recover his position, however, probably because Hooker knew that he could not remove the influential Republican dipsomaniac for incompetency.[9]

In front of the Federals, Johnston's army had stopped for the moment, deployed, and dug in. Along a low ridge, the Confederate line ran from Rottenwood Creek along the approximate course of today's Roswell-Smyrna Road to Smyrna Campground, then west along the approximate course of today's Concord Road to Ruff's Mill at Nickajack Creek. It totaled some seven miles and was manned by Loring's Corps on the east of the campground, Hardee's Corps in the center between the campground and

---

1992) 330–31; *The War of the Rebellion: A Compilation of the Official Records of the Union and Confederate Armies* (4 series, 70 vols. in 128 vols., Washington: Government Printing Office, 1880–1901), vol. 38, series V, ser. no. 76, 30–31. Hereafter referred to as *OR*.

[9]Castel, *Decision in the West*, 331; Charles H. Dickinson Diary, Wisconsin State Historical Society, Madison, Wisconsin Pre-1907 Vital Records Collection, R51 N168-Vol 1, and F587.C48-Vol. 2, Chippewa County, Wisconsin, past and present, 125–27; Alfred H. Trego Diary, 3 July 1864; on the label "Old Falstaff," see George F. Cram, *Soldiering with Sherman: The Civil War Letters of George F. Cram*, ed. Jennifer Cain Bornstedt (DeKalb IL: Northern Illinois University Press, 2000), letter to Mother, 23 April 1864, 76, 89, 190.

approximately today's South Cobb Drive, and Hood's Corps to the west overlooking Nickajack Creek. Hood's line refused strongly so that two-thirds of his force faced southwest. Cleburne's Division was posted along the Atlanta Road, while Walthall's Division and French's Division were to its right as Featherston's (Loring's) Division covered the extreme right of the Confederate lines.[10]

Albert Quincy Porter of the 22nd Mississippi of Featherston's Brigade explained the Confederate withdrawal from Kennesaw Mountain. "We left the place where we staid last knight and went within four miles and a half of Atlanta. Our forces commenced falling back this morning at 2 o'clock in the direction of Atlanta. The enemy are pressing them," continued Porter. "Fighting is going on all the time. We have heard guns all day and now while am writing we can hear artillery firing not far off, also the firing of small arms can be heard very distinctly."

Featherston's Mississippi Brigade was temporarily commanded by Colonel Thomas Mellon of the 3rd Mississippi because General Winfield Scott Featherston was commanding Loring's Division while Major General William Wing Loring was commanding Polk's Corps. Lieutenant General Leonidas K. Polk was killed on 14 June at Pine Mountain, and a permanent replacement had not yet been named. Meanwhile, a number of officers from Polk's Corps, which was still officially known as the Army of Mississippi, were away from their commands, attending the funeral service for their fallen leader at an Episcopal church in Augusta, Georgia. In addition to General Longstreet, who was recovering in Georgia from a wound he received in the Battle of the Wilderness, "it really seemed as if the whole Confederacy was trying to push their way into the Church. All the military were out…" to escort the body of their beloved general, recalled one staff officer.[11]

Meanwhile, back at the front above Smyrna, Sherman and members of Ward's Division were not the only ones who had a close call with the Rebel

---

[10]Scaife, *Campaign for Atlanta*, 74–75, 82–83; David Seibert, "Battle of Smyrna," Cobb County Historical Markers, http://georgiainfo.galileo.usg.edu/topics/historical_markers/county/cobb/battle-of-smyrna (accessed 6 July 2014).

[11]Albert Quincy Porter, diary, Z0565.000, Manuscript Collection, Mississippi Department of Archives and History (MDAH), Jackson MS, 21; L. H. Fleming to Lou Fleming at Augusta, 3 July 1864, Moseley Family Letters, Z0545.000, Manuscript Collection, MDAH.

lines during the march from Marietta on 3 July. General John King and Colonel William Stoughton, commanding a division and a brigade, respectively, in Palmer's XIV Corps rode with their staffs and found themselves about a hundred yards ahead of their men. They were not made aware that they were leading the corps on the route. Captain James Biddle was in the party of Federal horsemen when a volley of fire reached them from a Confederate line hidden in the woods ahead. It was too near for comfort. "Had the Rebs. not fired when they did, Genl. King…would have gone right into the enemy's rifle-pits. One of the balls struck me two inches below the knee & though the skin was not broken the leg turned black to the heel," explained the captain. Biddle witnessed the scene as Colonel Broughton rode forward to check on General King who was in the van of the group. "I thought other troops were in advance of us!" King shouted. Presently, General Thomas rode forward and told the party, "You are the advance. Throw out two or three companies of…skirmishers, and continue to push right along as you have been doing. Hooker is on the right and Howard is on the left." "Keep things steadily moving and if the rebels cause you too much trouble order up some of the artillery," he added.[12]

Behind the US Regulars, the balance of Palmer's XIV Corps moved up, stacked arms and set up camps. The weather had been so hot that many veterans simply gave out and collapsed along the side of the road. Colonel Benjamin Scribner, commanding the 3rd Brigade of Johnson's 1st Division, halted his brigade at 7:00 PM behind the Regulars. There, in an oat field, they camped while the steady rattle of artillery fire in front rocked them to sleep. Captain Robert Findley of the 74th Ohio recorded in his diary, "Slept soundly after partaking of supper of corn bread cakes."[13]

On the Confederate side of the lines, Dr. Edward Young McMorries of the 1st Alabama in Quarles's Brigade of Walthall's Division, which was put into line near Cleburne's Division, recorded his impressions of the day. "July 3 the Federals advanced in force to the edge of the timber in front, planted a Battery on our right, and about 2 PM made a fierce attack from their positions, but did not charge. Heavy sharp-shooting was kept up all night, and we slept on our arms." The Confederate physician described the Rebel lines, which they prepared in a relatively short period of time: "The

---

[12]Johnson, *That Body of Brave Men*, 510.
[13]Blackburn, *Letters from the Front*, 202–203.

rear of our position here was an old field; the front, recently a forest whose timber had been felled for 100 yards as an obstruction to the enemy. We found here a ditch ready for our occupancy."[14]

By dusk of 3 July, Thomas's three corps were aligned from east to west; Howard's IV Corps was east of the railroad along the edge of a cornfield just south of Ruff's (New Dow) Station, Palmer's XIV Corps was in the middle, just west of the railroad, while Hooker's XX Corps was still further west, with its right connecting by a series of vedettes to McPherson's Army of the Tennessee. In front of Palmer's Corps, General King deployed his division into a line of battle and put four companies out in skirmish, as Biddle described, "to feel the enemy & to see if he were in force." "We soon discovered," Biddle added, "by the long line of entrenchments that a large part, if not all his army was in our front." Biddle's skirmishers closed to within two hundred yards of the Confederate lines where they continued to keep a vigil through the night.

The Confederates opposite them were Alabamians and South Carolinians from Manigault's Brigade of Hindman's Division, which was on the right of Hood's Corps. In the van of Howard's Corps, Stanley's 1st Division rested its right on the railroad near the station. The balance of Stanley's Division was deployed along the edge of a cornfield facing the Confederate line across the field. Newton's 2nd Division and Wood's 3rd Division were first massed in column behind Stanley's force. Subsequently, they deployed with Newton's Division in the middle and Wood's Division on the left facing to the east. There, the men entrenched, laid down and rested while they waited for the evening to pass and for the nation's 89th birthday to unfold.[15]

4 July 1864

Independence Day broke warm along the Federal and Confederate forces near the little village of Smyrna Campground which, due to the close proximity of the opposing lines and artillery batteries, promised that the day

---

[14]Edward Young McMorries, *History of the First Regiment, Alabama Volunteer Infantry, C. S. A.* (Montgomery AL: Brown Printing Co., 1904) 74.

[15]*OR*, vol. 38, series I, ser. no. 72, 200; Johnson, *That Body of Brave Men*, 511; Castel, *Decision in the West*, 330–32; Scaife, *Campaign for Atlanta*, 74–83.

would see a lot of fireworks. Smyrna Campground was created as a meeting place by Methodist Pioneers in 1833 as white settlers moved into the area that had been taken from the Cherokee Indians and carved up via a lottery in 1832. There, "a brush arbor was built near a near a fresh water spring that once ran through the area" where "traveling ministers would hold services" and people in the area met and socialized.[16]

In the 1840s, as the Western & Atlantic Railroad was completed, a train stop called Varner's Station was created near the Methodist meeting place. The station was later relocated a bit north and named Ruff's Siding, Ruff's Station or Neal Dow Station (depending upon whom you ask). The battle that would be fought on 4 July would also be known by several names: the Battle of Ruff's Station (not to be confused with the Battle of Ruff's Mill, which was also fought on 4 July 1864 about three miles to the west), the Battle of Neal Dow Station, the Battle of Smyrna, the Battle of Smyrna Depot, and the Battle of Smyrna Campground. While the area was known by many names, the most common ones given at the time of the war was Smyrna or Smyrna Campground, but the name "Smyrna" was not officially adopted until 1872, via an act to recognize it as a municipality by the Georgia legislature.[17]

Despite Sherman's entreaties to attack with vehemence, Thomas's men spent the morning of 4 July celebrating Independence Day as bands played and troops cheered. By noon, however, Howard got his IV Corps in motion east of the railroad depot at Ruff's (Neal Dow) Station. Unsatisfied with the lack of activity, Sherman made another personal reconnaissance and returned to order Thomas to send a force to take what appeared to him to be merely a line of rifle pits manned by "unsupported skirmishers." General Howard and his staff tried to tell the impetuous Sherman that his assessment of the Southern lines was wrong, but the fiery chief would not be mollified. Insisting that Johnston was merely holding a weak line with a rear guard, Sherman insisted that Howard attack. The lot fell to Grose's 3rd Brigade of Stanley's Division to make the assault while the balance of Howard's men supported them with fire from a line of skirmishers.[18]

---

[16]"History of Smyrna," Smyrna Historical and Genealogical Society, http://www.smyrnahistory.org/_history_ofsmyrna.htm (accessed 6 July 2014).

[17]Ibid.

[18]*OR*, vol. 38, series V, ser. no. 76, 30–31; Castel, *Decision in the West*, 331.

Eighteen-year-old Sergeant Tighlman Jones of the 59th Indiana, which participated in Grose's attack, described the setting: "An open field lay before us extending to within 40 yards of the Rebs works." Jones explained that the Federals had to charge about four hundred yards of an open field to reach the Confederate lines, which were shielded by a wooded strip about forty yards wide. "Our skirmishers drove their pickets out of the field into the woods when two lines of battle was moved to the middle of the field on a slight elevation where we were ordered to build works. Rails was brought from the fences but could not be used," added Jones. "The Rebs artillery was giving us an ovation in shape of shell and cannister shot. We quit and laid now on the ground—their shells plowing up the dirt too close for comfort—in the open field with no shade, the heat about 100 degree F." Jones and his comrades looked for shelter in the exposed field. "Shelled until you have buried yourself in the ground to some depth with only your bayonet and paws, half choked by thirst, sometimes wishing it was somebody else." Sarcastically, Jones quipped: "We enjoyed our Fourth [of July]. Night came and brought relief. Our regiment was relieved and sent back to get something to eat and rest. Our loss July 4th was 19 killed and wounded." Noting that the Confederates had evacuated overnight once again, Jones added, "Next morning we could not find any body who was disposed to fight so we moved out." Had the imprudent Sherman not ordered the futile assault, Jones's men would have been spared the need to make an attack as Johnston's men would fall back during the night.[19]

Across the cornfield from Grose's men stood the veteran Texas brigade commanded by General Hiram M. Granbury from Cleburne's Division. One Texan described the charge: "The Yankee band had been playing all day, and about one o'clock one of their buglers sounded the charge. We all looked to the front, and soon saw our skirmishers just tearing through the woods. Co. A was ordered out to support them, and we went at the double-quick." The veteran continued:

> It was about 400 yards to the skirmishers' works, and we were anxious to get there before too many Yanks got into them. When we arrived within 100 yards of the works we saw that some of our skirmishers were trying to form a line. It was in an old field. The Yanks were in our works and some of them

---

[72]Glenn W. Sunderland, *Five Days to Glory* (Cranbury NJ: A. S. Barnes & Co., 1970) 151–52.

behind trees between us and the works. We deployed, raised a strong yell, and went at them. When we got to the works all we found was two Yankee knapsacks, two guns and a haversack fill of hard-tack and bacon. We did not get a man hurt in the charge.[20]

While Company A was spared any casualties during the action, the 10th Texas lost four men wounded and two captured.

To the left of Grose's attack, Reynolds's Arkansas Brigade directed a flanking fire on the exposed Federals. In the action, Private William J. Berry of the 9th Arkansas was killed as the left of Reynolds's skirmish line was driven in.[21]

Dr. McMorries of the 1st Alabama in Quarles's Brigade remembered, "July 4th the enemy fired National salutes with loaded shot and shell at us, their brass bands along the lines struck up National airs with loud huzzahs. To us it looked like a big gala day among the Federals. They were drinking whiskey and in high glee." The Alabama surgeon continued, "About 2 PM three double lines advanced about seventy yards over the felled timber, halted about seventy-five yards from us, when the men stringing out under a big oak log and picking it up, limbs and all, would swing it around parallel to our breastworks, forming a pretty good defense for themselves. They did this in 15 minutes, under a murderous fire from our lines. Nobody but a set of drunken fools would have attempted such a thing." The fighting continued on this part of the line between Stanley's Division and the Confederate right until after dark. During the fighting, Dr. Madding, the 1st Alabama's assistant surgeon to Dr. McMorries, was killed.[22]

At about 6:00 PM, the Federals made another attempt to take the Rebel works after thinking that the Confederate troops were evacuating. A Texas veteran remembered,

"the Yanks concluded to try us again. They came with the best yell I ever heard come out of Yankee throats, and at first I really thought they meant to interest us but when they came within a hundred yards our boys answered with a shout of defiance. This angered the Yanks, and the officers

---

[20]Chuck Carlock, *History of the Tenth Texas Cavalry (Dismounted) Regiment 1861–1865* (North Richard Hills TX: Smithfield Press, 2001) 151–52.

[21]James Willis, *Arkansas Confederates in the Western Theater* (Dayton OH: Press of Morningside Bookshop, 1998) 501–502.

[22]McMorries, *History of the First Regiment*, 122–23.

commenced shouting: 'Forward, men! Forward!' Our men answered by shouting: 'Come on, boys! Come on!' Just then a Dutch officer shouted to the Yanks, 'Trow away de knapsacks!' and our men shouted not to throw them off, as we wanted them. [The gritty Texans were spoiling for another chance at captured Yankee supplies.] The Yanks could not stand it any longer and they hid down in the bottom of a gully. The last command given by the Yanks was to hold that line. We knew where they were, and commenced firing on them, and about five minutes later the Yanks had gone and our videttes were in about a hundred yards of our works. One dead Yank and another who was mortally wounded fell into our hands. The one killed was as brave a man as ever lived. He was within 70 yards of us, loading his gun, perfectly cool, when 5 or 6 of the boys pulled down on him and killed him.

As dusk settled in along the lines, evening fires cast dark shadows across the battle-torn cornfield. The Texas soldier who had fought for Yankee knapsacks described the plight of the wounded Northern soldier: "The Yank that was wounded, as soon as he fell, shouted out to us that it was useless for us to fight them as they were too strong for us, but we soon showed him his mistake. He died in an hour or two, having been shot through the body."[23]

While the Federals sustained the majority of the day's casualties, the nation's birthday did not pass before the combat service of one of the South's division commanders was ended. Confederate General Thomas C. Hindman was injured in the eye during the day while riding his horse through a wooded area when he was struck by a tree limb. "As a result of being thrown from his mount, he suffered severe bruises and the blow from the branch caused a serious inflammation of the eyes that rendered him unfit for service in the field for an indefinite period of time," explained his biographers. He subsequently went to Atlanta and then to Macon to convalesce and would not return to active duty before the end of hostilities the following spring.[24]

Opposing Hindman's men were the veterans of King's Division, the Yankees continued to keep it warm on the skirmish line for the

---

[23]Carlock, *History of the Tenth Texas Cavalry*, 152.

[24]Diane Neal and Thomas Kremm, *The Lion of the South: General Thomas C. Hindman* (Macon GA: Mercer University Press, 1997) 196.

Confederates. With Federal artillery support, the Yankees were getting too many easy shots on their Rebel counterparts. One officer from Manigault's Brigade remembered being frustrated that they had to conserve their artillery ammunition and not return fire unless the Yankees in their front made an assault. Lieutenant Colonel C. Irvine Walker of the 10th South Carolina recorded, "In our line was a splendid Battery in breastworks and protected by well built works. But we had so little artillery ammunition that our batteries were only allowed to fire on advancing infantry. This afternoon the enemy moved up two batteries in an open field." Walker explained, "Our Battery was not allowed to fire until the infantry advanced. Consequently, the enemy's batteries concentrated on ours and eventually silence it. If it could have opened when these batteries first appeared, protected as it was, it could easily have driven them off."[25]

Some Confederate artillery was unleashed at King's men that day, however. One such shell gave a close call for Federals in the 2nd Battalion of the 18th Regular US Infantry Regiment. During a lull in the afternoon's fighting, Lieutenant Frederick Phisterer "took a walk of inspection to our extreme right and while conversing with the officer in command there, both of us of course lying down," explained Phisterer. "We saw a shell strike the ground in front of our line, jump over a little fence there and roll towards us, we kept low, it passed right between us and we hugged the ground still more." The Northern officer prepared to meet his maker. After a few heart-stopping moments, however, the shell had not exploded. Nerving himself up to chance a look, Phisterer peered behind him and found that "the shell was lying just a few feet from his boots." He again buried his head in the dirt, but found himself still alive after another minute. Collecting his wits, Phisterer crawled back to the shell and discovered that its fuse had fallen out. The lucky officer remembered, "Those were anxious moments."[26]

Other shells found their mark amidst the US Regular Brigade, however. One shell exploded directly over a part of 16th US Regular

---

[25]William Lee White and Charles Denny Runion, eds., *Great Things Are Expected of Us: The Letters of Colonel C. Irvine Walker, 10th South Carolina Infantry, C. S. A.* (Chattanooga: University of Tennessee Press, 2009) 127.

[26]Frederick Phisterer, manuscript, Larew-Phisterer Family Papers, US Army Military History Institute, Carlisle Barracks PA; Johnson, *That Body of Brave Men*, 511.

Infantry Regiment and took out half of the brigade's losses for the day. Earlier in the day, Colonel Stoughton was struck in the right leg by an exploding shell while he was making a reconnaissance in the morning. He would lose the leg and his brigade would lose their commander for the rest of the campaign. All told, the US Regular Brigade lost eight men killed and eleven men wounded during the action on the 4th. "If celebrating on the fourth consists in firing cannon we had plenty of it," remembered Lieutenant Arthur Carpenter of the 19th US Regular Infantry Regiment, "but I only wish the rebs had pointed their cannon the other way." Edgar Kellogg, another soldier from the US Regulars, simply recorded 4 July 1864 as "the liveliest anniversary of the Declaration of Independence I have ever seen."[27]

While Confederate batteries directed their fire toward King's lines, they were not the only ones. Federal artillerists also delivered some unintended fire upon the hapless Regulars. Lieutenant Walker of the 10th South Carolina recalled, "A very amusing incident occurred in our front at our last position near Smyrna Church. Our line made a very sharp angle at our Brigade." He explained,

> The Yankees came up to our front on two separate roads leading at more than a right angle to each other. They had not yet established a continuous line when our of their batteries opened upon our picket line taking it in flank and rear, just at the angle...during the fire they overshot our picket line and the shell went into their own lines on the other front. Another of their batteries thought that the first was rebel Battery opening fire upon it, and the two had a very brisk artillery duel for some time, and only ceased on one Battery silencing the other.

The Rebel officer continued, "It was very amusing to us although not so to the enemy who I supposed were very much chagrined when they discovered their mistake. I do wish we could see one half of the Yankee Army fighting the other, and we stand off and see the fun. I think I would enjoy that." Confederate General Arthur M. Manigault remembered seeing the two Federal batteries "engage each other with great spirit, firing round after round, each one under the impression that he was engaged with a rebel Battery. Our line was so tortuous that I am not surprised at the mistake

---

[27] Johnson, *That Brave Body of Men*, 511–12.

being made." Manigault added, "It was a very ludicrous sight, causing much merriment and shouts of laughter for the space of ten or fifteen minutes, until the two combatants found out their error."[28]

As it turned out, the Federal crossfire was between some guns of Hooker's XX Corps and Battery I, from the 2nd Illinois Light Artillery of Palmer's XIV Corps. Assigned to Jefferson C. Davis's 2nd Division, Battery I with its four three-inch ordinance rifles, had been ordered to the front to prepare to fire on the Rebel batteries early on 4 July, and "the men of the Battery were set to work building bastions for the guns," recalled Quartermaster Thaddeus C. S. Brown. "The morning was hot, the ground hard, but they worked faithfully till about nine o'clock with the Rebel breastworks in plain view, which showed a Battery bearing directly on our position, and every moment it was expected that it would open to prevent the building of the Union works," but the Confederates did not fire, apparently due to lack of ammunition.[29]

The Battery's captain, Charles M. Barnett, had a pet dog named Rosecrans who loved to chase Battery shells and rocks when thrown or flying. During this time, the dog was running around the Federal works yelping and carrying on while the men busily moved their guns into position. "In the afternoon the Battery was moved out of the works and taken still farther to the front," which was actually in front of Hooker's Corps and had come up and begun to entrench. "The Battery [accidentally] opened (against Hooker's men)," according to Quartermaster Thaddeus Brown of the Battery, firing to the right and front, but had not fired many rounds, when there came a volley of caseshot from the batteries of Hooker's Corps, fairly raking the ground in our immediate front, some pieces tearing their way through our Battery," Brown added. Meanwhile, Sherman and his staff had followed Battery I toward the front to gain a better view of the Rebel position and were within the line of fire of Hooker's batteries. It was the second time in as many days that Sherman had faced exposure to fire

---

[28]White and Runion, eds., *Great Things Are Expected of Us*, 128; R. Lockwood Tower, ed., *A Carolinian Goes to War: The Civil War Narrative of Arthur Middleton Manigault, Brigadier General, C. S. A.* (Columbia SC: University of South Carolina Press, 1983) 195.

[29]Thaddeus C. S. Brown, Samuel J. Murphy, and William G. Putney, *Behind the Guns: The History of Battery I, 2nd Regiment, Illinois Light Artillery* (Carbondale IL: Southern Illinois University Press, 1965) 98–99.

from his own men. Soon, he learned of the mistake, and sent for Hooker, who then "got one of the worst cursings from Sherman that he ever heard." Insulted, Hooker replied, "he was ready to take his corps and charge the rebels at any time to show that he was not afraid to be at the front, as Sherman intimated that Hooker did not know how far his line was from that of the enemy." Fortunately, Rosecrans and his comrades were spared from the friendly fire of Hooker's artillerists.[30]

In the rear of Howard's IV Corps, men from the 65th Ohio celebrated by cooking canned duck. They had expected to celebrate Independence Day eating the duck in Atlanta after capturing the city. Instead, amidst the rattle of Rebel skirmish fire and the lively artillery duel that occupied the attention of both sides and filled the day with incessant noise, the can was left unattended too long on the fire, and when the pressure in the can got too great, it exploded, sending soldiers in every direction. They thought that the Confederate artillerists had scored a direct hit on one of the Battery limbers posted nearby. So great was the duck explosion that overshadowed the artillery battle, that General Howard sent a staff officer to check on his men. The disappointed Ohioans "pocketed our disappointment and dined on hardtack, bacon and coffee," lamented one veteran.[31]

While the veterans from the 64th Ohio grieved over the loss of their Independence Day dinner, some of their comrades were busy with the war. The 42nd and 79th Illinois regiments were deployed as skirmishers while the 125th Ohio worked on improving the intrenchments for Bradley's Brigade.[32] One Federal private in Stanley's Division, Charley Brown of the 59th Illinois, received a shrapnel wound in the buttocks. Asked about his condition by his company commander, the private replied, "Captain, they have shot the ass off me this time."[33]

---

[30]Ibid., 98–100. However, the dog named Rosecrans did not survive the war; he was killed in front of Atlanta by a Rebel sharpshooter.

[31]Wilbur F. Hinman, *The Story of the Sherman Brigade* (self-published, 1897) 568.

[32]Charles T. Clark, *Opdyck Tigers, 125th Ohio* (Columbus: Spahr & Glenn, 1895) 284.

[33]Arnold Gates, ed., *The Rough Side of War: The Civil War Journal of Chesley A. Mosman* (Garden City NY: Basin Publishing Co., 1987) 235; Scaife, *Campaign for Atlanta*, 74.

In the center of Johnston's line near Smyrna Campground, Colonel Alfred J. Vaughan and his brigade of Tennessee veterans were resting behind a Battery when the Yankees opened up on the Battery and overshot it. One of the shells exploded near Vaughan and caused the loss of a leg; the Colonel was out of action for the remainder of the war.[34] Meanwhile, over to the far left of Johnston's lines, several miles away at Ruff's Mill, part of Stevenson's Division of Hood's Corps was being driven in, and Northern troops were threatening to turn Hood's exposed left flank. Johnston quickly dispatched portions of Hardee's Corps, including Cheatham's Division and Lowrey's Brigade of Mississippians and Alabamians from Cleburne's Division. Soon, however, Federals began massing for an apparent attack at the salient of the Southern line, and Lowrey's order was countermanded. Outnumbered nearly two to one, Johnston's men were used to being moved from one point to another to repel Yankee attacks.[35]

On the Confederate right, in Featherston's division, Colonel M. D. L. Stephens of the 31st Mississippi had a close call when "a shell fell in our trench right amongst the men with the fuse still burning. Sergeant Major Hightower picked up the shell and threw it in the air over our breastworks and it exploded, not more than ten feet high, a piece of the shell cut my bridle reigns that was on my arm holding my horse but did not injure me or my horse. We had several men wounded here," recalled Stephens.[36]

That evening, Johnston ordered another withdrawal. Quarles's brigade was ordered to guard the rear on the Atlanta Road and cover the retreat. "The men began filing silently to the rear by 9 PM, and by 11 PM the ditches were empty, and Quarles' brigade alone fronted Sherman's army," remembered Dr. McMorries of the 1st Alabama. "It was two hours later before we left, and they were two hours of anxiety. We knew that the enemy had but to advance to capture us, and all those indications of advance so well known to Confederates were in strong evidence. About 1 AM the command 'File right, march,' was whispered along the line," explained the Rebel

---

[34]Alfred J. Vaughan, *Personal Record of the Thirteenth Regiment, Tennessee Infantry, C. S. A.* (Parsons WV: McClain Printing Co., 1975) 34.

[35]David Williamson, *The Third Battalion Mississippi Infantry and the 45th Mississippi Regiment* (Jefferson NC: McFarland Publishing, 2009) 209.

[36]M. D. L. Stephens, *Recollections, 31st Mississippi*, MDAH, Special Collections, RG9, vol. 136 (R151, Box 20, File S3-289) 34.

surgeon. "We had moved out noiselessly; and stooping to conceal our movements, had gone but a few yards when Lieut. Knight was wounded by a bullet piercing his thigh and crushing his bone. He fell, but such was his pluck and presence of mind that not a groan escaped him," added McMorries. "Without a word being spoken, he was picked up by the litter-bearers and borne on with us."[37]

5 July 1864

One the morning of 5 July, it was discovered that the Rebels had once again vacated their works and fallen back, this time to the north banks of the Chattahoochee River where a new line of newly-designed and created works had been created for them under the direction of General Francis A. Shoup. Sherman ordered his commanders to press the retreating Confederates in the hopes of catching them unprepared for battle with a large river at their backs. The 41st Ohio from Wood's division of the IV Corps was detached to pursue a road that ran along the north bank of the Chattahoochee River. They learned from a railroad agent that the Southerners were attempting to evacuate their supply train and baggage over a pontoon bridge not far from them. "The regiment was put on the road and the march hastened," explained Lieutenant Colonel Robert L. Kimberly. "Approaching the river, the enemy's cavalry was found, but no trains."[38]

Meanwhile, in Featherston's Mississippi Brigade, some of the men forgot to wake one of their comrades before they slipped away in the night. Private George A. McGehee of Co. E, 22nd Mississippi, explained,

On the 5th of July, 1864 on a line about five miles south of Marietta, Georgia, I was awakened by a charge of Yankees on our empty breastworks and on jumping up three Yankee soldiers on top of the breastworks cried out "surrender" and on looking to see if there was any chance to get away—one said "Oh you cannot get away, I say surrender," which I did! They came to me and asked me when the army left and as I was left by the company sound

---

[37]McMorries, *History of the First Regiment*, 123.

[38]Robert L. Kimberly and Ephraim S. Holloway, *The 41st Ohio Veteran Volunteer Infantry in The War of the Rebellion 1861–1865* (Huntington WV: Blue Acorn Press, 1999) 92.

asleep, I did not know which I told them as I certainly would have gone with them if I had known the time of departure.

McGehee remembered that his captors were "part of [a] Sixty-odd Ohio Regiment."[39]

Johnston's staff officers had succeeded in hastening the withdrawal of his supply train, but they had left the pontoon bridge open for Wheeler's Cavalry to cross and then cut the moorings from both banks to allow the river's current to drift down the river to the right bank where at a bend in the river located at Montgomery's Ferry (now known as Bolton), it could be retrieved, collected, and stacked on wagons to preserve it for future use. Assigned the task of screening the Confederate wagon train were Martin's and Kelly's divisions of Wheeler's Cavalry. Wheeler's horsemen cut the moorings from the north bank, but when they attempted to cut the south bank's moorings, Federal sharpshooters from the 41st Ohio appeared on the north bank and laid down such a heavy fire across the river that the Rebel cavaliers were unable to cut the pontoon bridge loose. "The skirmish line, commanded by Major Williston, went forward at a run across the flat ground," explained Lt. Colonel Kimberly, "and so pushed the cavalry that the last man had barely time to cut the bridge loose and let it swing over to the Confederate side. The enemy opened up a lively fire across the river, and hurt some men, Major Williston receiving a shot in the shoulder." With the Southerners unable to recover the pontoons and with the crossing the river upstream at Roswell a few days later, the bridge was captured by the Federals on July 8th, thus depriving Johnston's army of that essential equipment.[40]

During the day, Lieutenant Rennolds of the 154th Tennessee of Vaughan's Brigade was in charge of the picket line. While he and a detachment from the regiment were busy exchanging skirmish fire with Yankees who soon arrived from across the field, several of the Tennesseans took the chance to bathe in the Chattahoochee River behind the large ridge on which the Confederate line rested, unaware of their proximity to the lines or of the Federal artillery's reach. Presently, a shell exploded among them,

---

[39]George A. McGehee, "Experience of Confederate Prisoner," *Gloster Record*, 17 March 1939, MDAH Civil War diaries, misc. collection, Z0371.002F, clipping.

[40]Scaife, *Campaign for Atlanta*, 78–79; Kimberly and Holloway, *41st Ohio Veteran Volunteer Infantry*, 92.

killing Lazarus Johnson and wounding privates Allen and Seth Speight. General Vaughan had been wounded on 4 July as his brigade also held a key salient in the Southern line at Smyrna Campground, and Colonel Michael Magevney replaced him. Two more Tennessee veterans, Bush Archer and M. B. Alexander, would be wounded on 7 July on the skirmish line as Vaughan's Brigade occupied an exposed part of the Confederate line.[41]

By 2:00 PM, after marching for more than five hours, Howard's IV Corps reached the Chattahoochee River. There, on a high hill, many Federal men took their first look at Atlanta, which was only nine miles away. As some of veterans from the 64th and 125th Ohio and other regiments from Bradley's brigade reached the summit, they stumbled into "the remains of a man completely mummified," who was hanging from the branch of a tree on top of the hill. "In the woods near the top of the hill there was a grewsome sight," recalled one Ohio veteran. "It was the body of a man, dressed in butternut, hanging by a hickory withe from a limb of a tree. Evidently he had been dead many days. Whether he committed suicide, or whether he was hanged by others—perhaps a captured Union scout or spy–we never knew." During the day, a squad of prisoners was captured by men from the 64th Ohio. Two or three of them were from the 65th Georgia and were happy to receive some hardtack and coffee. "That's the first grain of coffee I've seen in four months," explained one Georgian, who was carrying an Atlanta paper a couple of days old that boldly announced that "Sherman's campaign was near its end and would utterly fail; that his army was dispirited, discontented, and dwindling in numbers, and was in such a sad plight that it must soon retreat!"[42]

It must have made quite a contrast along the bank of the Chattahoochee River as thousands of eager Yankees took turns gazing from the hilltop southward toward Atlanta. Beneath them lay a score of beaten but content Rebels, sipping coffee and eating hardtack as other boisterous Federals shared the Atlanta newspaper that had proclaimed their demise.

---

[41]Edwin H. Rennolds, *A History of the Henry County Commands* (Kennesaw GA: Continental Books Co., 1961) 85; Scaife, *Campaign for Atlanta*, 174–75.

[42]Ralsa C. Rice, *Yankee Tigers: Through the Civil War with the 125th Ohio*, edited by Richard A. Baumgartner and Larry M. Strayer (Huntington WV: Blue Acorn, 1992) 121; Hinman, *Story of the Sherman Brigade*, 569.

Flapping in the wind above it all, the corpse of a butternut-clad Confederate seemed suspended against a deep blue sky.

4

RETREATING JOE

> Our army is sadly depleted, and now reports 10,000 less than the return of 10th June. I find but little encouraging.[1]

President Davis had followed the Georgia Campaign in earnest throughout the past three months, but when the Chattahoochee River came into the view of the armies, Davis became alarmed and got actively involved. He dispatched General Bragg to go to Atlanta personally to size up things and report back him, and he began a dialogue with Johnston where he searched for signs of an offensive spark from his commander and for a hope of saving Atlanta. Upon learning of the Confederate withdrawal from the Georgia Gibraltar, Kennesaw Mountain, Richmond journalists published a new moniker for Johnston—"Retreating Joe"—in a 4 July newspaper.[2]

For ten days President Davis had anxiously looked for assurances from his field commander that he and his army had a plan to repel Sherman's forces, but General Johnston continued to remain quiet about his plans and doubtful about the situation. On 7 July, Davis first learned that Johnston's army was nearing the Chattahoochee River. Although the president did not at the time know it, Johnston had already fallen back to the heights overlooking the river on 5 July, and, with his back to the river, Johnston was holding on 7 July a conference with his corps commanders to discuss withdrawing to the other side of the river, a move that he would make just two days later on 9 July.[3] Alarmed by the news that the Georgia Campaign was now so near the Chattahoochee River, with Atlanta so closely behind it, Davis sent a concerned telegraph to Old Joe.

---

[1] *OR*, series V, vol. 38, ser. no. 76, 878.

[2] John D. Wright, *The Language of the Civil War* (Westport CT: Oryx Press, 2001) 250; "Civil War Timeline Chronology for July 4," Blue and Gray Trail, http://blueandgraytrail.com/date/July_4 (accessed 6 July 2014).

[3] William R. Scaife, *The Campaign for Atlanta* (Atlanta: self-published, 1993) 81; F. A. Shoup, "Works at the Chattahoochee River," *Confederate Veteran Magazine* 3 (1895): 262–65.

General J. E. Johnston:

The announcement that your army has fallen back to the Chattahoochee renders me more apprehensive for the future. That river, if not fordable, should not be immediately in your rear, and if you cross, it will enable the enemy without danger to send a detachment to cut your communications with Alabama, and, in the absence of the troops of that department, to capture the cities, destroy the mines and manufactories, and separate the States by a new line of occupation. At this distance I cannot judge of your condition or the best method of averting calamity. Hopeful of results in Northern Georgia, other places have been stripped to re-enforce your army until we are unable to make further additions, and are dependent on your success. Efforts have been made and are still making to organize the reserves as an auxiliary force for State defense. You well know what progress has been made in Georgia and Alabama.

JEFFERSON DAVIS[4]

Johnston, appearing surprised by Davis's inquiry, responded to the president the next day, in a defensive reply:

Near Chattahoochee Railroad Bridge,

8 July 1864

His Excellency the PRESIDENT, Richmond:

SIR: I have received your dispatch of yesterday. Our falling back was slow. Every change of position has been reported to General Bragg. We have been forced to fall back by the operations of a siege, which the enemy's extreme caution and greatly superior numbers have made me unable to prevent. I have found no opportunity for battle except by attacking intrenchments. It is supposed in the army that Sherman's immediate objective is the capture of Atlanta. A part of our troops is on the north side of the river intrenched, and, having six bridges behind it, so that we do not think it exposed. It is believed here that there are 16,000 cavalry for defense of Mississippi and Alabama, and, therefore, that the enemy cannot make a detachment able to invade that department. Might not 4,000 of this cavalry prevent the danger by breaking up the railroad between the enemy and Dalton, thus compelling Sherman to withdraw?

J. E. JOHNSTON[5]

---

[4]*OR*, series V, vol. 38, ser. no. 76, 867.

[5]Ibid., 868–69.

General Johnston's response was not reassuring to the president. Not only did his general not appear to have a plan to reverse things in Georgia, he wanted to take more troops, some 4,000 cavalry, from neighboring Alabama and Mississippi, which had already been stripped of everything save this cavalry force and given to Johnston back in the spring. If Johnston believed that 4,000 cavalry operating in Sherman's rear and along his railroad and communications between the front and Dalton would reverse course, why couldn't he dispatch it from his own force? He had more than 12,000 cavalry at his own disposal. With General Joe Wheeler's Cavalry Corps of some 8,000 troops, Johnston also had General William H. Jackson's Cavalry Division from the Army of Mississippi with another 4,000 veteran cavalry.[6] Subsequently, this very plan to send a detachment of Wheeler's cavalry against Sherman's supply lines at and around Dalton was tried by General Hood during the siege of Atlanta with little or no positive results.

The war appeared to be going well for the Confederacy in all of the other theaters; at least it seemed that way to Davis during the weekend of 8–10 July. In Virginia, Lee had stopped Grant and had him in more or less a stalemate while vigorously contesting any attempt by Grant to flank him or gain more ground. A Confederate army was threatening Washington DC under General Jubal A. Early, who was dispatched by Lee even though Grant far outnumbered him. Lee had taken the war to the very gates of the Federal capital even while on the defensive at Richmond. On 9 July, General Early routed a Federal force near Frederick, Maryland, and was marching on Washington.

At Charleston, South Carolina, Federal troops were driven from their beachhead on James Island. In the west, General Forrest had twice beaten and hurled back superior Northern numbers, and he and others appeared to be more than holding their own against Federal forces despite being greatly outnumbered. And in Kentucky, Missouri, and Arkansas, the occupying Federal troops were literally ducking for cover as pro-Southern uprisings by large segments of the citizenry were common.

In the political arena, Northern papers and Democrats openly talked of the futility of continuing the conflict, and that a peaceful solution should be sought. Lincoln and his cabinet worried about the upcoming elections.

---

[6]*OR*, series III, vol. 38, ser. no. 74, 653–54, 679.

Everywhere the South was winning, or it appeared to be so to President Davis and the government in Richmond as they headed for church on Sunday, 10 July—except in Georgia. Johnston continued to fall back in the face of Sherman's approaching legions, despite having the South's largest army under his command, and despite having an army that was proportionally closer in terms of the number of men to Sherman's armies than any of the other principal armies facing each other during summer 1864.[7]

After receiving Johnston's Friday, 8 July, dispatch wherein he requested the 4,000 cavalry, President Davis sent off a telegram to Johnston with his initial reaction:

Richmond, Va., 11 July 1864
General J. E. Johnston:
Your telegram of the 8th received. You know what force you left in Alabama and Mississippi, and what part of it has, since you left that department, been transferred to re-enforce you in Georgia. You were, therefore, in condition to judge of the value of the belief that there are now for the defense of those States 16,000 cavalry, and of the conclusion drawn from that belief. The proposition to send 4,000 cavalry from that department to break up the railroad between the enemy and Dalton suggests the inquiry. Why not so employ those already sent to you from that department, or others of equal number, for the proposed operation, the importance of which has long been recognized, and the immediate execution of which has become a necessity? If it be practicable for distant cavalry, it must be more so for that which is near, and former experiences have taught you the difference there would be in time, which is now of such pressing importance. Will write to you and give information in relation to the condition of General S. D. Lee's department, which, I perceive, you cannot possess.
JEFFERSON DAVIS[8]

---

[7]John S. Bowman, ed., *The Civil War: Day by Day* (New York: Dorset Press, 1989) 168–70; Albert Castel, *Decision in the West* (Lawrence: University Press of Kansas, 1992) 345–46.

[8]*OR*, series V, vol. 38, ser. no. 76, 875. By adding the phrase "former experiences have taught you" that time is of the essence, Davis may have been referring to Johnston's Vicksburg performance where Johnston planned to attack Grant on 5 July, one day too late for the beleaguered city and its defenders.

Davis continued to stew on the matter, and the more he considered Johnston's note, the angrier he became. Later, Senator Benjamin H. Hill, an ally and friend of Joe Johnston, met with the president and urged a Confederate cavalry strike. Senator Hill had met the week before with Johnston at his headquarters in Georgia. There, Johnston relayed his oft-repeated request that General Forrest be sent from Mississippi with his cavalry force to operate on Sherman's rear, tearing up his supply line and communications. The Davis administration had heard from others on the subject, including the powerful Georgia politician Howell Cobb, who had written Secretary of War James A. Seddon on 1 July requesting that Forrest be unleashed on Sherman's line of communications. Cobb, an ally of Johnston, went on to volunteer that the people in Georgia "have the utmost confidence in General Johnston, which has not been shaken by his falling back, and they believe that the President will do all that any man can do."[9] Davis asked Hill if Johnston had told him how long Johnston could hold the defensive line north of the Chattahoochee River. Hill replied that he could hold for a month or more—"a long time."[10] The president then showed Hill a telegram just received from Georgia:

> Atlanta, July 10, 1864.
> On the night of the 8th the enemy crossed at Isham's, or Cavalry Ford; entrenched. In consequence we crossed at and below the railroad and are now about three miles from the river, guarding the crossings.
> J. E. Johnston.[11]

Davis then sent a more detailed telegraph to Johnston wherein he answered fully Johnston's query about the availability of troops from Mississippi and Alabama. The president explained to Johnston that they had their hands full and would not be giving up any more troops to Georgia. Davis went on to explain that he had met with Senator Hill and that Davis would get additional information and "exact statements from the War Department" and respond yet further to Johnston's request if he wished.[12]

---

[9]*OR*, series V, vol. 38, ser. no. 76, 858.

[10]Castel, *Decision in the West*, 344.

[11]*OR*, series V, vol. 38, ser. no. 76, 873; Castel, *Decision in the West*, 344.

[12]*OR*, series V, vol. 38, ser. no. 76, 875–76.

The president then had the following letter sent to the War Department:

> Executive Department, C. S. A.
> Richmond, Va., July 11, 1864
> General S. Cooper,
> Adjutant and Inspector General:
> GENERAL: I am directed by the President to request that you will furnish him at once with official information in reply to the following questions: What re-enforcements have been sent to General J. E. Johnston since he took command of the army in Georgia, and at what times have they been sent? What force had he when he assumed command? What force has he now of infantry, what of cavalry, what of artillery? What force is there in General S.D. Lee's department, specifying infantry, artillery, and cavalry, and dividing into the commands of General Maury, of General Forrest, of General Roddy, & c. ?
> Very respectfully, your obedient servant,
> BURTON N. HARRISON,
> Private Secretary.[13]

The president wasn't finished on this busy Monday. He had already dispatched General Bragg to Atlanta. He also heard from Secretary of State Benjamin and Secretary of War Seddon who, along with a number of congressmen, newspapers and concerned citizens and businessmen from Georgia, called for Davis to replace Johnston.[14]

Almost as if he meant to irritate the president further, Johnston sent the following telegraph to General Bragg on the same day:

> Near Atlanta, July 11, 1864
> General Bragg:
> I strongly recommend the distribution of the U. S. prisoners, now at Andersonville, immediately.
> J. E. JOHNSTON,
> General.[15]

---

[108]Ibid., 874.
[14]Castel, *Decision in the West*, 347.
[15]*OR*, series V, vol. 38, ser. no. 76, 876.

Johnston was probably unaware of how far over the edge his dispatches had pushed the Confederate commander in chief, but he likely didn't care. He also couldn't know that Bragg was on his way to spy on him and his army. Davis was already furious with Johnston's failure to act when he received this dispatch calling for the evacuation of Andersonville.

Andersonville, Georgia, was more than 150 miles away, and about as far away from a hostile army as any part of the Confederacy. Located in rural southwestern Georgia, the prisoner of war camp at Andersonville was created in the Deep South because of its remoteness. It was not close to anything of strategic value, and surely Johnston wasn't seriously considering its evacuation. However, in fairness to Old Joe, he had been given a report that a detachment of Federal cavalry was being sent to South Georgia and that Andersonville was the intended target. The report turned out to be false, but Johnston's timing couldn't have been worse. In reaction to Johnston's request, Davis turned to his most trusted general and advisor, General Robert E. Lee.

The next morning, Tuesday, 12 July, after receiving Johnston's Andersonville dispatch, the president telegraphed Lee at Petersburg, "General Johnston has failed, and there are strong indications he will abandon Atlanta. He urges that prisoners be removed immediately from Andersonville. It seems necessary to remove him at once. Who should succeed him? What think you of Hood for the post?"[16] Lee gave a quick reply. "I regret the fact stated. It is a bad time to relieve the commander of an army situated as that of Tennessee. We may lose Atlanta and the army too. Hood is a bold fighter. I am doubtful as to the other qualities necessary."[17]

While waiting on Lee's response, President Davis snapped off a reply to Johnston's Andersonville evacuation recommendation:

Richmond, July 12, 1864.
General J. E. Johnston:
Your telegram received. You have all the force that can be employed to distribute or guard prisoners; know the condition of the country and

---

[16]Ibid.; Castel, *Decision in the West*, 352.
[17]*OR*, series V, vol. 38, ser. no. 76, 876; Castel, *Decision in the West*, 352–53.

prospects of military operations. I must rely on you to advise General Winder as to the proper and practicable action in relation to U. S. prisoners.
JEFFN. DAVIS[18]

After reflecting more on the subject, Lee sent a letter to President Davis later that evening. Fully aware of the import of trying to keep Atlanta, Lee wrote freely to the president:

> Still if necessary it ought to be done [that is, the removal of Johnston from command].... If Johnston abandons Atlanta I suppose he will fall back on Augusta. This loses us Mississippi and communications to the Trans-Mississippi. We had better therefore hazard that communication to retain the country. Hood is a good fighter, very industrious on the battlefield, careless off, & I have had no opportunity of judging his action, when the whole responsibility rested upon him. I have a very high opinion of his gallantry, earnestness & zeal. Genl. Hardee has more experience in managing an army.
>
> May God give you wisdom to decide in this momentous matter.[19]

Lee reluctantly had concurred with the president's conclusion that a change might have to take place, but he, in his subtle approach, recommended Hardee to the president as if to dismiss Hood from consideration. Davis continued to worry about the state of things in Georgia, but he decided to hold off making a change. He wanted to hear from Bragg, who should be in Atlanta the next day.

The forty-seven-year-old Bragg stepped off the train in Atlanta on Wednesday morning, 13 July. In the opinion of one female observer, Bragg "is a tall, skinny, ungainly man...whose gray, spiked hair and beard make him look like 'an old porcupine.'"[20] A couple of staff officers accompanied him, and, before meeting Johnston or anyone from his staff, Bragg telegraphed the president: "Have just arrived without detention. Our army all south of the Chattahoochee, and indications seem to favor an entire evacuation of this place. Shall see General Johnston immediately."[21] Braxton

---

[18]*OR*, series V, vol. 38, ser. no. 76, 877.
[19]Ibid.; Castel, *Decision in the West*, 353.
[20]Ibid.
[21]*OR*, series V, vol. 38, ser. no. 76, 876; Castel, *Decision in the West*, 353.

Bragg didn't think much of Joe Johnston, and the feeling was mutual. Johnston once said, "I know Mr. Davis thinks he can do a great many things other men would hesitate to attempt, i.e. try to do what God failed to do. He tried to make a soldier of Bragg but it couldn't be done."[22] Braxton Bragg had left Georgia in disgrace just six months earlier. Now, he had returned as the president's chief of staff and was carrying orders to "confer with Genl Johnston in relation to military affairs there" and report back to the president as to his findings.[23]

It didn't take Bragg long to form his opinion; it had already been formed. He "finds but little encouraging," and at just 1:00 PM, before he has made any visit to Johnston—and only a couple of hours after he arrived in Atlanta—Bragg sent his second telegraph to Richmond:

> Atlanta, July 13, 1864—1 PM
> His Excellency JEFFERSON DAVIS:
> The enemy are reported by General Wheeler as having crossed two corps to this side of the river about nine miles above the railroad bridge. An official report has just reached General Wright that the enemy's cavalry, accompanied by artillery, crossed the Chattahoochee this evening nine miles from Newnan. Were at last accounts advancing on that place. Our army is sadly depleted, and now reports 10,000 less than the return of 10th June. I find but little encouraging.
> B. Bragg[24]

It is clear that Bragg was setting up Johnston for removal. This may have been the plan all along between Bragg and Davis, but Davis could have made the decision without sending Bragg to Atlanta. Moreover, the president was struggling not only with the decision to remove Johnston but also with finding his replacement. This was perhaps Davis's greater problem. Clearly, President Davis fretted over finding a suitable substitute. This dilemma likely explains why he sought Lee's advice on Hood as well as the council of his cabinet, congressmen, and others on the critical issue; Davis

[22]Stanley F. Horn, *Army of Tennessee* (Norman: University of Oklahoma Press, 1952) 343; James W. Rabb, *W. W. Loring: Florida's Forgotten General* (Manhattan KS: Sunflower University Press, 1996) 161.

[23]Castel, *Decision in the West*, 353.

[24]*OR*, series V, vol. 38, ser. no. 76, 878.

knew could this be the defining decision of his presidency and influence the outcome of the war. After the war, General French related a conversation he had with President Davis:

> In a private conversation with President Davis he told me that so great was the pressure made on him by deputations, committees, individuals, officials, and the press demanding to know if Atlanta and the State of Georgia were to be given up without a battle for its preservation, that he was reluctantly obliged to relieve Gen. Johnston to satisfy the clamorous demands made for a halt and a battle in defense of the State while the army was in the mountainous region, and so he yielded to the cry of the people.[25]

It was widely thought that General James Longstreet, who was born in South Carolina but raised in Georgia, would have been given command except for wounds to his throat and right shoulder suffered in May during the Battle of the Wilderness. In July, Pete Longstreet was convalescing from his wounds in Augusta and later at Union Point, Georgia, near Athens, but he would not be ready to return to duty until October. The Macon *Daily Telegraph*, quoting from the Richmond *Dispatch*, printed, "It is believed that Longstreet would have been appointed Johnston's successor but for his wound, from the neuralgic effect of which he is still suffering."[26]

It is unfair to Jefferson Davis to conclude that he merely took Bragg and Hood's opinion on the state of affairs in reaching his decision, or that the president let his disfavor of Johnston cloud his decision. Perhaps this is why the president dispatched Bragg and didn't immediately make a move to transfer command. "Jefferson Davis and Braxton Bragg were not stupid men,"[27] claims the well-respected apologist and historian Richard McMurry, who favors the president's move. Davis and Bragg understood full well the crisis, and they had to take other factors across the Confederacy into consideration, which Johnston, in their estimation, couldn't—or wouldn't—see.

---

[25]Samuel G. French, *Two Wars: An Autobiography of Gen. Samuel G. French* (Huntington WV: Blue Acorn Press, 1999) 218.

[26]Jeffry D. Wert, *General James Longstreet, The Confederacy's Most Controversial Soldier* (New York: Simon & Schuster, 1994) 387–91; Johnston and Hood, *Macon Daily Telegraph*, 4 August 1864.

[27]Richard M. McMurry, *Atlanta 1864: Last Chance for the Confederacy* (Lincoln: University of Nebraska Press, 2000) 133, 137–38.

5

SHERMAN

"War is cruelty. There is no use trying to reform it, the crueler it is, the sooner it will be over."[1]

All was quiet along the Chattahoochee River on Saturday, 16 July 1864, as the Federal armies of Major General William Tecumseh Sherman rested along its banks.[2] There, the general considered his options. Since 5 July, he had been contemplating how best to cross the river and take Atlanta, and on 6 July, Sherman began preparations for a set of crossings north and east of the Georgia capital. Born on 8 February 1820 at New Lancaster, Ohio, to Charles R. Sherman (a lawyer) and the former Miss Mary Hoyt, William Tecumseh Sherman was given the unusual middle name after the Shawnee chief, Tecumseh, whom had been both feared and admired for his tenacity and chivalry from Pittsburgh to the Mississippi River and throughout the Ohio Valley.

Tecumseh means "Crouching Panther" or "Shooting Star," depending upon the version of the white man's translation of the Shawnee name, and both were fitting for the Indian chieftain who tried to preserve his people's way of life through treaties and peaceful solutions but who was not afraid of war and used it to great effect when necessary. Quite often, stories of butchery and abuse against enemies, including women and children, were attributed to the white settlers, French traders, or British troops of Tecumseh's region, or to other rival Indian tribes, but not to Tecumseh and his tribe during his reign. Tecumseh denounced such barbarism and held his people as well as his adversaries to a higher standard. He was killed in 1812 at the Battle of the Thames in Canada, and he left both a void and a legacy for his leadership and civility in the white and Indian communities alike.

---

[1]Lloyd Lewis, *Sherman: Fighting Prophet* (New York: Smithmark Publishers, 1994) 360.

[2]*OR*, series I, vol. 38, ser. no. 76, 150–58.

For all of these reasons, father Charles felt it important to remember this warrior in one of his offspring.[3]

Nicknamed "Cump" when he was a child because the three syllable name "Tecumseh" proved too hard for his siblings to pronounce, Sherman was, like most Civil War generals, a West Point graduate (1840). So, too, were classmates Ulysses S. Grant from Ohio (1843) and Virginian George H. Thomas (1840). Cump would also later be called "Billy" by his friends and classmates, and by this point in the war, his men referred to him as "Uncle Billy."[4]

One hundred days of hard fighting and marching in the hot Georgia sun had brought Sherman's veterans to within sight of Atlanta. It was during this time that many of his men saw the Gate City of the South for the first time. Major James A. Connally, assistant inspector general for Absalom Baird, wrote his wife on 12 July:

> Mine eyes have beheld the promised land! The domes and minarets and spires of Atlanta are glittering in the sunlight before us, and only 8 miles distant. On the morning of the 5th, while riding at the extreme front with the General [Absalom Baird], and eagerly pressing our skirmishers forward after the rapidly retreating rebels, suddenly we came upon a high bluff [Vinings Hill] overlooking the Chattahoochee, and looking southward across the river, there lay the beautiful 'Gate City' in full view, and as the soldiers caught the announcement that Atlanta was in sight, such a cheer went up as must have been heard even in the entrenchments of the doomed city itself.

> In a very few moments generals Sherman and Thomas (who are always with the extreme front when a sudden movement is taking place) were with us on the hill top, and the two veterans, for a moment, gazed at the glittering prize in silence. I watched the two noble soldiers—Sherman stepping nervously about, his eyes sparkling and his face aglow—casting a single glance at Atlanta, another at the River, and a dozen at the surrounding valley to see where he could best cross the River, how he could best flank them. Thomas stood there like a noble Roman, calm, soldierly,

---

[3]Lewis, *Sherman: Fighting Prophet*, 20–22.

[4]Ibid., 23, 48–53; Albert Castel, *Decision in the West* (Lawrence: University Press of Kansas, 1992) 85–86.

dignified; no trace of excitement about the grand old soldier who had ruled the storm at Chickamauga.

> I felt proud that I belonged to this grand army, and that I was at the front instead of at the rear, doing fancy duty.[5]

There was an air of invincibility in the western armies of Sherman's command. The speed of his advances had also captured the imagination of the Confederates who faced him. When rumor spread that General Forrest had destroyed a tunnel in the Yankee's rear, a despondent Southerner replied that it wouldn't matter, for "Sherman carries a duplicate tunnel."[6] Sherman's armies seemed to move with one voice and in singleness of purpose. This was no accident. During the campaign, Sherman once wrote Grant,

> You may go on with the full assurance that I will continue to press Johnston as fast as I can overcome the natural obstacles and inspire motion into a large, ponderous and slow, by habit, army. Of course it cannot keep up with my thoughts and wishes but no impulse can be given it that I will not guide.[7]

Sherman once bragged to his superiors in Washington that his armies had his full confidence and that each knew his duty.

> We have good corporals and sergeants and some good lieutenants and captains, and those are far more important than good generals. They all seem to have implicit confidence in me. They think I know where every road and by-path is in Georgia, and one soldier swore that I was born on Kenesaw Mountain.[8]

While Sherman's men were confident of success, perceived Northern failures by Grant and the Army of the Potomac at the Wilderness, Spotsylvania, and Cold Harbor in Virginia as well as by Sherman's men at Resaca, New Hope, and Kennesaw had led to horrendous casualty lists, and no tangible results, at least to the casual eye. Looking at the picture more closely gave much reason for positive feelings about the results of Sherman's

---

[5]James A. Connolly, *Three Years in the Army of the Cumberland* (Bloomington: Indiana University Press, 1996) 234.

[6]Lewis, *Sherman: Fighting Prophet*, 360.

[7]*OR*, series I, vol. 38, ser. no. 75, 507.

[8]Lewis, *Sherman: Fighting Prophet*, 400.

campaign to date. Most of the newspaper correspondents who followed Sherman's legions "were impressed by the desolation of the country through which they had just passed by the 'Foot and Walker's Express.'"[9] A Chicago *Tribune* newspaper reporter wrote, "There is no adult male population in northern Georgia, except a few old men."[10]

There were other reports on the condition of the population, explaining that the women were "'lean, lank, and scrawny,' addicted to snuff dipping and tobacco chewing—most of them 'intense she-rebels.'"[11] A New York writer exclaimed, "The more I see of the social circle here, the more am I convinced that this is a war of democracy against aristocracy—that it is a war for the emancipation of the 'poor white trash' of the South as much as it is for the [African Americans].[12]

The same correspondent wrote about a time on the campaign when near Big Shanty, Georgia, he entered a house where an old lady was sharing a pipe with a Federal soldier:

> "You'ns fellows don't fight we'ns fair," the old lady reproached. "How so?" queried the soldier.
>
> "Why, you'ns fight wid bags, and that's not fair," said the old lady, drawing a very indignant puff from the pipe. "Besides," said she, "you'ns have furriners fightin'."
>
> "Not that I know of," came the reply from the trooper.
>
> "O, you'ns can't come over me that way. Wasn't there fellows from a place called New York here to-day?"[13]

Amusement aside, the North had plenty of reason for optimism, and, after four years of hard fighting, the war was going their way, even if only professional soldiers like Sherman and Grant and Thomas knew it.

---

[9]J. Cutler Andrews, *The North Reports the Civil War* (Pittsburgh: University of Pittsburgh Press, 1985) 558.

[10]"From the Front," Chicago *Daily Tribune*, 12 and 16 June 1864; Andrews, *North Reports the Civil War*, 559.

[11]Andrews, *North Reports the Civil War*, 559; Cincinnati *Daily Commercial*, 7 June 1864; "From the Front," Chicago *Daily Tribune*, 8 June 1864.

[12]"News from Georgia," New York *Herald*, 19 June 1864; Andrews, *North Reports the Civil War*, 559.

[13]"News from Georgia," New York *Herald*, 1 July 1864; Andrews, *North Reports the Civil War*, 559.

But politics is politics, and Abraham Lincoln needed victories. The nation had grown weary of the war, and the general population was not convinced that the North was winning or that it was worth the price they were paying even if they were succeeding. Lincoln needed something tangible to convince the voters to re-elect him; casting a ballot for the Lincoln administration meant affirming his position on the war for preserving the Union and freeing the slaves. It also meant continuing on with the war until the South capitulated, regardless of the cost. The price of war had been high that year, but there had been no glorious triumph over a Confederate army or capture of a Southern city to show for it. There had only been the dreadful, and seemingly endless, list of casualties. Grant and Lee had fought to a draw and were now stuck in the trenches around Richmond and Petersburg with no apparent prospect of a change in the circumstances any time soon.

Self-appointed emissaries from both sides seeking to negotiate a peace were calling for an audience with the other side's president, but neither president could afford to budge in his position. When asked to entertain a meeting with a couple of would-be Southern peacemakers who had gone to Niagara Falls, Canada, Lincoln correctly sensed that the men had no official authority from President Davis or the Confederate government. He responded to the request:

Executive Mansion,
Washington, July 18, 1864
To Whom it may concern:
Any proposition which embraces the restoration of peace, the integrity of the whole Union, and the abandonment of slavery, and which comes by and with an authority that can control the armies now at war against the Unites States will be received and considered by the Executive government of the United States, and will be met by liberal terms on other substantial and collateral points; and the bearer, or bearers thereof shall have safe-conduct both ways.
Abraham Lincoln[14]

---

[14]Carl Sandburg, *Abraham Lincoln: The Prairie Years & The War Years* (New York: Budget Book Service, 1993) 533–34.

The president had discerned the situation and the parties involved correctly, and he used the incident to re-enforce his position in prosecuting the war. These abilities to read people and to change the dialogue of an issue to favor his position served Lincoln well. A couple of years earlier, after McClellan's Army of the Potomac was defeated on the Virginia peninsula, when one of the veterans complained to Lincoln about his superior officer, the president merely told him, "Go home and read Proverbs XXX, 10." The man went and looked it up in his Bible and found "Accuse not a servant unto his master, lest he curse thee, and thou be found guilty."[15]

It may not have made him popular, but Lincoln used his wisdom well. During the long, hard summer months of fighting in 1864, he studied the military situation. With Grant's forces stalemated in Virginia, Forrest's Confederate cavalry keeping Mississippi swept of any Federal advances, and Southern gains in the Trans-Mississippi Department, his eyes shifted to the Deep South with hopes that Sherman's men would provide him with victories in the only theater of the war that appeared to have any prospect of success during the summer. Lincoln needed Sherman to strike a decisive blow, to make a splash in the papers, and to give the North something to convince themselves that the war had been worth fighting and that the end was in sight.

Also approached by an envoy of would-be emissaries, President Jefferson Davis met with a Methodist clergyman from Illinois, Colonel James Fraizer Jaquess, who had raised the 73rd Illinois Infantry, and a journalist, James R. Gilmore. When asked for acceptable terms from the Confederate leader, Davis replied:

> I worked night and day for twelve years to prevent it [war], but I could not. The North was mad and blind, would not let us govern ourselves, and so the war came; now it must go on until the last man of this generation falls in his tracks and his children seize his musket and fight our battles, *unless you acknowledge our right to self-government*. We are not fighting for slavery. We are fighting for independence, and that, or extermination, we *will* have.[16]

The Confederate president alluded to his service in two terms as a United States senator before the war, but it was clear that he, like Lincoln,

---

[15]Ibid., 299.
[16]Ibid., 535.

felt the weight of the static military situation that had developed by July 1864. During the Atlanta Campaign, the 73rd Illinois, nicknamed "The Preacher Regiment," would do its part to ensure the Confederacy's extermination.[17]

Like a pair of champion poker players, Lincoln and Davis were both "all in," meaning that each had bet all of his chips on the hand that was dealt to him during summer 1864. Both men had won and lost battles and armies during the previous three years of war, and while Lincoln held more chips by winning battles with larger pots and by having a larger bankroll, Davis could still win if he could catch a few pots, and even the chip count. Perhaps then, he could win the war, but it would take some bold gambling, he reasoned. With the few chips that he had left, Davis believed that there was no use wasting them; he should risk them on the chance that he could win the pot that summer, and with it, independence for the Confederacy.

Lincoln, by contrast, had more chips and ordinarily could afford to be more cautious, but he was working on a deadline. The presidential election was coming in early November; if he had not won the war by then, or guaranteed its outcome, he believed that he would be defeated, and the war would thus be lost. Moreover, in both the North and South, large portions of the armies were made up of three-year volunteers who had joined during late 1861 or the first half of 1862. Their terms of enlistment would expire before the warm weather came in 1865. Therefore, if either man were to win with such a hand, he needed to do so during the summer and fall 1864—

---

[17]W. H. Newlin, D. F. Lawler, and J. W. Sherrick, eds., *A History of the Seventy-Third Regiment of Illinois Infantry Volunteers* (Decatur IL: Regimental Reunion Association of Survivors of the 73rd Illinois Infantry Volunteers, 1890) 20–21, 289, 350. The 73rd Illinois earned its nickname "the Preacher Regiment" because, in the communities where the ten companies of the regiment were raised, ministers led the call to arms. In fact, other regiments (including the 115th and 117th Illinois) at Camp Butler made such a call for the nickname "Preacher Brigade." On 17 September 1862, Henry A. Castle, the adjutant's clerk for the 73rd Illinois, sent a letter to the Cincinnati *Commercial* and described the unit as the "Methodist Preacher Regiment" and identified the colonel, lieutenant colonel, major, and six of the ten captains as preachers. He added, "Six or seven of the twenty lieutenants are also licensed Methodist preachers. Being thus officered, you may rest assured we are a good set of boys." Newlin, Lawler, and Sherrick, eds., *A History of the Seventy-Third Regiment of Illinois Infantry Volunteers (1890)*, 645. It was also nicknamed "the Persimmon Regiment."

before the winter weather set in. Sure, both leaders could, and did, continue to draft men to fill the ranks, but the willingness and quality of the service of men conscripted into duty was never as good as those who had volunteered and experienced some of the campaigns and battles of the war, and it would take time to train any new troops.

In the South all able-bodied men between eighteen and thirty-five had already been brought into service. There were no more "chips" for the Confederacy to spend unless they allowed slaves to serve in exchange for their freedom, a concept that some Southern leaders were beginning to consider. In the North, a steady supply of European immigrants, particularly from Germany and Ireland, continued to come to its shores, giving the Lincoln administration at least some chips in reserve. But the people in the North were growing weary of the war, and a feeling of despair was prevalent after each battle as the long roll of casualties filled local newspapers. For both leaders, time was running out. The battles of the long 1864 summer would decide the outcome of the war.

6

THE GATE CITY

While the number of good, moral citizens was increasing...the town was characterized as tough. It grew distinctively a railroad center with the vices common to rough frontier settlements. Drinking, resorts, gambling dives and brothels were run wide open...and the sporting element were insolent in their defiance of public order. There were more saloons than churches; more bawdy houses than banks.[1]

The march from Chattanooga to the gates of Atlanta, "The Gate City of the South," or, the "Gate City," had been a series of flanking movements for Sherman and his legions as they slipped around the right or left of the smaller Confederate army, forcing Johnston to fall back and give up one strong defensive position after another without a general engagement. The Gate City was a fitting description for Atlanta as it held the key to the Deep South and the rich farms and crops in central and southern Georgia. Johnston's constant withdrawals increasingly worried the Confederate leaders in Richmond about the prospect of losing Atlanta with its factories and mills and its strategic location as the Confederacy's hub for transportation and communications.[2]

Atlanta was a young city at the outbreak of the Civil War, even by American standards. Originally named Terminus, the city came about after

---

[1]Franklin Garrett, quoted in Cathy Cox, "History of Atlanta," IEEE SENSORS Conference 2007, http://ewh.ieee.org/conf/sensors2007/atlanta/history.html (accessed 6 July 2014).

[2]Laurence Urdang, *Names and Nicknames of Places and Things* (New York: New American Library, 1987) 241; Michael D. Shook, *By Any Other Name* (Hoboken NJ: Wiley & Sons, 1994) 137–8; Although sometimes referred to as "The Gateway City," this nickname is more commonly associated with St. Louis, the "Gateway to the West." Atlanta seems to hold the keys to the deep South and thus has been called the Gate City to the South. Today, one can hardly travel by air or on the interstates in the South without traveling through Atlanta; so, too, during the Civil War in the railroad era did travelers have to go through the city during their journey through the deep South.

the Georgia General Assembly in 1836 voted to create a state railroad from the Tennessee River near Chattanooga south "to a point on the southeastern bank of the Chattahoochee River."[3] The Georgia legislature hoped to link Georgia and its coastal and river cities and farms with the Midwest. With the removal of the Creek Indians from middle Georgia in the 1820s and the Cherokee Indians from north Georgia in the 1830s after the discovery of gold near Dahlonega around 1828, the fledgling state began carving up and giving out the newly acquired lands of northwest Georgia to white settlers in a series of land lotteries.[4]

Further, as the state's population rapidly grew, westward expansion and the need for new roads, particularly the new railroad for train travel, was inevitable. "The new railroad was to be called The Western & Atlantic Railroad of the State of Georgia," an appropriate name describing the legislators' goal of joining the two regions across the state. Colonel Stephen Harriman Long, an experienced army engineer, was commissioned to choose the best and "most practical route for the new rail line." Beginning on the Tennessee River at Rossville, Long mapped out several routes through the southern Appalachians toward the center of Georgia and the Chattahoochee River and carefully surveyed each one. In 1837, after considering a half-dozen routes, he finally settled on an ending point about eight miles south of the Chattahoochee River "where connecting ridges and Indian trails converged. He drove a stake into the red clay near what is now Five Points in Downtown Atlanta."[5] This location would mark the ending place for the new rail line through northwest Georgia.

In 1839, after receiving a contract from the Monroe Railroad to build an embankment that would enable the future junction of the Monroe Railroad from Griffin and Forsyth from the south with the Western & Atlantic Railroad, John Thrasher built a settlement called Thrasherville near the peg that marked the planned terminus of the Western & Atlantic

---

[3] Cox, "History of Atlanta."

[4] See also Charles A. Overby, "Georgia Gold," *Gems and Minerals* (Cocoa Beach FL: Big Ten, 2007); "Georgia Gold Mines, Prospecting, Panning, Treasure Hunting and Rockhounding," www.goldmaps.com/east/georgia_gold_mines.htm (accessed 7 July 2014); David Williams, *The Georgia Gold Rush: Twenty-Niners, Cherokees, and Gold Fever* (Columbia: University of South Carolina Press, 1994).

[5] Kenneth Coleman, ed., *A History of Georgia* (Athens: University of Georgia Press, 1982) 153–73; Cox, "History of Atlanta."

Railroad. "The Monroe Embankment, a $25,000 project, required about two years to complete. To fulfill his contract John Thrasher brought in many laborers, built rough shelters to house them and opened Atlanta's first store. Atlanta's first religious service, labor trouble, social event and baby are associated with this settlement."[6]

As construction of the Western & Atlantic Railroad from this southernmost point, or "Terminus," progressed to the northwest toward Chattanooga, other railroad construction began, linking the Terminus of the Western & Atlantic Railroad to the rest of Georgia.[7] The Georgia railroad was the first such link, connecting the Terminus with Augusta. Subsequently, the Macon and Western Railroad would link the Terminus with Macon and south Georgia, and the Memphis and Charleston Railroad would link the Terminus with the west to Alabama and Mississippi. Later, the Atlanta and La Grange Railroad would link the Terminus with La Grange and Columbus so that by the time of the outbreak of the Civil War there were four rail lines with five railroad companies sending trains regularly to the Gate City.[8]

The Terminus began as a settlement of railroad workers and engineers. Soon, merchants and craftsmen, opportunists and land speculators began to arrive. While the Terminus continued to grow, it remained a rough town filled with railroad workers and prostitutes. Still, it had not yet earned a name to call itself save the railroad's moniker, Terminus. In December 1842, the little village was ready to test its first rail line when the section of the Western & Atlantic Railroad was completed between Terminus and Marietta, the county seat of Cobb County. After searching for a locomotive, the *Florida* was found in Madison, Georgia, located about fifty miles to the east, but there was no rail link to bring it to Terminus. The leaders of the

---

[6]"Thrasherville," Fulton County Historical Markers, http://georgiainfo. galileo.usg.edu/topics/historical_markers/county/fulton/thrasherville (accessed 7 July 2014).]

[7]"In 1842 the terminus was changed to the place now marked by the Zero Mile Post," "Thrasherville," Fulton County Historical Markers.

[8]William Key, *The Battle of Atlanta and the Georgia Campaign* (Atlanta: Peachtree Publishers, 1981) 6; Webb Garrison, *Atlanta and the War* (Nashville: Rutledge Hill Press, 1995) 16–19; "Atlanta Old and New: Prehistory to 1847," Roadside Georgia, http://roadsidegeorgia.com/city/atlanta01.html (accessed 7 July 2014).

new railroad contracted for a large wagon to be built to carry the iron horse to Terminus by pulling it with the more traditional kind of horse. The wagon was the largest one ever seen in the South and would take sixteen mules, not horses, to pull it. After several weeks of planning and moving the *Florida* to Terminus, she was ready to take her maiden trip. Pulling only an empty box car, the *Florida* chugged to Marietta and back home again to a waiting and cheering throng of men and women who had gathered in front of Mr. John Thrasher's little store at Terminus on Christmas Day 1842 to watch.[9]

Almost overnight, shops sprang up at the southern Terminus of the Western & Atlantic Railroad. As Terminus continued to grow, it became apparent that the little rail village needed a name more befitting the growing citizenry. It had at times been referred to as Thrasherville, after the early railroad contractor and merchant, John Thrasher, but it appeared that a name more befitting a growing rail center was needed. Hence, when a charter for the town was presented the next year at the state capital in Milledgeville, some clerks decided to rename the town in honor of the daughter of former governor and railroad proponent, Wilson Lumpkin. Her name was Martha Atalanta Lumpkin, and "Marthasville" was given her charter in 1843.[10]

Marthasville soon saw sawmills, factories, warehouses, banks, and some textile mills and ironworks among her businesses. While she continued to grow, Marthasville remained a rough town holding on to her early railroad and prostitute roots. According to Atlanta historian Franklin Garrett,

> While the number of good, moral citizens was increasing…the town was characterized as tough. It grew distinctively a railroad center with the vices common to rough frontier settlements. Drinking, resorts, gambling dives and brothels were run wide open…and the sporting element were insolent in their defiance of public order.[11]

Garrett added that "There were more saloons than churches; more bawdy houses than banks."[12]

---

[9]Garrison, *Atlanta and the War*, 16–17; "Atlanta Old and New"; Cox, "History of Atlanta."

[10]Garrison, *Atlanta and the War*, 17; Cox, "History of Atlanta."

[11]Franklin Garrett, quoted in Cox, "History of Atlanta."

[12]Ibid.

As Marthasville grew in the 1840s, new chief engineer of the Georgia railroad, J. Edgar Thompson and many other citizens thought the name was too bucolic for the growing city. They believed the former governor's daughter's middle name "Atalanta" was more fitting. Atalanta was the fleet-footed woman in Greek mythology who had been raised by a bear and could out run, out fight, and out hunt any man. Thinking the name Atalanta better symbolized the growing rail city with its fast locomotives, Thompson and others recommended the change, and in 1847, the town of nearly three hundred settlers received a new charter under the name Atlanta. Whether the second "a" was dropped by a scrivener's error or whether it was omitted by design, would never be known, but the city's third try at a name would last.[13]

Atlanta grew from three hundred folks in 1847 to more than 2,500 people in 1850. In just three years, the city's first census recorded 1,063 white males, 997 white females, 277 female slaves, and 216 male slaves lived in the Gate City. Additionally, there were 13 free black females and 6 free black males who resided in Atlanta in 1850. Because the city was growing so rapidly, an unofficial census taken in 1854 revealed that the population had increased to 6,025, more than double the count of the 1850 census.[14]

Over the next ten years, the city grew into an important place of industry and commerce, but it became clear that its location at the end of the Southern Appalachians had made her a vital rail center.

> By 1861 Georgia had an extensive railroad system, the best in the Deep South and second only to Virginia in the whole South. Over fourteen hundred miles of tracks, mostly 5-foot gauge, crisscrossed central Georgia, spilled over into the northern and southern sections of the state, and linked

---

[152]Garrison, *Atlanta and the War*, 17; Garrett, quoted in Cox, "History of Atlanta"; "Atlanta Old and New: Prehistory to 1847," Roadside Georgia, http://roadsidegeorgia.com/city/atlanta01.html (accessed 7 July 2014); "Atalanta," www.paleothea.com/Myths/Atalanta.html (accessed 7 July 2014).

[14]US Census Records, 1850, National Archives; Garrison, *Atlanta and the War*, 18–19; Garrett, quoted in Cox, "History of Atlanta"; "Atlanta Old and New: Prehistory to 1847," Roadside Georgia, http://roadsidegeorgia.com/city/atlanta01.html (accessed 7 July 2014); Coleman, *A History of Georgia*, 153–73; *Funk & Wagnalls New Encyclopedia*, 1986 ed., vol. 3, 37–38.

up with other lines snaking out into the rest of the nation.[15]

In contrast, "older and wealthier states such as New York and Pennsylvania failed to match railroad expansion in the southern state that her citizens proudly called 'The Empire State of the South.'"[16] While each state developed their own rail lines as the industrial revolution spread across the nation, Georgia out-spent her sister states by pumping some $26 million into rail lines, including over $6 million in the Western & Atlantic Railroad during this time.[17] The ratio of railroad miles to inhabitants in Georgia was 1 to 744 in an 1860 study, compared to 1 to 1,083 miles for the rest of the country. As one historian wrote, "In Georgia and the rest of the Cotton Belt, railroads were designed to serve two functions: transportation of cotton to the coast and importation of manufactured goods and foodstuffs to the interior."[18] As Georgia's railroads continued to spread across the state, Atlanta grew at an increasing rate.

The 1860 Census revealed that Atlanta had grown to 9,554 inhabitants of which approximately 20 percent were black. The city was growing so fast that it was impossible to obtain an accurate figure, and some accounts even placed the population of Atlanta as high as 20,000.[19] By the time that war broke out, the city boasted more than "3,800 homes, iron foundries, mills, warehouses, carriage and wheelwright shops, tanneries, banks and various small manufacturing and retail shops."[20] Atlanta contained an iron plant that was able to roll out over 18,000 tons of rails each year.[21] While Richmond continued to produce the majority of the Confederacy's iron works, Atlanta produced a considerable amount of iron for military purposes during the war. Moreover, Atlanta produced many other materials vital to the war effort, including shoes, wagons, clothes, knives, buttons, canteens, spurs, bridles, belt buckles, accouterments, and food stuffs. Much of this production during the war years can be attributed to the forward-thinking

---

[15]Coleman, *A History of Georgia*, 161.

[16]Garrison, *Atlanta and the War*, 21.

[17]Coleman, *A History of Georgia*, 161–62.

[18]Garrison, *Atlanta and the War*, 21.

[19]US Census Records, 1860, National Archives; Coleman, *A History of Georgia*, 172; Garrison, *Atlanta and the War*, 23.

[20]Cox, "History of Atlanta."

[21]Coleman, *A History of Georgia*, 172.

governor Joseph E. Brown, who had helped to make Atlanta the center of the state's industrial war effort.[22]

There was another, more personal, reason that made Atlanta a goal of capture for Sherman and his men. Up to this point in the war, Sherman and his armies had seen the brand "made in Atlanta" on virtually every captured wagon, weapon, box, article of clothing, or war material. By summer 1864, the Yankees in the western theater of the war had come to view Atlanta as the heart of the Confederacy, and they were ready to stop its pulse. As he and his men eyed the distant spires of Atlanta in early July, their focus changed from destroying Johnston's army to destroying the Gate City. To them, Atlanta had become the Richmond of the west.

With refugees from other parts of the South, particularly Tennessee and north Georgia, and with displaced journalists from several refugee papers that somehow continued to be issued daily, including the Knoxville *Register*, the Chattanooga *Rebel*, and the Memphis *Appeal*, and with the five daily newspapers, the Atlanta *Appeal*, the *Intelligencer*, the *Southern Confederacy*, the *Reveille*, and the *Commonwealth*, Atlanta was a busy and crowded place. Atlanta "had become the supply and shipping center of the Confederacy" and Sherman had to take her.[23]

General Sherman did not plan his famous March to the Sea strategy at Chattanooga before leaving for Georgia, although the journey began there. He could not have hoped for more than to celebrate Christmas that year with his men in sight of the Atlantic Ocean at Savannah, but his plan to pursue, engage, and destroy Johnston's Army of Tennessee and penetrate deep into Georgia would result in just that. In what has become known as the Atlanta Campaign, Sherman's mission began as an effort to go after Johnston's army, wherever it could be found and cornered, and then destroy it. Perhaps the campaign should have been more appropriately termed the Georgia Campaign. His plan to capture Atlanta did not mature until well into the campaign when it became clear that the Gate City was central to the South's war effort, both physically and psychologically.[24]

---

[22]Garrison, *Atlanta and the War*, 22–23.

[23]Key, *Battle of Atlanta*, 4–6, 15; Cox, "The History of Atlanta."

[24]Lloyd Lewis, *Sherman: Fighting Prophet* (New York: Smithmark Publishers, 1994) 345; Williams, *Lincoln and His Generals*, 306–307; *OR*, Grant to Sherman, 4 April 1864, series I, vol. 38, ser. no. 74, 245–46.

7

WAR IS CRUELTY

You I propose to move against Johnston's army, to break it up and to get into the interior of the enemy's country as far as you can, inflicting all the damage you can against their war resources. I do not propose to lay down for you a plan of campaign, but simply lay down the work it is desirable to have done and leave you free to execute it in your own way. Submit to me, however, as early as you can, your plan of operations.[1]

As the war progressed, Sherman and his superior, General Grant, came to realize that as long as the Confederacy could put an army in the field, it still had life. This was a concept that President Lincoln understood early in the war, but it took three years of fighting until he found generals to implement it. Lincoln was strong in his assessment that the war could not be won until the principal Confederate armies in the field were destroyed. When General George Gordon Meade, commanding the Army of the Potomac, proposed to capture Richmond in fall 1863 after his army was victorious at Gettysburg, the president replied,

To avoid misunderstanding, let me say that to attempt to fight the enemy slowly back into his intrenchments [sic] at Richmond, and then to capture him, is an idea I have been trying to repudiate for quite a year.

My judgment is so clear against it that I would scarcely allow the attempt to be made if the general in command should desire to make it. My last attempt upon Richmond was to get McClellan, when he was nearer there than the enemy was, to run in ahead of him. Since then I have constantly desired the Army of the Potomac to make Lee's army and not Richmond, its objective point. If our army cannot fall upon the enemy and hurt him where he is, it is plain to me it can gain nothing by attempting to follow him over a succession of intrenched lines into a fortified city.[2]

---

[1]Ulysses S. Grant, *The Civil War Memoirs of Ulysses S. Grant* (New York: Tom Doherty Associates, 2002) 276.

[2]T. Harry Williams, *Lincoln and His Generals* (New York: Alfred A. Knopf,

Shortly before his death, Grant wrote about the North's plan to end the war in spring 1864 after he took command of all of the Federal armies: "My general plan now was to concentrate all the force possible against the Confederate armies in the field.... Accordingly, I arranged for a simultaneous movement all along the line."[3] Grant wanted Sherman to strike for Johnston at the same time that he would have the Army of the Potomac strike at Lee's army, thus preventing either Southern army from re-enforcing the other. This concept of coordinated action in two theaters had been much discussed during the war, and in Grant and Sherman, Lincoln had finally found the leaders to make it happen.

Thus, after their visit, Sherman received his orders from Grant in a confidential letter from Washington DC on 4 April 1864:

> General:—It is my design, if the enemy keep quiet and allow me to take the initiative in the spring campaign, to work all parts of the army together, and somewhat towards a common centre. For your information I now write you my programme, as at present determined upon....
>
> You I propose to move against Johnston's army, to break it up and to get into the interior of the enemy's country as far as you can, inflicting all the damage you can against their war resources.
>
> I do not propose to lay down for you a plan of campaign, but simply lay down the work it is desirable to have done and leave you free to execute it in your own way. Submit to me, however, as early as you can, your plan of operations.[4]

Years after the war Sherman stood in the Burnet House in Cincinnati, Ohio, where he and Grant met in March 1864 for the last time before each left for the spring offensive, pointed at the room where they planned the "grand strategy," and exclaimed, "Yonder began the campaign...we finally settled on a plan. He was to go for Lee and I was to go for Joe Johnston. That was his plan. No routes prescribed.... It was the beginning of the end as Grant and I foresaw right here...."[5]

1952) 286–87; Lincoln to Halleck, 19 September 1863, *Works of Lincoln*, IX, 128–30.

[3] Grant, *Civil War Memoirs*, 275–77.

[4] Ibid., 276.

[5] Lloyd Lewis, *Sherman: Fighting Prophet* (New York: Smithmark Publishers,

While President Lincoln and his principal commanders, Grant and Sherman, understood that in order to win the war the Southern field armies had to be destroyed, many leaders on both sides never understood this concept. In the North, Lincoln was constantly given plans by his generals on how they would capture Richmond and thus end the war. Lincoln had suffered from a long line of generals who devised plan after plan to take the Army of the Potomac into the gates of Richmond only to suffer defeat at the hands of the Army of Northern Virginia. From generals McDowell and McClellan, to Pope, Burnside, Hooker and Meade, Lincoln constantly found that his generals in the eastern theater mistook the key to winning the war as the capture of Richmond instead of the destruction of the Confederate army in the field opposing it. In the end, he proved to have a better military mind that most of his subordinates. He even had to open Grant's eyes a bit before his greatest warrior bought into the concept.[6]

On the Southern side, Johnston understood that as long as he commanded a viable and effective army in the field in front of Sherman, and Lee did the same against Grant in Virginia, the Confederacy lived. By 1864, the notion that the South could win the war with bold offensive movements against a vastly superior foe was no longer realistic. It was for this reason that after the failures at Chickamauga and Chattanooga to reverse through offensive means the misfortunes of the Gettysburg and Vicksburg defeats, many informed men of the South knew that they no longer possessed the ability to win the war outright, merely the chance to prolong it. Winning the war by not losing it, and causing the North to grow weary of its savagery and high price in men and money, became the strategy employed by some learned Southerners like Joe Johnston who had embraced this theory since the beginning of the war. President Davis did not agree.

To Davis, and a number of equally respected Southerners, the Confederacy had a limited supply of resources in terms of men, war materials, and money, and they had to win before these resources ran out. For the Southern president, these precious resources were dwindling in the face of overwhelming Federal forces, weaponry, and funding, and thus, the South was running out of time. If he did appreciate the concept of winning the war by not losing through a long and drawn-out war of attrition and

---

1994) 344–45.

[6]Williams, *Lincoln and His Generals*, 291–306.

survival, the president was not willing to accept it. It is probable that Davis was guilty of the latter and not the former, for the well-reasoned and educated president surely knew that a morose end was in sight after the devastating setbacks of 1863. Faced with the responsibility of holding the patchwork Confederacy together and winning its independence, the weary Davis was faced with limited options.

The country won its first independence by adopting the policy of attrition. Perhaps the South could win its second independence this way, too, reasoned some. Others saw the quick strike and bold victories accomplished by Stonewall Jackson and Robert E. Lee in the east, and Nathan Bedford Forrest in the west as evidence that the offensive policy was best. Moreover, constant withdrawals meant that much of the South would suffer under the capture and control of the Yankee invaders, which made the give ground policy unpopular. For a number of compelling reasons, including the rapidly failing economy, the lack of resources and limited supply of manpower, and the waning interest by the Southern citizens in continuing the costly and bloody struggle, Davis looked to Johnston to reverse the Confederacy's failing fortunes by engaging Sherman north of the Chattahoochee, and not to lose Atlanta without a fight. The president wanted the offensive option. His general had chosen the other.

Since the opening rounds of early May, Johnston had shrewdly prepared and fallen back to countless lines of strong defensive works, but Sherman would not commit his forces to a full scale assault; instead, he used his forces to flank the Southerners, causing Johnston to withdraw during the night, taking everything with him save the trench works. By daylight Sherman would again face an empty line, and thus the cat-and-mouse game would repeat itself, closer and closer to Atlanta with each successive move. The constant digging, flanking, and withdrawing prompted one Rebel officer to remark, "I think Sherman and Johns[t]on have cut parallel ditches across three counties."[7]

Although outnumbered two to one during most of the campaign, Johnston had been moving his smaller forces across the northwest Georgia chessboard, blocking Sherman's various flank movements with great skill

---

[7]Walter A. Rorer to Cousin Susan, 9 June 1864, vertical files, 20th Mississippi Infantry, Carter House Library and Archives, Franklin TN, courtesy T. Glover Roberts, Historian.

and audacity. He had bloodied Sherman a few times where he had been able to maneuver his forces so that more or less equal numbers faced each other in a smaller and isolated area. To be sure, each leader made mistakes. Johnston was slow to withdraw from Dalton when Sherman flanked him and nearly took Resaca in Johnston's rear before the Southern leader could react. Johnston had also failed to carry out any effective counterattack while Sherman was spread out on the march, although he attempted to do so once in what has come to be known as the Cassville Affair.

For his part, Sherman failed to press his advantage at Resaca, allowing Johnston to retreat from a near trap. Sherman failed to appreciate his opportunity to bag the Confederate army at Dalton by closing the back door at Resaca. At New Hope, Sherman's men had gotten tangled up in deep woods that were much like the Wilderness region in Virginia, where the vast forested areas rendered Sherman's superior artillery useless and neutralized his advantage in numbers, thus permitting Johnston to fall on the Federal forces and bloody them. At Kennesaw, Sherman lost his patience in the flanking moves, and, like Grant at Cold Harbor in Virginia, he needlessly sacrificed his men against the Confederate works.

From a rational viewpoint, it is hard to imagine asking more of Johnston than he had done to this point of the campaign. For three months his men had been employing the battle tactic of withdrawing fighting in the face of the larger and equally skilled blue force. Arguably, the Yankees opposing him were perhaps the largest, most cohesive and effective fighting machine created by the Federal forces in the entire war. But, President Davis and the people of Richmond had come to expect the unexpected. In its own front yard, the Confederate high command had witnessed the audacity of the Southern legions as Lee and his lieutenants and the men of the Army of Northern Virginia had won one improbable victory after another for three years in the face of long odds. In fighting Sherman to a tactical draw, Johnston was certainly competent. Unfortunately, the Rebel leader had been expected to do the exceptional.

Sherman's men had been feeling their way to the stony Chattahoochee since Independence Day.[8] By pushing Johnston quickly from the Chattahoochee River line, Sherman hoped to gain Atlanta before Old Joe could get into strong defensive positions around the Gate City. On 3 July,

---

[8]*OR*, series I, vol. 38, ser. no. 76, 73.

Sherman pressed his generals to attack and push Johnston's army as much as possible as Johnston's back was to the Chattahoochee River. In a letter to Major General George Thomas on the same date at 6:45 PM, Sherman explained,

> The more I reflect the more I know Johnston's halt [along the heights immediately to the west and north-west of the Chattahoochee River] is to save time to cross his material and men. No general such as he, would invite battle with the Chattahoochee behind him. I have ordered McPherson and Schofield to cross Nickajack at any cost and work night and day to get the enemy started in confusion toward his bridges. I know you appreciate the situation. We will never have such a chance again, and I want you to impress on Hooker, Howard, and Palmer [Thomas's three corps commanders] the importance of the most intense energy of attack tonight and in the morning and to press with vehemence at any cost of life and material. Every inch of his line should be felt and the moment there is a give, pursuit should be made—by day with lines, but by night with a single head of column and section of artillery to each corps, following a road. Hooker should communicate with McPherson by a circuit if necessary and act in concert. You know what loss would ensue to Johnston if he crossed his bridges at night in confusion with artillery thundering at random in his rear.... But still we have now the best chance ever offered, of a large army fighting at a disadvantage with a river to his rear. Send copies of this to Hooker, Palmer, and Howard. I have instructed Schofield, McPherson, and Garrard.[9]

Whether Sherman was upset at Thomas and the other commanders for failing to press with vehemence Johnston's veterans in another costly frontal assault before the Rebel positions north of the Chattahoochee River will never be known. The Southerners were dug in along a well-fortified line of earthworks on the high ground just above the Chattahoochee River and any such all out assault at any cost of life and material by Sherman's generals would have resulted in the slaughter of his men. Sherman had managed his campaign well, taking advantage of his superior numbers by out-flanking Johnston from Dalton to the Chattahoochee, except for an ill-considered charge at Kennesaw Mountain. Sherman ordered the attack there because he thought that the Confederates were spread too thin and that if he had been successful, his troops could have cut off much of Johnston's army from

---

[9]Ibid., 30–31.

its retreat line to Marietta and subsequently to Atlanta. He also thought that both Johnston and his own men "had settled down into the belief that flanking alone was my game."[10]

Having previously commanded the Federal army of the Tennessee, Sherman was familiar with its men and officers who had been with him during the bloody struggle at Shiloh and the arduous Vicksburg campaigns. Subsequently, these men came with him to Chattanooga in November 1863. His hand-picked commander of the Army of the Tennessee was Major General James Birdseye McPherson, a fellow Ohioan. Sherman trusted his old army, which consisted of the veteran XV, XVI, and XVII Corps commanded by Major generals John A. Logan, Grenville M. Dodge, and Francis P. Blair respectively, to handle the tough assignments. By July, everyone in the Federal armies knew that these men were Sherman's "pets."[11]

Sherman frequently sent McPherson and his "pets" on the daring flank movements, while using Major General George H. Thomas's Army of the Cumberland with its IV, XIV, and XX Corps, commanded by Major generals Oliver O. Howard, John M. Palmer, and Joseph Hooker respectively, to do the less glorious work of demonstrating in front of the Rebel trenches to occupy Johnston's attention. Sherman also quite often sent his third army, the small Army of the Ohio, commanded by the young but eager Major General John M. Schofield, with its lone XXIII Corps, to flank Johnston's defenses.[12] Schofield, just thirty-two years old, was a fellow mid-westerner and held the confidence of General Grant, who had promoted him to command of the tiny Army of the Ohio in January. In time, Schofield's desire to please his superior during the Georgia Campaign would win Sherman's trust as well.[13]

General Thomas, the Rock of Chickamauga, was another story. The veteran Thomas was an old friend and West Point roommate of Sherman, and the two had served together early in the war. While they worked well together for the most part during the Georgia Campaign, there were some

---

[10]Ibid., 123.

[11]Ibid.

[12]Ibid., 123–26.

[13]Albert Castel, *Decision in the West* (Lawrence: University Press of Kansas, 1992) 78–88.

difficult moments. Thomas was a bit older and had been in command of the Army of the Cumberland longer, while Sherman had only commanded the XV Corps in Grant's Army of the Tennessee. Thomas had fought well during the war, including winning an important early war victory at Mill Springs, which rid eastern Kentucky of Confederates. He had also helped to steady the Federal line at Stone's River and stave off disaster at Chickamauga, where he earned the title "Rock of Chickamauga" by holding off the victorious Confederate assailants while the remainder of the Federal army fled to Chattanooga. Thomas's men had been largely responsible for breaking the Confederate hold on Chattanooga. They were bitter about the defeat at Chickamauga and unhappy with the unfortunate and undeserving heckling that was heaped upon them by the Army of the Tennessee, which had been sent from Vicksburg to liberate them and the besieged Scenic City. Making bold and determined assaults on Orchard Knob, Lookout Mountain, and Missionary Ridge, Thomas's men had broken the Southern grip on Chattanooga in November 1863, opening the door for the spring 1864 campaign into Georgia.[14]

In contrast, Sherman's war record could be viewed with mixed results. He was at First Manassas where his green troops fought as well as could be expected until they fled the field with the rest of the Federal army. At Shiloh, he and his men were totally unprepared for a surprise attack but rallied to help General Grant turn the tide of battle. And at Vicksburg, though ultimately victorious while serving as part of Grant's invading force, Sherman had been unsuccessful at Chickasaw Bayou, the Delta Expeditions, and Snyder's Bluff when he had independent commands.[15]

If Sherman hadn't proven himself by victories in battle, he had certainly proven that he understood the concept of total war on the population and property of the enemy, a concept that he and Grant had adopted during the Vicksburg Campaign. By February of 1864, Sherman's Army of Tennessee had occupied and burned the Mississippi capital of Jackson three times. The city had come to be called "Chimneyville," for chimneys were virtually the

---

[14]Ibid., 85–86; Lewis, 343–45; James R. Sullivan, *Chickamauga and Chattanooga Battlefields* (Washington DC: United States Department of the Interior, 1961) 36–37, 40–41.

[15]Edwin Cole Bearss, *The Campaign for Vicksburg*, 3 vols. (Dayton OH: Press of Morningside Bookshop, 1991) vol. 1, 175–192, 213, 224..

only structures that remained in the city. Grant knew Sherman would deliver this style of war to Georgia as he pursued Johnston.

After having been given command of the western armies, Sherman met Thomas on 28 March 1864 to discuss the upcoming Georgia Campaign. He no doubt worried about how Thomas would receive him, despite his subsequent assertions to the contrary. To his old roommate's credit, Thomas was the true gentleman and greeted Sherman warmly. If Thomas was hurt by Grant's passing over him to place Sherman in command of the western Federal armies, he didn't show it. Once when responding to an officer's complaint at being passed over for promotion, Thomas retorted "I have educated myself not to feel."[16]

Sherman's friendship with Thomas cooled during the war, perhaps due to Grant's influence. They had grown apart, both personally and professionally. Certainly their view on how to best win the war differed. Sherman also knew of Grant's distaste for Thomas, and while he and Tom, which he was sometimes called, remained friends, sometimes Sherman, who was able to differentiate between friendship and business, would unfairly complain to Grant about him. Sherman's hot temper also likely compelled him to fire a few barbs now and then to his lieutenants, even at an old friend. Sherman sulked when he felt that Thomas and his Army of the Cumberland, the largest of his three armies, and his cavalry had acted too slow in advancing against Johnston. Writing to General Grant on 18 June, Sherman complained,

> ....Garrard is over-cautious and I think Stoneman is lazy...[but] my chief source of trouble is the Army of the Cumberland, which is dreadfully slow. A fresh furrow in a plowed field will stop the whole column and all begin to intrench. I have again and again tried to impress on Thomas that we must assail and not defend; we are the offensive, and yet it seems the whole Army of the Cumberland is so habituated to be on the defensive that, from its commander down to the lowest private, I cannot get it out of their heads.[17]

By all rights, Thomas should have been given command of the western armies. He was senior to Sherman, both in terms of rank in the pre-war army, and in the provisional ranks of the Civil War. His war record certainly

---

[16]Richard O'Connor, *Thomas: Rock of Chickamauga* (New York: Prentice Hall, 1948) 195.

[17]*OR*, series I, vol. 38, ser. no. 75, 507.

had been as good as, if not better, than Sherman's to that point in the war. The fact that he was from Virginia could not have helped him, but Thomas did not lose the chance at promotion because of it. He lost it because Grant did not like him, and it was Grant who decided who would replace him. Sherman had the good fortune of being Grant's most trusted lieutenant while Grant piled up successes in the western theater at Forts Donelson and Henry, at Shiloh and Memphis, at Vicksburg and Jackson, and at Chattanooga and Missionary Ridge, and when Grant went east to take command of the entire Federal effort, he felt comfortable leaving command of the western Federal armies to his old friend Sherman.

Wars produce leaders and heroes, whether by design or by accident, and this war was no exception. What made the stories of the Civil War's generals so intriguing, at least in part, was the contrast in their leadership styles and personalities. The romantic period was fast coming to a bloody and sad end; an era that epitomized the virtues of Old South and the pre-war gentleman officer of the United States Army was slipping away. With it, the country was losing a way of life as the noble and traditional qualities of manhood found in the old and long-valued genteel traits like chivalry, honor, restraint, dignity, fairness, courage, nobleness, and gentleness gave way to the uncultured, the unorthodox, the unelaborate, the often unfair, the unrestrained, and sometimes, the uncouth. At odds in this war, in terms of leadership style, were the old ways of the aristocratic South and the new ways of some from the energetic and industrious North. Perhaps more accurately put, the old east coast traditional, highly educated, and romantic school of thought contrasted with the western, plain, simple, uneducated—but practical—school of thought. Nowhere was this more poignant than the contrast between the Old Dominion's romantic military leaders such as Lee, Jackson, Joe Johnston, and Federal general George Thomas, and the Midwestern armies' common-looking and common-acting commanders Sherman, Sheridan, McPherson, and Grant, and Southerner Nathan Bedford Forrest.

George Thomas, despite his loyalty to the Union, and his faithful and most competent and trusted service to the North, was cast from an old-style Virginia mold, where the finer romantic qualities found in man were of the purest part. Sherman and Grant were made of something new and different in the fledgling nation, found in the growing Midwest and west of the Allegheny Mountains. Cut more out of leather and burlap sackcloth than silk or fine wool, these western men understood the concept of total war and were not too modest to apply it upon the land and people of the enemy. Whether the gentle Southern heroes such as Robert E. Lee, Thomas J. "Stonewall" Jackson, and Joseph E. Johnston of Virginia and the Northern hero George Thomas understood the concept of total war is unclear. What is clear, however, was that these men were not made to fight that way. It was not in their character to act with such barbarism, in their minds, as to engage in total war upon the enemy's lands, people and property. There was still a certain amount of gamesmanship in the act of war, and no finer honor could be had than to show restraint to a conquered foe.

Confederate Major General Samuel G. French, a Quaker and native of New Jersey, chose the Southern romantic way of life after graduating from West Point and marrying a Philadelphian. On Sunday, 17 July, French wrote in his diary of Sherman,

> It does seem strange that we cannot have one quiet Sabbath. Sherman has no regard for the Fourth Commandment. I wish a Bible society would send him a prayer book, instead of shipping them all to the more remote heathen: but it would be the same in either case. The one is wicked by nature; the other, I fear, is becoming so from habit. Perhaps "Tecumseh," has something to do with it. There is much in a name.[18]

There is much in a name, but French could not have known that the Shawnee chief who first bore the name was much more like the Quaker general's ideal of a warrior than his image of Sherman was—at least in terms of chivalry and restraint in battle, making French's remarks about the Indian Tecumseh not only disingenuous, but also unfounded.

Why Grant disliked Thomas, and vice versa, is unknown. For all of his fine qualities and proven record, Thomas was not Grant's man. Perhaps the feud began after the Battle of Shiloh when General Henry Halleck briefly removed Grant from command and placed Thomas in charge of his men after they captured Corinth, Mississippi. Thomas never sought to take Grant's place.[19] According to Thomas's biographer, by the time that Grant took command of all of the Federal armies, his feelings toward Thomas had thawed, at least somewhat.

---

[18]Samuel G. French, *Two Wars: An Autobiography of Gen. Samuel G. French* (Huntington WV: Blue Acorn Press) 216.

[19]O'Connor, *Thomas: Rock of Chickamauga*, 170–71.

Many men who knew them both well believed that Grant no longer harbored a grudge against Thomas for the Corinth episode, which certainly had reflected no inclination on the latter's part to supersede him, but Grant doubtless was irritated by him; they were alike in their reticence and underlying sensitivity, but their viewpoints were so dissimilar they could never be sympathetic.[20]

Why Grant chose Sherman is clear. Grant understood Sherman and Sherman understood Grant. They understood that to end the war, they had to bring the South to its knees, and the quicker they did so, the less bloodshed in the end would be spilled. A woman in Tennessee once chided Sherman for the thefts from private homes perpetrated by his soldiers during a march to Knoxville and back. After ignoring the woman until her persistence finally compelled his reply, Sherman snorted,

> Madam, my soldiers have to subsist themselves even if the whole country must be ruined to maintain them. There are two armies here; one is in rebellion against the Union, the other is fighting for the Union...if either must starve to death, I propose it shall not be the army that is loyal. There is nothing too good for the soldiers who wear the blue.
> War is cruelty. There is no use trying to reform it, the crueler it is, the sooner it will be over.[21]

The woman was the mother-in-law of one of Sherman's officers, General Gordon Granger.[22] By permitting his men to make "total war" upon the Southern people and their property, Sherman clearly did not exude the same noble qualities of his Indian namesake, Tecumseh.

As biographer Richard O'Connor observed,

> Sherman and Thomas had grown apart to a considerable extent, not only in their personal relations but in military thinking. Sherman was obsessed with the drive-ahead-and-let-nothing-stop-you theory, which reduced war to terms of objectives and expendables and disregarded all human factors. It was not that he was a brutal, bloodthirsty man; indeed he had a high order of intelligence, imagination and a gift for prophecy; he believed himself ahead of his time. In his view "Old Tom" was a step behind the times, too much

---

[20]Ibid., 263.
[21]Lewis, *Sherman: Fighting Prophet*, 330.
[22]Ibid., 329.

given to Old Army ways and West Point teachings, too slow-witted to grasp new methods, not possessing enough "impetus" as he phrased it to Inspector General Warner. Sherman believed that the war would be ended only by great expenditures of men and material and "t'were best it were done quickly." Thomas held that careful preparation and evaluation of all potentialities, moving into battle with deliberation, and then striking with every ounce of power at his command, would result in lower casualties and a more complete victory. It was not merely a matter of the one callously disregarding the lives of his men, and the other nobly concerned with them, for Sherman believed that if the war ended quickly it would result in the conservation of life in the final accounting.[23]

Thus it was that Grant appointed Sherman to succeed him in the west. When asked by an officer if Thomas appeared dissatisfied with Sherman's appointment over him, Sherman replied, "Not a bit of it. It don't make any difference which of us commands the army. I would obey Tom's order tomorrow as readily and cheerfully as he does mine today. But I think I can give the army a little more impetus than Tom can."[24] Grant thought so, too.

---

[23]O'Connor, *Thomas: Rock of Chickamauga*, 263.
[24]Lewis, *Sherman: Fighting Prophet*, 346.

CHAPTER 8

ROSWELL FACTORY

I repeat my orders that you arrest all people, male and female, connected with these factories, no matter what the clamor, and let them foot it, under guard to Marietta, whence I will send them by cars to the North.... The women will make a howl. Let them take along their children and clothing, provided they have the means of hauling it or you can spare them. We will retain them until they can reach a country where they can live in peace and security.[1]

On the evening of 4 July, Sherman sent General Kenner Garrard and his Federal cavalry Division to Roswell, located on the west bank of the Chattahoochee River where there were several factories and stores including paper mills, flouring mills, machine shops, a woolen mill on the east side of town, and several cotton mills just north of the little village. On 5 July, the 7th Pennsylvania led the Yankee parry into the town where they found the wagon road bridge across the Chattahoochee River in flames. General Joseph Wheeler's Rebel cavalry had just set fire to the bridge as the enemy approached, destroying the bridge for any further purpose that could be had by the Federals.[2]

When the Northern cavalry came into Roswell, they found Theopholie Roche, a Frenchman and the head weaver of the mills, flying a French Tricolor flag over the woolen factory. With him were about four hundred mill workers, mostly women and children, busily producing uniforms and clothing for the Confederate cause. Another mill flew the British Union Jack over its doorway nearby. Undaunted by the arrival of the Yankee troopers, Roche refused to shut down and instead pointed to the Tricolor

---

[188]*OR*, series I, vol. 38, ser. no. 76, 76; William Key, *The Battle of Atlanta and the Georgia Campaign* (Atlanta: Peachtree Publishers, 1981) 41.

[2]*OR*, series I, vol. 38, ser. no. 72, 70; ser. no. 73, 813; & ser. no. 76, 76; Jacob D. Cox, *Campaigns of the Civil War: Atlanta* (Dayton OH: Morningside House, 1987) 137.

and asserted his neutrality.[3] Learning of Roche's defiance, Garrard ordered the French flag struck down and wrote to his commander, recommending that the mills be burned. He did not have to wait long for Sherman's reply. Ratifying his cavalryman's actions, Sherman went a step further:

> Your report is received and is most acceptable.... Their utter destruction is right and meets my entire approval, and to make the matter complete you will arrest the owners and employees and send them under guard, charged with treason, to Marietta, and I will see as to any man in America hoisting the French flag and then devoting his labor and capital in supplying armies in open hostility to our government.... Should you under the impulse of anger, natural or contemplating such perfidy, hang the wretch, I approve the act beforehand.
>
> I repeat my orders that you arrest all people, male and female, connected with these factories, no matter what the clamor, and let them foot it, under guard to Marietta, whence I will send them by cars to the North.... The women will make a howl. Let them take along their children and clothing, provided they have the means of hauling it or you can spare them. We will retain them until they can reach a country where they can live in peace and security.[4]

Fortunately for Roche, General Garrard did not act "under the impulse of anger," but instead started Roche and the some four hundred workers by foot to Marietta the next day where Sherman's trains awaited them. Garrard then turned to the factories and burned everything in sight, destroying over a million dollars in material and equipment. Garrard did spare the finer homes from the torch in Roswell, however.[5]

One man in the 100th Indiana Infantry Regiment, which had been temporarily reassigned from the front line to guarding the stores and trains in Marietta, saw the refugee women and families as they were marched from Roswell to the railroad at Marietta. This man, Private Theodore F. Upson of Indiana, had just returned to his unit from Chattanooga where he had

---

[3]Scaife, *Campaign for Atlanta*, 79; Cox, *Campaigns of the Civil War*, 137.

[4]*OR*, series I, vol. 38, ser. no. 76, 76; Key, *Battle of Atlanta and the Georgia Campaign*, 41.

[5]*OR*, series I, vol. 38, ser. no. 76, 76; William R. Scaife, *The Campaign for Atlanta* (Atlanta: self-published, 1993) 79.

seen some sixteen carloads of Confederate prisoners of war who were being sent North. Upson noticed they had to place only one guard for each car because the Southerners appeared to have no fight left in them, and "they had no desire to escape. I think the most of them are glad their fighting is over for a while at least."[6] As for the refugee women, Upson observed that they had plenty of fight left in them.

> We have some 400 young women in the old Seminary Building near town. They have been working in a factory at Rossvill [Roswell] making cloth for the Confederate government. The factories were destroyed and the girls are to be sent South or North whichever way they want to go. Some of them are tough and it's a hard job to keep them straight and to keep the men away from them. General Sherman says he would rather try to guard the whole Confederate Army, and I guess he is right about it.[7]

Private Upson was misinformed about the refugee women's choice to "be sent south or north" as the Yankee train from Marietta only went north. Considering them contraband, Sherman sent these poor refugees by train, together with their children, where they were unceremoniously released north of the Ohio River in Indiana, far away from their homes and families. Many of these displaced Southern ladies and children never returned to the South; they married Northerners and settled down in the towns of Ohio and Indiana or in nearby Kentucky. Some never remarried, but could not afford to return to their homes or husbands, who never learned of their fate after the war.[8]

During the sacking of Roswell, the Northern troops set fire to buildings up and down the banks of the Chattahoochee River, and the entire area to appear aglow in the inferno. Sherman's men had burned towns throughout Mississippi the year before, and they had partially burned Rome and Marietta during this campaign, so some of the men had become fond of burning towns. When some of the Northern troops neared the banks of the Chattahoochee River and saw the village ablaze with smoke billowing above

---

[6]Theodore F. Upson, *With Sherman to the Sea: The Civil War Letters, Diaries and Reminiscences of Theodore F. Upson* (Indianapolis: Indiana University Press, 1958) 118–19, courtesy Zack Henderson Library, Georgia Southern University.

[7]Upson, *With Sherman to the Sea*, 119.

[8]Scaife, *Campaign for Atlanta*, 79; Key, *Battle of Atlanta and the Georgia Campaign*, 41.

the town and the adjoining river, it cast an eerie glow, causing one soldier to remark to another, "Charley, I believe Sherman has set the river on fire."[9]

Another episode during the capture and destruction of Roswell factory involved an unusual discovery of food. While they sacked the mill town, a squad of some Yankees went through a cemetery and one of them stopped and exclaimed,

> "I smell meat!" Following his nose, the men knocked a hole in a burial vault and were extracting ham, bacon, and molasses when, as the Seventy-Second Indianans told it, an old woman pounced on the men, shouting, "I allus heerd you-uns robbed the cradle and the grave but I never expected to see it."[10]

On 7 July, Sherman wrote to Major General Henry W. Halleck, chief of staff in Washington, about the Roswell incident in an apparent attempt to justify his nineteenth-century brutality on the non-combatants and civilian women and children. Sherman explained that "They had been for years engaged exclusively at work for the Confederate Government" and even though they were "exempt from conscription, they are as much governed by the rules of war as if in the ranks."[11] Perhaps foretelling his plans to "make Georgia howl," a statement Sherman would later exclaim during his famous, or infamous, March to the Sea just four months later, Sherman wrote to Halleck, "This whole region was devoted to manufactories, but I will destroy every one of them."[12]

After Garrard's Cavalry destroyed Roswell Factory, Sherman sent General Schofield to reconnoiter the Chattahoochee River between Pace's Ferry and Roswell. Pace's Ferry was just northeast of where the main Confederate line was drawn up to defend the railroad crossing on the Chattahoochee River, some twenty miles below Roswell. Sherman considered his options as well as those of his opponent. By Saturday, 9 July, he had decided that Johnston "will be forced by the present situation to either attack or withdraw." With his back to Atlanta and no more room to maneuver without being eventually boxed in and trapped in the Gate City, Johnston would have to either risk battle or be faced with losing the city to

---

[9]Lloyd Lewis, *Sherman: Fighting Prophet* (New York: Smithmark, 1994) 380.
[10]Ibid.
[11]*OR*, series I, vol. 38, ser. no. 76, 73.
[12]Ibid.

Federal hands. By Sunday, 10 July, Sherman concluded, "If he [Johnston] neglect his right or center we get on his Augusta road. If he neglect Atlanta we take it. If he assume the offensive we cover our roads and base and can make as good use of Peach Tree Creek as he."[13] Interestingly, Sherman had foreseen the importance that Peach Tree Creek would have in the ensuing days.

---

[13]Ibid., 108; Webb Garrison, *Atlanta and the War* (Nashville: Rutledge Hill Press, 1995) 124.

9

SHOUPADES: A NEW KIND OF DEFENSE

I took a long look at the works into which my heart had gone to such a degree, and felt that the days of the Confederacy were numbered. I could not then, and have never been able since, to see why the position should not have been held indefinitely.[1][end block]

Johnston's men were provided with some unique trenches and "fresh furrows," as Sherman put it, for their defense as they fell back to the Chattahoochee River line from Kennesaw Mountain and Marietta during the last days of June and first few days of July. The battle-hardened Southerners took one look at the unique trenches and immediately began improvising and changing them to make the works more like the typical trenches and works that they had been using for the past three months. For four miles along a ridge line that intersected and protected the rail line and railroad bridge over the Chattahoochee River and anchored on each end by the river and facing to the northwest, the works were a series of tiny forts that could be defended by small groups of men. Thus other soldiers were freed for use on different parts of the line or for offensive purposes against the enemy's flanks.

Named "Shoupades" for their creator, Brigadier General Francis Asbury Shoup, chief of artillery in Johnston's Army of Tennessee, these works were ahead of their time.[2] Each Shoupade was a separate small fort that could be defended by a company of men, and each was further protected by interlocking gunfire from neighboring fortifications or earthworks. Each Shoupade could operate independently or in concert to repel an intruder by pouring gunfire on the attackers from a multitude of

---

[1]F. A. Shoup, "Works at the Chattahoochee River," *Confederate Veteran Magazine* 3 (1895): 262.

[2]Greg Biggs, "*The 'Shoupade' Redoubts: Joseph E. Johnston's Chattahoochee River Line,* 82–93, Civil War Regiments," *Civil War Regiments: A Journal of the American Civil War* 1/3 (1991): 12–24.

angles and directions. The renowned Confederate general Patrick R. Cleburne, upon reviewing the works with his men, remarked,

> I knew [Shoup] had built the thing and felt sure there must be some sense to it, so I began to study the scheme. In a moment the whole plan flashed upon me. I got up in one of those redoubts with a crowd of men about me, anxious to hear what I thought. I first directed their attention to the redoubt itself, pointed out how it was entirely enclosed with perpendicular sides, and asked them if they did not think a company of men could hold it against any force that could be brought against it? They said yes, they could hold it against the world. I then pointed out how it was defended by a cross fire from half a dozen other works within easy range, and the re-entering angles of the stockades.[3]

When the Civil War began, earthen fortifications had been limited chiefly to the defense of coastal regions.[4] After three years of bloody fighting, many officers—and all foot soldiers—had come to see the value of field fortifications. By the Atlanta Campaign and spring 1864, it was common for soldiers to dig in and prepare defensive positions any time they stopped marching, unless ordered not to do so if they were expected to recommence marching shortly. According to historian and engineer William Scaife, by 1864 the entire system for field fortifications, or defensive works, was "based upon the concept of *digging in* for protection." Scaife explained,

> But General Shoup's design was a radical departure from the then accepted method of *digging in* and embraced the system of log forts built above grade. Each fort was diamond shaped in plan with its two outer faces pointing in the direction of the enemy like an arrowhead. The forts were constructed after the fashion of log cabins, using double walls of logs filled with compacted earth. The exterior face walls were 10 to 12 feet thick at the base and extended to a height of 10 to 12 feet—surmounted by an infantry parapet or banquette for riflemen, for a total height of some 16 feet. These massive earthen structures could readily absorb the impact of artillery fire and were therefore virtually impregnable. Each fort was designed to be

[3]Shoup, "Works at the Chattahoochee River," 262–65.

[4]Robert J. Fryman, *Fortifying the Landscape: An Archaeological Study of Military Engineering and the Atlanta Campaign* (Gainesville: University Press of Florida, 1991) 43–55; Clarence R. Geier and Stephen R. Potter, eds., *Archaeological Perspectives on the American Civil War* (Gainesville: University Press of Florida, 2002) 43–55.

manned by a company of 80 riflemen and the strange looking structures became known as *Shoupades* in honor of their designer.[5]

During this time there was considerable concern in Washington that the Confederates would send troops from Virginia to reinforce Johnston and destroy Sherman's armies, which had penetrated deep into Georgia. General Grant wrote Sherman, warning him to look out for Confederate reinforcements from Virginia with perhaps as much as 25,000 men.[6] On 12 July, Rebel General Jubal A. Early was turned back from his raid on Maryland and Washington, and by the evening of 13 July, Early's Corps of barely 8,000 weary veterans were south of the Potomac River, and the Washington was out of danger.[7] Thus, on 16 July at 10:00 AM, Grant telegraphed Sherman:

> The attempted invasion of Maryland having failed to give the enemy a firm foothold North, they are now returning, with possibly 25,000 troops. All the men they have here, beyond a sufficiency to hold their strong fortifications, will be an element of weakness to eat up their supplies. It is not improbable, therefore, that you will find in the next fortnight re-enforcements in your front to the number indicated above. I advise, therefore, that if you get to Atlanta you set about destroying the railroads as far to the east and south of you as possible; collect all the stores of the country for your own use, and select a point that you can hold until help can be had. I shall make a desperate effort to get a position here which will hold the enemy without the necessity of so many men. If successful, I can detach from here for other enterprises, looking as much to your assistance as anything else.[8][end block]

Major General Henry W. Halleck, Lincoln's chief of staff, also wired Sherman on 16 July, at 4:30 PM, repeating Grant's fears and advising him to stock up on his supplies and make ready a possible defense of this new threat.[9]

---

[5]William R. Scaife, *The Campaign for Atlanta* (Atlanta: self-published, 1993) 76.

[6]*OR*, series I, vol. 38, ser. no. 76, 149.

[7]Jubal A. Early, *Autobiography* (Wilmington NC: Broadfoot Publishing, 1989) 380–94; *OR*, series I, vol. 38, ser. no. 76, 144–50.

[8]*OR*, series I, vol. 38, ser. no. 76, 149.

[9]Ibid., 150.

Grant reasoned that if Lee could afford to dispatch Early's Corps from his defenses around Richmond and Petersburg to raid up the Shenandoah Valley and into Maryland, he could send Early and his men to Georgia to help Johnston repel Sherman. Grant and the Northern high command also believed Early's force was some 25,000 strong.[10] No doubt the Federal leaders in Washington had been given grossly exaggerated reports of the invading Rebel force as Early swept north up the Shenandoah Valley and into Maryland. Earlier in the war Confederate corps typically contained 20,000 to 25,000 men at full strength although their size varied widely. However, by 1864, Lee's Army of Northern Virginia had been much depleted. Perhaps Grant and Halleck could not fathom that a Southern force would be so bold as to threaten Washington with only 8,000 men. In any event, Early's men were in no condition to be sent by trains to Georgia to reinforce Johnston. Instead, they were to suffer the inglorious defeat at the hands of General Phil Sheridan in the Shenandoah Valley two months later.[11]

If Grant and Halleck were afraid that the South would send significant reinforcements to Johnston to overwhelm Sherman, Uncle Billy was not. In response to Grant's and Halleck's admonitions on 16 July, Sherman wired back to Halleck that evening at 11:00 PM,

> I have yours and General Grant's dispatches. I had anticipated all possible chances and am accumulating all the stores possible at Chattanooga and Allatoona, but I do not fear Johnston with re-enforcements of 20,000 if he will take the offensive; but I recognize the danger arising from my long line and the superiority of the enemy's cavalry in numbers and audacity. I move to-morrow from the Chattahoochee toward Decatur and Stone Mountain, east of Atlanta. All well. Copy of this to General Grant.[12]

Sherman did not have a defensive-minded bone in his body. He was already on the move, ready to encircle Atlanta and cut off the Gate City from the outside world. Offense was the only way that the North would win the war, Sherman reasoned, and he would employ whatever means he had at his disposal to carry the war to the South. By maintaining pressure on

---

[10]Ibid., 149.

[11]Roy Morris, Jr., *Sheridan: The Life and Wars of General Phil Sheridan* (New York: Crown, 1992) 197–222.

[12]*OR*, series I, vol. 38, ser. no. 76, 150.

Johnston's men and thus pinning them down in front of him, Sherman could remain on the offense and keep Johnston from launching his own attack. This strategy had worked during the past three months as Sherman had prevented Johnston from having time to mount a counterstrike. It had also permitted Sherman to use his superior numbers to outflank Johnston and force the Rebels to fall back or be surrounded. Now, Sherman was on the move again and already reaching out with his men to flank Atlanta from the east and her link to Virginia and the Carolinas.

The common soldier of both armies was well aware of the circumstances that faced each army commander. Private J. B. Sanders of the 37th Mississippi Infantry in Cantey's Brigade of Walthall's Division wrote in a letter to his wife on 15 July:

> Sherman is too strong for Johnston's force to attack him, he will march around our army again which he does he will compel Johnston to fall back into the city and then if Sherman gets the railroad from West Point to Macon he [Johnston] will have to fall back where to I have no idea. Johnston is having everything moved out of Atlanta to Macon so as to lose nothing but the place if he has to abandon it. I believe Johnston is doing all in his power to save our country and unless the people do turn out and stand by those who are risking their health and lives to drive this enemy hard back we are a Lost and Ruined People....[13]

Sherman was quite adept at flanking Johnston's lines and he understood and applied this tactic methodically during the Georgia Campaign. Only at Resaca and Kennesaw did he lose his patience and strike the Confederate works. At Resaca, at the onset of the Georgia Campaign, Sherman probed the Southern defenses for two days before he flanked Johnston's men to the right by crossing the Oostanaula River below the little village forcing the Rebels to fall back. At Kennesaw, Sherman lost his patience and attacked the Southern trenches. He did so because he felt the Confederates were stretched thin and to the breaking point. He soon realized his error and once again took to the flank of Johnston's lines, forcing the evacuation of the Confederates from Marietta. Much to the

---

[13]J. B. Sanders, papers, Z0598.000, Manuscript Collection, Mississippi Department of Archives and History (MDAH), Jackson MS; Illene D. Thompson and Wilbur E. Thompson, *The Seventeenth Alabama Infantry: A Regimental History and Roster* (Berwyn Heights MD: Heritage Books, Inc., 2003) 87.

consternation of President Jefferson Davis and the Southern high command in Richmond, by July Sherman had Atlanta in his sights.

If Richmond did not appreciate or accept the concept of flanking the enemy rather than making headlong assaults against prepared works, the common soldier of both sides in Georgia certainly did. A captured Southerner during the Georgia Campaign told his captor in the 103rd Illinois, "Sherman'll never go to hell; he will flank the devil and make heaven in spite of the guards."[14] The lowliest private appreciated the significance of flanking the enemy. Federal stretcher-bearer C. E. Benton heard a Rebel prisoner complain, "You-ons swings around on your ends like a gate."[15]

In General French's Division of newly appointed Lieutenant General A. P. Stewart's Army of Mississippi, the Confederate line swung out on a wooded knoll, putting it closer to the Federal line than at other points. Also, the field works had not been completed to the same degree as at other parts of the line. Shovels, pick axes and entrenching tools were not to be found anywhere in the division. The Mississippians in Sears's Brigade used shingles from a nearby house as shovels to deepen the trenches and dig rifle pits.[16] Nearby, Ector's Texas Brigade did not have any tools or nearby houses with shingles that could be pressed into service to strengthen the Texans' portion of the line. Needing to obtain some shovels and pick axes, Brigadier General Mathew Duncan Ector obtained permission from Major General French to send a regiment from his Texas Brigade forward to some woods in front of his line to catch some unsuspecting Yankees as the Federal line advanced to form a skirmish line. According to General French, "This he [Ector] did successfully, and returned with good picks, spades, and steel axes (ours were cast iron) that will cut wood.[17]

The hot, humid, and muggy climate began to take its toll on Northern troops as they neared the Chattahoochee River. Most of the men in the

---

[14]Lloyd Lewis, *Sherman: Fighting Prophet* (New York: Smithmark Publishers, 1994) 360; C. W. Willis, *One Hundred and Third Illinois* (Washington DC: Globe Printing Co., 1906) 78.

[15]Lewis, *Sherman: Fighting Prophet*, 360.

[16]David V. Stroud, *Ector's Texas Brigade and the Army of Tennessee, 1862–1865* (Longview TX: Ranger Publishing, 2004) 162.

[17]Ibid.; Samuel G. French, *Two Wars: An Autobiography of Gen. Samuel G. French* (Huntington WV: Blue Acorn Press) 215.

Federal army were used to being in the outdoors, but many were not accustomed to the extreme heat found in the Deep South. In July the temperature in Georgia can climb to near 100 degrees; the temperature combined with the high humidity causes such miserable, sweaty conditions that it is hard for men to accomplish much in the heat of the day. The wool uniforms worn by the soldiers in both armies did not allow for perspiration to dry well and left the men soaked with sweat after just a bit of activity. Thus, seemingly routine marches or brief work details left men fatigued and often unfit for combat action. For this reason, the Federal army had gotten in the habit of being on the march by 5:00 AM and stopping for the day by 1:00 PM or so to let the men entrench, build campfires, and rest until the following morning.

The constant fighting since mid-May had made many in the Federal ranks weary. One veteran, Private James S. Pressnall, from the 63rd Indiana in General Schofield's Army of the Ohio remembered, "Here both armies seemed to be in kind of [a] lethargic condition. The picket lines mostly in plain view of each other, and within easy rifle range, seemed more intent on finding a good place to rest than shooting at the other fellow."[18] The soldier noted that from Cassville, below Resaca and Calhoun, to the outskirts of Atlanta the armies had fought 13 separate battles, and over the "course of sixty days, the boom of cannons and rattle of musketry along the picket lines was constant night and day; the enemy gradually falling back from one fortified position to another."[19] Pressnall lamented, "For a period of fifty-two consecutive days, our company lost a man every day either killed or wounded, the common average of about four wounded to one killed prevailing."[20]

Many Northern soldiers wrote especially about the conditions around the Chattahoochee River, where Georgia's sub-tropical climate creates a jungle-like environment. One such soldier from the 6th Iowa Infantry Regiment in Major General John A. Logan's XV Corps penned:

> No former position occupied by the regiment had ever compared with the one at Nickajack in density of small growth of timber, canebreak, tangling

---

[18]James S. Pressnall, memoirs, vertical files, filed under "Union 63rd Indiana," Carter House Library and Archives, Franklin TN.

[19]Ibid.

[20]Ibid.

vines, and rank growth of vegetation covering the whole surface along the creeks, in the swamps and on the bottom lands of the Chattahoochee River. The presence of myriads of insects, venomous worms and reptiles, caused great annoyance, and the added persistent and deadly fire of the enemy's sharpshooters made the position very uncomfortable. The locality was a genuine fever breeder and many strong men who had withstood all the hardships up to that point were compelled to give up on account of raging fever, and seek the cheerless comforts of the field hospitals.[21]

Federal Major Fredrick C. Winkler wrote home on 10 July about the conditions along the front,

The rebels have a line of works about a mile this side; It would be Impregnable against an infantry attack, on account of stockades that were built some twelve to fifteen feet high along the rifle pits, but I think an artillery would have set it flying. Our pickets are on the northern bank and have agreed with the rebel pickets on the other side not to shoot. There they were this morning, within talking distance of each other, not the least bitter feeling disturbing the friendly intercourse.

The Yankee major seemed amused by the scene. "The rebels were freely walking about on the south bank, washing their clothes and spreading them in the sun to dry, while our men were doing the same on this side; some of ours had even been across and traded off coffee and sugar for tobacco." Winkler added, "The weather is hot, still quite endurable. General Hooker says this is the healthiest part of the whole south."[22]

As Sherman's men drew near to the Chattahoochee, Johnston pulled his troops from the west side of the river before Sherman could test the Shoupade works. It was a blow to Francis Shoup, who had staked his reputation on their merit. Worried by Sherman's cavalry and infantry crossings upriver, Johnston called a meeting of his leaders on 7 July. General Shoup later recorded his recollections about the meeting:

---

[21]Henry H. Wright, *A History of the Sixth Iowa Infantry* (Iowa City IA: The State Historical Society of Iowa) 299.

[22]"Civil War Letters of Major Fredrick C. Winkler, 1864," Sons of the 26th Wisconsin Infantry Volunteers, http://www.russscott.com/~rscott/26thwis/26pgwk 64.htm (accessed 8 July 2014).

General Johnston called a council of the corps commanders to consider the situation, and I was invited to be present. General Hood stated his position, and urged that the army be moved across the river. He did not seem to understand the design of the works; and I doubt he ever stopped to think much about them. When I was called upon to say what I thought ought to be done, I said that, in my opinion it [the Chattahoochee River line] ought to be provisioned, so as to stand a siege, if necessary, of a considerable period. No definite conclusion was reached, but the tone in favor of holding on to the side of the river next the enemy was not such as I could have wished.

It was the second day after this, I think (we abandoned the works on the 9th of July), while I was working hard to make our left flank strong...information reached me that the whole army was leaving that side of the river. I need not attempt to say what a blow it was to me. I took a long look at the works into which my heart had gone to such a degree, and felt that the days of the Confederacy were numbered. I could not then, and have never been able since, to see why the position should not have been held indefinitely.[23]

Private Phillip Daingerfield Stephenson of the Washington Artillery in Hardee's Corps reflected as his unit crossed the river: "It was a gloriously beautiful moonlight night." As the Battery traversed the bridge that carried them to the eastern shore of the quiet river on that balmy July night, the St. Louis native pined, "With me the thoughts engendered were melancholy. The bloody struggles, the horrid scenes, the frightful passions at play, all of these made a dreadful contrast to the beauty all about us. What a monster man is!"[24]

Later, after seeing the works, Sherman admitted that the Confederate works were most formidable and that it would have been a blunder to try to assail them. "I confess I had not learned beforehand of the existence of this strong place.... During the night Johnston drew back his army and trains inside the 'tete-du-pont' at the Chattahoochee, which proved one of the strongest pieces of field fortifications I ever saw."[25] An Iowa soldier

---

[23]Shoup, "Works at the Chattahoochee River," 262.

[24]Nathaniel Cheairs Hughes, Jr., *The Pride of the Confederate Artillery: The Washington Artillery in the Army of Tennessee* (Baton Rouge: Louisiana State University Press, 1997) 193.

[25]*OR*, series I, vol. 38, ser. no. 72, 69.

remarked, "The abandoned works were found to be the strongest encountered during the campaign."[26] General Jacob Cox, upon seeing the works and others used during the Georgia Campaign, commented that "Johnston had always confronted them with impregnable fortifications."[27] According to historian Gordon L. Jones of the Atlanta History Center, the Shoupades were ahead of their time:

> The remains of the Chattahoochee River Line of Confederate fortifications designed by Francis A. Shoup in 1864 constitute some of the most significant [and neglected] historic structures in the United States. Unlike other Civil War fortifications, Shoup's design of the arrowhead-shaped earth-and-log infantry forts, arranged in tandem with artillery forts to produce a deadly overlapping field of fire, was years ahead of his time; indeed, this design would not be used again until World Wars I and II.[28]

Meanwhile, on the Southern side of the Chattahoochee, while Sherman's legions were busy, tired veterans of Johnston's armies took time to rest and reflect. One such soldier, Lieutenant Emmitt Ross, who was engaged to marry Miss Mary V. Collins of Canton, Mississippi, took time to write a poem to his sweetheart:

I'll Think of Thee

> I'll think of thee, when morning lifts it[s]
> Upon the hills, far o'er the lee,

---

[26]Wright, *A History of the Sixth Iowa Infantry*, 299.

[27]Jacob D. Cox, *Campaigns of the Civil War: Atlanta* (Dayton OH: Morningside House, 1987) 148; Fryman, *Fortifying the Landscape*, 47.

[28]Gordon L. Jones, Memorandum on Shoupades, part 2, 10 June 1998, Unpublished manuscript in author's possession, author's vertical file no. 270. According to Jones, "There are no other fortifications like this in the world. Of the 36 earth-and-log infantry forts (or 'Shoupades') that once comprised the defensive line running from the mouth of Nickajack Creek northeast toward Vinings Station (The Chattahoochee River Line) and none of them are legally protected from destruction. Because of the tremendous historical significance of these 'Shoupades' and the impossibility of preserving all the remaining examples from eventual destruction, it is imperative that at least one example be set aside for historical research and educational appreciation.... A long term plan for its preservation and interpretation would add immeasurably to the historical record of the Civil War...." Plans for a new Atlanta Braves baseball stadium and additional construction in this area threaten the future existence of these works.

When flow'rets wake to sip the dew-drops bright,
I'll think of thee, I'll think of thee—
2
I'll think of thee, when all seems dark and drear
When toss'd upon life's fretful sea;
Though clouds arise, and anxious fears appear
I'll think of thee, I'll think of thee.
3
I'll think of thee and not forget the heart,
Which thou hast promised, Love, to me:
All clouds will fade and anxious fears depart
I'll think of thee, I'll think of thee,
4
I'll think of thee when soft sleep shuts mine eyes
And stars light up the canopy
Of midnight; Dreaming 'neath the cloudless skies
I'll think of thee, I'll think of thee.
5
I'll think of thee, while in the ranks of War,
I fight for home and Liberty,
Thy name my watch-word and my guiding star
I'll think of thee, I'll think of thee.[29]

The young Lieutenant was severely wounded on 28 July at the Battle of Ezra Church, but he would survive to return and marry his sweetheart in Mississippi in August.[30]

---

[29]John K. Bettersworth, ed., *Mississippi in the Confederacy as They Saw It* (Clinton MA: Louisiana State University) 326–27.
[30]Ibid., 169–71.

10

CROSSING THE CHATTAHOOCHEE

This is a delicate movement and must be done with caution.[1]

Georgia poet Sidney Lanier best described Georgia's largest river in his famous and majestic poem *Song of the Chattahoochee*:

> Out of the hills of Habersham,
> Down the valleys of Hall,
> I hurry amain to reach the plain,
> Run the rapid and leap the fall,
> Split at the rock and together again,
> Accept my bed, or narrow or wide,
> And flee from folly on every side
> With a lover's pain to attain the plain
> Far from the hills of Habersham,
> Far from the valleys of Hall.
>
> All down the hills of Habersham,
> All through the valleys of Hall,
> The rushes cried *Abide, abide,*
> The willful waterweeds held me thrall,
> The laving laurel turned my tide,
> The ferns and the fondling grass said *Stay,*
> The dewberry dipped for to work delay,
> And the little reeds sighed *Abide, abide,*
> *Here in the hills of Habersham,*
> *Here in the valleys of Hall.*
>
> High o'er the hills of Habersham,
> Veiling the valleys of Hall,
> The hickory told me manifold

---

[1]*OR*, series I, vol. 38, ser. no. 76, 66.

Fair tales of shade, the poplar tall
Wrought me her shadowy self to hold,
The chestnut, the oak, the walnut, the pine,
Overleaning, with flickering meaning and sign,
Said, *Pass not, so cold, these manifold*
Deep shades of the hills of Habersham,
These glades in the valleys of Hall.

And oft in the hills of Habersham,
And oft in the valleys of Hall,
The white quartz shone, and the smooth brook-stone
Did bar me of passage with friendly brawl,
And many a luminous jewel lone
—Crystals clear or a-cloud with mist,
Ruby, garnet and amethyst—
Made lures with the lights of streaming stone
In the clefts of the hills of Habersham,
In the beds of the valleys of Hall.

But oh, not the hills of Habersham,
And oh, not the valleys of Hall
Avail: I am fain for to water the plain.
Downward the voices of Duty call—
Downward, to toil and be mixed with the main,
The dry fields burn, and the mills are to turn,
And a myriad flowers mortally yearn,
And the lordly main from beyond the plain
Calls o'er the hills of Habersham,
Calls through the valleys of Hall.[2]

The rambling stream that cuts across the Peach State was sometimes quiet and peaceful, while at other times rocky and violent, but it was always wild and unpredictable, and Sherman's men had to cross it before they could reach Atlanta. One Iowa veteran, upon seeing the river at Roswell, noted, "The river at this point is 200 yards wide, with a rapid current, rocky

---

[2]Sidney Lanier, *Yale Book of American Verse*, ed. Thomas R. Lounsbury (New Haven CT: The Elizabethan Club, Yale University, 1912).

bottom, shallow water, and is very muddy."[3] Cutting its way from the northeast part of Georgia to the southwest corner of the Empire State of the South, the Chattahoochee River screens the Gate City from oppressors who would seek to enter it from the northwest. For this reason Johnston was admonished by his president to keep Sherman and his legions on the other side of the river. Unfortunately, that task would prove easier said than done. While the Chattahoochee was wide, and filled with rocky and impassible points throughout its length, it was not very deep and contained a number of fords. Each passable crossing would have to be guarded, and defending them would be like trying to figure out from which hole the weasel would pop.

By 6 July, Sherman had changed his view of how he would conduct his offensive against Atlanta from pressing his armies to assault works to severing the rail lines into the city and thus cutting off the food and supplies reaching it and its defenders. He had decided to feint a move to the right, or west, of Atlanta with McPherson's Army of the Tennessee and some of his cavalry, while he sent Schofield and his small Army of the Ohio over the Chattahoochee River at Roswell. Sherman planned to press Thomas with his largest force, the Army of the Cumberland, to attempt crossings at the center, around Power's Ferry, to hopefully occupy General Johnston's attention and thus keep the Southerners busy defending Thomas while he made his push for Atlanta from the north and east. Once Schofield's men were across, Sherman would then swing McPherson's army around from the extreme right of his lines, to the extreme left, following the Army of the Ohio at or near Roswell across the river. Then, as he had done at Snake Creek Gap when he was in front of Dalton, and again in front of the Etowah River and the Allatoona Mountains, Sherman would send his beloved Army of the Tennessee on a flanking move, striking out to the east of Atlanta.[4]

In doing so, Sherman would also be able to prevent quick reinforcement by rail to Johnston with troops from Virginia via the Augusta Railroad. General Grant was concerned about this prospect, so much so that

---

[3] Henry H. Wright, *A History of the Sixth Iowa Infantry* (Iowa City IA: The State Historical Society of Iowa) 300.

[4] Albert Castel, *Decision in the West* (Lawrence: University Press of Kansas, 1992) 216–18, 348–50.

he wrote to General Halleck in Washington to warn Sherman.[5] General Sherman had already considered this possibility a week before Grant had and was taking steps to prevent it. Perhaps deriving the idea from Johnston, who had left the Western & Atlantic Railroad in disrepair at Marietta and Vining's Station and thus caused some delay in bringing supplies to the Northern commander's troops, Sherman knew how important the Augusta rail line was to the Confederates in Atlanta. In a dispatch to General Halleck, Sherman contended,

I propose to study the crossings of the Chattahoochee, and when all is ready to move quick. As a beginning I [will] keep the wagons and troops well back from the river, and display to the enemy only the picket-line, with a few batteries along at random. Have moved General Schofield to a point whence he can in a single march reach the Chattahoochee, at a point above the railroad bridge, where there is a ford. At present the waters are turbid and swollen by the late rains [it rained nearly every day from June 2 to June 22]; but if the present hot weather lasts the water will run down very fast. We have pontoons enough for four bridges, but, as our crossing will be resisted, we must maneuver some. All the regular crossing places [over the Chattahoochee River] are covered by forts, apparently of long [log] construction; but we shall cross in due time, and instead of attacking Atlanta direct, or any of its forts, I propose to make a circuit, destroying all its railroads. This is a delicate movement and must be done with caution. Our army is in good condition and full of confidence....[6]

Thus, on 7 July, Sherman ordered Major General John M. Schofield to take his Army of the Ohio, which consisted of the western troops of the veteran XXIII Corps, to move from Smyrna Campground east, across Rottenwood Creek and effect a bridgehead over the Chattahoochee River near the mouth of Sope Creek (known today as Soap Creek)[7] at Phillip's Ferry.[8] On 8 July, Schofield sent General Jacob Cox's 3rd Division, which was in the van, to quietly take positions on the west bank of the Chattahoochee River and prepare to cross and take the east bank. Cox

[5]*OR*, series I, vol. 38, ser. no. 76, 143–44.

[6]Ibid., 66.

[7]Castel, *Decision in the West*, 336.

[8]William Key, *The Battle of Atlanta and the Georgia Campaign* (Atlanta: Peachtree Publishers, 1981) 41; *OR*, series I, vol. 38, ser. no. 76, 66 and ser. no. 73, 679–85.

discreetly placed his troops and artillery in the woods opposite the ferry, a move done so efficiently that the Southern sentries did not learn of their approach.[9]

General Cox discovered a fish dam further upstream and sent Colonel Daniel Cameron's 2nd Brigade to take it and cross the river if possible and then take the Rebel position in flank from the north. The fish dam was near a paper mill along Soap Creek, just north of its mouth at the Chattahoochee River. According to Cox, "Soap Creek, near the mill, runs in a rocky gorge with precipitous sides, and Cameron's men had to cross it by clambering down the dangerous rocks and by picking their way along the edge of the slippery dam above."[10]

Meanwhile, Colonel George P. Buell commanding the Pontoon Train, with the 58th Indiana under Lieutenant Colonel Joseph Moore and the Pontoon Battalion led by Captain Patrick O'Connell, was ordered to bring the pontoon boats down to Soap Creek where they were launched near the paper mill at the mouth of the Creek and its confluence with the Chattahoochee River.[11] Cox wanted Cameron's men to cross the river over the rocks at the fish dam at the same time as another crossing would be effected with the pontoon boats downstream.

General Jacob Cox ordered Colonel Robert K. Byrd's 3rd Brigade to lead the direct attack at the mouth of Soap Creek with the pontoon boats. At the point where Soap Creek and the Chattahoochee River meet, there was a ferry known as Phillip's Ferry. Byrd selected Lieutenant Colonel Laurence H. Rousseau and his 12th Kentucky Regiment to be ferried over the swift flowing river in the boats as his striking force while the balance of his brigade supported in firing position along the west bank. Oarsmen from General Milo S. Hascall's 2nd Division who were from the Great Lakes Region were recruited to take Rouseau's Kentuckians across. Opposing them was a small Confederate cavalry unit under General Joseph Wheeler and one piece of artillery placed at Phillip's Ferry—more for show than

---

[9]Jacob D. Cox, *Campaigns of the Civil War: Atlanta* (Dayton OH: Morningside House, 1987) 137–41; William R. Scaife, *The Campaign for Atlanta* (Atlanta: self-published, 1993) 80.

[10]Cox, *Campaigns of the Civil War*, 138–39.

[11]Ibid., 136–40; Scaife, *Campaign for Atlanta*, 68–69; *OR*, series I, vol. 38, ser. no. 73, 679–85.

strength—to oppose a crossing. The Confederate cavalry's chief job, however, was to keep a lookout for Federal movements, and to report any northern efforts to cross the river. The time set for the crossing was 3:30 PM: "At that hour a careful reconnaissance from the top of the ridge showed that there were no symptoms of alarm on the opposite bank."[12] On the Confederate side, the men were preoccupied with cooking supper and writing to loved ones. No one was watching the river.[13]

> The signal to advance was given. Cameron's advance guard, led by Colonel [John S. "Jack"] Casement, One Hundred and Third Ohio, entered the water at the fish-dam, scrambling along the broken rocks in the swift current. Immediately twenty white pontoon boats shot out from the mouth of the creek, pulled by expert oarsmen selected from Hascall's division, and loaded with Colonel Rousseau's Kentuckians. The rest of Byrd's brigade, which had been deployed under cover of the woods along the base of the hills, rushed forward across the bottom land and lined the margin of the stream. A single cannon-shot was fired from the enemy's outpost, and the gun was reloaded and run forward to fire again; but so completely was it now covered by the rifles of Byrd's men, that no one could aim it or fire. The mounted men, conscious of their inability to cope with the force before them, galloped away to carry the news.[14]

The Confederate artillerists soon followed their cavalry comrades, and Cox's men captured the Rebel gun without losing a single man. At the deserted Southern camp, Cox and his men found a half-cooked supper awaiting them, along with an unfinished letter from one of the Confederate soldiers to his wife, in which he tells her "that he was almost as free from peril as if he were at home on his plantation: that the solitude about them was rarely broken, even by the appearance of a single horseman on the opposite side of the river...." His sentence was interrupted, and the letter was never completed.[15] Cox's Division soon erected a pontoon bridge, and his men entrenched a bridgehead along a ridge overlooking the crossing.[16]

---

[12]Cox, *Campaigns of the Civil War*, 138; *OR*, series I, vol. 38, ser. no. 73, 679–85.

[13]Cox, *Campaigns of the Civil War*, 138–39.

[14]Ibid., 139.

[15]Ibid., 140; Scaife, *Campaign for Atlanta*, 80.

[16]Cox, *Campaigns of the Civil War*, 140; Scaife, *Campaign for Atlanta*, 80.

Thus, on 8 July, Sherman had secured a crossing over the Chattahoochee River, the last natural barrier between him and Atlanta, and his men had done it without a single loss.

The next day, on 9 July, Colonel John T. Wilder's 3rd Mounted Infantry Brigade of General Kenner Garrard's 2nd Division of Cavalry, effected a crossing of the Chattahoochee River at Shallow Ford, a mile below the Roswell bridge. Wilder's Lightning Brigade was aided by the Chicago Board of Trade Battery, and, since Wilder departed from command on 14 June due to illness, his command was ably led by Colonel Abram O. Miller.[17] Leading the movement, two companies of the 17th Indiana and two companies (companies D and I) of the 72nd Indiana "were deployed as skirmishers right along the edge of the water, and secreted in the brush" with Captain Thomson of Company D, 72nd Indiana commanding. Also, the Chicago Board of Trade Battery with its six ten-pounder Parrott rifles "quietly got into position on the high hill overlooking the river."[18]

After getting his brigade up at 3:30 AM, Miller moved his men to near the creek and the point of the crossing. Colonel Miller described the movement of his cavalry force: "at the first dawn of day I moved out on foot. After passing through the town of Roswell, I moved the 17th Indiana, Major Vail (commanding), and the 98th Illinois, Lt. Colonel Kitchell (commanding), forward on the main road leading to the ford of the river...." Miller dispatched the 72nd Indiana under Captain Pinkerton and the 123rd Illinois led by Lieutenant Colonel Biggs "on a road to the left, so as to strike the river about 200 yards above the main road." The brigade commander then deployed his force for the crossing: "As soon as the advance reached the river two companies of the 72nd Indiana were deployed on the left and 2 companies of the 17th Indiana on the right, forming a line of skirmishers extending along the bank of the river for 300 yards." Miller took the additional precaution to deploy a protective line to cover his advance. "At the same time one company from the 72nd [Indiana] and two from the 17th [Indiana] were deployed as sharpshooters on the bluffs on this side, to

---

[17]Scaife, *Campaign for Atlanta*, 79–81.

[18]B. F. McGee, *History of the 72nd Indiana Volunteer Infantry of the Mounted Lightning Brigade, 1882* (Lafayette IN: S. Vater & Co., Printers, 1882) 333–34.

engage the attention of the enemy and protect my skirmishers while crossing."[19]

The Federal activity in the early dawn of 9 July attracted the attention of the Confederate pickets. "During these arrangements the enemy's sharpshooters on the opposite shore were very active, shooting whenever our men exposed themselves. The main column having been moved as close to the river as possible, and everything being in readiness, I ordered the skirmishers forward," Miller proudly explained. "And every man moved promptly into the water, when the enemy opened with a heavy fire, which was vigorously replied to by our sharpshooters from this side, and which attracted their attention from the men in the water," he continued. The Chattahoochee River "was running very swift, with a rough bottom, and in some places, up to the arms in depth, but the skirmishers moved steadily forward, keeping a good line, and before they reached the opposite shore the enemy fled in confusion, with the exception of a few who were captured before they could escape." Miller continued his line forward on the eastern shore of the river until his men secured the crest of a ridge some three hundred yards from the river. There, his men dug in and secured a lodgment for Sherman's forces.[20]

According to one veteran of the famous Lightning Brigade, "The river was four hundred yards wide, and the fog so heavy upon the water that the men could not see across, and it seemed so deep that scarcely a man dreamed they were expected to cross."[21] Captain Thomson climbed half way up the hill to view the Rebel lines on the other side. It was just getting light enough to see the other shore a little and Thomson could make out the silhouettes of the enemy sentinels at regular intervals along the river, and there were "others passing up and down the hill in numbers sufficient to convince him that it would be hazardous to undertake to cross...." Moreover, there were a number of Rebels sleeping on the porch of a large white house on a hill overlooking the river. Captain Thomson then met with Colonel Abraham O. Miller to inform him that his men were deployed in line of skirmish along the base of the river. At this point Colonel Miller replied, "Well, as soon as the artillery opens, move your men right across."

---

[19]*OR*, series I, vol. 38, ser. no. 73, 850–51.

[20]Ibid.

[21]McGee, *History of the 72nd Indiana Volunteer Infantry*, 334.

The astonished captain retorted, "You don't mean to say that we are expected to wade that river?" Miller then said, "Yes, that is what we have been sent here for, and we expect to do it." With that, Thomson replied, "If you order it, we will try it."[22]

When Thomson got back to his men, they were debating their chances, and when the captain relayed their orders, someone cried out, "We'll never cross it." Another responded with, "If they order us to, we'll do it; but I don't believe Col. Miller will ever order us to." Captain Thomson finally convinced the men that they were, in fact, ordered by the beloved Colonel Miller to make the river crossing, so the boys nerved themselves up to the task. Suddenly, the early dawn silence was broken as the artillery "belches forth a volley of shells which burst among the sleeping sentinels with the sound of mighty thunder." Thomson ordered "Forward," and without hesitation, "the men plunge into the water up to their arm-pits. Not a faltering one; not a laggard! But with a cheer they rush into the water and charge for the other shore."[23]

As the men proceeded, Brigadier General Kenner Garrard rode up to the water's edge and cheered the attackers on, shouting, "Bully boys! Bully boys! Whisky in the morning!" Sergeant B. F. McGee of Company I in the 72nd Indiana, recorded the scene:

> The whole brigade now rises up, and with cheer after cheer urges them forward, while the Battery men work away at their guns, determined that the expedition shall not fail for want of energy on their part. However, it is not all smooth sailing with our brave men in the water. As the shells burst among the sleeping rebels on the opposite bank, they start up in the wildest flight, and realize for the first time that the Yankees are upon them. They seize their guns and rush to the water's edge and open upon our men in the river, but, as frightened men usually do, they shoot clear over their heads, but the men are having a rough time of it; the water is so deep and the current so swift that they can scarcely stand on their feet, let alone make any advancement, and as they attempt to move forward step into the numerous trenches and holes, and go under. Still on they rush; the rebels firing volley after volley at them; and if you divest your mind for a moment of all thought of danger, the motion of the line would appear laughably comical and

---

[22]Ibid.
[23]Ibid., 334–35.

ridiculous. As the line moves forward a comrade suddenly steps into a hole or trench, and under he goes, as if dodging the rebel bullets, and open fire on the rebels in the brush along the shore.

As our men rush up out of the water and immediately open fire with their Spencers, the river is all ablaze, the rebels think that pandemonium has broken loose, and all the imps of the lower regions are now coming for their lawful prey, and they break and run up the hill, our men shooting them in the back. Now there is a race who of our brave men shall reach the shore first. The water has gradually become shallower, and now is scarcely to their hips, and such another running, shooting, cheering, and splashing, was never witnessed before. Sergt. James A. Mount, Co. D, ever anxious to excel, was perhaps the first to reach the shore, and David Frazier, Co. I, was but little behind him. But where every man of those four companies did his noble, clean best, and each and every one got there just as quick as he could, we will not be invidious with further distinctions. As our men reach the shore they rush for the top of the hill and capture three or four prisoners as they ascend, who are blanched and trembling with fright, declaring that our men had just raised up out of the water and commenced to shoot at them. From these prisoners we learn that Martin's whole brigade of cavalry is camped near by as support for the pickets, and we immediately take to trees, and stumps, and logs, for defense. The whole brigade now moves across in column, and our skirmishers are peering into the woods and brush ahead, momentarily expecting Martin's Brigade to move upon them; but the frightened fugitives had told the General that Wilder's whole brigade was already across, and he thought discretion was the better part of valor, and contented himself with simply watching our movements. The whole brigade got across in a few minutes, moved out to a good position and went to work throwing up defensive works, and in half an hour could not have been driven from them by all Johnston's army. Our brigade were the first troops to cross the Chattahoochie, and although it was effected without the loss of a man, we cannot help shuddering when we think of the fearful peril we were in when first ordered to pitch into the water.[24]

The next day, as promised, the men were given their ration of whiskey and allowed to make their camp in the town of Roswell. Unfortunately, some men managed to get more than their draw of about a gill. After a few

---

[24]Ibid., 335–36.

of them got drunk, they began to get into mischief. "Upon this occasion their delirium took the form of making love to the women, and before night Colonel Miller found it necessary to move the brigade a mile north of the town."[25]

Another account of the Federal crossing comes from Minty's 1st Brigade of Garrard's Division, which also participated in the attack with Miller's 3rd Brigade ("The Lightning Brigade"). Supporting the 3rd Brigade, Colonel Robert H. G. Minty's Brigade "dismounted and waded the Chattahoochee in rear of [the] Third Brigade; threw up breast-works and held the ground until dark, when General Newton's Division of the IV Corps relieved us."[26] One veteran remembered,

> As the rebel bullets began to splash around pretty thick, the boys sought to keep in this deep water with only the head exposed; they soon discovered that they could throw the cartridge from the magazine (of the Spencer) into the chamber of the piece, by working the lever as well under water as in the air; hence, all along the line you could see the men bring their guns up, let the water run from the muzzle a moment, then taking a quick aim, fire his piece and pop down again, with only his head exposed. Now, the rebels had never seen anything of this kind before, nor, for that matter had we, and their astonishment know no bounds. We could hear them calling to each other, "Look at them Yankee sons of bitches, loading their guns under water!"

Minty's biographer added, "More than 200 Confederate soldiers forthwith surrendered in order to get a closer look at the Spencers."[27]

Also on 9 July, a portion of Colonel James P. Brownlow's 1st Tennessee (Federal) Cavalry Regiment from the 1st Brigade of General Edward McCook's Division successfully crossed the river at Cochran's Ford, located about a half-mile below Soap Creek. General McCook wrote of the odd crossing:

> It was deep and he [Brownlow] took them over naked, nothing but guns, cartridge boxes and hats. They drove the enemy out of their rifle pits,

---

[25]Ibid., 337–38.

[255]*OR*, series I, vol. 38, ser. no. 73, 813.

[27]Theodore W. Blackburn, *Letters from the Front: A Union "Preacher" Regiment (74th Ohio) in the Civil War* (Dayton OH: Press of Morningside Bookshop, 1981) 210–211.

captured a non-commissioned officer, 3 men and two boats on the other side. They would have got more, but the rebels had the advantage in running through the bushes with clothes on. It was certainly one of the funniest sights of the war, and a very successful raid for naked men to make.[28]

On the Southern side of the river, Confederate cavalry opposing Brownlow's naked attack tried to fire from the banks of the river at the Yankees, who had chosen to swim across without their bulky, woolen uniforms. Many of the surprised Southerners were dismayed at the immodest Yankees, who would drop under water or behind a rock and then surface and fire with their repeating rifles, which contained cartridges with self-contained shells of powder and bullets that did not let the powder get wet. Carrying either Spencer or Henry rifles, the Federal attackers had the advantage of firing up to fifteen rounds for Henry rifles, or eight rounds for Spencers, without having to reload or worry about water damaging the cartridges. In this comical but deadly attack, frustrated Confederates would marvel at the Yankees with their special "week long" rifles, saying, "they could load them on Sunday and fire them all week long without having to reload them."[29]

The historian for the 1st Tennessee Volunteer Cavalry (Federal), gave a slightly more embellished version of the infamous naked crossing:

Colonel Brownlow was given orders to cross the River, but due to the depth of the water and the enemy snipers on the opposite shore was unable to do so. There was much "cussed and discussed" by the men, both before and after this attempt. After Colonel Dorr, commanding the brigade, discussed the matter with Colonel Brownlow and gave him peremptory orders to move across the River at once and uttered unnecessary threats in the event his orders were not made, Colonel Brownlow was truly in a "fighting-mad" frame of mind. Colonel Brownlow took nine men and went up the river where they stripped to the skin, and using several logs lashed

---

[28]OR, series I, vol. 38, ser. no. 73, 760; Scaife, *Campaign for Atlanta*, 80.

[29]OR, series I. vol. 38, ser. no. 73, 760; Scaife, *Campaign for Atlanta*, 79–81; Schuyler, Hartley & Graham, *Illustrated Catalog of Civil War Military Goods* (New York: Dover Publications, 1985) 132–33; Jack Coggins, *Arms & Equipment of the Civil War* (Garden City NY: Doubleday, 1962) 35–36; Tennessee Historical Commission, *Tennesseans in the Civil War*, 2 vols. (Nashville: Civil War Centennial Commission, 1964) 1:318–20.

together to hold their carbines and cartridge boxes they swam the river. One man was left to guard the raft while the others donned their cartridge boxes and belts and took up their carbines. They did not have any uniforms, hats, boots, etc. Colonel Brownlow with his eight men were able to get in the rear of the enemy and turned their carbines loose on them, after which several escaped, but they took twelve prisoners which they made swim back across the river.

The next morning, a Reb yelled out across the river; "Hello, Yank!" "What do you want, Johnny" "Orders to dry up." "What for, Johnny?" "Oh, Jim Brownlow with his damn Tennessee Yankees swam over upon the left last night and stormed our rifle-pits naked, captured sixty of our boys and made 'em swim back with him. We'uns have got to keep you'uns on your side of the river now."[30]

According to Brigadier General Edward McCook, they captured only four of the surprised Southerners, "but the rebels had the advantage in running through the bushes with clothes on." But, reasoned McCook, it was "a very successful raid for naked men to make."[31]

Meanwhile, as Garrard's 1st and 3rd Brigades were busy surprising the Confederates at Roswell, his 2nd Brigade under Colonel Eli Long were ordered to take and hold McAfee's Bridge, some eight miles upriver. For this purpose Long dispatched the 4th Ohio Cavalry at 3:00 AM "With instructions to hold it [the bridge] and prevent the enemy from crossing or destroying it." Long followed up with the balance of his brigade in support soon thereafter. According to Colonel Long, "The enemy held the farther end of the bridge, and skirmishing with them was continued until evening, when they fell back, and the 4th Ohio held the bridge entire, having no loss except 1 man wounded." Long noted that the next day Lieutenant P. B. Lewis from the 3rd Ohio Cavalry, his topographic engineer, together with four men of brigade scouts, were captured by a company of Rebel cavalry while exploring at Alpharetta. Also on 10 July, Long's brigade suffered the

---

[30] W. R. Carter, "History of the First Tennessee Cavalry, First Division, First Brigade, Army of the Cumberland, Cavalry Corp, United States Volunteers," http://www.1sttennesseecavalry.com/history2.aspx (8 July 2014); "General Sherman's Advance," *Harper's Weekly* 13 August 1864, 525.

[31] Phil Noblitt, "Confederate Breakout Attempt at Peachtree Creek" *America's Civil War* 11/4 (September 1998): 54.

loss of four more men captured, also from the 3rd Ohio Cavalry, while guarding the wagon train as part of the rear guard. The Federal colonel balanced the losses, however, by adding that "during the month 6 prisoners have been taken and 21 deserters from the rebels received."[32]

Historian Phil Noblitt noted that Sherman had "expected every possible resistance in the crossing the Chattahoochee River," and he was delighted with the lack of Southern opposition.[33] In a twist of fate, the bold subordinate Corps commander, John Bell Hood, had determined that his position was "untenable and urged the army to fall back. After learning of the Federal crossings to the east, Johnston characteristically obliged. On the moonlit evening of 9 July, the Army of Tennessee slipped quietly across the Chattahoochee."[34] The move would seal the fate of Joe Johnston, who would be removed from command a week later for failing to give battle north of the Chattahoochee, and the young Hood would be propelled to lead the surprised army.

After marching more than thirty miles from Green and Howell's Ferry, on the extreme right of Sherman's Chattahoochee River line to Roswell, Major General Grenville M. Dodge's XVI Corps crossed the Chattahoochee River in support of General Garrard's cavalry and fortified. According to Henry Sawyer of the 18th Missouri Infantry Regiment, the boys crossed on "a stone foundation, knee deep under water so swift that walking and standing were difficult."[35] There, the pioneers of the XVI Corps began rebuilding the bridge that had been burned by Wheeler's Confederate cavalry.

Pleased with the quick and efficient crossings over the Chattahoochee by Schofield's Corps at Phillips Ferry and Garrard's Cavalry at Roswell, on 12 July Sherman wrote Grant,

> The moment I got Johnston to the Chattahoochee I sent Schofield to a ford above, and he effected a crossing without the loss of a man, and has two pontoon bridges. About the same time, Garrard's cavalry crossed, still above, at Roswell Factory, and has been relieved by Dodge's corps, so that I now

---

[32]*OR*, series I, vol. 38, ser. no. 73, 838.
[33]Noblitt, "Confederate Breakout Attempt at Peachtree Creek," 3–4.
[34]Ibid.
[35]Leslie Anders, *The Eighteenth Missouri* (Indianapolis: Bobbs-Merrill Company, Inc., 1968) 230.

cover the Chattahoochee and have two good crossings well secured; by tonight I will have a third.[36]

At 5 AM on 12 July, Howard crossed the Chattahoochee with his IV Corps by sending General Stanley's 1st Division up the river to the pontoon bridge at Phillips Ferry that had been laid by Schofield's men. There, Stanley's Division crossed the river, and swept south down the east bank of the river until it reached the ground opposite Wood's 3rd Division at Power's Ferry where Wood's engineers were busily preparing their own pontoon bridge. By midday Wood's men were over and together with Stanley's men, the two divisions began to dig in on the high ridge covering the river crossing, with Wood's Division on the left and Stanley's Division on the right. Newton's 2nd Division crossed over the following morning. [37]

Palmer's XIV Corps remained on the west side of the river further to the south at Pace's Ferry on July 12th, some nine or ten miles southwest of Roswell while Hooker's XX Corps continued the Federal line south along the Chattahoochee to Palmer's right, from opposite Montgomery Ferry, approximately to the mouth of Proctor's Creek. Logan's XV Corps and Blair's XVII Corps from McPherson's Army of the Tennessee were still further to the right and posted along the Chattahoochee River and Nickajack Creek from near Mayson's and Turner's Ferry all the way to Howell's Ferry.[38] Turner's Ferry was about nine miles southwest of Power's Ferry, which was approximately the center of Sherman's line. Thus, half of Sherman's troops were on the west side of the river, and the other half were spread along the Chattahoochee River Basin with Dodge's XVI Corps at Roswell, Schofield's XXIII Corps at Phillips Ferry below, and Howard's IV Corps at Powers Ferry, all having crossed the river and established bridgeheads.

From Roswell to the northeast, to Turner's Ferry to the southwest, Sherman's forces were spread out roughly along a twenty-mile front with half of his men on each side of the river. There were only five or six passable fords in the twenty-mile stretch. Moreover, there were no connecting roads along the banks of either side of the river over which one part of Sherman's armies could support another part in the event one became threatened. Any

---

[36]*OR*, series I, vol. 38, ser. no. 76, 123.
[37]*OR*, series I, vol. 38, ser. no. 72, 155, 898–99.
[38]Ibid.; Scaife, *Campaign for Atlanta*, 83, 86–87.

movement by one of Sherman's forces would necessarily require a withdrawal from the Chattahoochee River line and back toward Marietta before being rerouted to the threatened area. Any such move would likely involve a rough march of some fifteen or more miles and take the better part of a day to accomplish. Sherman's aggressive thrusts across the river had placed three corps, each about 10,000 men strong, in isolated bridgeheads, miles apart from each other and from any reinforcements that might be called upon from the west side of the river. Thus, Johnston had a golden opportunity to strike a blow at one or more of Sherman's exposed positions while he had one foot on the east side of the Chattahoochee River and his other foot on the west side. But the Johnston was not even considering seriously such a blow, despite numerous cries from Richmond that he do so. Instead, Johnston appeared to be preoccupied in withdrawing stores of supplies from Atlanta and in preparing the Gate City for battle.

Following up on General Garrard's successful crossing of the Chattahoochee River at Roswell and, in support of General Dodge's XVI Corps, which had crossed the river there, Sherman sent the remainder of McPherson's Army of the Tennessee from the far right of his line along the Chattahoochee River below Nickajack Creek, to Roswell on the extreme left of his line. These troops, Logan's XV Corps and Blair's XVII Corps had to backtrack through Marietta to get to Roswell, which they did between 12 and 15 July. Brigadier General William Harrow's 4th Division of Logan's XV Corps crossed the Chattahoochee River on 14 July, and Logan's remaining two divisions followed suit the next day.[39]

Meanwhile in Atlanta, news that the Confederate army had crossed the Chattahoochee River was causing chaos. "Our presence on the south side of the Chattahoochee caused considerable alarm in Atlanta, and the good people of that city have been getting to the rear in a hurry," remembered Irenus Watson Landingham, clerk for the assistant adjutant general for Hood's Corps. "I was in town a few days after we crossed, and there was so much confusion that is was a relief to get back to the Army again," explained the soldier from the 5th Texas Infantry. "Citizens hurrying to and fro with anxious faces, drays and wagons running about with furniture, engines

---

[39]*OR*, series I, vol. 38, ser. no. 74, 100–101, 280–81, 332–33; Steven E. Woodworth, *Nothing But Victory: The Army of the Tennessee* (New York: Alfred A. Knopf, 2005) 326–27.

whistling, & puffing and blowing, and shrieking, Hotel gongs ringing...."
Landingham continued, "Cavalry dashing about over the streets, artillery
rumbling, and everything generally in such a high state of hast and
confusion, that it did not present a very lovely scene to a lover of
tranquility."[40]

---

[40]Irenus Watson Landingham (Co. A, 5th Texas Infantry and clerk for the A.
A. G., Hood's Corps) Papers, letter to Mother, 14 July 1864, folder 5, Special
Collections, Auburn University Library, Auburn AL.

11

OLD JOE JOHNSTON

We privates loved you because you made us love ourselves.[1]

The confidence of the men of General Stewart's Corps, which was still called the Army of Mississippi, had been high during the Georgia Campaign. Under the leadership of General Joseph Eggleston Johnston, the Southerners had met, stopped, and bloodied Sherman's invading armies at every step. Even though they had fallen back repeatedly, the men seemed to understand and appreciate Johnston's strategy. Most of the soldiers of the Army of Mississippi believed in Old Joe—or "Marse Joe" as they affectionately referred to him. They knew that he would not needlessly send them in an ill-planned assault and that he would strike only when the timing was right and when the odds favored them.

While Johnston's practice of falling back from one position to another was worrying President Davis and the Confederate high command, the privates and noncommissioned officers fighting Sherman's legions appreciated it. Sergeant Robert W. Banks, in a letter to his parents on 23 May wrote, "The Army of Tennessee has been forced to fall back because of Sherman's superiority in numbers. It may turn out for the best—let us trust so at all events. Remember that McClellan once said, beware of *Johnston's retreats*. The troops are in fine spirits and eager for a decisive fight."[2] Johnston's veterans had lived long enough through the war to learn that their chances of survival were substantially greater when they fought from behind defensive works such as trenches, logs and earthworks rather than when they were sacrificed through pell-mell charges against the enemy's works. Southern soldiers also reasoned that if they continued to survive, so did the Confederacy. Moreover, the longer they continued to survive as an effective fighting force, the better the chances of the war ending in their

---

[1]Samuel R. Watkins, *Company Aytch* (New York: Simon & Schuster, 1997) 171.

[2]Robert W. Banks, Letters, in Albert Castel, *Decision in the West* (Lawrence: University Press of Kansas, 1992) 217.

favor became, perhaps from the intervention of European powers like Britain or France, or from a tired North simply giving up.

By summer 1864 the Northern Democratic Party was openly promoting a peace treaty and an end to the war that would give the South its independence. The Federal draft of soldiers had been met with outrage and even riots, including a vicious riot in New York City. One Federal soldier gave his opinion of those in the North who did not support the war in a letter home from the Georgia front, "Exterminate all copperheads if a million die, how I detest them.... If I had my wish it would be that every traitor in the north be confined in such an infernal place, that hell would be a heaven to it."[3] President Lincoln feared that the continuation of the war without any appreciable progress by his armies in the field in summer 1864 would mark the end of his presidency and doom his chances at re-election in November. Two years earlier Lincoln had written his secretary of state, William H. Seward, of his will to see the war through until the nation was reunited: "I expect to maintain this contest until successful, or till I die, or am conquered, or my term expires, or Congress or the country forsakes me"[4]

Lincoln was so concerned about not being re-elected and not having the chance to see the country reunited through winning the war that he brought this note to his cabinet on 23 August:

> Executive Mansion,
> Washington, Aug. 23, 1864.
> This morning, as for some days past, it seems exceedingly probable that this administration will not be re-elected. Then it will be my duty to so co-operate with the President elect, as to save the Union between the election and the inauguration; as he will have secured his election on such ground that he can not possibly save it afterwards.
> A. Lincoln.[5]

---

[3]Charles Harding Cox, "'Gone for a Soldier': The Civil War Letters of Charles Harding Cox," ed. Lorna Lutes Sylvester, *Indiana Magazine of History* 68/3 (September 1972): 218.

[4]Carl Sandburg, *Abraham Lincoln: The Prairie Years and The War Years* (New York, Budget Book Service, 1993) 296.

[5]Ibid., 543.

Lincoln had every cabinet member sign the back of the folded paper, but he did not permit them to see or read its contents.[6] He hoped that he would never have to use it.

The Federal armies were being constantly re-filled by immigrants, particularly from Germany and other northern European states, and their will to fight for their new home could wane in the face of constantly attacks on fortified Southern positions at fearful and uneven costs. The general feeling in the Confederate army was that while they had been giving ground to Sherman, they had been bleeding his army at every step, thus reducing his forces to a number more equal to the Southerners. Colonel Virgil S. Murphy of the 17th Alabama Infantry in Walthall's Division writing from Kennesaw Mountain on 21 June had this to say about the campaign:

[We] fought them in all our ditches, as the enemy very prudently avoids them. The weather has been very unfavorable for Military Operations recently. We have dug nine ditches in the campaign and only fought in one of them [at New Hope Church]. We are well entrenched now [at Kennesaw] and have plenty loose rocks. And I think it would take more Yankees than you could pack into a fifty acre field to move us from our position.... It is not our fault however that we have not rain every day, but one or two since the 31st of May. The roads are almost impassable and it still continues to rain. It is bad on soldiers. We have no tents and no covering but "the canopy of Heaven." And it leaks mighty bad when it rains....

We continue to fight after the same fashion. Shelling and skirmishing daily. Occasionally the Yankees make a feeble effort to charge our works, but invariably get so badly used that they are losing all taste for such sport. And prisoners say that an order has been read to them saying they would not be required to charge breastworks anymore. If that is so I can't imagine how General Sherman proposes to get to Atlanta. Some men are killed and wounded every day. And as General Johnston said in his report some time ago, the aggregate fighting and casualties are as great as if a general battle had been fought.[7]

---

[6]Ibid.; T. Harry Williams, *Lincoln and His Generals* [New York: Alfred A. Knopf, 1952] 334–35.

[7]Virgil S. Murphy, to cousin from Kennesaw Mountain GA, 21 June 1864 in Illene D. Thompson and Wilbur E. Thompson, *The Seventeenth Alabama Infantry: A Regimental History and Roster* (Berwyn Heights MD: Heritage Books, 2003) 85–

Major T. J. Burnett from Butler County, Alabama, also of the 17th Alabama Infantry, explained the advantage of fighting behind earthworks: "we have killed more of their men because we are above them and have the best chance, and our men can beat them shooting. We are not falling back because the Yankees can whip us but because they won't fight, but go round us...."[8] According to Lieutenant Colonel Walter A. Rorer of the 20th Mississippi Infantry of Adam's Brigade in Loring's Division:

> Sherman has been flanking first one way then the other for thirty days or more, and it has been a continual fight on some part of our line all the time, the loss to the enemy at some points has been very great. I think they must number at least twenty-five thousand men less now than when they left Chattanooga. If that be so our numbers nearly equal now.[9]

Lieutenant Colonel Rorer's accurately estimated Federal casualties sustained by Sherman from the start of the Georgia Campaign until 17 July; the actual number was 29,104. Unfortunately for Rorer and the Confederates, however, Sherman had received reinforcements nearly equal to his losses during the three months of the campaign. At the start of the Georgia Campaign, Sherman had present for duty in the Army of the Cumberland, 60,773; the Army of the Tennessee, 24,465; and the Army of the Ohio, 13,559. This amounted to 108,797 infantry, artillery, and cavalry. Including field and staff, commissary, quartermaster staff, and other non-combatants, Sherman had with him a total of 110,123 at the start of the campaign.[10]

Assuming Rorer's calculations and that of the Confederate army were correct, Sherman's forces (108,797 combatants) should have been reduced to a mere 69,693 fighting men of all arms facing Johnston's legions. This figure did not include those who were sick, absent without leave, or who had been

---

86.

[8]Major Thomas J. Burnett, *Marietta* (GA) *Journal*, 13 November 1924; Thompson and Thompson, *Seventeenth Alabama Infantry*, 85.

[9]Walter A. Rorer to Cousin Susan, 9 June 1864, vertical files, 20th Mississippi Infantry, Carter House Library and Archives, Franklin TN, courtesy T. Glover Roberts, Historian.

[10]*OR*, series I, vol. 38, ser. no. 72, 62–63, 85, 115–17, 145, 152, 158–59; ser. no. 73, 510, 520, 749; ser. no. 74, 28, 48, 85, 87–89, 113, 373–74, 389–90, 488–89, 550–51, 566–67.

discharged when their time had expired. A number of units in Sherman's armies had enlisted in summer 1861 for three years, and their periods of enlistment were now expiring. Many of them did not re-enlist, so Sherman lost whole units, including companies and regiments, of veterans whose experience would be sorely missed. In contrast, as of 10 July's Abstract of Returns for the Confederate army, Johnston had about 73,013 men of all forces to defend Atlanta against Sherman, but this number included all those who were sick, slightly wounded, assigned to some duty away from the front line, or were non-combatants. Thus, 73,013 was the total number that Johnston had available on paper. Reducing his army by all of the non-combatants and sick, Old Joe only had about 50,932 "effective total present for duty," and of that amount, only about 41,000 were infantry in his three corps.[11]

Moreover, Johnston had lost some 9,972 men killed and wounded from 6 May to 9 July compared to Sherman's loss of 29,104 men during that time, proving that by fighting behind defensive works, the Confederates had bled the Yankees three times heavier than they themselves had been bled during those ninety days of fighting.[12] This number of Rebel casualties did not include those who were captured or who deserted. The Federal reports reveal that in May a total of 610 Rebel deserters and 1,795 prisoners were taken, and in June 1,839 deserters and 1,308 prisoners were captured, for a total of 5,552 men. This number, coupled with the 9,972 men killed and wounded, reveal that Johnston's losses from the start of the campaign until about 17 July were 15,524, approximately half of Sherman's losses. Moreover, a large part of the 2,449 Confederate deserters were from North Georgia and Tennessee because these veterans who had grown weary of the war, saw their army retreating farther from their homes, leaving families and farms at the mercy of the advancing Yankees.

Taking these losses into consideration, it was clear to Johnston's veterans that they were bleeding down Sherman's forces and that the Yankees were growing somewhat disheartened. Lieutenant Colonel Rorer reported,

> Our cavalry are daily bringing in a number of prisoners; they captured the Yankees' homeward mail a few days ago containing letters to the first of

---

[11]*OR*, series I, vol. 38, ser. no. 74, 679.
[12]Ibid., 687.

June—they are all despondent and feel themselves whipped all ready, in some of their assaults on our lines they have suffered dreadfully according to their accounts. We have maneuvered and dug ditches back and forth across the country until many think we are digging "our last ditch," and that here we must fight.[13]

Actually, Sherman had been adding to his forces during the ninety days of hard campaigning, so that by 17 July, he had about 105,000 men present for duty, roughly the same number that he began with in Chattanooga in April. Sherman's forces were supplemented by the addition of the XVII Corps to the Army of the Tennessee from North Alabama by 10 June, a force of some 10,024 fresh veteran troops; plus 5,713 were added to the Army of the Ohio during this time, and the Army of the Cumberland was increased by another 5,000–10,000 men who were returning from leave, illness, or who had recovered from wounds during the Chickamauga and Chattanooga campaigns the previous fall. According to Sherman, "About these figures have been maintained during the campaign, the number of men joining from furlough and hospitals about compensating for the loss in battle and from sickness."[14] Moreover, Sherman gained another 5,000–10,000 men from newly arrived regiments that had never before seen combat. Thus, as Johnston continued to try to bleed out Sherman's army, Uncle Billy continued to replace his losses, but Johnston would not be able to do the same.[15]

Sherman's forces can be followed during the first ninety days of the Georgia Campaign as follows: In the Army of the Tennessee: the XV Corps began the campaign with 12,101 men, lost about 3,273 men through 17 July, leaving about 8,828 before accounting for re-enforcements; the XVI Corps began with 13,120 men, lost about 1,155 men by 17 July, and had about 11,965 men remaining before allowing for those who were added to their number during the campaign; and the XVII Corps with some 10,024 men were added by 10 June to the Federal forces, they lost about 677 men

---

[13]Walter A. Rorer to Cousin Susan, 9 June 1864, Carter House Library and Archives.

[14]*OR*, series I, vol. 38, ser. no. 72, 63.

[15]*OR*, series I, vol. 38, ser. no. 72, 62–63, 85, 115–117, 145, 152, 158–59; ser. no. 73, 510, 520, & 749; ser. no. 74, 28, 48, 85, 87–89, 113, 373–74, 389–90, 488–89, 550–51, 566–67.

by 17 July, and had about 9,347 in front of Atlanta before taking into consideration additions to their number by Sherman. In the Army of the Ohio, the XXIII Corps began with 13,565 men, lost about 3,969 during the entire campaign, and added 5,713 in re-enforcements to their number during the campaign for a total number of men who served in the XXIII Corps during the Georgia Campaign at 19,268. In the Army of the Cumberland: the IV, XIV, and XX Corps mustered some 60,773 at the start of the campaign, lost 20,030 infantry and 938 cavalry, and gained about 5,000–10,000 in men returning to their units from wounds, sickness, and furlough, and another 5,000–10,000 men from newly created units. Thus, Sherman had an effective strength on 30 April some 88,833 infantry and 110,123 men of all arms, on 31 May, 89,659 infantry and 112,819 men of all arms, and on 30 June, 83,637 infantry and 106,070 men of all arms, so that when Johnston faced Sherman on 17 July, he was outnumbered about 80,000 to 40,000 in infantry and 105,000 to 53,000 men of all arms.[16]

By 17 July, Johnston's army was approximately 73,013 on paper and 50,932 in the trenches. He had begun the campaign in Dalton in April with only the two corps of Hood and Hardee, and the cavalry of General Joe Wheeler, an effective total present of some 43,887 men of all arms. His only significant re-enforcements during the campaign came with the addition of the Army of Mississippi under General Polk, which began arriving during the eve of the Battle of Resaca in the second week of May. With the Army of Mississippi came some 19,245 veteran infantry, artillery, and cavalry, bringing Johnston's total fighting force at its height during the latter part of May at 60,000 men. He never had more than this number in the field at any time during the campaign; he fought with 40,000–60,000 effective troops against a Yankee force that never numbered fewer than 90,000 until after Johnston was no longer in command.[17] Thus, Old Joe believed that he had fought against two- or three-to-one odds for ninety days, given up ninety miles, and inflicted two or three to one casualties on his foe in the process.

One problem with calculating the size and strength of the Rebel army is in the method of counting used by the Confederate states' army during the war. The Federal army's calculations provided the total of men available for service, that is, those who were present in the field, slightly sick but at or

---

[16]Ibid.
[17]Ibid., 679, 687.

near the field, and pioneers, teamsters, guards and others who were perhaps detached on duty nearby or in the rear. In contrast, the Confederate army's calculations do not always include them, and as a rule, did not. Confederate tabulations provided the number "present for duty" and also included the figure for those "aggregate present." Historian and author Richard McMurry has completed an excellent and challenging study of this issue by concluding that taking a percentage of these relative figures into account, one may arrive at a truer number of Confederates actually in the zone of fire, or available for fighting by Johnston.[18]

If the administration in Richmond didn't like Old Joe's defensive strategy, the Southern boys in the red clay trenches of Georgia, at least those from General Stewart's Army of Mississippi, certainly did. They had followed Old Joe in Mississippi during summer 1863 and believed his leadership and organizational abilities were beyond question. When they were led by Old Joe they had plenty to eat; were given sufficient equipment, arms, and ammunition; and were skillfully put into strong defensive positions before the numerically superior foe. This had not always been the case when they had been under the command of other generals such as Bragg, Van Dorn, Pemberton, and Polk. When they were withdrawn it was understood that they had been flanked by the overwhelming numbers of Yankees, but that Old Joe would have another surprise for the Yankees just around the next hill.

The Rebel army at Atlanta was a rag-tag outfit, but there was a cohesiveness among them and a sense of purpose that General Johnston had managed to create and maintain despite their hardships. They did not enjoy any comforts during the campaign, but they had been well fed, at least in terms of quantities of beef and bread. According to Major Walter Rorer in a letter to his cousin:

> The men and nearly all the officers are without a change of clothing. None carry more than one blanket and some only carry a blanket for their men; raw meat and cold corn bread or crackers have been our only diet for more than a month, the ration is abundant and the men in good health; though the

---

[18]Richard M. McMurry, *Atlanta 1864: Last Chance for the Confederacy* (Lincoln: University of Nebraska Press, 2000) appendix 2, 194–97; McMurry also has discovered that in June, 1864 around Kennesaw Mountain, Johnston ordered 75,000 daily rations to feed his army.

exposure and dirt would have killed us all at the commencement of the war.[19]

The spirit of the Confederate army had been reasonably high during June and July, as evidenced by the letter of Private James K. Watson of Company B, 31st Mississippi from Choctaw County, who had written with confidence and hope to his father on 1 July from Kennesaw Mountain:

> I think we will be shure to whip them at this place. Some of the Yanks we have taken said they was going to Atlanta by the 4th of July but I think there will be sevrel that will go like them did—under guard. I could write a week if I had time and paper, but I think it not worthwhile to write, but I think we will whip them hear and General Lee is whiping them at Richmond so I think we will have peace soon.[20]

Not all of the soldiers were as cheerful about their conditions, and many Southerners despaired of the hardships brought about by the arduous campaign. Private Frank Copeland Robertson of the 17th Alabama wrote home to his wife during this time:

> ...we don't get to sleep a bit hardly tall we are up night and day and rite under the shells and bullets all the time but I am getting use to them all tho I am very tired of hearing them ther is a grate many killed and wounded. Ever day that passes by this company is all rite yet all though tha is here a grate many wounded but none killed.... Martha I will tell something concerning our fate here we don't get nothing to eat but a little meat and bread and not more than half a nough of it a tall Martha I have got on the same clothes that I wore off from home yet and never had them washed at all and now we is low as hogs....[21]

For Private Robertson the war would soon be over. Apparently his despair led him to defect on the evening of 4 July after hearing the Federal army's bands play patriotic music all day. Private Robertson was listed as

---

[19]Walter A. Rorer to Cousin Susan, 9 June 1864, Carter House Library and Archives.

[20]James Watson, Pvt., Co. B, 31st Miss. Infantry, to father, "Private Watson Winter Home," *The Webster* (Eupora MS) *Progress*, 15 July 1937, Confederate Files, 6, Kennesaw Mountain National Battlefield Park Library, Kennesaw GA; copy in author's possession, author's vertical file no. 130.

[21]Frank Copeland Robertson to Martha Robertson, June–July 1864 from Georgia, in Thompson and Thompson, *Seventeenth Alabama Infantry*, 86.

captured by the Federal army on 5 July. He would pay a dear price for his capture. On 3 February 1865, Private Robertson died of pneumonia at Camp Douglas, in Chicago, after the brutal winter there.[22]

Georgia historian Kenneth Coleman aptly described the mood that had begun to take hold among some Georgians by 1864:

> Conscription, impressment, inflation, numerous shortages, and fiery denunciations of Confederate authorities by the Brown-Stephens-Toombs clique intensified war-weariness in Georgia. Increasing dissension led to numerous desertions from the army and some disloyalty at home. Some areas, especially in north Georgia, temporarily defied Georgia and Confederate authority, and a peace movement centered in western Georgia made headway. In the spring of 1864, with Sherman's massive army poised to slash into Georgia, a special session of the legislature adopted the resolution of Brown and the Stephens brothers; it was a very vague call for peace negotiations based on the Declaration of Independence and states' rights and only part of a complex procedure that condemned the Confederates but praised President Davis. The Georgia State Legislature continued to waffle in its support of Davis vs. the states' rights maverick [Governor Brown], but in the last chaotic months of the war the morale of the people crumbled and near anarchy prevailed in many areas.[23]

While there were very few desertions reported in Johnston's army during the Atlanta Campaign, it is revealing that disproportionate and considerable numbers of deserters are found in north Georgia and Tennessee units during the summer of 1864, particularly after the change in command to General Hood. A comparison to Mississippi, Louisiana, Missouri, Texas, Arkansas, and Alabama units of Polk's Army of Mississippi (later called Stewart's Corps) reveals that after General Polk marched his corps toward Resaca and the Atlanta Campaign began, there were hardly any desertions in his ranks at all, but during winter 1863–1864, his men left camps around Canton, Meridian, and Enterprise, Mississippi; and Selma, Demopolis, and Mobile, Alabama in droves. This phenomenon of close-to-home desertions in the Army of Mississippi certainly gave credence to General Forrest's belief that soldiers should serve as far from

---

[22]Thompson and Thompson, *Seventeenth Alabama Infantry*, 274.

[23]Kenneth Coleman, ed., *A History of Georgia* (Athens: University of Georgia Press, 1991) 193.

home as possible to reduce the temptation of desertion. Forrest's theory does *not* explain the increase in desertions in units of men who periodically received desperate and pitiful letters from their starving and threatened loved ones and whose homes had recently been occupied by the enemy other than the obvious concerns for the safety of their homes and families.[24]

It was said that by this point of the war, rural counties in the South were so full of deserters that there was no tree or bush in the woods or swamps that did not have a deserter behind it. One man noted in his diary as early as 3 February 1863 that "some runaway Negroes in Choctaw County [Mississippi] have come in and report the woods so full of runaway white men that there is no room for them."[25] Another Mississippian of the same region, Mr. George Washington Dudley, who served in the 11th Mississippi, was nineteen years old when the war ended.[26] He wrote,

> During the war a large number of men took up their abode in the dense swamps. An organization was effected among them called "Hutto's Battery," named for one of their leaders. [This was Aaron Hutto, who served as a scalawag public official of Choctaw County during Reconstruction.] These men had an organized camp and kept pickets out to prevent being taken by surprise by the Confederate cavalry. A number of them built a boat and floated down the Big Black [River] to a point opposite Vicksburg, then in possession of the Federal army. They then went north until the war was over. Mr. Dudley had talked personally with one of those who had thus expatriated themselves for a time.[27]

In Georgia, it was observed that letters from wives and mothers to loved ones in the service had a huge impact.

> Perhaps the greatest challenge for Georgia's white women was the awful loneliness in isolated rural areas. They tried to resist this by working hard

---

[24]Robert Selph Henry, *First with the Most: Nathan Bedford Forrest* (New York: Smithmark Publishers, 1995) 368; Coleman, *A History of Georgia*, 187–204.

[25]J. P. Coleman, *Choctaw County Chronicles: A History of Choctaw County, Mississippi 1830–1973* (Ackerman MS: J.P. Coleman, 1973) 71, quoting diary of Jason Niles of Kosciusko MS.

[26] Dudley had four brothers serve in the Confederate army, three of them who each lost their lives with the 31st Mississippi in Featherston's Brigade.

[27]"Mississippi Soldiers and Sailors in the War of the Rebellion," Compiled Service Records, Record Group 269, Rolls 341–6, Mississippi Department of Archives and History, Jackson, MS; Coleman, *Choctaw County Chronicles*, 75–76.

and writing long letters to loved ones at the front. These letters powerfully affected army morale, the positive ones encouraging renewed optimism and the negative ones encouraging a host of deserters. In the later stages of the war some rural areas were harassed by deserters and bushwhackers and then overrun by Union forces that sent great hordes of men, women and children, black and white, "refugeeing" into more secure regions like southwest Georgia.[28]

Joseph Eggleston Johnston was a man of great skill and military training. A native Virginian, Johnston attended the West Point Military Academy where he graduated in 1829. Serving with excellence in the United States Army, he held positions in the artillery and engineering departments. During the Mexican War, Johnston was wounded five times and proved to be a gallant officer in battle who could be trusted with command. By the end of the Mexican War, Johnston had risen to the rank of Brevet Lieutenant Colonel. By June 1860, less than a year before his beloved Old Dominion State would leave the Union, Johnston had risen to the rank of brigadier general and was the quartermaster general of the United States Army. Competent, efficient, reliable and prudent were trademarks that defined Joe Johnston's pre-Civil War career.

When he resigned his post to offer his services to the Confederacy, Johnston was the ranking officer in the South and expected to be given this distinction. However, on 31 August 1861, when President Jefferson Davis nominated his five leading officers to full generalship to the Confederate Congress, he specified the order of their rank as follows: first, Samuel Cooper; second, Albert Sidney Johnston; third, Robert E. Lee; fourth, Joseph E. Johnston; and fifth, P. G. T. Beauregard. The Confederate Congress had previously passed a law on 14 March 1861, which provided that any former United States officer who entered the Confederate service would have the same relative rank that they had previously enjoyed in the Federal army.

As Johnston was the only one in the Southern army who held a general's commission with the pre-war army, he certainly expected to rank first among the generals in the new Confederacy. When he learned that he was fourth in seniority, he wrote President Davis, exclaiming, "I still rightfully hold the rank of first general in the Armies of the Southern

---

[28]Coleman, *A History of Georgia*, 195.

Confederacy."[29] Clearly offended, Davis snapped back a quick reply in which he remarked of Johnston's letter, "Its language is, as you say, unusual; its arguments and statements utterly one sided, and its insinuations as unfounded as they are unbecoming."[30] Avoiding an explanation in his letter, Davis reminded Johnston that he was president and the commander in chief of the Confederacy, and the dispute sparked or re-kindled ill-feelings that would continue between the two throughout the war. In reality, Davis did not want Johnston to outrank Samuel Cooper, Albert Sidney Johnston, and Robert E. Lee who were his friends and whom he trusted over Johnston.

It didn't help Johnston that he and Davis had been rivals at West Point. It was rumored that the two had their first quarrel—a fist fight—over a girl. Never able to see eye to eye, the two tried to work together earlier in the war. By fall 1863, their rivalry and opposing views on the defense of the South had blossomed into an open and ugly rift. Mutual suspicion grew so much that by December 1863, President Davis found no comfort in appointing Johnston to command of the Army of Tennessee, but the Confederate leader felt he had no other option.[31]

---

[29]Bell Irvin Wiley, *Embattled Confederates* (New York: Harper & Row, 1964) 56.

[30]Ibid. For a good discussion of this issue, see Craig L. Symonds, *Joseph E. Johnston: A Civil War Biography* (New York: W. W. Norton & Co., 1994) 127–29. Civil war historian and president of the Georgia Battlefields Association, Charles Crawford of Atlanta, a retired Air Force colonel, makes a good argument that Joe Johnston should have been cashiered and discharged from the Confederate army in September 1861 after his outburst to President Davis, the commander-in-chief of all Confederate forces. Crawford adds that had Johnston been removed from command at that time, the Confederacy might have been better off (personal communications between Crawford and the author, 2011).

[31]Shelby Foote, *Fort Sumter to Perryville*, vol. 1 of the *Civil War, A Narrative* (New York: Vintage Books, 1986) 7; Stanley F. Horn, *The Army of Tennessee* (Norman: University of Oklahoma Press, 1952) 305–309; Thomas Lawrence Connelly, *Autumn of Glory: The Army of Tennessee* (Baton Rouge: Louisiana State University Press, 2001) 281–89. The story about a fight over a girl appears to be apocryphal. Craig Symond's biography on Johnston provides a detailed account of Johnston's West Point experience; he mentions the incident only in a footnote: "The nineteenth-century rumor that Davis and Johnston quarreled over a girl is almost certainly false" (Symonds, *Joseph E. Johnston*, 390).

When General Braxton Bragg resigned from command after the defeats at Chattanooga, Missionary Ridge, and Lookout Mountain, and the Army of Tennessee fell back to Dalton, Georgia, Davis searched for a replacement. After first offering command to Hardee, who refused it, Davis turned to Robert E. Lee. Twice declining the offer to go himself to Georgia, Lee then suggested P. G. T. Beauregard. For Davis, that recommendation was out of the question as Davis disliked Beauregard more than Johnston, if that were possible. General Johnston was the other obvious choice, but Davis continued to look, convinced he must be overlooking the right man. From 30 November to mid-December, Davis searched the nation. Seeking counsel from his cabinet, his political friends, Braxton Bragg, and General Lee, Davis kept looking. The president called Lee to Richmond. The two met for a week behind closed doors. Apparently Lee thought the president would order him to Georgia anyway, for he wrote a curious letter to General J. E. B. Stuart, his trusted cavalry commander, before leaving the Army of Northern Virginia to go see the president. In the letter, Lee lamented, "my heart and thoughts will always be with this Army."[32]

Perhaps the Confederate president had other options, including promoting a junior officer to the rank of full general or creating a new cadre of leadership by elevating a group of rising stars among his western generals, but passing up superior ranking officers was likely beyond the his imagination. Historian Steven Woodworth argues in his article, "A Reassessment of Confederate Command Options During the Winter of 1863–1864," that Davis had a number of attractive options available to him in December 1864 to lead the Confederate forces. Those included selecting Lieutenant General Edmund Kirby Smith and pressing Lieutenant General William Joseph Hardee into relenting and taking field command. Woodworth also soundly points out that the Confederacy held back worthy officers from promotion. Generals Alexander Peter Stewart, Stephen Dill Lee, and Patrick Ronayne Cleburne, Woodworth explains, should have been promoted to corps command under a newly created structure of the Southern forces in Georgia and Mississippi during winter 1863–1864, a structure which had been suggested by Joe Johnston. Then, argues Woodworth, should Johnston (or whoever Davis had placed in command of the Army of Tennessee in December 1863) have failed, Davis would have a

---

[32]Connelly, *Autumn of Glory*, 281–88.

wide range of available options among the new corps commanders. Instead, by failing to promote his rising stars, the president was left with the limited option of promoting Hood to command when Davis felt a change was necessary.[33]

Davis's old friend and roommate at West Point, Bishop-General Leonidas Polk, writing from his post in Mississippi, weighed in on the subject. Fully aware of Davis's anxiety over Johnston, the bishop wrote,

> When, there is so general a desire on the part of the army and the country as there is to have General Johnston placed in that command, a part of your duty seems to your friend to be to yield to this general desire, that those whose all is staked upon the issue may have something to say as to the hand in which it shall be saved or lost.[34]

Davis finally relented. On 16 December, three weeks after the vacancy of command of the Army of Tennessee occurred, Johnston's appointment was sent. After all of Davis's effort to find someone else, he was not sure that Johnston would accept. It was widely known that Lee had met in private with Davis and that Davis had been reluctant to follow Lee's advice to appoint Johnston. Johnston knew that his support in Richmond would be mixed. Johnston received the order on 18 December to turn over his department in Mississippi to General Polk and report to Dalton to take command of the Army of Tennessee. His friends in the Richmond government convinced him to take the post, despite misgivings and the lack of full support from the president and cabinet. Senator Louis Wigfall, Davis's greatest detractor and Johnston's strongest political ally, wrote Johnston, "you will not again decline this offer."[35] He referred to Johnston's previous reluctance to take command of the Army of Tennessee during spring 1863 when Wigfall declared that he and his anti-Davis and anti-Bragg crowd, "had been moving heaven and earth to have you put in

---

[33]Steven Woodworth, "A Reassessment of Confederate Command Options during the Winter of 1863–1864," in Theodore P. Savas and David A. Woodbury, eds., *The Campaign for Atlanta & Sherman's March to the Sea*, vol. 1, Essays of the American Civil War (Campbell CA: Savas Woodbury Publishers, 1994) 18–19.

[34]Horn, *Army of Tennessee*, 308.

[35]Connelly, *Autumn of Glory*, 283.

command of their Army."[36] Johnston packed his bags, left Bolton, Mississippi, and arrived in Dalton on 27 December. [37]

On the evening of Sunday, 17 July 1864, Johnston found himself near Bolton, Georgia, quartered at Dexter Niles's abandoned old farmhouse below Peach Tree Creek. With the general was his wife, Lydia, who had been in Atlanta for two months until joining her husband, now only a short ride from the Gate City.[38] Mr. Niles was a slave trader and speculator who had come from Boston, Massachusetts, before the war and during the pre-war growth of Atlanta. He had bought the old Benjamin Thurman pioneer homestead and, according to neighbors,

> turned it into a slave plantation, or maybe it was a wholesale slave market. We had never seen so many dark skinned people in all our lives. Perhaps two years went by and then all at once the residence was vacated and all the cabins were bare. It was said that when it became evident that the institution of slavery was doomed these bondsmen, women and children, were rushed to a slave market beyond the shores to the south of us and sold before Confederate money entirely lost its value. Dexter Niles went back to Boston...."[39]

After two and a half months of falling back across north Georgia since the opening of the Georgia Campaign, Johnston's Fabian Policy became an increased concern for President Davis. The Southern army had repeatedly retreated and given up territory in north Georgia without committing to a full-scale fight. Indeed, in less than three months, the Confederates had gone all the way from near the Tennessee state line at Dalton to the outskirts of Atlanta. Without engaging in a general battle or providing a reasonable explanation for the absence of one to Davis, Johnston's army had fallen below the Chattahoochee River, the last natural barrier before the Gate City. Johnston had given the president little reason for his failure to bring on a general engagement, despite repeated requests from Davis to

---

[36]Ibid.

[37]Ibid., 289.

[38]Samuel Carter III, *The Siege of Atlanta, 1864* (New York: St. Martin's Press, 1973) 176; Sarah Huff, *My 80 Years in Atlanta*, http://www.artery.org/08_history/UpperArtery/CivilWar/SaraHuff/My80YearsInAtlanta_All.pdf, 1937 (18 November 2014) 4–5.

[39]Huff, 4–5.

Johnston for information and action. Further, Johnston offered no reports on the state of affairs or his plan for the defense of Atlanta including how he intended to defeat Sherman.[40]

The president had previous experience with Johnston's failure to bring on a decisive battle in the Peninsular Campaign in Virginia in spring 1862. Johnston had fallen back to the defenses of Richmond without giving battle, and he came near to losing the Confederate capital before his wounding at the Battle of Fair Oaks (or Seven Pines) compelled his temporary removal from command. Johnston's injury resulted in Robert E. Lee being given command of the Virginia forces.[41]

By spring 1862 Johnston had earned both respect and high esteem from his fellow officers and men for his quiet, calm, gentle, efficient, reassuring, and even stoic presence. At the same time, he had earned a reputation for caution, slowness, evasiveness, and uncooperativeness with his superiors. Capable of simultaneously projecting both pure Southern romanticism and punctiliousness, Johnston proved an enduring and perplexing enigma in the life of the Confederacy. He kept his plans to himself, neither seeking nor receiving counsel from Davis, much to the president's vexation. As Johnston would later explain, "I could not consult him [Davis] without adopting the course he might advise, so that to ask his advice would have been, in my opinion, to ask him to command for me."[42]

During the Peninsular Campaign, Johnston eventually made an effort to defend the Confederate capital with an aggressive battle plan that was, as expected, competent, reasonable and well-drawn, but which was carried out so inefficiently and piecemeal that it failed to bring on the rout Johnston had desired. Whether the blame for its miscarriage lay with Johnston or with subordinates who had taken their own interpretation of orders for the charge at Fair Oaks, or whether the assault was as effective as could reasonably have been expected of relatively green troops, would not matter. As dusk brought about the end of the day's fighting, Old Joe's career in Virginia ended with a painful bullet wound to his right shoulder, followed

---

[40]Horn, *Army of Tennessee*, 309–340; Connelly, *Autumn of Glory*, 286–89, 326, 402–407, 420–21.

[41]Foote, *Fort Sumter to Perryville*, 438–41; Wiley, *Embattled Confederates*, 57–58.

[42]Foote, *Fort Sumter to Perryville*, 440.

by a shell fragment in his chest. Johnston's assault had, however, checked Federal general George McClellan's advance on Richmond, which allowed the Confederates to organize and eventually mount a counter-offensive under General Robert E. Lee, Davis's replacement to Johnston. By the time Johnston had recovered from his wounds, Lee had removed McClellan from the peninsula, cleared most of Virginia of the Federals, and even carried the war into Maryland. Lee had in just three short but busy months done the incredible; there was no way Richmond was going to replace Lee. Thus, even after Johnston had recovered from his injury, Lee remained in command.

Again, in the Mississippi Campaign during spring 1863, Johnston failed to coordinate the Southern troops in middle Mississippi and bring about an assault against General Grant and the invading Federal force at either Vicksburg or Jackson. In his defense, he had been ordered to take command of the Confederate forces in the Mississippi theater too late to stop Grant from destroying Jackson and then turning and laying siege on Vicksburg. Johnston was given some 30,000 men during the latter part of May and first of June 1863, with specific instructions from President Davis to attack Grant and try to break his hold on Vicksburg. Johnston continued to give excuses why he could not and should not attack. When around 1 July, he finally moved toward Vicksburg from his base at Canton, located some twenty miles north of Jackson and forty miles east of Vicksburg, he was too late. By the time that he got to the outskirts of Vicksburg with his dubiously named "Army of Relief," General John C. Pemberton had surrendered the Confederate forces in Vicksburg on, of all days, the Fourth of July. For many years, Vicksburg turned a blind eye to the national holiday and its citizens did not celebrate it.

The some 30,000 disheartened and starved troops under Pemberton were bottled up in Vicksburg since mid-May. Daily, they expected to hear Johnston's guns coming from the east to rescue them. Through a bold chess-like move, Grant was able to catch the Confederate forces in Mississippi in detail during the month of May; that is, he was skillful enough to attack portions of the Southern troops with his whole army, which numbered at the start of Grant's movements only about 32,000 officers and men in seven well-trained divisions. Various Rebel units continued to remain idle or chase after Grant's shadow. After scattering a few small Southern units near Jackson, Grant turned toward Vicksburg and caught Pemberton unawares about halfway between Jackson and Vicksburg at the Battle of Champion Hill (or the Battle of Baker's Creek). Grant then slugged it out with Pemberton, first at Champion Hill on 16 May and again at Big Black River on 17 May before pushing Pemberton and most of his army into the defenses of Vicksburg. There, believing Johnston would come, Pemberton and his men waited. After waiting more than six weeks for Johnston and with dwindling food and ammunition (including the percussion caps needed to fire their rifles), Pemberton and his men finally gave up.

If Johnston had acted quickly, he would have enjoyed numerical superiority. In fact, on 7 June, Johnston had some 60,000 men including his 31,000-man Army of Relief and Pemberton's force of nearly 30,000 to just 56,000 in Grant's army. By the time Johnston determined to move, Grant had strengthened his position and formed a line to meet Johnston coming from behind him. By late June, Grant had amassed some 77,000 men by bringing in more troops from Memphis through his naval transports and rendered Johnston's efforts virtually meaningless.

Clearly, Johnston knew what was expected of him during the Vicksburg Campaign. When asked whether additional troops should be given to him from General Braxton Bragg's Army of Tennessee, stationed in middle Tennessee on 12 June, Johnston replied that do to so would "involve yielding Tennessee. It is for the Government to decide between this State and Tennessee."[43] After more prodding from Richmond, Johnston telegraphed Richmond on 15 June and explained that he considered "saving Vicksburg hopeless." The next day, James A. Sedden, secretary of war, responded,

> Vicksburg must not be lost without a desperate struggle. The interest and honor of the Confederacy forbid it. I rely on you still to avert the loss. If better resources do not offer, you must hazard attack. It may be made in concert with the garrison, if practicable, but otherwise without, by day or night, as you think best.[44]

The dialogue continued until it became too late. Johnston simply had ignored orders to try to lift the Vicksburg siege by force, and, the year

---

[43]*OR*, series I, vol. 24, part 1, ser. no., 226.
[44]Ibid., 227.

before, he had given up the Virginia Peninsula without a fight until his back was to the Confederate capital and the church bells of Richmond could be heard within his lines. During spring and summer 1864, Johnston fell back from the mountain country of north Georgia without a general engagement, and it seemed he might give up Atlanta without a fight. Certainly, Johnston's track record was not encouraging to President Davis.

In his defense, Johnston was really in a no-win situation. Faced with defending Georgia and Atlanta against a well-organized, experienced and equipped force that was more than twice the size of his own, Johnston had limited options to stop the Federal forces, which were led by the very capable and well-respected commander, General William Tecumseh Sherman. Johnston had to bide his time and try to draw Sherman into either assaulting the Southerners in a strong defensive position or leading Sherman deep into Georgia and away from his communications and supply line and then strike a decisive blow against an exposed part of the Yankee force. Sherman, Johnston's friend before the war, was proving a worthy foe as he constantly shifted his forces around the Southern flanks, forcing Johnston to continually fall back across Georgia.

Johnston tried many times to lure Sherman into an attack, and indeed he succeeded, at least in part, at the battles of Resaca, New Hope, and Kennesaw, costing Sherman disproportionate casualties. With a few more results like the ill-fated Federal assault at Kennesaw Mountain, Johnston could cut Sherman's force down to size and give his own men better odds.

Johnston's tactics were not always defensive as counter-assaults at Resaca, New Hope, Dallas, and Pickett's Mill had proved. He had even tried to turn and attack a wing of one of Sherman's vast armies at Cassville on 19 May, but a rare display of timidity by General Hood that day disrupted the intended assault. Hood was to lead the striking force when some aggressive Yankee cavalry appeared on the wooded ridges to the east of his marching columns where no enemy was expected.[45]

After withdrawing from Resaca on the night of 15 May, Johnston fell back to Adairsville. From there, on the morning of 18 May, Johnston sent General Hood and General Polk with two-thirds of his army southeast toward Cassville over a lightly traveled road. He then sent General Hardee

---

[45]William R. Scaife, *The Campaign for Atlanta* (Atlanta: self-published, 1993) 55–79; Castel, *Decision in the West*, 76–82, 195.

140

with the remaining one-third of the Confederate army on the main road that led south toward Kingston. To further disguise the trap, Johnston sent all of the baggage wagons and ambulances with Hardee, making it appear that most of the Confederate army was heading to Kingston. By separating his corps and sending them down a couple of roads that joined farther south, Johnston hoped that General Sherman would also divide his forces as they pursued.[46]

The scheme appeared to work as Sherman took the bait and sent most of his infantry forces after General Hardee's Corps as it fell back from Adairsville to Kingston. Only Major General John M. Schofield's XXIII Corps, which formed the little Army of the Ohio, followed Hood and Polk toward Cassville. Schofield's force consisted of about 14,000 men in his XXIII Corps. Johnston planned to bag Schofield's XXIII Corps as it traveled southward following trails of dust created by the Southerners' apparent retreat. The combined corps of Hood and Polk totaled about 40,000 men who were full of confidence under Old Joe Johnston. The only other Federal infantry close enough to Schofield that could provide any assistance was Major General Joseph Hooker's XX Corps from the Army of the Cumberland, and they were several miles away and on the other side of a creek. Further, there were no roads that could bring Hooker's men into support of Schofield without a lot of counter-marching and a considerable loss of time. By then, Schofield's men would be crushed by Hood and Polk.[47]

The surprise presence of Federal troopers to the east was discovered by the Southerners just before Hood's men were preparing to turn west to begin the ambush on Schofield's column. The Northern cavalry units were the brigades of Colonel Joseph B. Dorr and Lieutenant Colonel James W. Stewart in General Edward M. McCook's Division. They had been ordered to swing out to the east and south to probe and try to reach the Western & Atlantic Railroad at or below Cass Station and tear it up.[48] Not finding any roads that would lead to Cass Station from the east, McCook turned west, where he found himself uncomfortably close to Hood's Corps. His timing

---

[46]Castel, 76–82.
[47]Ibid.
[48]Scaife, *Campaign for Atlanta*, 45.

could not have been better for the North because Schofield's unsuspecting divisions were marching right into Johnston's trap.

After stumbling into the rear of Hood's column, McCook ordered an attack by Stewart's Brigade. While it would amount to little more than a skirmish, it would completely disrupt Johnston's plans. Rather than proceed with the ordered attack and dispatch a few regiments or a brigade to deal with the menacing blue cavalry, Hood had his entire corps turn around and chase McCook. Hood apparently believed that this enemy force consisted of infantry and artillery.[49] Then, worried by the unexpected Yankees on his right flank, Hood nervously pulled back without telling Johnston until he had already begun to withdraw to the heights below the village of Cassville.[50]

Incredibly, that evening Hood then succeeded in talking General Polk and General Johnston into retreating further south during the night, away from the heights between Cassville and Cass Station, giving up perhaps the best defensive position in all of the campaign without a fight. Johnston had let the brash young Hood talk him out of the stronghold below Cassville, a decision he would subsequently regret. Johnston had also lost an opportunity to strike a blow against a portion of Sherman's force as Hood failed to bring about the planned attack. The incident would later be appropriately termed the "Affair at Cassville," where the Confederate high command seemed to suffer a loss of nerve.[51]

In mid-July, Johnston considered his options. Still faced with an intimidating enemy force, he reasoned that Sherman would spread his force in a wide arch when the Yankees crossed the Chattahoochee River. When Sherman's separated armies were too far apart to be able to come to each other's aid, he would strike. Johnston had kept his army intact for this purpose. He remained so secretive about it that both President Davis and General Sherman both thought he would continue withdrawing and perhaps even give up Atlanta without a fight.

---

[49]Connelly, *Autumn of Glory*, 347–48; *OR*, series I, vol. 38, ser. no. 74, 621–22.
[50]Castel, *Decision in the West*, 195.
[51]John P. Dyer, *The Gallant Hood* (Indianapolis: The Bobbs-Merrill Co., 1950) 235; Samuel G. French, *Two Wars: An Autobiography of Gen. Samuel G. French* (Huntington WV: Blue Acorn Press) 196–98; Connelly, *Autumn of Glory*, 347–48.

Johnston had reasons for being secretive. He didn't trust the president to keep things out of the Richmond papers. He had been burned before by telling Davis of his plans only to find hints of his intended move in the press. He also didn't discuss his plans much with his corps commanders, Hood, Hardee and Polk, which created an unnecessary lack of confidence between Johnston and his lieutenants, particularly Hood. Both Polk and Hardee apparently supported Johnston's defensive philosophy, leaving Hood as the lone advocate for aggressive offensive action. After General Polk was killed at Pine Mountain, Hardee and Hood were Johnston's only experienced lieutenant generals although Major General William W. Loring temporarily commanded Polk's Corps until Major General A. P. Stewart was promoted. Hardee seemed to favor Johnston's defensive plans and did not appear to have any better idea of his own. The president, his cabinet, and the War Department in Richmond believed that Johnston had no plan to repel Sherman other than to fall back in the face of the Northern thrusts, further confirming Davis's fears.[52]

The Confederate president had served in the United States military and drew on his own experience. In addition to being a West Point graduate, Davis was a Mexican War veteran, and he thought he knew a thing or two about soldiering. Johnston didn't care for Davis's micromanaging. Old Joe found the president annoying and often disregarded him. He further distrusted the president's cabinet, which appeared to Johnston as merely an extension of the president's reach. And then there was Braxton Bragg; Davis had removed his confidant and friend from command of the Army of Tennessee before Johnston took over, but as a consolation, Bragg was placed in Richmond as Davis's adviser. Bragg had some old scores to settle with the Army of Tennessee, and worse, he had the president's ear.[53]

When Johnston wouldn't communicate adequately with Davis about his intentions concerning Atlanta, the president felt he had no choice but to take action. Thus, on the evening of 17 July 1864, while General Johnston was speaking with his chief engineer, Colonel Stephen Presstman, and his chief of staff, General William W. Mackall, he received an order at his headquarters in the Dexter Niles (Niall) house northwest of Atlanta on the Marietta Road. The order was from adjutant and inspector general Samuel

---

[52]Connelly, *Autumn of Glory*, 281–85, 314–17.
[53]Ibid., 347–48.

Cooper in Richmond. Cooper was President Davis's right-hand man and voice to the army. It was about 9:00 PM:[54]

> Lt. Gen. John B. Hood has been commissioned to the temporary rank of general under the late law of Congress. I am directed by the Secretary of War to inform you that you have failed to arrest the advance of the enemy to the vicinity of Atlanta, far in the interior of Georgia, and express no confidence that you can defeat or repel him, you are hereby relieved from the command of the Army and Department of Tennessee, which you will immediately turn over to General Hood.[55]

The news brought shock, disbelief, and anger among the men. One Tennessee soldier lamented, "Farewell, old fellow! We privates loved you because you made us love ourselves."[56]

---

[54]Ibid., 421; Johnston recorded that he received the order at around 10:00 PM, but Lieutenant Thomas B. Mackall, an aide de camp on Johnston's staff and younger cousin to chief of staff Brigadier General William W. Mackall, recorded in his pocket diary that the order was received at 9:00 PM; Diary of Thomas B. Mackall, Joseph E. Johnston Papers, Mss. 3.9.1.J63, Box 3, Folder 2, Special Collections, Earl Gregg Swem Library, College of William and Mary, Williamsburg VA. Further, the original order may be seen as part of the Joseph E. Johnston Papers in the Henry E. Huntington Library in San Marco CA; see Joseph E. Johnston, *Narrative of Military Operations* (New York: D. Appleton & Company, 1874) 348; McMurry, *Atlanta 1864*, 139, 217, 221; Symonds, *Joseph E. Johnston*, 320, 421; Samuel Cater, III, *The Siege of Atlanta, 1864,* (New York: St. Martin's Press, 1973) 188–89.

[55]Order from Adjutant and Inspector General Samuel Cooper, *OR*, series I, vol. 38, ser. no. 76, 885.

[56]Watkins, *Company Aytch*, 171.

12

THE FABIAN POLICY

I shall not re-enlist, and my reasons are, first, I have no desire to monopolize all the patriotism there is, but am willing to give others a chance. My second reason is that after I have served three years my duty to my country has been performed and my next duty is at home with my family.[1]

Johnston's fallback strategy has traditionally been called the "Fabian Policy," named for the famous Roman soldier, who, for eighteen years, managed to hold a numerically and materially superior foe in check by skillfully using his force and the available geographic features such as mountain ranges. Eventually, Fabian wore out his opponent and won the day.[2] History teaches that the weaker South could not have won a war of attrition against the wealthier, stronger, and more populous North, and perhaps only by bold offensive strokes could they have ever hoped for independence. But, George Washington had won some eighty-seven years before by stalling the British Redcoats and by preserving his army during the American Revolution against a much stronger power in England. Who could know in 1864 that the Fabian Policy might not be the best way to win Southern independence? For that matter, an argument could be made today that by slowing the Federal armies as they invaded the South, and by not trying to take the offensive so frequently (and thus depleting their precious, small supply of manpower), the Confederacy may have ultimately won.

Many Southerners believed that if they carried on the war long enough and prayed long and hard enough, something good would happen, like foreign recognition, a collapse of the North's will to continue, or Divine Providence would intervene and give them victory. One officer in the Army of Mississippi wrote on 31 March 1864, "My hopes are in divisions amoung

---

[1]D. L. Day, *My Diary of Rambles with the 25th Massachusetts Volunteer Infantry* (Milford MA: King & Billings, 1884) 110.

[2]"Fabian Policy," *Funk & Wagnall's New Encyclopedia*, 1990 ed., vol. 10, 68; "Fabian Policy," Freedictionary.com

the northern people, and recognition and intervention by France; I can at present see no other way to end the war."[3] While the Southern tactic of winning the war by not losing it is not generally embraced today among historians and followers of the War between the States—perhaps it should be. Johnston had several good reasons for following it.

First, the deeper into the South that Sherman's armies went, the more tenuous his communications and supply lines became. Further, Sherman's prolonged campaign required more teamsters, engineers, wagons, and trains to supply his men. Sherman also needed to continually dispatch units to cover his rail and supply lines, further depleting his force.[4] Johnston contended that the further South Sherman went, the smaller his army became. In contrast, the further Johnston fell back down his line of communications, the larger his army grew as he picked up more men from posts and garrisons and teamsters who were no longer needed in the rear.[5] Thus, by the time that the opposing armies faced each other along the Chattahoochee River on 17 July, they were nearer the same size than at any other time in the campaign. Johnston could not have known that through reinforcements and re-enlistments, Sherman's armies remained about 100,000 strong throughout the campaign, while Johnston's mobile infantry force was never more than about 60,000.

Second, a number of Sherman's units were made up of three-year men, meaning that in summer 1864, or by that fall, their term of enlistment would be up and they would be going home unless they reenlisted. While Sherman was having better success in getting his men to "re-up" than the Federal armies in the East, including the principal force there, the Army of the Potomac, the loss in experienced men to the Federal armies in both the eastern and western theaters was becoming critical.[6] One such soldier in the East explained his decision:

---

[3]Walter A. Rorer to Cousin Susan, 9 June 1864, vertical files, 20th Mississippi Infantry, Carter House Library and Archives, Franklin TN, courtesy T. Glover Roberts, Historian.

[4]Henry Steele Commager, *The Blue and the Gray* (New York: Random House, 1996) 930.

[5]Ibid.

[6]Bruce Catton, *Bruce Catton's Civil War*, "A Stillness at Appomattox," 480–81.

I shall not re-enlist, and my reasons are, first, I have no desire to monopolize all the patriotism there is, but am willing to give others a chance. My second reason is that after I have served three years my duty to my country has been performed and my next duty is at home with my family.[7]

Third, President Abraham Lincoln was up for reelection in November. Many in the North had grown weary of the war and were ready to get it over with, win or lose. Johnston was fully aware of the political pressures faced by Lincoln, and those pressures clearly played a role in his strategic planning: "The importance to the Confederacy of defeating the enterprise against Atlanta was not to be measured by military consequences alone. Political considerations were also involved, and added much to the interest of that campaign."[8] Daily, the rolls of wounded, missing, and dead filled Northern newspapers. Financially, the war was taking its toll on the merchants and citizens, and the Conscription Act was forcing men to join a war and a cause that they did not believe in. If it were fought today, the national polls might likely show about one-third of the people in support of continuing the war to its bitter end whatever the cost, one-third ready to sue for peace and stop the futile killing, and the final third on the fence, waiting to see what happened next before casting an opinion. These ratios would have been just as common during the Civil War as they are today as rarely have Americans agreed on an issue or conflict over the history of the United States.

It was in this climate that the popular former Federal general George B. McClellan was being advanced by the Democratic Party as an alternative to Lincoln's War Party and the Radical Republicans who, they exclaimed, had gotten the country into this terrible conflict in the first place. Should the "Little Napoleon," as his men had earlier called McClellan, be elected, perhaps the North could find a peaceful and quick end to the war, either with the Southern states back into the Union as slave states, or by recognizing the Confederacy if the North had to, but setting up favorable trade and defense treaties with them. The weary president feared if "Mac Napoleon," as Lincoln dubbed him, should win, then the country would be hopelessly and permanently divided—and the war lost.

---

[7]Day, *My Diary of Rambles*, 110.

[8]Joseph E. Johnston, *Narrative of Military Operations* (New York: D. Appleton & Company, 1874) 362–63.

Fourth, by holding on to Atlanta and not permitting Sherman to draw him into a decisive battle, Johnston hoped to swing the opinion of the North against Lincoln and his generals. Newspaper reporters following Sherman's armies did not favor Sherman or his results, in no small part because Sherman did not want them there and they knew it. Sherman made it very hard for the reporters to cover events at the front. He screened the mail and telegraph messages newspaper reporters attempted to send to their editors in the North. The reporters often could not get any information or news of the armies' progress, which resulted in many gloomily reporting that Sherman was in a hopeless stalemate.[9] One such reporter wrote in a private letter to his editor,

> We are making no headway. And—(I may be mistaken)—I fear the enemy have it in their power to prevent our further advance upon Atlanta. Perhaps we are only threatening that place to hold the Army here from assisting Lee, and…the actual taking of Atlanta is to follow the capture of Richmond.[10]

Fifth, fighting a defensive campaign required fewer men than fighting offensively. Johnston had skillfully used the advantages of entrenchments and natural terrain barriers such as rivers and mountains over the hundred days of fighting that had marked the Georgia Campaign, much to the consternation of his old friend Sherman. The trench-style warfare that Johnston employed was being echoed in Virginia by General Lee's army beginning at Spotsylvania, and continuing to Cold Harbor, Richmond, and Petersburg. This type of war became a precursor to the trench-style warfare employed in Europe during the World War I just fifty years later.

The great German-Prussian military theorist, Klaus Von Clausewitz, described the great dilemma between fighting an offensive versus a defensive campaign. According to von Clausewitz, when a nation seeks to destroy the opposing country's ability to wage war (such as what the Federal army was trying to do to the Confederacy), the offensive strategy is required. The offensive strategy was the total war concept that Sherman and Grant understood and applied to the South. This style ultimately brought the rebellion to a bitter—but convincing—end. According to the Prussian

---

[9]J. Cutler Andrews, *The North Reports the Civil War* (Pittsburgh: University of Pittsburgh Press, 1985) 552–66.

[10]Elias Smith to Sydney Howard Gay, 31 May 1864, Gay Papers, Butler Library, Columbia University, 14–15.

strategist, when a nation simply desires to hold on to its own territory or people and seeks only to sting their attackers enough to make them stop fighting, a defensive strategy should be employed. Von Clausewitz added,

> Here lies the origin of that difference of *Offensive* and *Defensive*, the influence of which prevails over the whole province of war. We cannot at present pursue this subject further than to observe that from this negative intention are to be deduced all the advantages and all the stronger forms of combat which are on the side of the *Defensive*, and in which that philosophical-dynamic law which exists between the greatness and the certainty of success is realised...
>
> If then the negative purpose, that is the concentration of all the means into a state of pure resistance, affords a superiority in the contest, and if this advantage is sufficient to *balance* whatever superiority in numbers the adversary may have, then the mere *duration* of the contest will suffice gradually to bring the loss of force on the part of the adversary to a point at which the political object can no longer be an equivalent, a point at which, therefore, he must give up the contest. We see then that this class of means, the wearying out of the enemy, includes the great number of cases in which the weaker resists the stronger.[11]

Frederick the Great during the Seven Years War was never strong enough to overthrow the Austrian monarchy, so he simply outlasted it.

By simply dragging out the war and inflicting more casualties on Sherman's attacking armies from prepared defensive positions, Johnston was bleeding his foe. By keeping his army in the field as a viable, and undefeated force, the North would eventually give up. President Lincoln and his generals were fighting a race against time, and they knew it. They needed victories, and they needed them quickly before support for the war effort faded. Johnston was aware that the North needed to beat his army in the field and do it quickly. Johnston also reasoned that Sherman's army could better take a defeat on the battlefield than could his own force. Sherman could simply re-enforce his army and take the offensive again, but if Johnston's men were defeated in a risky offensive move, they might be

---

[11]Karl von Clausewitz, *On War*, trans. J. J. Graham (London: N Trübner, 1873) 24–36.

destroyed, leading to the destruction of the Confederacy. This prophecy would be fulfilled just four months later, on 30 November 1864, when Hood's disastrous Tennessee Campaign ended in the bloody conflicts at Franklin and Nashville and after which the Army of Tennessee was virtually wiped out and the fate of the South was sealed.

Perhaps no greater insight into Johnston's thoughts about how he planned to conduct the remainder of the Georgia Campaign can be found than what Old Joe himself wrote in his memoirs some ten years later and in comparing it to what he wrote President Davis the day before his removal from command. Johnston's postwar reflections were as follows:

> In transferring the command to General Hood I explained my plans to him. First, I expected an opportunity to engage the enemy on terms of advantage while they were divided in crossing Peach-Tree Creek, trusting to General Wheeler's vigilance for the necessary information. If successful, the great divergence of the Federal line of retreat from the direct route available to us would enable us to secure decisive results; if unsuccessful, we had a safe place of refuge in our intrenched lines close at hand. Holding it, we could certainly keep back the enemy, as at New Hope Church, and in front of Marietta, until the State troops promised by Governor Brown were assembled. Then, I intended to man the works of Atlanta on the side toward Peach-Tree Creek with those troops, and leisurely fall back with the Confederate troops into the town, and, when the Federal army approached, march out with the three corps against one of its flanks. If we were successful, the enemy would be driven against the Chattahoochee where there are no fords, or to the east, away from their communications, as the attack might fall on their right or left. If unsuccessful, the Confederate army had a near and secure place of refuge in Atlanta, which it could hold forever, and so win the campaign, of which that place was the object. The passage of Peach-Tree Creek may not have given an opportunity to attack; but there is no reason to think that the second and far most promising plan might not have been executed.[12]

While Johnston watched and hoped for an opportunity to attack Sherman as he crossed Peach Tree Creek, he had not apparently matured any such plan to carry it out. He would not have an opportunity to do so, either, because President Davis fired him before Sherman's army reached Peach Tree Creek. Some historians contend that Johnston never had a plan

---

[12]Johnston, *Narrative*, 350–51.

to attack Sherman along the Peach Tree Creek line.[13] He appeared totally committed to the defensive strategy, marking time with space and inflicting counter-strikes only when conditions were perfect. One war correspondent pointed out in his article from Sunday, 24 July 1864, that, "There are no sutlers in Atlanta, nor government stores, nor magazines, nor arsenals. Everything has been removed before Gen. Hood assumed command, and nothing is retained, save what we have here in our immediate vicinity, along our lines."[14]

> It has been said, with tongue in cheek, that if Johnston had been left in command at Atlanta, the war would still be going on, with Johnston holding out in one of the Florida Keys. Many historians have held that Johnston really had no plan, other than to try not to lose.[15]

There were plenty of his contemporaries who held the same view. One official in Richmond, Colonel Josiah Gorgas in the Confederate Ordnance Bureau, wrote in his journal back on 21 May, "Johnston is falling back as hard as he can.... It is surmised that he will reach Macon [one hundred miles south of Atlanta] in a few days at the rate he is retreating. I trust the country will find out sooner or later what kind of General he is. I don't think he will suit [in] the emergency.[16]

On 25 May, as the Federal and Confederate armies struggled in the woods around New Hope Church, Gorgas added, "Johnston verifies all our predictions of him. He is falling back just as fast as his legs can carry him....

---

[13]Stephen Davis, *Atlanta Will Fall*, book 3 of the American Crisis Series: Books on the Civil War Era (Washington DC: Rowman and Littlefield Publishers, 2001) 133; Richard M. McMurry, *Atlanta 1864: Last Chance for the Confederacy* (Lincoln: University of Nebraska Press, 2000) 138–39, 146–47; Richard M. McMurry, *John Bell Hood and the War for Southern Independence* (Lincoln: University of Nebraska Press, 1992) 126–28; and Philip L. Secrist, *Sherman's 1864 Trail of Battle to Atlanta* (Macon: Mercer University Press, 2006) 142–43.

[14]Chattanooga *Daily Rebel*, 27 July 1864, roll 1, microfilm 1045, Tennessee State Library and Archives, Nashville TN.

[15]See the works of historians Richard McMurry; Steve Davis; Charlie Crawford, president, Georgia Battlefields Association and Atlanta historian and tour leader; and Johnston's biographer Craig Symonds.

[16]*The Journals of Josiah Gorgas, 1857–1878*, ed. Sarah Woolfolk Wiggins (Tuscaloosa: University of Alabama Press, 1995) 109, 111, 119–120; McMurry, *Atlanta 1864*, 130.

He is falling back behind the Chattahoochie and will I fear give up Atlanta.... Where he will stop only heaven knows."[17] It is clear that Johnston's constant fall backs and Sherman's constant flanking took a toll on the Southern morale. While the two armies were separated by the Chattahoochee River, "one day a Johnny asked, 'Who commands the army across the river?' 'General Sherman,' was the reply. 'Well, he commands ours, too,' said Johnny, 'for every time you are ordered to move we move too.'"[18]

Robert G. H. Kean, a clerk in the War Department, recorded in his diary on 22 May:

> Johnston has retreated still further.... The Secretary [of War, James A. Seddon] is dissatisfied. He told me this morning that General Johnston's theory of war seemed to be never to fight unless strong enough certainly to overwhelm your enemy, and under all circumstances merely to continue to elude him. This is a very just criticism upon all of General Johnston's campaigns.[19]

A just criticism indeed! With such a strategy, it was impossible to be assured that Johnston would have committed everything to the defense of Atlanta, as described in his memoirs, for his belief that keeping his army intact and in the field was clearly his first priority.

Perhaps the letters of Private J. B. Sanders of the 37th Mississippi in O'Neal's Brigade provide some insight on the evolving mood of the common soldier during the campaign. At the outset of the fighting, Sanders wrote his wife on 18 May, near Cassville: "the army is slowly falling back fighting evry inch of ground we ar only falling back to change persision we ar not whiped nor never will be we hav only bin flanked on the left we are on the right wing they is no telling when this fight will end I have not bin in eny ingagement since the 9th [of May]."[20] On 5 July from the hospital at Barnesville where he was recovering from illness, Sanders wrote,

---

[17]Ibid.; McMurry, *Atlanta 1864*, 130–31.

[18]John R. McBride, *History of the 33rd Indiana Veteran Volunteer Infantry* (Indianapolis: Wm. B. Buford Printers, 1900) 127.

[19]Robert Garlick Hill Kean, *Inside the Confederate Government: The Diary of Robert Garlick Hill Kean* (New York: Oxford, 1957) 151, 154; McMurry, *Atlanta 1864*, 130–31.

[20]J. B. Sanders, papers, Z0598.000, Manuscript Collection, Mississippi

We have fell back some 80 miles we ar not discourrage I yet beleave we will concur him before he reaches his prise...we held Shurman at bay on the Kennesaw Mountain 15 days altho he fill the side with shell and shot he never kill but 2 men in the 37th [Mississippi] and wounded some 4 or 5 now of our campany have bin hurt since the first of June....[21]

By the next week, the weary Mississippi soldier was clearly despondent about the Southern army's condition and the survival of the Confederacy. On 13 July from Barnesville, Sanders wrote,

I beleave Johnson is doing all in his power to save our cuntry and unless the people do turn out and stand by the side of those [who]...we ar a lost and ruin people...the govener of this state has caul every man out that is able tho bare arms from 16 to 55 years of age and ordered them to report to atlanta by the 20th of this month which will swell ou numbers some 12 or 15 thousan, but that aint anuf.... Let the men from Ala., Miss. and South Carolina all turn out at once and come and stand by Johnson just 10 days and we will all drive the last vistage of a enemy out of our land and have peace..."[22]

Lieutenant Colonel Frank Alexander Montgomery, commander of the 1st Mississippi Cavalry Regiment of Armstrong's Brigade, explained Davis's plight well when he recorded,

Whatever was the real cause of General Johnston's removal, I am sure it was not because of any prejudice, if he had any, against him in the mind of President Davis, as too many thought and said. He was too great a man, and had too much at stake. It must be remembered that of all the men of the confederacy Mr. Davis had the most at stake. Failure meant not only ruin to the cause he loved, but disaster to his own great fame, for upon his devoted head was to be poured out all the reproaches, for a time at least, not only of his enemies, but of many who ought to have been his friends, more loyal in defeat than if success had crowned his efforts and his hopes. He could not, brave soldier though he had been and would gladly have been again, even have the comfort of knowing that he had exposed his own life to danger on the battlefield with his devoted friends and followers. It was said at the commencement of the war, and I have no doubt it was true, that Mr. Davis preferred and even desired the command of the army in the field rather than

---

Department of Archives and History (MDAH), Jackson MS
[21]Sanders, papers.
[22]Ibid.

the presidency, but this could not be, for all eyes turned to him, and no other man could in his place have done more or better, none I believe so well.[23]

Looking critically at the president's options, he could leave Johnston in place and likely lose Atlanta in the next several days. In that event, Mississippi and Alabama and communication with the western states would be lost, as well as supplies, clothing, food, and munitions produced from the Gulf states and Western states. Moreover, political opinion would shift in favor of the Republican Party in the North, and the upcoming elections would confirm Lincoln's continuation of the war, which would doom the Confederacy. Hope that Johnston would actually hold out at Atlanta "indefinitely," as Johnston would later retort, was not justified by his war record.[24]

Old Joe would later lament that if he were unsuccessful in beating off Sherman, his army "had a place of refuge in Atlanta too strong to be assaulted and too extensive to be invested."[25] However, Johnston's track record told a different story. Joe Johnston had fallen back from the peninsula to Richmond in 1862; he had failed to interrupt Grant's siege and subsequent capture of Vicksburg in 1863; and now, he had failed to arrest Sherman's advance deep into Georgia in 1864, losing more than one hundred miles in fewer than one hundred days. In all three campaigns, from Virginia, to Mississippi, to Georgia, Johnston had failed to mount any kind of effective offensive action, except for the one at Fair Oaks where he was wounded but managed to check the Federal advance. In the past three months, his habit of withdrawing in the face of conflict continued. Davis could not take the chance of leaving Johnston in command and losing Atlanta without at least "hazarding" a fight, as General Lee had put it.[26]

Braxton Bragg did go and see Johnston, first on the afternoon of 13 July, and then again the next day. However, Bragg did not inform the field commander of the purpose of his trip, instead choosing to tell Johnston that he was merely passing through Atlanta on his way to see generals S. D. Lee

[23]Frank Alexander Montgomery, *Reminisces of a Mississippian in Peace and War* (Chicago: Acheron Press, 2012) 184.

[24]*OR*, series I, vol. 38, ser. no. 74, 618–19; Johnston, *Narrative*, 350–51.

[25]*OR*, ser, I, vol. 38, ser. no., 74, 619; Johnston, *Narrative*, 350–52.

[26]*OR*, ser, I, vol. 38, ser. no., 74, 619; Albert Castel, *Decision in the West* (Lawrence: University Press of Kansas, 1992) 353.

and E. K. Smith in Mississippi and the far Western theater.[27] If Johnston was aware of his impending removal, he did not show it. Even his friend, Senator Hill, who had met with the president and pleaded with him to deploy Forrest against Sherman, realized the desperation of the situation and the burdens caused by Johnston's failure to act. On 14 July, Hill wrote, "General Johnston: You must do the work with your present force. For God's sake do it. B. H. Hill."[28] Still, Johnston did not act.

While Johnston remained idle northwest of Atlanta, tracking the moves of Sherman's forces at his headquarters, General John Bell Hood was certainly busy advancing his opinion on what to do. He took the opportunity of Bragg's visit to write a strongly worded letter that blamed the army's failures on Johnston and Hardee. He expressed that he alone had advocated offensive action during the campaign. Bragg encouraged Hood to write the note that leveled unfair and untrue assertions against Johnston. Further, Hood let Bragg and Davis know that he was offering his services to command the army if offered to him.

> Near Atlanta, Ga. July 14, 1864.
> General Braxton Bragg,
> Commanding Armies Confederate States, Richmond, Va.:
> GENERAL: During the campaign from Dalton to the Chattahoochee River it is natural to suppose that we have had several chances to strike the enemy a decisive blow. We have failed to take advantage of such opportunities, and find our army south of the Chattahoochee, very much decreased in strength. Our loss cannot be less than 20,000, without having fought a decisive battle. I deem it of the greatest importance that General Kirby Smith should be ordered at once, with at least half, if not a larger portion, of his army, on this side of the Mississippi River. Our success west of the Mississippi River has proven a disadvantage to us, since the enemy has re-enforced his army on this side, and we have failed to do so. The strength of the Army of Tennessee is such at this time as to render it necessary to have aid from General Kirby Smith—allowing that we should gain a victory over Sherman—to follow up our success and regain our lost territory. Our present position is a very difficult one, and we should not, under any circumstances, allow the enemy to gain possession of Atlanta, and deem it

---

[27]*OR*, series I, vol. 38, ser. no. 74, 620–21.
[28]*OR*, series I, vol. 38, ser. no. 76, 879.

excessively important, should we find the enemy intends establishing the Chattahoochee as their line, relying upon interrupting our communications and again virtually dividing our country, that we should attack him, even if we should have to recross the river to do so. I have, General, so often urged that we should force the enemy to give us battle as to almost be regarded reckless by the officers high in rank in this army, since their views have been so directly opposite. I regard it as a great misfortune to our country that we failed to give battle to the enemy many miles north of our present position. Please say to the President that I shall continue to do my duty cheerfully and faithfully, and strive to do what I think is best for our country, as my constant prayer is for our success.

Respectfully,

J. B. Hood,

Lieutenant-General.[29]

Hood was unfair in his assessment of Johnston's performance and his own conduct during the campaign, but his conviction was heartfelt. He clearly believed he was in the right as to his opinion on how to conduct the campaign. He "forgot" to include in his letter, however, that he had blundered the surprise attack at Adairsville entrusted to him by Johnston, that he had urged falling back from Cassville (perhaps the strongest defensive line Johnston had in north Georgia), and that he had botched other assaults at New Hope and at Kolb's Farm near Kennesaw.[30] His estimation of losses during the campaign to date, 20,000 men, was about double the true number, but Johnston later admitted that he had lost from battle casualties about 10,000 men killed and wounded, and another 4,700 men from "all other causes, mainly slight sickness produced by heavy cold rains, which prevailed in the latter half of June," which, Johnston added, for the most part returned to their units.[31]

Braxton Bragg, having completed his work in Atlanta, sent two telegrams on 15 July before he departed for Alabama. The first one continued to paint Bragg's dim view of matters.

Atlanta, July 15, 1864.

---

[29]Ibid. 879–80.

[30]Johnston, *Narrative*, 333–34, 340; Castel, *Decision in the West*, 291–95.

[31]*OR*, series I, vol. 38, ser. no. 74, 619.

His Excellency Jefferson Davis, Richmond, Va.:

The enemy were driven back across the Chattahoochee near Newnan this morning by our cavalry before they reached the West Point railroad. Another corps of infantry has crossed above. Nearly all available stores and machinery are removed, and the people have mostly evacuated the town.

Braxton Bragg.[32]

Then, before leaving the Gate City, Bragg sent a summary of his trip, with perhaps his fairest report of his assessment:

Atlanta, July 15, 1864.

His Excellency Jefferson Davis, Richmond:

I have made General Johnston two visits, and been received courteously and kindly. He has not sought my advice, and it was not volunteered. I cannot learn that he has any more plan for the future than he has had in the past. It is expected that he will await the enemy on a line some three miles from here, and the impression prevails that he is now more inclined to fight. The enemy is very cautious, and intrenches immediately on taking a new position. His force, like our own, is greatly reduced by the hard campaign. His infantry now very little over 60,000. The morale of our army is still reported good.

Braxton Bragg.[33]

Bragg was wrong about Sherman's force. In fact, Sherman had about 88,000 infantry, another 12,000 cavalry, and 6,000 artillery, for a total force of some 106,000 men during the first part of July.[34] Bragg sent a third letter to the president that day via a special courier that contained many details and impressions that he did not feel prudent to send by telegraph. In it, Bragg expounded on his telegraph dispatches and urged offensive action as the only solution. He told the president that Hood, Wheeler, and Stewart concurred in this position, but Johnston and his subordinate, Hardee, did not. Thus, merely removing Johnston from command would not improve things and might make them worse. In Bragg's estimation, while the army had confidence in Johnston, it did not have confidence in Hardee. Bragg

---

[32]Ibid., 881.

[33]*OR*, series I, vol. 38, ser. no. 76, 881.

[34]*OR*, series I, vol. 38, ser. no. 72, 115–17.

related his incorrect estimates that Johnston lost 20,000 men, and that Sherman's forces numbered only about 60,000 infantry, 5,000 artillery, and 10,000 cavalry, for a total opposing force of about 75,000. Sherman actually had about 30,000 more men than Bragg figured. Braxton Bragg also estimated the available Confederate force at 52,000.[35] Johnston's 10 July Abstract of Returns reflected that there were 59,196 officers and men present for duty.[36] Therefore, Bragg intentionally narrowed the gap between his estimates of Sherman's strength and Johnston's strength by claiming that Sherman had only some 60,000 infantry against Johnston's force of 52,000. In reality, Sherman had almost exactly twice the available infantry force of Johnston as the two forces opposed each other along the banks of the Chattahoochee River. As can be seen in a captured document,[37] the available Confederate infantry force on Monday, 18 July, was just 44,400 as compared to some 88,000 infantry available to Sherman at the same time.

Instead of being outnumbered only six to five as Bragg and the president believed, the Southerners were actually out-manned nearly two to one at Atlanta. Bragg included a copy of Hood's letter to him, which Bragg may have even solicited. Hood was all too eager to provide it and bolster Bragg's contentions. Bragg added,

> If any change is made Lieutenant-General Hood would give unlimited satisfaction, and my estimate of him, always high, has been raised by his conduct in this campaign. Do not understand me as proposing him a man of genius, or a great general, but as far better in the present emergency than any one we have available.[38]

After receiving Bragg's two telegraphs of Friday, 15 July, President Davis had his fears confirmed. Johnston could very well evacuate Atlanta without a general engagement, and Alabama, Mississippi, and the Trans-Mississippi would be lost. Having learned that the stores and machinery had been removed from Atlanta, and the citizenry had largely evacuated, it would be only a matter of time before Johnston lost the Gate City to

---

[35]Ibid., 712–14.

[36]*OR*, series I, vol. 38, ser. no. 74, 675–79.

[37] See Exhibit C, which contains the contents of a memorandum inscribed "Estimated Strength of Hood's Army" which was found at an abandoned Confederate cavalry camp near Paces Ferry.

[38]*OR*, series I, vol. 38, ser. no. 72, 712–14.

Sherman. There was still a prospect of hope, however, as Bragg reported that the army was still in fine spirits and awaited an order to assault. Moreover, Bragg relayed that Johnston now appeared more inclined to act. Perhaps he would strike, like he did outside of Richmond at Fair Oaks in spring 1862. After a week of worrying about the state of things in Georgia, and after having his fears confirmed by the reports of General Bragg, Davis was at the end of his rope. Since first learning that Johnston had his back to the Chattahoochee River the previous Friday, events had snowballed to the point that by Friday, 15 July, the president was desperate for news of aggressive action from Johnston to stop Sherman.

Alarmed by the news that Sherman was entirely across the Chattahoochee River and was moving to cut the railroad and telegraph lines to Augusta that connected north and east to Richmond, the president sent a final request for information to Johnston.

Richmond, July 16, 1864.
General J. E. Johnston:
A telegram from Atlanta of yesterday announces that the enemy is extending intrenchments from river toward railroad to Augusta. I with to hear from you as to present situation, and your plan of operations so specifically as will enable me to anticipate events.
JEFFERSON DAVIS[39]

Johnston's reply was less than encouraging:

Near Atlanta, July 16, 1864.
His Excellency the President,
Your dispatch of to-day received. The slight change in the enemy's dispositions made since my dispatch of the 14th to General Cooper [wherein Johnston informed the President that at least three of Sherman's seven corps were across the Chattahoochee River and digging in between Roswell and the railroad] was reported to General Bragg yesterday. It was a report from General Wheeler that Schofield's corps had advanced eastwardly about three miles from Isham's Ford and intrenched. As the enemy has double our number, we must be on the defensive. My plan of operation must, therefore, depend upon that of the enemy. It is mainly to watch for an opportunity to

---

[39]*OR*, series I, vol. 38, ser. no. 76, 882.

fight to advantage. We are trying to put Atlanta in condition to be held for a day or two by the Georgia militia, that army movements may be freer and wider.

> J. E. JOHNSTON[40]

There it was. "We are trying to…[hold Atlanta]…for a day or two…" was clear evidence that Johnston was committed to the Fabian Policy, even when his back was to the wall. A *"day or two!"* For more than a week the president had been following with angst the developments in Georgia, hanging on every dispatch for news and information, as well as some proof that Johnston would act. He found none. Instead, on three separate occasions Davis heard alarming news from his general. On 8 July, Johnston asked for help from Forrest's Cavalry in Mississippi and stated that he had found no opportunity for battle in one hundred miles and one hundred days. On 11 July, Johnston even recommended the evacuation of Andersonville. And, on 16 July, the field commander suggested that the militia may hold Atlanta for a day or two. The president justifiably felt that he must act immediately if he were to have any chance of saving Atlanta from capture and destruction.

One article, which appeared in the Macon, Georgia, *Journal & Messenger* on 27 July 1864 sounded more like a "pep talk than news, but made a good point." Titled "Lived through It," the article pointed out how gloomy the Confederacy had felt when Joe Johnston was replaced by R. E. Lee two years earlier, but how that sadness was soon forgotten when Lee began to bring victories:

> A little more than two years ago the Confederate mind was convulsed with the tidings that Gen. Lee had, in effect, superceded Gen. Johnston in the command of the Army of Virginia. The discontent was great and almost universal. The clamor was not so loud as it was deep. Readers may not so well recollect the fuss made about it as we do, because, in common, (as we suppose), with every other conductor of a public press, we were much importuned to give instant and earnest expression to the public dissatisfaction. The country was betrayed—the army was outraged and would be demoralized by the change. Lee was an 'old granny'—a red tape

---

[40]Ibid., 883.

martinet, and the gravest doubts were expressed even of his integrity, patriotism and fidelity to the cause of the Confederacy."[41]

Continuing, the editor reasoned that in time, the populace could grow to believe in Hood like it had come to love and admire Lee: "The grandeur of Lee's character and the splendor of his military achievements have dispersed these doubts and suspicions as bats fly to their holes before the rays of the morning sun. Nobody owns them now, because such proprietorship would betray equal injustice and want of sagacity," added the journalist. "The public confidence and admiration of Lee exceeds all bounds—but the man who conceived and dictated that change, and braved the fearful hazard of making it, since he boldly assumed the responsibility and for a time dared popular and military opinion," he reasoned, "should not be defrauded of the honor and the confidence the result is well calculated to inspire." Unwittingly foreshadowing the impending demise of the Confederacy, the writer concluded,

Let the public and the army reflect upon this passage in history, while they ponder upon the change in the command of the Army of Tennessee. If anybody says now—"the country is ruined—the army is betrayed and turned over to incompetent hands"—ten to one that man said the same thing when Lee assumed the command of the Virginia army. Suspend opinion. The President was right then—he may be so now. The country and cause lived through that removal—it may do the same now.[42]

Historians still debate the decision of President Davis to replace Johnston with Hood.

In a letter to the editor of a Macon paper published on 30 July, in response to an assumption by the paper that Johnston had been relieved because he was planning to abandon Atlanta without a fight, a citizen of Atlanta reported his observations around the Gate City during the days and weeks preceding Johnston's removal:

Macon, July 29th, 1864.
Editor of the Macon Telegraph:

---

[41]*Georgia* (Macon GA) *Journal & Messenger*, 27 July 1864.
[42]Ibid.

...Unless I and other citizens of Atlanta with whom I have conversed have come to wrong conclusions from what we saw and heard, (I must refute your assertion that Johnston was not going to fight to save Atlanta). I was in Atlanta when Gen. Johnston was relieved, and remained there for several days after. Some time before, and on the very day he received the order (of removal), a large number of negroes had been and were at work on the fortifications around Atlanta, strengthening and modifying them in important particulars, preparing them to receive six or eight heavy rifled cannon, which were in the town and ready to be mounted. So far as outsiders could judge, there was no indication that Gen. Johnston had an intention to abandon Atlanta, without a struggle to avert such a calamity. It was the common talk and believe of such of the army, officers and privates, as I came in contact with, that Atlanta would be held at every risk and sacrifice, save that of the army. My object in writing is not to call in question the action of the President in relieving Gen. Johnston and assigning Gen. Hood to the command of the Army and Department of Tennessee, but simply to ask you to correct an error, which, if uncorrected, may affect the truth of History.

Citizen of Atlanta.[43]

Davis had to fear that Johnston would give up Atlanta before the president could do anything about it. This latest response from Johnston that "We are trying to put Atlanta in condition to be held for a day or two by the Georgia militia, that the army movements may be freer and wider"[44] had given no better plan for reversing things in Georgia than he had a hundred days ago and a hundred miles ago in Dalton. Putting Atlanta in "condition...to be held by the Georgia militia"? "To be held for a day or two"? So that his armies' movements could "be freer and wider"? Just what did Johnston intend to do? Was he seriously going to leave Atlanta and her defense to a force of just 5,000 militia, consisting of old men and boys, while he took the army away so that their movements could "be freer and wider"? To the president, Old Joe had no plan other than to fall back. For Davis, it was all the justification he needed to make the change and he had better do it immediately if Atlanta had any chance to be saved. Another week would be too late, he reasoned. Thus, on Sunday, July 17th, Davis gathered his cabinet, and by that evening, he had his Adjutant issue the order that,

---

[43]Macon *Daily Telegraph*, 30 July 1864.
[44]*OR*, series I, vol. 38, ser. no. 76, 883.

according to Private J. M. Miller of the 20th Mississippi Infantry in Adams' Brigade, "was as unexpected as a peal of thunder from a cloudless sky."[45]

Johnston played the hand that had been dealt to him, and he had been playing it well in the eyes of his men as well as in the view of his adversary. Perhaps one of his admiring troopers, John A. Miller of the 6th Texas Cavalry in Ross's Brigade, put it best when, upon learning of Johnston's removal, he lamented that Johnston was "the safest general the Confederacy had."[46] Unfortunately for Old Joe, he had not played the hand the way President Davis and Braxton Bragg thought it should be played and that ultimately led to his removal as commander of the Army of Tennessee. His defensive strategy was simply not in line with the president's plans on how the Confederacy should win its independence. The two men were not only personal rivals, they held diametrically opposing views. Historians will continue to debate who was right, or which view promised the best chance or success for the South. In any event, the transfer was a shock to the Confederate army, and, in the opinion of Lieutenant General Stewart, "a stupendous blunder which, in my judgment, was the coup de grace of the Confederate cause."[47]

Earlier in the long summer of 1864, General Johnston promised President Davis and the Atlantans that he could hold the Gate City forever. But, with the ambitious General Hood in command of her defense, she lasted only forty-five days. Whether Old Joe could have done any better is debatable, but public sentiment was clear. John DuBose, of Wheeler's Cavalry staff wrote about receiving the news of the transfer, "Thus perished the southern Confederacy."[48]

---

[45]Quoted in Montgomery, *Reminisces of a Mississippian in Peace and War*, 186–87.

[46]]Martha L. Crabb, *All Afire To Fight: The Untold Story of the Ninth Texas Cavalry* (New York: Avon Books, 2000) 229.

[47]Broomfield L. Ridley, *Battles and Sketches, Army of Tennessee, 1861–65* (Mexico MO: Missouri Printing and Publishing Co., 1906) xii; John B. Lindsley, ed, *Military Annals of Tennessee*, vol. 1 (Wilmington NC: Broadfoot Publishing, 1995) 95–99, 100; Sam Davis Elliott, *Soldier of Tennessee: General Alexander P. Stewart and the Civil War in the West* (Baton Rouge: Louisiana State University, 2004) 200–201.

[48]John Witherspoon DuBose, *General Joseph Wheeler and the Army of Tennessee* (New York: Neale Publishing Co., 1912) 360.

13

THE TRANSFER

The clear-hearing statesmen of the Southland heard the doom bells ringing the death knell of the Southern Confederacy.[1]

Miss Sarah Huff, an eight-year-old who lived just a quarter of a mile away from the Niles House where Johnston's headquarters lay, remembered the evening of 17 July:

> "The transfer," came right home to mother and me, out on our front porch. Mother, a lover of music, said that the music of the military bands on that brilliant moonlight night was the sweetest she ever heard. I, who stood by mother's chair, have always thought of that lovely moonlight night whenever I have heard music on a beautiful summer evening.

> Pathos was furnished by the weeping and angry soldiers, as they strolled about mother's front yard, and told her and each other of the despair they felt on account of the approaching discharge of their idolized commander, General Joseph E. Johnston.

> The music over the way became more lively, and mingled with strains of "Dixie" came the rhythmic sound of dancing feet. The wives and lady friends of some of the officers were visiting headquarters and, as is usual with army people, even if comes a Waterloo tomorrow, there is a sound of revelry by night.

> At midnight when the old Atlanta watchman's voice rang out: "Twelve o'clock, and all's well!" The clear-hearing statesmen of the Southland heard the doom bells ringing the death knell of the Southern Confederacy.[2][end block]

While the men of Hotchkiss's Artillery Battalion sojourned around the home of Jeremiah C. Huff (where he and his daughter Sarah sat on the

---

[1]Sarah Huff, *My 80 Years in Atlanta*, http://www.artery.org/08_history/Upper-Artery/CivilWar/SaraHuff/My80YearsInAtlanta_All.pdf, 1937 (18 November 2014) 11.

[2]Ibid.

front porch), a Confederate regimental band serenaded the crowd with such favorites as "Dixie," "The Bonnie Blue Flag," and "The Homespun Dress." Just down the road, General Johnston conferred with his staff about the disposition of his troops and Atlanta's defenses when Major Charles Hubner of the telegraph corps, who had ridden from the telegraph office in Atlanta to the general's headquarters northwest of town, interrupted them. Hubner was bearing the order for Johnston's removal. Soon, General A. P. Stewart arrived, and Johnston showed him the order. While Stewart implored Johnston and his staff to contain the shocking news until they could discuss it further the next day, it was too late. Johnston had already prepared his farewell address to the soldiers and had delivered a reply to Richmond acknowledging receipt of the order.[3] The news of Johnston's removal spread quickly among the officers, soldiers, and civilians nearby.[4]

Samuel Pearce Richards, a book dealer and choir singer of Atlanta, recorded in his diary:

> We have again been permitted to meet at the sanctuary for the worship of God. The enemy draws nearer and nearer tho' to our city. All of a sudden Gen. Johnston has been relieved of the command of the Army and Gen. Hood or "Old Pegleg" as the soldiers style him placed in command, so that there is thought to be a prospect for a fight before Atlanta is given up, as Hood is said to be a fighting man, if he has only one leg. The ordinance of baptism was administered in our church this morning to two candidates, a lady and a deaf-mute young man.[5]

Who knows if Richards went to the dance outside the Huff House and near Johnston's headquarters after choir practice that evening, or if he heard the spreading news and gossip on Atlanta's streets?[6]

---

[3]*OR*, series I, vol. 38, ser. no. 76, 885.

[4]Huff, *My 80 Years in Atlanta*, 11; Wilbur G. Kurtz, Kurtz Papers, file MSS-130, Scrapbook 28, Special Collections, Kenan Research Center, Atlanta History Center, Atlanta GA; William R. Scaife, *The Campaign for Atlanta* (Atlanta: self-published, 1993) 84; Samuel Carter III, *The Siege of Atlanta, 1864* (New York: St. Martin's Press, 1973) 188–89; Melancthon Smith, Journal of Campaign from Dalton to Atlanta, B. F. Cheatham Papers, Tennessee State Library and Archives, Nashville TN, 7.

[5]A. A. Hoehling, *Last Train From Atlanta* (New York: Thomas Yoseloff Publisher, 1958) 100.

[6]Carter, *Siege of Atlanta*, 193, 242; Hoehling, *Last Train From Atlanta*, 100.

Perhaps indication of the high public regard for Johnston can be found in the pages of the Macon and Columbus, Georgia, newspapers in the weeks following his removal from command. One such article commended the general for his kindness displayed toward a woman at the Macon train depot. There,

> a poorly clad, humble woman approached [a crowd of men] saying "For the love of heaven gentlemen, aid me in putting the coffin of my dead husband on the train." Gen. Johnston was the first, and about the only one, who moved to her assistance, and he saw that the coffin was deposited in the cars. In such little acts as these do we often distinguish the qualities that characterize our greatest, purest men, and such Gen. J truly is.[7]

It has been argued by some modern historians that the army welcomed Johnston's removal from command.[8] One point is that much of Johnston's support from his men is found in post-war manuscripts and reminisces after the soldiers had an opportunity to reflect on the war, and that some of the diaries and letters written during the Atlanta Campaign were not as optimistic about the state of affairs with the army. The examples of contemporary letters and diaries given by President Davis's apologists do not criticize Johnston and his leadership necessarily, and the handful cited mostly come from Georgia soldiers who faced occupation of their homes and destruction of their property for the first time in the war, and the attendant demoralization caused thereby.

One such soldier from Georgia, Celathiel Helms, penned on 6 July, "The men is all out of heart and say that Georgia will soon have to go under and they are going to the Yankees by the tens and hundreds most every night. Johnson's army is very much demoralized as much as a army ever gets to be."[9] Another Georgian, from the 65th Georgia Regiment in Hardee's Corps, wrote his sister on 11 July as the Confederate army's back was to the Chattahoochee River: "Sister I am getting a little scared about home...there

---

[7]Macon *Daily Telegraph*, 22 September 1864, quoting from the Columbus *Sentinel*; Genealogical and Historical Room, Washington Library, Macon GA.

[8]See Richard M. McMurry, *Atlanta 1864: Last Chance for the Confederacy* (Lincoln: University of Nebraska Press, 2000) 129–31 and Stephen Davis, *Atlanta Will Fall*, book 3 of the American Crisis Series: Books on the Civil War Era (Washington DC: Rowman and Littlefield Publishers, 2001) 131.

[9]McMurry, *Atlanta 1864*, 130.

are prospects of us leaving Atlanta and if we do I will be a little demoralized for if we cant stop them at...[the Chattahoochee River] it is not reasonable that we can stop them any other place and an other thing 1/3 or 2/3 of our men will desert and go home."[10]

After being captured during the campaign, one Rebel trooper, flustered with Sherman's prowess, said, "Sherman gits on a hill, flops his wings and crows, then yells out, 'Attention! Creation! By kingdoms right wheel! March!' And then we git!"[11] Federal soldiers recounted finding many signs along their path from below Kennesaw Mountain to Atlanta during the campaign, informing them that they would not make it to the Gate City. After the Confederates evacuated their works near Dallas, Georgia, they left a board nailed to a tree that read, "Till here and no further."[12] Maurice Marcoot, a German immigrant fighting with the 15th Missouri, remembered, "After we had crossed the Chattahoocha [Chattahoochee] river we saw many more similar arranged messages."[13]

Lieutenant A. J. Neal wrote his father on 20 July about the transfer of command,

> I had a full history of the removal of Gen. Johnston this morning from one of Cheatham's Brigadiers who is an old friend and schoolmate at the University of Virginia and at the Lebanon Law School. Pres. Davis has been wanting Johnston to give battle ever since he crossed the Etowah and thinks he could have afforded it at Dallas and New Hope. Johnston would not divulge his plans to the president but told him he intended to fight the first opportunity. As soon as Johnston crossed the Chattahoochee it was resolved to relieve him from command of the Army.[14]

---

[10]Ibid.

[11]Donald Allendorf, *Long Road to Liberty: The Odyssey of a German Regiment in the Yankee Army: The 15th Missouri Volunteer Infantry* (Kent OH: Kent State University Press, 2006) 204.

[12]Ibid.

[13]Ibid.

[14]A. J. Neal to father, 20 July 1864, Confederate Files, Georgia, vertical files, Kennesaw Mountain National Battlefield Park Library, Kennesaw GA; Wilbur G. Kurtz, Kurtz Papers, file MSS-130, Special Collections, Kenan Research Center, Atlanta History Center, Atlanta GA. The brigadier general with whom Neal conversed appears to have been General George Maney, who studied law near Nashville before the war.

Neal correctly guessed that "Hood was placed at the head because Hardee had refused command at Dalton last winter and the president was incensed at it. The change was very unexpected in the Army and deeply regretted but I cannot regard it as calamity. Johnston has never stood well with the administration." He explained, "he had obtained no favors in this campaign. With an Army of little over fifty thousand of all arms he has had to confront a host of one hundred and fifty thousand." The young lieutenant was exaggerating, but his point was well founded. Neal's next remark would prove prophetic: "Since the appointment of Hood I think the Administration will feel bound to sustain him and their own honor and capacity being involved will do every thing to sustain him."[15]

While certainly there were some demoralized men in Johnston's ranks, and surely some disapproved of Johnston, the great weight of the available letters, diaries, and other primary source records, written both at the time that the events transpired and subsequently, indicate that the western armies had tremendous faith in Joe Johnston the man and in General Johnston the leader. General Polk wrote President Davis in the fall of 1863, encouraging Johnston's appointment because of the strong support among the officers and men of the western Confederate armies. After all the battles and marches that had occurred since, the men and officers still had the utmost faith in Johnston.[16]

Most of the men realized that the odds were against them, but in the first six months of the Georgia Campaign under Johnston, they had not lost a battle (at least in their minds, every battle had either been won or fought to a draw); they had traded territory for casualties inflicted on Sherman's forces; and they had kept their army intact, in good order, and undeterred. Under Old Joe, their orders were logical, understood, and generally cheerfully followed (except in some instances by General Hood), and for the most part they produced good results. Many of the men and soldiers of both the Army of Mississippi and the Army of Tennessee felt for the first time in the war that they had a leader worthy to command them. Even one of Johnston's greatest detractors, General Braxton Bragg, who had been sent

---

[15]Ibid., Kurtz Papers; MSS-130, Kenan Research Center, Atlanta History Center, Atlanta GA.

[16]Stanley F. Horn, *The Army of Tennessee* (Norman: University of Oklahoma Press) 308.

by President Davis to Atlanta in July, wrote to the president, "The morale, though damaged of course, is still good, and the army would hail with delight an order for battle."[17]

A writer with the dubious pen name "Appomattox" wrote to a Richmond newspaper about Johnston's removal: it was picked up and published by the Macon *Daily Telegraph*. In his letter, he appears to support President Davis's decision:

> In conclusion, the President was reduced to the alternative of retaining Johnston and losing Atlanta, or losing Johnston and the possibility of saving Atlanta. He could not but be satisfied that Johnston had already made up his mind to abandon the place as untenable. If he did not fight Sherman at the Chattahoochee, would he have done so in the open country around Atlanta? Sherman could turn his position at Atlanta more easily than at Kennesaw. It may be, and I fear is, too late now to save Atlanta; but do not place the blame on the wrong shoulders. And especially do not say Johnston could not but retire because Forrest was not sent to him. Forrest was not idle in the West; he was beating back column after column of reinforcements going to Sherman. The order for him to move to Georgia was given, nevertheless; but before he could obey it, the enemy were again moving from Memphis to the support of Sherman, and it became necessary to fight him. Forrest has been assisting Johnston in Mississippi. He could have done no more in Georgia.[18]

Interestingly, throughout the armies of Mississippi and Tennessee, the letters and diaries depicted a despair about the condition of the war, a resolve about the writers' roles and the ultimate outcome, and confidence in General Johnston's leadership. Captain Solomon M. Thornton, commander of Company B, 31st Mississippi, and Private James K. Watson also of Company B, 31st Mississippi, wrote home expressing confidence in their army and commander and are but two of many such examples.[19] One soldier from the 35th Alabama in Scott's Brigade penned in his diary near 9 July:

---

[17]Richard McMurry, *John Bell Hood and the War for Southern Independence* (Lincoln: University of Nebraska Press, 1992) 120.

[18]Macon *Daily Telegraph*, 4 August 1864, quoting Appomattox from the Richmond *Dispatch*, Genealogical and Historical Room, Washington Library, Macon GA.

[19]Solomon M. Thornton to Sarah F. Thornton, 7 March 1864 (from camp near Demopolis AL), Letters, Thornton, Solomon M., courtesy of Special Collections, Mitchell Memorial Library, Mississippi State University, Starkville

Today we are throwing up new fortifications that run from the Chattahoochee to Peach Tree Creek. Dig, dig, dig. Retreat, retreat, retreat. What can you do when you are outnumbered more that[n] two to one. Every time the Union troops come at us head on, we give them a licking. I guess that is the reason the Federals are afraid to take on our General Johnston and instead they just move around our flank.[20]

Another diarist from Scott's Brigade, Dr. J. P. Cannon of the 27th Alabama, wrote on 15 July:

General Bragg arrived from Richmond. I guess they are getting uneasy about Atlanta and have sent him to see if something can be done to check Sherman's invasion. It is getting to be a serious matter, but we have the utmost confidence in General Johnston and feel like he will devise some plan to hold the city, if we can't whip the Yankees in a fair fight.[21]

The historian for the 27th Alabama, Harry V. Barnard, found that "Morale among the men of the Twenty-seventh was high as June passed into July."[22] After General Hood took command, the mood of the men changed.

Their new commander, General Hood, had not been able to stop the Union advances and the casualties continued to mount.... The weather...combined with being constantly in the line of battle [during July and August in the defense of Atlanta under Hood], exhausted the men. The casualty rate grew, desertions mounted, and by the end of August the effective force of some of the companies was so reduced that some of them had to be combined and the officers assigned to other commands.[23]

One of the Kentucky Orphan Brigade's soldiers wrote in his diary about the retreat across the Chattahoochee during the night of 9 July: "We did not entrench here but kept strict watch of the enemy. Us Eleven Dollar

---

MS; James Watson, Pvt., Co. B, 31st Miss. Infantry, Confederate Files, 6, Kennesaw Mountain National Battlefield Park Library, Kennesaw GA.

[20]Leroy F. Banning, *Regimental History of the Thirty-Fifth Alabama 1862–1865* (Westminster MD: Heritage Books, 2005) 50.

[21]J. P. Cannon, *Bloody Banners and Barefoot Boys* (Shippensburg PA: Burd Street Press, 1997) 82–83.

[22]Harry Vollie Barnard, *Tattered Volunteers: The Twenty-Seventh Alabama Regiment, C. S. A.* (Northport AL: Hermitage Press, 1965) 30.

[23]Ibid., 33.

Generals, as the boys in the trenches called themselves, said, 'Now watch Mars Joe [Johnston] fall on Sherman when he crosses this river & eat him up.'"[24] In less than ten days the mood of the army changed dramatically. The same soldier wrote upon learning of the transfer that there was a gloom among all of the men.[25] In the Washington Artillery, an elite Battery in Hardee's Corps from New Orleans, news of the transfer was received with shock and anger. Some of the men "wept like children, others seemed speechless, and others poured forth denunciations and curses upon our deluded and infatuated President." One private in the Battery wrote of his gun's sergeant, Thomas C. Allen's, reaction. Sergeant Allen, a native Virginian who had made New Orleans his home before the war, was "a superb soldier." He "mounted a stump and passionately advised going in a body to Johnston's headquarters to protest his leaving."[26] Similar speeches were heard throughout the Confederate camps.

Sergeant William Pitt Chambers of the 43rd Mississippi in Sears's Brigade recorded in his journal:

> On Monday [July] 18th we again formed a line of battle along the hills said to be on the south side of Peach Tree Creek. We had barely got in position when the rumor came flying like wildfire down the line that Gen. Johnston had been superseded as chief commander of the Army of Tennessee by Lt. Gen. John B. Hood. There was great indignation among the rank and file, and there were open threats of insubordination. For nearly three months we had been retreating, but the morale of the army was better than when the campaign opened. We knew that while we were losing ground the enemy was losing men much more rapidly than we were, and that after a few weeks more his available force would be no greater than our own. We had seen the retreat conducted without the loss of even a broken wagon wheel, and we had unlimited faith in the generalship of "Old Joe," as we liked to call him.

---

[24]Johnny Green, *Johnny Green of the Orphan Brigade: The Journal of a Confederate Soldier*, ed. A. D. Kirwan (Louisville: University of Kentucky Press, 1956) 141; Eleven dollars was the monthly pay received by the Confederate privates during the war, hence the remark "Eleven-dollar generals" which was a reference often made by the Southern soldier.

[25]Ibid., 142.

[26]Nathaniel Cheairs Hughes, Jr., *The Pride of the Confederate Artillery: The Washington Artillery in the Army of Tennessee* (Baton Rouge: Louisiana State University Press, 1997) 195.

We were willing to fight at any time and place he said so, believing that he would not ask us to fight unless the advantages were clearly on our side. Of Gen. Hood we knew but little; only the impression prevailed that he was rash to a criminal extent. We knew him to be a splendid corps commander, brave and reliable, but somehow we judged him to be lacking in those higher qualities that fit one for handling an independent army.[27]

"Old Joe was our idol," exclaimed Private J. B. Gracey of Company G, 51st Tennessee: "I can bear witness to the spirit of mutiny that filled the minds of the troops, who to a man were ready to throw down their arms and quit."[28] This sentiment was echoed by Private David B. Morgan, 5th Georgia Cavalry, who said, "When Johnston was removed from the army his soldiers almost mutinied. Not that they did not trust Hood, but their love for Johnston was so great, and they knew he had such consideration for their welfare, that they felt no one else could take his place."[29] One Texan recorded in his diary on the day of his learning the news, 19 July, that Johnston "was always looking after our comfort and safety. He would investigate our breastworks in person, make suggestions as to any little addition or improvement that would make them safer or more comfortable."[30]

Others in the Army of Tennessee described their displeasure in Old Joe's removal. The transfer "is regretted by the whole army as Gen. Johns[t]on had won the respect and admiration of all, and especially the love of the men by his untiring efforts to save his men and feed them well."[31] A second soldier wrote, "The War Department perhaps knows best, but the troops are dissatisfied with the change, for Gen. Johnston was the idol of the

---

[27]William Pitt Chambers, *Blood and Sacrifice: The Civil War Journal of a Confederate Soldier*, ed. Richard Baumgartner (Huntington WV: Blue Acorn Press, 1994) 156.

[28]*Confederate Veteran* 26 (September 1918): 385.

[29]*Confederate Veteran* 26 (July 1918): 302.

[30]Samuel T. Foster, *One of Cleburne's Command: The Civil War Diary of Captain Samuel T. Foster, Granbury's Texas Brigade, C. S. A.*, ed. Norman D. Brown (Austin: University of Texas Press, 1980) 106.

[31]Mumford H. Dixon, Diary, 17 July 1864, Rubenstein Library Dept., Sec. A, Box 36, William R. Perkins Library, Duke University, Durham NC.

army...."[32] A Texas officer explained "Gen. Johns[t]on could not have issued an order that these men would not have undertaken to accomplish."[33]

Another Texan, 1st Lieutenant R. M. Collins of Company B, 15th Texas (Dismounted) in Granbury's Brigade of Cleburne's Division, remembered that 18 July was a bright, sunny day and the boys were all lying "loose under the shades of the great oaks," where "they had their blankets spread and were playing draw-poker or shaking dice." While many soldiers thought that card games and dice were sinful, many a bored Yankee or Rebel passed the long hours of camp life with these activities, including many of Granbury's wild Texans. "Along with the majority of my company, I was playing a little game in the deep shade of a great oak, on a big, moss-covered flat rock for a table, when Adjutant John Willingham came up," the Texan explained; "[He] read the order from President Davis removing Gen. Jos. E. Johnston from command and putting Gen. John B. Hood in command of the Army of Tennessee." Collins could not believe the news. "The boys all threw down their cards and collected in little groups discussing the new move. They were all dissatisfied, but soon dismissed the whole with the remark 'Hell will break loose in Georgia sure enough now.' Hood was a bulldog fighter from away back, and," according to Collins, "President Davis could not have suited Gen. Sherman better had he commissioned him to have made the appointment."[34]

In the Army of Mississippi, General A. P. Stewart's staff had to bring all of the division and brigade commanders together to try to calm the men for fear of a revolt after they learned of Johnston's removal. One of Stewart's staff officers recalled, "I believe that a word from any Col. of good standing would have induced the army to stack arms then and there unless their old Gen. was restored." The officer lamented some three years after the war, "I am free to say I now regret that word was not spoken."[35]

---

[32]J. N. Wyatt to J. B. Cunningham, 10 August 1864, *Confederate Veteran* 5, 1897): 521.

[33]Foster, *One of Cleburne's Command*, 106.

[34]R. M. Collins, *Echoes of Battle: The Atlanta Campaign, An Illustrated Collection of Union and Confederate Narratives*, ed. Larry M. Strayer and Richard A. Baumgartner (Huntington WV: Blue Acorn Press, 1991) 212.

[35]J. C. Thompson to A. P. Stewart, 8 December 1867, folder 5, box 1, Joseph E. Johnston Collection, Earl Gregg Swem Library, College of William & Mary, Williamsburg VA.

In the 15th Mississippi Regiment of Adams's Brigade, Private Tom Gore wrote, "From the hour the news of the change of commander reached the men in the pits, a mark of sentiment was discernable. Whatever may have been said or may be said in the future...General Johnston at least had the unqualified confidence of his men."[36] James Binford of the same brigade said, "President Davis never made a more serious mistake than he did by removing General Johnston."[37] Lieutenant Colonel Columbus Sykes of the 43rd Mississippi, also in Adams's Brigade, wrote his wife about the transfer saying, "This is the 80th day of the 'On to Atlanta movement.... The army was astonished yesterday when it was announced that Gen. Johnston had been relieved of command and Gen. Hood placed in command. We are not yet informed of the cause of his removal, whether dissatisfaction with his management of the campaign or whether other influences operated. Hood has been made a full general."[38]

In the 27th Alabama of Scott's Brigade, in his diary entry for Monday, 18 July 1864, J. P. Cannon recorded,

> About 1 PM a circular order was brought around the lines and read, imparting the sorrowful news that our beloved commander had been removed and General J. B. Hood placed in command. This is a great blow to our cause and has cast a gloom over the whole army. Strong men wept, while others cursed, and not one approved the change.[39]

The Alabamian went on to write that the men "felt it a terrible mistake of our president."[40] Captain Isaac Jasper Rogers, commander of Company B, 27th Alabama, explained that Johnston's removal was "surprising" to the men. Rogers said, "We hated very much to part with old Joe as all familirly

---

[36]Ben Wynne, *A Hard Trip: A History of the 15th Mississippi Infantry, C. S. A.* (Macon GA: Mercer University Press, 2010) 122.

[37]James R. Binford, "Recollections of the Fifteenth Regiment of Mississippi Infantry, C. S. A.," p. 50, vol. 5, box 2, Patrick Henry Papers, Mississippi Department of Archives and History (MDAH), Jackson MS.

[38]Columbus Sykes (lieutenant colonel, 43rd Mississippi Volunteer Infantry) to his wife, Subject File, MI-4, Kennesaw Mountain National Battlefield Park Library, Kennesaw GA, 30A.

[39]Cannon, *Bloody Banners and Barefoot Boys*, 83.

[40]Ibid.

called him but we had to give him up and trust to an inexperienced officer."[41]

The reaction in the Army of Tennessee was the same. Major General William H. T. Walker, a division commander in Hardee's Corps and a close friend of Joe Johnston, led a division that consisted predominately of Georgians. After learning of the transfer, Walker wrote his wife, "I thought when I saw Bragg come that he had come to relieve him but I knew he had something on hand. I have feared this all along." Walker had not approved of the army's constant fallbacks from Dalton, and he believed correctly "that if Johnston fell back behind the Chattahoochee he would be relieved." He assumed that Bragg would take over command when he arrived. "A fight now is obliged to come off for if Johnston has been relieved for falling back (as I take it for granted he was)," said Walker; "it is as much as to say to Hood, don't you try the same game." The Georgia general added, "Hood has 'gone up like a rocket.' It is to be hoped…that he will not come down like the stick. He is brave, whether he has the capacity to Command armies (for it requires a high order of talent) time will develop. I will express no opinion."[42] Walker would be dead within a week, struck down while leading one of Hood's rocket-like assaults at Decatur.

Colonel Ellison Capers, commander of the 24th South Carolina in Gist's Brigade of Walker's Division was so moved by the transfer that he included in his official report,

A courier handed me a circular order from General Hood, announcing General Johnston's removal.… It is due to truth to say that the reception of these orders produced the most desperate feelings in my command. The loss of the commanding general was felt to be irreparable.… Passing by his [Johnston's] headquarters, Walker's Division passed at the shoulder [arms],

---

[41]Charles E. Wilson in Cannon, *Bloody Banners and Barefoot Boys*, appendix 3, 125–36; Barnard, *Tattered Volunteers*, 64.

[42]Richard M. McMurry, *John Bell Hood and the War for Southern Independence*, 123; David V. Stroud, *Ector's Texas Brigade and the Army of Tennessee, 1862–1865* (Longview TX: Ranger Publishing, 2004) 164; Scott Walker, *Hell's Broke Loose in Georgia: Survival in a Civil War Regiment* (Athens: University of Georgia Press, 2007) 149.

the officers saluting and most of the latter and hundreds of the men taking off their hats.[43]

A. P. Adamson of the 30th Georgia Regiment in Stevens's Brigade wrote that it was a "staggering blow" when Old Joe was removed. He exclaimed, "They all loved him and believed he was doing the best he could under the circumstances…. Gen. Johnston will go down in history as one of the greatest generals of the age."[44] On 21 July 1864, Private Angus McDermid of the 29th Georgia in Stevens's Brigade wrote his father, "They have made old J. Johnston quit us because he falls back. I am sorrow of it."[45] Also on 21 July, Captain Charles Manning Furman of the 16th South Carolina in Gist's Brigade, wrote his wife from the trenches near Atlanta: "The army parts with Johnston, their beloved leader with great Regret. I hope that Hood may prove competent to the work assigned him."[46]

In Mercer's Brigade, Lieutenant Hamilton Branch of the 57th Georgia wrote his mother on 19 July: "We learned yesterday to our great surprise and sorrow that our beloved gallant commander had been relieved from the command of this army. I never have seen or heard of an army so wrapped up in a commander as this army proved itself to be on yesterday." Branch continued, "When it was announced everyone seemed to feel as if they had lost their best friend and the general remark was, well this army is lost, and everyone seemed to be whipped. As for myself I have never felt so downhearted in my life as I did on yesterday." The young Lieutenant exclaimed, "and if we had not have been ordered off, I know that I could not have helped from crying. Genl. Johnston had the love and confidence of every man in his army, and not one doubted but that he would annihilate Sherman before he had finished the campaign." Branch finished with a note about the new commander: "Genl. Hood the present commander of this army is a fighting man and no doubt a fine officer and under him we will

---

[43]*OR*, series I, vol. 38, ser. no. 74, 720; Scaife, *Campaign for Atlanta*, 86.

[44]A. P. Adamson, *Brief History of the 30th Georgia Regiment* (Jonesboro GA: Freedom Hill Press, 1987) 41.

[45]Angus McDermid, *Letters from a Confederate Soldier*, ed. Benjamin Rountree, *Georgia Review* (1964): 266–67.

[46]"Captain Charles Manning Furman, Company H, Sixteenth South Carolina," http://batsonsm.tripod.com/letters/letters9.html (accessed 15 August 2014).

gain the victory, but he is not Genl. Johnston."[47] Also in Mercer's Brigade, Colonel Charles H. Olmstead, commander of the 1st Georgia Infantry, would write in his memoirs years after the war, "The removal of Genl. Johnston at the crisis of the campaign was one of the most lamentable events of the entire war. Its effect upon the morale of the Army was immediately disastrous; it took the heart out of the men for he was their idol."[48]

In the Kentucky Orphan Brigade of General Bate's Division of Hardee's Corps, Private Johnny Green wrote, "Genl. John B. Hood has been placed in command. The boys have no objection to him but they don't think there is another General in the world eaqual to Genl. Joseph E. [Johnston]—except Genl. R. E. Lee. The removal has cast a gloom over the army."[49] Another member of the Kentucky Orphans, Lieutenant L. D. Young, recorded,

> While Hood was a Kentuckian as well as we Orphans, & we priding in everything pertaining to the history of Kentucky, we had unbounded confidence in General Johnston. But once before had we felt such sadness & regret—when General Breckenridge was taken from us and sent to Virginia. This feeling was intensified by the belief that Bragg was responsible.[50]

The displeasure with the change in command was particularly great among the Tennessee soldiers. In Cheatham's all Tennessee Division, there was a near mutiny. Many officers threatened to resign in protest. By 20 July, a number of them did.[51] On Monday, 18 July, Martin Van Buren Oldham of Company G, 9th Tennessee wrote,

---

[47]Walker, *Hell's Broke Loose in Georgia*, 148.

[48]Ibid., 149.

[49]Green, *Johnny Green of the Orphan Brigade*, 142.

[50]L. D. Young, *Reminiscences of a Soldier of the Orphan Brigade*, 26 June 1916, Paris, Kentucky. Copy available at David Library, UNC Chapel Hill, E605.Y7, address printed for the Richard Hawes Chapter of the United Daughters of the Confederacy, Paris KY, Lt. L. D. Young, 1916, 90.

[51.]First Lieutenant John W. Hodges of Company B, 51st Tennessee, and 2nd Lieutenant William R. Jones and 2nd Lieutenant J. W. Seaton of Company F, 52nd Tennessee, all of Carter's Brigade, each resigned, as did 1st Lieutenant James A. McFerris of Company K, 32nd Tennessee, Major William C. Morelock of the 3rd Mounted Tennessee Infantry, and Captain A. C. Gardner of Company G, 9th Tennessee. Supplement to the *OR*, part II, Record of Events, vol. 66, series no. 78 (Wilmington NC: Broadfoot Publishing, 1997) 152, 468, 485, 488, 490, 580, 590,

Today we were completely dumbfounded at the announcement that Gen. Johnston had been removed, and superseded by Lt. Gen. Hood. General dissatisfaction exists and I doubt whether it is possible to find another man in whom the army would place such implied confidence as Gen. Johnston. Whether fighting or retreating the men were satisfied that their Gen. knew best and wherever he led they were willing to follow. It will no longer be the case with the Army of Tenn. Hood's fighting quality, as demonstrated by his total disregard of human sacrifice, does by no means suit the men. If the change could have been made at another time when the crisis was not so near at hand, a better opportunity for winning the confidence of the soldiers would have been offered. But he takes command on the eve of a battle with a force numerically inferior to the enemy and dispirited from the removal of a General whom they had learned to admire for his superior skill and sagacity and who shared their utmost confidences. Whatever Johnston has done to deserve such treatment by the Dep. is left a secret. He alludes to nothing that would enlighten us in his farewell address. We feel (and it is the common feeling of the army that he has been the object of gross injustices) that Gen. Bragg and Pres. Davis are alone responsible for the evil which is likely to result. The enemy has succeeded in crossing nearly his whole force six miles above and our army has moved to confront him. All our Div. has gone except ours and one other Brig. A battle is expected tomorrow or next day. Gen. Hood will probably teach the army other tactics than fortifying.[52]

"Monday, July 18…. Genl. Johnston relieved by Genl. Hood, causing great gloom in the army," wrote Private John T. Kern of Company K, 45th Mississippi in Lowrey's Brigade, one of Cleburne's four brigades.[53] Private William E. Bevens of the 1st Arkansas Regiment in Polk's Brigade, also in Cleburne's Division, wrote,

The great military genius was thrown out on the eve of his final and greatest assault upon Sherman, an assault which could have saved Atlanta to the

---

658,

[52]Martin Van Buren Oldham, *Civil War Diaries of Van Buren Oldham, Company G, 9th Tennessee, 1863–1864*; http://www.utm.edu/departments/acadpro/library/departments/special_collections/E579.5_Oldham/text/vboldham_indx.htm (29 November 2008).

[53]David Williamson, *The Third Battalion Mississippi Infantry and the 45th Mississippi Regiment* (Jefferson NC: McFarland Publishing, 2009) 214–15.

Confederacy. Hood's and Davis' tactics prevailed after that, and the splendid, unconquered army was swept off the earth into the grave.[54]

In another of Cleburne's brigades, Granbury's Texas Brigade, the news of the transfer was not received well:

In less than an hour after this fact becomes known, groups of three, five, seven, ten or fifteen could be seen all over camp discussing the situation—Gen. Johnston has so endeared himself to his soldiers, that no man can take his place. We have never made a fight under him that we did not get the best of it. And the whole army had become so attached to him, and to put such implicit faith in him, that whenever he said for us to fight at any particular place, we went in feeling like Gen. Johnson knew all about it and we were certain to whip.[55]

Captain Samuel T. Foster recorded these words in his diary and added that Johnston had "never deceived us once," the men "always had something to eat," and after an "extra hard march" or "in bad weather" he "would have a little whiskey issued."[56] Captain Foster recorded that if the Confederate president had ventured in to their camp that evening, "he would not have lived an hour."[57] The Texas captain went on:

For the first time, we hear men openly talk about going home, by tens (10) and by fifties (50). They refuse to stand guard, or do any other camp duty, and talk open rebellion against all Military authority—All over camp, (not only among Texas troops) can be seen this demoralization—and at all hours in the afternoon can be heard Hurrah for Joe Johnston and God D_ _ n Jeff Davis.[58]

If anyone in either the Army of Tennessee or Army of Mississippi wanted Johnston removed, or was unhappy about his conduct during the six

---

[54]Daniel E. Sutherland, *Reminiscences of a Private: William E. Bevins of the First Arkansas Infantry C. S. A.*, ed. Daniel E. Sutherland (Little Rock: University of Arkansas Press, 1999) 56–58; Scaife, *Campaign for Atlanta*, 86.

[55]Samuel T. Foster, *One of Cleburne's Command: The Civil War Diary of Captain Samuel T. Foster, Granbury's Texas Brigade, C. S. A.*, ed. Norman D. Brown (Austin: University of Texas Press, 1980) 106.

[56]Ibid.

[57]Williamson, *Third Battalion Mississippi Infantry*, 215.

[58]Ibid.; Foster, *One of Cleburne's Command*, 106–107.

months in Georgia (except for General Hood, who wrote often to Bragg and Davis asserting his opinion), this researcher has not yet found it.

A kind of pre-funeral wake overtook the Confederate army on Monday, 18 July as shocked and disbelieving officers and men discussed and debated their future and the future of the army, and along with it, Atlanta and the Confederacy. A Texas captain from Cleburne's Division recorded the mood. "The noise and confusion was kept up all night. Genl. Johns[t]on was serenaded, and if Jeff Davis had made his appearance in this army during the excitement he would not have lived an hour."[59] During the day, while marching to another position toward Atlanta, Walker's Division received the news of Johnston's removal. As rumor spread that Johnston had been relieved, the men could not believe it until a courier arrived with a circular order from General Hood confirming the news. The order "produced the most despondent feelings" in the men, according to one Colonel.[60]

> Continuing the march and passing by his (Johnston's) headquarters Walker's Division passed at the shoulder, the officers saluting, and most of the latter and hundreds of the men taking off their hats. It had been proposed to halt and cheer, but General Johnston hearing our intention requested that the troops march by in silence.[61]

Other generals tried to get the order countermanded when they learned of the change in command. Among them was Lieutenant General Alexander P. Stewart, who had served under Hood as one of his division commanders. Known as "Old Straight" for his steadfastness in battle, Stewart rode to Johnston's headquarters at the Dexter Niles House on the evening of 17 July after deploying his Corps south of Peach Tree Creek. It was after dark. When Stewart got there, Johnston showed him the order:

> Astounded by the order, Stewart asked Johnston to suspend its execution until the army made the planned attack, but Johnston refused. Stewart then rode to Hardee's headquarters. Old Straight found Hardee primarily interested in seeing if he was mentioned in the change order. When Stewart

---

[59]Samuel T. Foster, *One of Cleburne's Command: The Civil War Diary of Captain Samuel T. Foster, Granbury's Texas Brigade, C. S. A.*, ed. Norman D. Brown (Austin: University of Texas Press, 1980) 107.

[60]*OR*, series I, vol. 38, ser. no. 74, 717.

[61]Ibid.

said he was not, Hardee suggested Stewart find Hood. Stewart agreed, but asked Hardee not to publish the existence of the order, perhaps hoping that it could be reversed before the word got out to the troops. Hardee agreed, but subsequently leaked word.[62]

Whether Hardee, the Old Reliable, leaked word or whether a sulking Johnston who was busily preparing his farewell address to the Army, let the news of his removal out is unclear. In his Journal entry for 17 July, Colonel Melancthon Smith, Hardee's chief of artillery, wrote, "At night received General Johnston's address bidding the troops farewell, General Hood taking command."[63] Johnston, perhaps relieved to be relieved of command wasted no time in carrying out the president's order. In his postwar narrative, Johnston asserted, "Orders transferring the command of the army to General Hood, were written and published immediately...."[64]

Old Straight sent a note to Hood, and the new commander agreed to meet him early the next morning. At sunrise, Stewart and Hood met on the road on the way to Johnston's headquarters. It appeared to Stewart that Hood genuinely agreed to try to have the order countermanded. Perhaps Hood realized that many of the soldiers might not support his command or that the weight of responsibility might be too much to bear. Or, it may have simply been that Hood wanted to appear supportive of Stewart's proposal, for to act otherwise would appear to be too eager to take command. However, one comment apparently made by Hood to Johnston seems to point to the conclusion that the attack of Thomas's forces along Peach Tree Creek was imminent. According to John DuBose, Hood told Johnston to "pocket the order and fight your battle," meaning the anticipated assault upon Sherman's exposed forces as they crossed Peach Tree Creek.[65] Johnston and Hood then held a meeting outside of Stewart's presence. While Stewart waited, General Hardee arrived. After the meeting between Johnston and Hood concluded, Hood, Hardee and Stewart wrote and

---

[62]Sam Davis Elliott, *Soldier of Tennessee: General Alexander P. Stewart and the Civil War in the West* (Baton Rouge: Louisiana State University, 2004) 200.

[63]Supplement to *OR*, part I, vol. 7, ser. no. 7 (Wilmington NC: Broadfoot Publishing) 79.

[64]Joseph E. Johnston, *Narrative of Military Operations* (New York: D. Appleton & Company, 1874) 349.

[65]John Witherspoon DuBose, *General Joseph Wheeler and the Army of Tennessee* (New York: Neale Publishing Co., 1912).

delivered a telegram to Adjutant General Samuel Cooper in Richmond, who had sent the order on behalf of the president.[66] The letter was sent from General Hood, but was endorsed by generals Hardee and Stewart:

> General S. Cooper:
> GENERAL: I have the honor to acknowledge the receipt of my appointment as general of the Army of Tennessee. There is now heavy skirmishing and indications of a general advance. I deem it dangerous to change the commanders of this army at this particular time, and to be to the interest of the service that no change should be made until the fate of Atlanta is decided.[67]
> J. B. Hood, General.

Hood, Hardee, and Stewart waited for a reply. Johnston agreed to remain while Hood issued orders under Johnston's name to the troops. Monday passed while the Confederate army remained idle, its leaders anxiously awaiting a response from Richmond. Finally, at 5:20 PM, a reply came from Richmond to General Hood, this time from President Davis. The president also copied Hardee and Stewart:

> General Hood:
> Your telegram of this date received. A change of commanders, under existing circumstances, was regarded as so objectionable that I only accepted it as the alternative of continuing in a policy which had proved so disastrous. Reluctance to make the change induced me to send a telegram of inquiry to the commanding general on the 16th instant. His reply but confirmed previous apprehensions—that is, what will best promote the public good; and to each of you I confidently look for the sacrifice of every personal consideration in conflict with that object. The order has been executed, and I cannot suspend it without making the case worse than it was before the order was issued.
> JEFFERSON DAVIS[68]

---

[66]Elliott, *Soldier of Tennessee*, 200.
[67]*OR*, series I, vol. 38, ser. no. 76, 888.
[68]Ibid.

The last portion of Davis's letter was clearly addressed to Hardee and Stewart to support Hood and Davis's decision for "the public good." Davis no doubt was aware that Hardee would probably be upset at being passed over for appointment, but the president had already considered the "Old Reliable" as Johnston's replacement and decided against it. This is clear in his correspondence with General Bragg in the days leading up to the change. It has been argued that because Hardee had declined the position after Bragg's removal in November 1863 he would not have accepted it if offered to him a second time. Hardee declined the promotion the year before because the army was in a state of demoralization, and he believed that a fresh face and outside leader such as Joe Johnston could better rebuild the army and bring back its morale. In this opinion it appears that Hardee was right. He perhaps felt that his own ability to renew the army's vigor would be impeded because he had been part of the in-fighting by the officers under Bragg's command and because he might not have the full support of all of the officer corps. Hardee did not have the same reservation, apparently, to promotion in July. Moreover, he clearly was unhappy about being passed up for a junior grade officer like Hood, whom he had commanded in the pre-war United States Army.[69]

Elsewhere in the Confederate army, generals were learning of the transfer with disbelief. In addition to General Stewart, Loring, French, Stevens, Manigault, and others tried to get the order countermanded. Brigadier General Arthur Middleton Manigault explained that,

> The removal of General Johnston from the command of the Army of Tennessee, was one of those hasty and ill-judged steps on the part of Mr. Davis, which, I believe, contributed materially to the downfall of the Confederacy, and possibly caused it…[Hood is] incompetent, and entirely unfit for the responsible position he occupied.[70]

---

[69]*Macon Daily Telegraph*, 10 August 1864.

[70]R. Lockwood Tower, ed., *A Carolinian Goes to War: The Civil War Narrative of Arthur Middleton Manigault, Brigadier General, C. S. A.* (Columbia: University of South Carolina Press, Charleston Library Society, 1983) 200; James W. Rabb, *W. W. Loring: Florida's Forgotten General* (Manhattan KS: Sunflower University Press, 1996) 161–63.

Major General Samuel G. French, upon hearing of the transfer "rode down to army headquarters and bade Johnston good-by."[71] While there, French had a conversation with General Hood. According to the Quaker general,

> I told him that I was sorry Johnston had been relieved; that I had often, when in Mississippi, talked with him concerning the manner of conducting the war; but "now that you are in command, I assure you I will serve under you as faithfully and cheerfully as with him." Although he took my hand and thanked me, I was ever afterwards impressed with the belief that he never forgave me for what I said.[72]

To Mrs. Fannie A. Beers, who was serving as a volunteer nurse at a Confederate hospital in Atlanta, the news of Johnston's removal was a sad turning point.

> The whole post seemed as if stricken by some terrible calamity. Convalescents walked about with lagging steps and gloomy faces. In every ward lay men who wept bitterly or groaned aloud or, covering their faces, refused to speak, or eat. From that hour the buoyant, hopeful spirit seemed to die out. I do not think anything was ever the same again.

The alarmed Beers admitted that she knew little "of the relative merits of the two commanders," but the responses of the men told the story.[73]

First Lieutenant Claudius Virginius H. Davis, Adjutant of the 22nd Mississippi on the announcement to Featherston's Brigade of Johnston's replacement on the morning of July 18th described the scene:

> The men were astonished beyond expression and for the first time appeared disheartened. General Hood's order assuming command of the army was read to our command in line, and it was received in absolute silence. Not a cheer was heard and after breaking ranks many unfavorable comments and direful forebodings were indulged in, for our boys felt that a fatal mistake had been made.[74]

---

[71]Samuel G. French, *Two Wars: An Autobiography of Gen. Samuel G. French* (Huntington WV: Blue Acorn Press, 1949) 217.

[72]Ibid.

[73]Webb Garrison, *Atlanta and the War* (Nashville: Rutledge Hill Press, 1995) 143, quoting Beers.

[74]*Echoes of Battle: The Atlanta Campaign, An Illustrated Collection of Union and*

History has recognized Lee as a brilliant strategist and Johnston as only a competent but perhaps unimaginative commander, but Old Joe had the confidence of his men in a way that no one else who commanded a Southern force in the Deep South ever did. To be successful, the men in the ranks needed to feel good about themselves and their leaders. The men in both the Army of Tennessee and Army of Mississippi had suffered from poor leadership in the past. Generals Bragg and Pemberton had not inspired the kind of confidence in the common soldier of these armies that Johnston did. In Old Joe, they found a mature, confident, father figure who seemed to care about them and their sufferings. He also seemed to be judicious in his use of them, rarely committing them to futile attacks or foolish risks. "He was loved, respected, admired; yea, almost worshiped by his troops. I do not believe there was a soldier in his army but would gladly have died for him," said one veteran of the Army of Tennessee.[75]

In the decades after the war, as participants and historians reflected, various leaders in the North and South were either vilified or elevated depending on the writers' agendas. As Americans sought for deeper reasons for the war and Southerners needed to find meaning for their cause, heroes like Stonewall Jackson and Robert E. Lee were raised to untouchable heights. By the middle of the twentieth century, they were portrayed as god-like figures who were above criticism. Lee became the focus of such deification, so much so that a number of historians have written books about it.[76]

It is fitting, then, that Lee, Davis, and Jackson thus appear on the impressive stone carving on the side of Stone Mountain, Georgia, east of Atlanta. Though highly praised during the war when his armies were successful, Lee was not on such a pedestal, but Stonewall Jackson's untimely

---

Confederate Narratives, ed. Larry M. Strayer and Richard A. Baumgartner (Huntington WV: Blue Acorn Press, 1991) 220.

[75]Samuel R. Watkins, *Company Aytch* (New York: Simon and Schuster, 1997) 126–27; General Alexander P. Stewart to General Joseph E. Johnston, 11 February 1868 in Joseph E. Johnston, *Narrative of Military Operations* (New York: D. Appleton & Company, 1874) 367–69.

[76]Michael Fellman, *The Making of Robert E. Lee* (Baltimore: Johns Hopkins Press, 2003); Thomas L. Connelly, *The Marble Man: Robert E. Lee and His Image in American Society* (Baton Rouge: Lousiana State University, 1977) 163. In his book, Connelly adopts the moniker that he credits Stephen Vincent Benet for coining.

death placed him on a lofty perch in the Southern cause during the war. The people and the soldiers revered Joe Johnston as ardently as anyone else in that period. Certainly, time and bickering between Johnston and President Davis, as well as criticism leveled by Bragg and Hood, eroded the folk-like status Old Joe held in Southern lore. In fact, the only statue of Joseph Eggleston Johnston that exists today can be found on a downtown street corner in Dalton, Georgia, where he began his defense of the Georgia Campaign. A veteran or a junior officer who had served with Johnston during the war would have felt that Old Joe's place on the top shelf of Southern generalship would have been secured.

General Alexander P. Stewart, who had been with the Army of Tennessee since just before the Battle of Shiloh, later commanded the Army of Mississippi after the death of General Polk, and continued to lead it through its merger with the Army of Tennessee to the end of the war was perhaps in the best position to judge the morale of these armies during the war. In a postwar letter to General Johnston on the subject, General Stewart explained,

> I do not know that its [the Army's] *morale* was ever before equal, certainly never superior, to what it was when the campaign opened in Georgia in 1864, under your command. *You* were the only commander of that army whom *men* and *officers* were disposed to trust and confide in without reserve. While at Dalton, I frequently heard this subject, of the unbounded confidence of the men in "Old Joe," discussed among the officers, who seemed but little, if any, exceeded by the rank and file in this respect. The officers seemed to regard this feeling as a great element of strength (*as it certainly was* [added Stewart]), and looked upon it as a part of their duty to cherish and promote it. The army had confidence in whom they could place reliance. The consequence was, that the army *surrendered to you*; they gave you their *love* and *unlimited confidence*, were willing to follow you, advancing or retreating, and you could have led them wherever you chose. At the time the retreat from Resaca, and perhaps for a few days following, this feeling of *entire trust* in you somewhat abated; but it speedily revived, and was as perfect as ever when you retired. I cannot imagine it possible for an army to entertain more personal affection for a commander, or to place more implicit

reliance on one, than that army did for you. I believe the last man of them would have willingly died at your bidding.[77]

And so it was, with this reception, that the young commander Hood, with his battle-torn body, took the helm of the armies of Tennessee and Mississippi and the Confederate forces at Atlanta. His first action was to deliver the following dispatch to the men:

> In obedience to orders from the War Department I assume command of this army and department. I feel the weight of the responsibility so suddenly and unexpectedly devolved upon me by this position, and shall bend all my energies and employ all my skill to meet its requirements. I look with confidence to your patriotism to stand by me, and rely upon your prowess to wrest your country from the grasp of the invader, entitling yourselves to the proud distinction of being called the deliverers of an oppressed people.[78]

---

[77]General Alexander P. Stewart to General Joseph E. Johnston, 11 February 1868 in Johnston, *Narrative*, 367–69.
[78]*OR*, series I, vol. 38, ser. no. 76, 889.

14

OLD SLOW TROT

Whichever way I turned the matter over in my mind, my oath of allegiance to my Government always came uppermost to my mind.[1]

No, no, no. Mix them up. I am tired of state's rights.[2]

Tuesday, 19 July 1864, was supposed to be the day that General Joe Johnston would unleash his surprise assault on the scattered portions of Sherman's armies. Instead, it was the first full day on the job for the new commander, John Bell Hood, just three weeks removed from his thirty-third birthday. While General Hood got acclimated to his new post, Johnston prepared to leave Atlanta. When it became clear that Davis would not reverse the order, Johnston packed his bags. By the evening of 18 July, he and his wife, Lydia, quietly boarded the southbound train for Macon, Georgia, to sojourn at the home of Major General Howell Cobb.[3] In fairness to Old Joe, however, it was probably best for him to leave and clear the path for Hood to begin his regime. To remain would invite a possible mutiny, and, despite his flaws, Johnston was above such contrivance.

Rather than a Confederate attack, Tuesday saw much of Wheeler's gray cavalry on the move and Sherman's men draw closer to Atlanta.[4] Colonel George G. Dibrell, commanding one of Wheeler's Brigades, remembered that his Tennesseans were camped at Poplar Springs on the Peach Tree

---

[1]John Bowers, *Chickamauga and Chattanooga: The Battles that Doomed the Confederacy* (New York: Harper Perennial, 2001) 70; Richard O'Connor, *Thomas: Rock of Chickamauga* (New York: Prentice Hall, 1948) 110.

[2]Bowers, *Chickamauga and Chattanooga*, 239.

[3]Samuel Carter III, *The Siege of Atlanta, 1864* (New York: St. Martin's Press, 1973) 196–97; A. A. Hoehling, *Last Train From Atlanta* (New York: Thomas Yoseloff, 1958) 106–107.

[4]John P. Dyer, *The Gallant Hood* (Indianapolis: The Bobbs-Merrill Co., 1950) 20.

Road northeast of Cross Keys when news of the transfer arrived on Monday. Later that day, his brigade was ordered to fall back to the south side of Peach Tree Creek, which it reached by dusk.[5]

This move, coupled with a similar order to Anderson's and Hannon's Brigades, which were covering the Chattahoochee River crossings at Shallow Ford and McAfee's Bridge northeast of Atlanta, unknowingly opened the road for Sherman's forces to begin their encirclement of the city from the northeast and left the Georgia railroad to Augusta exposed. One of the few dispatches issued during the day from headquarters was to inform Wheeler about the importance of having all infantry and cavalry south of Peach Tree Creek in coordination with the burning of all bridges over the creek. In Hood's message, Wheeler was told that all Confederate "infantry at each bridge" has been ordered to prepare the bridges for burning and that Wheeler should instruct, "if forced back," for "a body of cavalry to cross at each bridge" with the "last that crosses" burn it. Unfortunately for Hood, Wheeler took the message to mean to break off surveillance of the Federal armies and withdraw to the safety of the Confederate lines south of Peach Tree Creek except for the brigades that faced Thomas.[6]

Wheeler subsequently reported that Kelly's Division was assigned to protect the Georgia railroad to Augusta while he led four brigades in front of Thomas. However, during the critical time during the change in Confederate command and Sherman's advance on Atlanta, Wheeler was busy micro-managing four brigades, a force of some 1,600 troopers who were assigned the relatively easy job of harassing and delaying the slow and careful moving Army of the Cumberland. During this time, the balance of his cavalry, another seven brigades consisting of three-fourths of his force, were either miles to the east or southwest of Atlanta, far away from contact with Wheeler or the Confederate high command. Hannon's and Anderson's brigades of Kelly's Division leisurely fell back to the east, away from Atlanta, as McPherson's Army of the Tennessee approached. Meanwhile, Dibrell's Brigade fell back with the balance of Wheeler's Cavalry below Peach Tree

---

[5]J. B. Lindsley, ed., *Military Annals of Tennessee*, vol. 2 (Wilmington NC: Broadfoot Publishing, 1995) 651–79, at 668.

[6]*OR*, series I, vol. 38, ser. no. 76, 889–90; Lindsley, ed., *Military Annals of Tennessee*, 668; John Witherspoon DuBose, *General Joseph Wheeler and the Army of Tennessee* (New York: The Neal Publishing Co., 1912) 362–70.

Creek and was subsequently ordered to Decatur to try and link up with the balance of Kelly's Division. The result was three-fold: Kelly's Division (1) failed to defend the railroad as assigned as they were much too light a force to offer McPherson's army any meaningful resistance; (2) lost direct communication with Wheeler, Hood, and anyone in Atlanta, so that news of McPherson's fast-moving forces that were threatening the railroad and Decatur did not reach Hood for twenty-four more hours; and (3) became isolated from the remainder of the Confederate forces so that when Hood directed Wheeler to move to the Decatur road east of Atlanta around 2:15 PM on 19 July, Wheeler only had three brigades—Ferguson's, Allen's and Iverson's—available. At the time, Williams's Kentucky Brigade was heavily engaged with Howard's IV Corps from Buckhead to Peach Tree Creek. Wheeler thus ordered Williams to report directly to General Cheatham, who had just assumed command of Hood's Corps, which was posted just east of the Buckhead Road. Kelly's Division remained busy with Garrard's Federal cavalry far to the east of the scene of McPherson's force. By 20 and 21 July, Kelly's three brigades would be pressed all the way to Covington so that while Wheeler was busy fending off McPherson's Army of the Tennessee from taking Atlanta on 20 July, the Confederate cavalry commander only had about 2,500 cavalry with him.[7]

While Wheeler's Cavalry was busy on 18 July, the Confederate infantry and its leaders remained idle. According to John Witherspoon DuBose, a noncommissioned staff officer from the 1st Alabama Cavalry who had been converted into a recruiter, General Hood told Johnston to disregard the order [to transfer command?]. The Confederate high command contemplated their options in light of Davis's order. Johnston's plan to strike Sherman when he crossed Peach Tree Creek needed to be executed soon if it was to work as the Federal crossings appeared eminent. "Put your order in your pocket and fight your battle, General Johnston," Hood insisted. Hood,

---

[7]*OR*, series I, vol. 38, ser. no. 74, 951–52; ser. no. 76, 221, 890–93; Edwin L. Drake, "Summary of Lt. General Joseph Wheeler's Cavalry Engagements, Nashville: Tavel, Eastman & Howell, 1879," Appendix, *The Annals of the Army of Tennessee and Early Western History*, vol. 1 (Jackson TN: The Guild Bindery Press, April-December, 1878) 67–73, 91, 98.

Hardee, Stewart and Johnston were all present at Confederate headquarters, which remained at the Niall House throughout the day.[8]

Except for the Rebel cavalry in front of the Army of the Cumberland, which continued to harass and slow Thomas's slow-moving legions between Power's Ferry and Pace's Ferry, the remainder of Sherman's forces were left to roam the Georgia countryside unmolested. At this critical time during the change in command, Sherman's right-wheel movement commenced unhindered.

After crossing the Chattahoochee River on Saturday and Sunday, 16 and 17 July, General Thomas and his Army of the Cumberland was ready to press on toward Peach Tree Creek. Forming the right or hub of the wheel of Sherman's armies as they crossed the Chattahoochee, Thomas was ordered to keep a grip on the river at its intersection with Peach Tree Creek and to cross his three corps over to the south side of the creek and press the Confederates toward Atlanta while Sherman's other four corps threatened the Gate City from the east and northeast. As historian John Cannan states, "one of the most competent generals and army commanders on either side, and truly the most unrecognized, was...the imperturbable George H. Thomas."[9]

Federal Major General George H. Thomas looked the part of an old soldier. At six feet tall and well over two hundred pounds, he made an imposing figure in the saddle of the unfortunate horse that had to carry him. Described as a "portly, whiskered old gentleman," and being "moon faced and bulky in girth," the native Virginian was known by a number of nicknames.[10] Called "Pap," "Old Pap," and "Uncle George" by his soldiers, Thomas was respected and revered by his men. His fellow officers and friends called him "Old Tom." At forty-seven years old, he was like a father

---

[8]Thomas McAdory Owen, *History of Alabama and Dictionary of Alabama Biography*, vol. 3 (Chicago: S. J. Clarke Publishing Co., 1921) 511; DuBose, *General Joseph Wheeler and the Army of Tennessee*, 363, 369; Dyer, *Gallant Hood*, 247, quoting post-war correspondence between Hood and Stewart; John Bell Hood, *Advance and Retreat* (Boston: Da Capo Press, 1993) 144.

[9]John Cannan, *The Atlanta Campaign: May—November, 1864* (Boston: Da Capo Press, 1991) 112.

[10]O'Connor, *Thomas: Rock of Chickamauga*, 3; Bowers, *Chickamauga and Chattanooga*, 71, 140; John Fitch, *Annals of the Army of the Cumberland* (Mechanicsburg PA: Stackpole Books, 2003) 56–66.

to the men, so many of whom were homesick teenagers or young men barely in their twenties. Born on 31 July 1816, in Tidewater, Virginia, Thomas was raised on the fringe of the Southern aristocratic planter class. His father, John Thomas, was a prosperous farmer with sizeable lands producing tobacco, corn, and cotton. He also had a fair number of slaves to work his land, but John Thomas was hardly considered part of the elite class of land barons and planters of the Southampton County, Virginia, aristocracy.[11]

Few stories of Thomas's childhood have survived, but one story sheds light on his feelings about slavery and the aristocracy in the South who perpetuated it: "Years after the Civil War had provided his freedom, an old Negro named Artise recalled that young George [Thomas] had secretly gathered the children of the Thomas's slaves every day after his own attendance at school and taught them to read and write—against his father's wishes."[12] This story was confirmed by Thomas's friend and classmate at West Point, Billy Sherman, who used to tell after the war and Thomas's death that, "As a boy, Thomas felt the South was wrong in denying education to the slaves and after school he led the pickaninnies of his father's slaves to a grove where he taught them what he had learned during the day."[13]

When war clouds gathered in November 1860, Thomas was literally on his back in Norfolk, Virginia, near his boyhood home. In November 1860, he had left his post with the 2nd Cavalry in Texas, where he served as major, to go to New York City to be with his wife and to recover from a Comanche arrow wound he had received that fall. The wound had come from an arrow that went through his jaw and sank into his chest. It would be his only war wound, despite serving in a number of vicious battles in the Mexican War and the Civil War. On his way to New York, his train stopped at a station in Norfolk, Virginia. He stepped off the train in the darkness just as the train unexpectedly lurched forward. He landed awkwardly in a ditch, injuring his back. Thomas remained in Virginia where he visited with his family, including his two sisters, while he recovered from his temporarily paralyzing injury. Thomas wrote for his wife, Francis Kellogg Thomas, a native New Yorker, to come to him in Virginia where he

---

[11]O'Connor, *Thomas: Rock of Chickamauga*, 3, 53–55, 199.
[12]Ibid., 55; Fitch, *Annals of the Army of the Cumberland*, 56–65.
[13]O'Connor, *Thomas: Rock of Chickamauga*, 55.

recuperated for the next six weeks as his country and command, the 2nd Cavalry, fell apart around him.[14]

Choosing to remain in the United States Army was not an easy decision for Thomas. By December 1860, his back ailing him, he left Virginia to go to New York. For the next three and a half months, Thomas remained in New York, wondering if his back would heal, if his country would heal and avoid war, if he would still have a job in the United States Army, if his back would even allow him to return, and if his Southern nativity would prevent his service. During this time, he watched South Carolina and six other states in the Deep South break from the Union; Virginia's decision to secede or remain with the United States remained in doubt. However, many Virginia citizens prepared themselves for war and began to mobilize their resources as the state authorized the creation and implementation of an army. Thomas was offered a position as the chief of ordnance, but he turned it down. Unsure that the United States government would keep a native Southerner in its army, Thomas thought that he might be left without a country or a job.

In the uncertain days between Lincoln's election in November 1860 and the firing on Fort Sumter in Charleston, South Carolina, in April 1861, many Southern officers in the United States military left the service. All native Southerners were suspected of disloyalty by the United States' government. Thomas even sought appointment as superintendent of the Virginia Military Academy before learning that his position in the US Army was safe. By spring 1861, his back had recovered, and it appeared he would not suffer a permanent injury from the fall. In the first week of April 1861, Thomas was ordered to meet the remnants of the 2nd Cavalry, which had left Texas, frustrated after being stripped of their arms and equipment and ridiculed for their Unionist stance by pro-Southern officers who had left them. Officers in the army could resign; soldiers in the ranks could not. Thus, while a Southern officer could go home to join or help form a new unit in his own state, a soldier in the ranks was tied to his commitment to the armed service. By the time that the demoralized men and the few officers who remained with them reached the North, the professional soldiers became galvanized to the Northern cause because of mistreatment at the hands of their former Southern officers during the winter of 1860–61.

---

[14]Ibid., 96–101.

On 10 April 1861, Thomas met them on the wharves of New York's City's harbor. He led them to Carlisle Barracks, Pennsylvania, to refit.[15]

As Thomas led the men to Pennsylvania on 12 April, he appeared to be torn between the Union and his native state, but on the way to Harrisburg, Pennsylvania, he learned that the secessionists at Charleston had fired on Fort Sumter, a United States fort. He was infuriated. The more he thought of the Rebels firing on his country's flag, its property, and its servicemen, the angrier he became. During his visit to Virginia in November, he apparently had told his sisters that he would return to the Old Dominion State to lead its troops in her defense. However, the firing on Fort Sumter changed his mind. He wired his sisters in Virginia from the Harrisburg depot telegraph station that he would not be coming home. It's unclear whether his wife and his winter in New York changed his mind, or if finding his demoralized fellow soldiers at the docks of New York harbor made him more resolute. Thomas explained, "he could not in all conscience join the Secessionist movement and would remain in the Federal army." His sisters never forgave him. They returned his Christmas cards, destroyed his portraits, and never spoke his name again. Before wiring his sisters in Virginia of his decision, Thomas had already that day written a letter to his wife in New York to tell her that he would remain with the Union. "Whichever way I turned the matter over in my mind, my oath of allegiance to my Government always came uppermost to my mind."[16] Thomas's resolve to the Union is best illustrated by a question he answered after the Battle of Missionary Ridge at Chattanooga. When asked if the dead should be buried by the states they represented, the general replied, "No, no, no. Mix them up. I am tired of state's rights."[17]

Old Pap was also called "Old Slow Trot," a name perhaps first coined by his men because his stoic and portly figure on his distinguished—but equally slow—horse appeared never to be in a hurry. Still bothered by his back injury, Thomas often looked like he was in excruciating pain while riding along on marches. The methodical and phlegmatic general remained

---

[15]Ibid., 96–101; Bowers, *Chickamauga and Chattanooga*, 70–71; Fitch, *Annals of the Army of the Cumberland*, 56–66.

[16]Bowers, *Chickamauga and Chattanooga*, 70; O'Connor, *Thomas: Rock of Chickamauga*, 109–110.

[17]Bowers, *Chickamauga and Chattanooga*, 239.

liked and respected by his men, however; they trusted his cool judgment, and his calm and confident nature inspired his troops. Others, like generals Schofield and Grant, who did not care for Thomas, didn't mind using his nickname to reflect their opinion of his lack of speed in moving his men, either on the march or in battle. The deliberate, but sturdy and dependable Thomas made quite a contrast to Grant and Sherman. His steadiness, both with respect to his command and his harmonious behavior under these two fiery leaders, proved critical for his Army of the Cumberland, which had been much maligned since its defeat at Chickamauga. Thomas proved his reliability again at that battle by helping to stave off disaster at Snodgrass Hill when the rest of the Federal line had given way and fled to Chattanooga. His efforts earned him another nickname, "The Rock of Chickamauga," although U. S. Grant and John M. Schofield continued to be skeptical of him.[18]

To Grant, Thomas was the epitome of everything wrong in an officer. Thomas personified everything that Grant was not. Thomas was a refined, educated, Southern aristocrat. He was methodical, slow to act, and reserved. Grant was aggressive, vain, plain, and barely educated except in military matters. He was a Westerner and a commoner. John M. Schofield, the commander of the rival Army of the Ohio, had a petty reason for disliking Thomas. While Schofield was a student at West Point and Thomas was an instructor there, Schofield was brought before a court of inquiry when three of four freshmen entrusted to Schofield, an upperclassman, failed the entrance examination in mathematics. Schofield clearly was not cut out to be a math teacher, and he was dismissed from the academy because of the incident. Two weeks later, the court reconvened and gave Schofield a second hearing. The court readmitted Schofield to the academy by a vote of thirteen to two. Schofield believed that Thomas was one of the two dissenting votes, and he never forgave Thomas for it.[19]

---

[18]Peter Cozzens, *The Battle of Chickamauga, This Terrible Sound* (Champaign: University of Illinois Press, 1992) 9; Bowers, *Chickamauga and Chattanooga*, 70–71, 140–41; O'Connor, *Thomas: Rock of Chickamauga*, 84, 199; Glenn Tucker, *Chickamauga: Bloody Battle in the West* (New York: Smithmark Publishers, 1995) 324–25.

[19]Van Horne, Thomas B., History of the Army of the Cumberland, vol.ume I, vii-ix; O'Connor, *Thomas: Rock of Chickamauga*, 84.

It is said that Thomas, not a man of humor, only laughed once during the war, and that was over a joke about a jackass. Usually the general was available and receptive to requests from his men, including administrative matters and requests for furloughs, which were supposed to be handled by staff officers. Once, however, while his army was posted at Murfreesboro, Tennessee, Thomas was asked for a pass from a soldier who, among other reasons, explained, "I ain't seen my old woman, General, for four months." The stoic General replied quickly, "And I have not seen mine for two years. If a general can submit to such privation, surely a private can." The soldier quipped, "Don't know about that, General. You see, me and my wife ain't made that way."[20]

---

[20]Tucker, *Chickamauga*, 325.

15

NANCY CREEK

This is fulton countey georgey Sill in the woodes ande Have Bin ever Sence lefte Dalton.[1]

Palmer's XIV Corps Crosses Nancy Creek

On 17 July, the XIV Corps advanced from Vining's Station to Pace's Ferry, then crossed the Chattahoochee River and proceeded to Nancy Creek, the 16th Illinois serving in the van. The Illinois regiment came from Morgan's 1st Brigade in Davis's 2nd Division and was constantly fighting with the enemy as they tried to advance through the Georgia wilderness. During this fighting, the 16th Illinois lost a first lieutenant, James Donaldson of Company C; two corporals, Alex Peterson of Company F, and John McGovern of Company D; and three privates, Whicker, Montgomery and Peterson. Two privates, Shaw and Nelson of Company F, were wounded.[2] First Lieutenant Donaldson had been shot six times and "lay suffering with his wounds for about 2 hours between the two lines," according to John Hill Ferguson of the neighboring 10th Illinois, which relieved the 16th Illinois. "The Rebs charged and compelled the 16th [Illinois] to fall back a short distance," leaving Lieutenant Donaldson between the lines. "It was in this charge the Lieutenant was shot," Ferguson recalled. "At last the 16th determined to get him and charged the Rebs, drove them back killing 8 which were left for them to buirry."[3]

While Morgan's Brigade led Davis's Division into the subtropical jungle that made up this part of North Georgia, to his left, Johnson's 1st

---

[1]William Cline Diary, 73rd Ohio, University of Notre Dame Library, Special Collections, http://www.rarebooks.nd.edu/digital/civil_war/diaries_journals/cline/8007-081.shtml (18 November 2014) 159–60.

[2]*OR*, series I, vol. 38, ser. no. 72, 662.

[3]John Hill Ferguson, *On to Atlanta: The Civil War Diaries of John Hill Ferguson, 10th Illinois Regiment of Volunteers,* ed. Janet Correll Ellison and Mark Weitz (Lincoln: University of Nebraska Press, 2001) 62–63.

Division felt their way through the rough terrain. In the van of this division, General Richard Johnson placed Colonel Moore's 3rd Brigade, which connected with the left of Davis's Division, and Johnson's 1st Brigade under Colonel Anson G. McCook and proceeded to the left of Moore's men. In reserve, he held the 2nd Brigade of General John H. King with his regular United States Army veterans. Johnson kept his artillery in reserve with King's Brigade because he could not risk putting them forward amid the vast wooded ridges and ravines ahead. According to Johnson, "at 4 PM Colonel Moore advanced his line southeast on the Buckhead road, over a very rough and rugged country, to Nancy's Creek, where he bivouacked for the night."[4]

According to Colonel Moore, "after moving up the road [toward Buckhead] a few hundred yards," he was compelled to form a "line of battle to the left of the road [where he] threw out skirmishers in front and on the left flank" to fend off the Confederate cavalry, which was contesting their advance.[5] Companies A, B and F of the 74th Ohio formed the skirmish line. The next morning, companies D and G relieved the skirmishers. According to one veteran of the 74th Ohio's Preacher Regiment, "at 8 o'clock we moved out of our works and advanced slowly and cautiously, our skirmishers driving the enemy from their lines of works of logs and rails. About 5 o'clock we were ordered to halt and fortify, and make the works wide and strong." Corporal John H. Forbes of Moore's Division explained, "We spent the evening and most of the night in building the strongest one, of the 27 lines, that we have thrown up during the campaign, which, if in one line, would be about three miles long, which the 74th [Ohio] have built." That evening Company I relieved the skirmishers.[6]

Palmer's advance toward Moore's Mill was part of the Army of the Cumberland's wide sweeping movement toward Buckhead and Peach Tree Creek from its positions along the Chattahoochee River. With Howard's IV Corps at Powers Ferry, Hooker's XX Corps at Paces Ferry, and Palmer's XIV Corps below it, Thomas's Army of the Cumberland was posted along a six-mile front. The terrain north and west of Buckhead was a series of

---

[4]*OR*, series I, vol. 38, ser. no. 72, 524.
[5]Ibid., 601.
[6]Theodore W. Blackburn, *Letters from the Front: A Union "Preacher" Regiment (74th Ohio) in the Civil War* (Dayton OH: Press of Morningside Bookshop, 1981) 213–14.

wooded ridges and deep ravines riddled with significant creeks and tangled vines; this part of the Georgia wilderness had been sparsely settled prior to the war. Charged with defending this force was Confederate cavalry commander General Joseph Wheeler. Wheeler had already dispatched Hume's Division, less Williams's Kentucky Cavalry Brigade, "to protect the ferries at Sandtown and at Campbellton and to patrol the river below Mayson-Turner Ferry.... After detaching Kelly's Division to cover the right of the army and the roads leading down from Roswell and McAfee's Brigade, and Jackson's Division, less Ferguson's Brigade, to cover its left," Wheeler had just four brigades at his disposal to check the advance of Thomas's Army of the Cumberland.[7]

These four brigades were Iverson's Georgia Cavalry Brigade, Ferguson's Cavalry Brigade (consisting of Alabamians and Mississippians), Allen's Alabama Cavalry Brigade, and Williams's Kentucky Cavalry Brigade. Ferguson's Brigade had the task of checking the advance of Palmer's XIV Corps, which headed toward Moore's Mill and the mouth of Nancy Creek. Williams's Kentucky Brigade covered the Powers Ferry Road and Howard's IV Corps advance on Buckhead from the north. Iverson's Georgians were assigned the role of covering the crossings of Nancy Creek by Hooker's XX Corps from the west along Paces Ferry Road, while Allen's Alabama Brigade covered the space between Iverson and Williams.[8]

Palmer's XIV Corps was fighting the Mississippians of Adams's Brigade to their left, and Sears's Mississippi Brigade to their right, with elements of Ferguson's Alabama and Mississippi Cavalry Brigade, led by General Samuel W. Ferguson, nipping at them in the Georgia wilderness. Ferguson's veteran cavalrymen had been fighting alongside of Nathan Bedford Forrest and William H. "Red" Jackson throughout Mississippi, Alabama and Tennessee for two years before being sent east to Georgia. Included in Ferguson's brigade were the 2nd Alabama Cavalry commanded by John H. Carpenter, the 56th Alabama Cavalry under the direction of

---

[7]OR, series I, vol. 38, ser. no. 74, 951; Allen P. Julian, *Operations through the Present Ridgewood Community, July 1864*, pp. 8–10, folder 4, box 4, mss 130, Wilbur G. Kurtz Collection, Keenan Research Center, Atlanta History Center, Atlanta GA.

[8]OR, series I, vol. 38, ser. no. 74, 951; Julian, *Operations through the Present Ridgewood Community*, 10, author's notes.

Colonel William Boyles, the 9th Mississippi led by Colonel Horace H. Miller, the 11th Mississippi Cavalry under Colonel Robert O. Perrin, and the 12th Mississippi Battalion Cavalry directed by Colonel Robert M. Inge.[9] The nearly all-Mississippi force kept Palmer's Corps bottled up between Nancy Creek and the Chattahoochee River on 17 July and most of 18 July until General Loring called back General Adams, who was preparing for an attack as portions of Johnson's 1st Division and Davis's 2nd Division crossed Nancy Creek. The 3rd Division under General Absalom Baird followed Johnson's Division, which forced a crossing over Nancy Creek at Kyle's Bridge. Kyle's Bridge crossed Nancy Creek along today's West Paces Ferry Road just north of Westminster High School.[10]

According to Ferguson, the 10th Illinois was ordered to advance about 3:00 PM with Companies C, D, and I deployed as skirmishers: "After advancing about a mile we found the enemy again but they fell back without much resistance. Companies I and D came to [Nancy Creek]. A bridge was built with rails, and Co. I crossed over with the understanding that the creek would be the guide for both companies to go by." The bridge was erected in the area of today's West Wesley Road. "But the creek forked with out being noticed by eather of the two companies and after advancing some distance, Company D was fiared into from the left. This seemed strange. Cap. Mason thought Co. I had got turned round and was firing at his company, supposing them to be Rebs," explained Ferguson. "He started off to the left to finde Co. I, and to notify them of his being there. He had not went but a little ways when the bullits came at him pritty thick and close. So he had to go back."[11]

Ferguson then witnessed a curious scene:

In the meantime Capt. Race, Brigade Inspector, was crosing along in rear of our picket line and road right up to the Rebel works. The Rebs looked

---

[9] William R. Scaife, *The Campaign for Atlanta* (Atlanta: self-published, 1993) 88–89; http://www.archives.state.al.us/referenc/alamilor/2ndcav.html (21 December 2008); Julian, *Operations through the Present Ridgewood Community*, 8–10.

[10] Julian, *Operations through the Present Ridgewood Community*, 9; *OR*, series I, vol. 38, ser. no. 72, 524, 634, 742; Georgia Historical Markers, "Federal Right Wing," and "Federal Right Wing to Peachtree Creek," both located at West Pace's Ferry Road [Atlanta GA]; Scaife, *Campaign for Atlanta*, 86–87, 149–53; Albert Castel, *Decision in the West* (Lawrence: University Press of Kansas, 1992) 367–68.

[11] Ferguson, *On to Atlanta*, 63.

surprised at his uneform, not expecting any Yankees there. A Reb officer inquiared what regiment he belonged to. Cap. Race made no reply but stuck his spurs to his horse and got out of there in the quickest possable time. The Rebs fired after him, but did not hit him. In his hurrie, dashing through the woods his hors fell and throwed him on his shoulder, but he got up and so did his horse. He mounted and dashed a head again leaving his hat behinde him and the Rebs fireing after him heavely. When he came back and told his tale, other officers laughed at him and said there were no Rebs in there. It was impossible. Race was shoure of it, but none els could see it.

So, Adjutant "Race" went out to prove the veracity of his story and to establish the Rebel line. Captain George A. Rave was the acting inspector general for Morgan's Brigade during the Atlanta Campaign.[12]

Meanwhile, companies D and I were still receiving an unusually heavy amount of incoming fire from the Georgia woods. According to Major Samuel J. Wilson, who was severely wounded in the action, "Fireing was still going on. Seemed to be in every direction, so our major concluded it was companys D and I had got turned some was and was fighting each other. So he started to go down to where he supposed Co. D was when he was fiared at and shot through the thigh. He was carried to the rear and Captain Lusk of Co. K took command of the regiment."[13] The men were no longer laughing at Adjutant Race.

"Everything was in confusion," explained Ferguson. "The companies on the skirmish line could not account for any but them selves. They had all sepperated and were faceing every way and most any way, and a vacancy of about 200 yards between each company. Company H and E were sent out to learn the trouble and straighten the lines." They were commanded by Captain Franklin A. Munson, who "was shot through the arm and the bone chattered. In the forks of the two creeks, the Rebels had there main lines facing both ways." His last journal entry for the fateful 18 July for his 10th Illinois regiment: "It is not yet assertained how the rebel lines runs but the vacancy is filled up, and our lines will be arranged tomorrow, if not to night." Ferguson and his regiment had run into a beehive of Rebels at the mouth of Nancy Creek where it deposits into Peach Tree Creek. There, Ector's Texas and North Carolina Brigade had deployed and entrenched

---

[12]Ibid.

[13]Ferguson, *On to Atlanta*, 63; *OR*, series I, vol. 38, ser. no. 72, 659.

along a ridge that protruded from the south bank of Peach Tree Creek as the creek made an unusual bend around it in the form of an upside down "U" with the center of the U at the end of Nancy Creek and near a little mill called by locals Moore's Mill (but known the Yankees as "Durant's Mill").[14]

As soon as Johnson's and Baird's Divisions crossed Nancy Creek, they turned south. Following the Howell Mill Road, and feeling their way along the east bank of Nancy Creek, they moved cautiously in the tangled Georgia jungle replete with wooded ridges and swampy and vine-riddled ravines. General Richard W. Johnson ordered Colonel Anson McCook's Brigade to take the lead on the morning of 17 July at 7:00. By 9:00 AM, skirmishing with Confederate cavalry commenced and continued until about 2:00 PM when Johnson had to form a line of battle just east of Nancy Creek at Kyle's Bridge at the intersection of the Buckhead Road (today's West Paces Ferry Road) and Howell Mill Road (today's Northside Parkway). One man from the 104th Illinois was wounded in the action; in the 33rd Ohio, which served in the lead most of the day, two were wounded. According to Captain T. A. Minshall, the 33rd Ohio (led by Lieutenant Colonel James H. M. Montgomery) found that "the enemy resisted the advance of our skirmishers with considerable obstinacy." After driving away the Rebel cavalry beyond Peach Tree Creek, the Northerners "constructed works along a road near Donelson's shanty."[15]

Howard's IV Corps Crosses Nancy Creek

Howard's IV Corps received orders at midnight 18 July to march at daylight from their position at a bridgehead below the Chattahoochee at Powers Ferry. At 4:30 AM the van of Newton's Division left camp, and by 5:00 AM General Howard had received orders that Buckhead was his destination.[16] The 3rd Brigade, commanded by General Luther P. Bradley, led the way.[17] By 6:30 that morning, the rear of Newton's column, General Nathan Kimball's 1st Brigade, was underway, "taking the direct road to Atlanta

---

[14]Ferguson, *On to Atlanta*, 63; *OR*, series I, vol. 38, ser. no. 72, 659.

[15]*OR*, series I, vol. 38, ser. no. 72, 524, 531, 537, 551.

[16]Ibid., 201.

[17]W. H. Newlin, D. F. Lawler, and J. W. Sherrick, eds., *A History of the Seventy-Third Regiment of Illinois Infantry Volunteers* (Decatur IL: Regimental Reunion Association of Survivors of the 73rd Illinois Infantry Volunteers, 1890) 322; Scaife, *Campaign for Atlanta*, 148.

[but] found no signs of an infantry force of the enemy."[18] Howard's men had been given rations the night before and knew that a move toward Atlanta was imminent, but all appeared to be confident and ready. Newton's Division was in front, and he pushed out flankers to his front and right—meaning that he placed a few men out in advance to screen his movements and to alert him of the presence of any enemy troops—while Stanley's Division came up next, with Wood's Division following.[19] Lieutenant Chesley Mosman recorded in his diary that his brigade and Gross's 3rd Brigade of Stanley's 1st Division started at 7:30 AM, and Mosman's brigade was in rear of the 2nd Division in the line of march. Thus, it took an hour before the rear of the 2nd Division in line to move.[20]

The line was necessarily stretched out to allow for the entire column to follow on the same road through the Georgia wilderness north and west of Buckhead that covered the lands north of the Gate City in the tangled ridges and valleys that held the beds of Nancy Creek, Green Bone Creek, and others that fed into Peach Tree Creek below. The area now houses many of Atlanta's finest homes, including the governor's mansion. It was 10:00 AM before Wood's Division in the rear began to move. Wood's men had barely moved a half a mile by noon, the tail of the line moving so slowly through the forest because the front faced unusually stiff resistance.[21]

Mosman remembered, "Marched very slowly, with frequent halts, showing that we are feeling our way up against the enemy again." He added, "Well, we have had 13 days of practical freedom from the whiz of the Minnie during which time Sherman has crossed a large stream with his army in this presence of the enemy without any serious fighting." The Illinois lieutenant was in charge of the 59th Illinois Pioneer Corps, and during the day his unit, together with the pioneers of the 30th Indiana, were "ordered to the front to rebuild bridges over small streams, and we lead our Brigade on the march." As they drew further south, Rebel resistance stiffened. Mosman recorded, "Cannonading in front. A major comes back

---

[18]Ibid.

[19]Alexis Cope, *The 15th Ohio Volunteers and Its Campaigns: War of 1861–5* (Charleston SC: Nabu Press, 2011) 523.

[20]Chesley A. Mosman, *The Rough Side of War: Civil War Journal of Chesley A. Mosman* (Garden City NY: Basin Publishing Co., 1987) 244.

[21]Cope, *Fifteenth Ohio Volunteers and Its Campaigns*, 523.

from the front who reports that Harker's Brigade has the advance for our Corps and connects with Hooker's Corps on the right. See the effects of cannister shot on the trees, fences and buildings."[22]

Hooker's XX Corps Crosses Nancy Creek

While Howard's IV Corps advanced on Buckhead and Palmer's XIV Corps continued to move down the eastern side of the Chattahoochee River, Hooker's XX Corps got the task of advancing through the jungle-like country between these two points. One veteran from Ward's 3rd Division, William Cline of the 73rd Ohio, entered in his diary, "contery [countryside] cute to peaces with Hills ande Holowes Bute litel clearde lande a Rounde Here."[23] Hooker's soldiers struggled down country lanes and footpaths and over creek bottoms. The first such tributary was Nancy Creek. Cline recorded on the evening of 17 July, "Juste ate Darke orders cam to moove all trains ande mooved 8 oclock ate nighte marchede all nighte croste Railroade in a north este Direction from olde camp ande closte to the River we move to Hour lefte stoped fore Breckfast."[24] While the men of Palmer's XIV Corps fought their way southward toward Peach Tree Creek, Hooker's XX Corps moved to the east along today's West Paces Ferry Road to form a juncture with Howard's IV Corps.[25]

On 18 July, Hooker's men moved in earnest through the wooded ridges and ravines as his columns cut their way through the Georgia rain forest. Cline jotted down in his diary, "ate Daylighte this nighte wea moovede 8 miles so this Beinge the 18 sunshines verey worm ande Heavey skermishing going on in front."[26] Originally, Hooker had been ordered to send his three brigades forward during the night of 18 July, but as the Confederate resistance was stiffening on both flanks, his order was withdrawn. Cline noted, "ordederds came to moove the nighte of the 18 Bute [were]

---

[22]Mosman, *The Rough Side of War*, 244.

[23] Cline Diary, 165.

[24]Ibid.158.

[25]Julian, *Operations through the Present Ridgewood Community*, 8–13; Georgia Historical Markers, "Federal Right Wing," and "Federal Right Wing to Peachtree Creek;" Scaife, *Campaign for Atlanta*, 86–87; *OR*, series I, vol. 38, ser. no. 72, 524, 634, & 742, ser. no. 73, 33, 136, & 327.

[26]Cline Diary 159.

countermanded." The Ohio soldier added, "this is fulton countey georgey Sill in the woodes ande Have Bin ever Sence lefte Dalton."[27]

Opposing Hooker's advance across the middle valley of Nancy Creek was the veteran Georgia Cavalry Brigade of General Alfred Iverson. Iverson's Brigade consisted of the 1st Georgia Cavalry under Colonel Samuel W. Davitte, the 2nd Georgia Cavalry led by Colonel Charles C. Crews and Major James W. Mayo, the 3rd Georgia Cavalry commanded by Colonel Robert Thompson, the 4th Georgia Cavalry temporarily directed by Major Augustus R. Stewart (covering for the recovering Colonel Isaac W. Avery who was wounded on 26 May near New Hope Church), and the 6th Georgia Cavalry under Colonel John R. Hart.[28] Fighting dismounted, the Georgia Cavalry played havoc with Hooker's Corps as they "fought behind successive lines of breastworks in an attempt to slow Thomas's advance." Iverson's Georgians reported capturing some sixty Federals in the fighting of 18 July. During the action of the 18th, "Lt. James T. Newsome of the 2nd Georgia's G Company was captured here, but soon managed to escape." On 19 July, Wheeler took this force, together with the remainder of his cavalry to check McPherson's advance on Decatur and Atlanta from the east. This move left no Confederate force north of Peach Tree Creek to check Thomas's approach to the creek.[29]

On 19 July, Hooker had his men up early and on the march before daylight. His sights were on reaching and crossing Peach Tree Creek before dark. Hooker and Thomas were feeling pressure from Sherman, who was accusing Thomas's men of moving too slowly toward Atlanta while McPherson and Schofield raced toward Decatur to the east. During the day, rumors of Atlanta's fall to McPherson the previous evening filled the conversations of the men of the XX Corps as they marched. Cline remembered, "ande all upe to moove ate 5 this morninge pulde out ate sunupe ...travelde Som 9 miles and in campede closte to Atlanta verey wormee Bute a plesente winde Hour Boyes tooke posesion of Atlanta the

---

[27]Ibid., 159–60.

[28]*OR*, series I, vol. 38, ser. no. 74, 657, 665; Scaife, *Campaign for Atlanta*, 187.

[29]*OR*, series I, vol. 38, ser. no. 74, 951; John Randolph Poole, *Cracker Cavaliers: The 2nd Georgia Cavalry under Wheeler and Forrest* (Macon GA: Mercer University Press 2000) 128–29; W. D. Dodson, ed., *Campaigns of Wheeler and His Cavalry* (Atlanta: Hudgins Publishing Co.) 199.

eveninge Of the 18."[30] During the day, Ward's Division "pioneers and working parties were busily engaged building bridges across Peach Tree Creek."[31] By morning of 20 July, it was evident that the rumors of Atlanta's demise had been premature, and those who had eagerly spread it were shamefaced. More work lay ahead for them. The Rebels were not going to quit that easily. Cline noted in his journal early on 20 July, "worme with Heavey Canon adinge in fronte Hour Boyes note in atlanta as war Reported yesterday the 19 Bute within two miles of the place this morninge traines all quiete Bute troopes mooves to the fronte."[32]

Meanwhile, opposite the Federal XX Corps, Private M. D. McQueen of the 29th Alabama of O'Neal's (formerly Cantey's) Brigade found time to write a few lines to his wife, Axis, in Wilsonville, Alabama.

Johnson's Army, Atlanta, Ga.
July 18, 1864

Dear Wife and Children: —I this day try to send you a line from our line of battle. This leaves me well, and I hope this will soon reach you, and find you all well. Our army is between Atlanta and the Chattahoochie River, in line of battle. We are expecting hard fighting to-day. I heard this morning that the enemy are now crossing the river; if so, we will be fighting in a few minutes. Our regiment has been fighting over two months, and the enemy has backed us all the time. We have lost a great many men, and what men we have left are worsted and bad, and very lousey, and nearly naked. I have stood it very well so far. I have one coat, one shirt, one pair pants, two pair drawers, one pair shoes, and a piece of a hat, and a good blanket. I want all of you to eat some fruit and think of me. If I had ever so many clothes I could not take care of them.

This is a long and hard fight. I have had to move about a mile through the woods since I commenced writing this letter, and now I do not know whether I can get to send it to you. I want you to write to me oftener; and when I am here, direct your letters to J. E. Johnson's Army, Cantie's Brigade, 29th Ala. Reg., Co. H. I have not had any news from you in a long time. You must all try and take good care of yourselves. Good bye.
M. D. McQueen[33]

---

[30]Cline Diary, 160–61.

[31]*OR*, series I, vol, 38, ser. no. 73, 327.

[32]Cline Diary, 160–61.

[33]Ithaca *Journal*, 24 August 1864.

Writing from his post along Peach Tree Creek on the morning of 18 July, McQueen was still unaware of Johnston's removal from command. He was also unaware that he would have only two more days to live. McQueen was killed during a charge at the Battle of Peach Tree Creek on 20 July when his regiment attacked through the forests located near the intersection of today's Northside Drive and Collier Road.[34]

---

[34]Ibid.

16

THE BATTLE OF MOORE'S MILL

I am damned tired and ready to give up![1]

The 2nd Division of General Palmer's XIV Corps of the Army of the Cumberland were among the last of Sherman's men to cross over to the southern shores of the Chattahoochee River at Pace's Ferry. The 2nd Division, commanded by General Jefferson C. Davis, sent the 1st and 2nd Brigades over on Sunday, 17 July, while the 3rd Brigade crossed before daylight on 18 July.[2] Driving the Rebel pickets before them, the 1st and 2nd Brigades managed to push back Wheeler's Confederate Cavalry beyond Nancy's Creek on 17 July. On Monday, 18 July, "skirmishers from the 22nd Indiana drove the enemy to Peach Tree Creek, near Howell's Mill."[3]

William H. Berryhill, 1st Lieutenant in the 43rd Mississippi, commanded the Pioneers Corps for Adams's Mississippi Brigade. He wrote his family on Monday, 18 July:

> Gen. Adams prepared to fight them but Gen. Loring stopped him and ordered him to fall back across Peachtree Creek which is a half mile from where we were yesterday. Adams had a man or two killed and several wounded. I was not with the Brigade. I was ordered across the creek with the wagons and went across the bridge before the Yankees came up. I and 12 of my corps [Pioneers Corps] are at a large bridge for the purpose of burning it if the Yankees advance upon it.

Berryhill explained that his detachment had arrived the night before at the bridge over Peach Tree Creek at Moore's Mill. He wrote, "We came here at dark last night and piled up dry rails upon the bridge and under it.

---

[1]W. C. Thompson, "From the Defenses of Atlanta to a Federal Prison Camp," *Civil War Times Illustrated* 10 (February 1965): 40.

[2]Henry J. Aten, *History of the Eighty-Fifth Regiment, Illinois volunteer Infantry* (Hiawatha KS: Henry J. Aten, 1901) 196; John Hill Ferguson, *On to Atlanta: The Civil War Diaries of John Hill Ferguson, 10th Illinois Regiment of Volunteers,* ed. Janet Correll Ellison and Mark Weitz (Lincoln: University of Nebraska Press, 2008) 62.

[3]Aten, *History of the Eighty-Fifth Regiment,* 196

We had lots of pine split up and every man had a handful." Berryhill described their vigil at the bridge all Sunday evening: "We kept fire burning all night ready to light our torches and put fire to the bridge, but the Yanks have not come up yet so we have not burned the bridge and the sun is 2 hours high. Our brigade is in line of battle on the hill close to the bridge."[4]

On Tuesday, 19 July, while passing the time away before the anticipated Yankee thrust over Peach Tree Creek, Lieutenant Berryhill wrote his wife. "We thought this morning that there would be a battle today," he wrote, "but up to this hour, 12 o'clock, I see no more sign of it than there was yesterday." Berryhill and his compatriots had not seen any evidence of a Federal advance in the tangled woods on the other side of Peach Tree Creek. "Adams' brigade had like to have gotten into a fight Sunday evening," he wrote;

> I expect would if Gen. Loring had not come up just in time to stop Gen. Adams, who then fell back across Peachtree Creek at Brown or Moors Mill (I forgot which). [Actually, it was at Moore's Mill.] It is a large creek and had a long bridge on it but I burned it up last night. Our men hold our side of the creek and the enemy the other.[5]

Reynolds's Arkansas Brigade was among the last Confederate infantry to cross to the south side of Peach Tree Creek. As "the last Rebel soldiers crossed...the bridge was set on fire. Just at the fire was set, Federal skirmishers arrived and began shooting at them. As skirmishing continued into the night, Reynolds extended his brigade along a mile long line to protect against any Federals crossing the creek."[6] A section of Yates's Battery of Artillery also aided in keeping the Yankees at bay.[7]

While the Confederates burned all of the bridges across the creek, the Yankees spent the morning "searching for a place where that stream could

---

[4]William H. Berryhill, *The Gentle Rebel: The Civil War Letters of William Harvey Berryhill, 1st Lieutenant, Company D, 43rd Regiment, Mississippi Volunteers*, ed. Mary Miles Jones and Leslie Jones Martin (Yazoo City MS: The Sassafras Press, 1982) 56.

[5]Berryhill, *Gentle Rebel*, 57.

[6]Ronald R. Bass, *History of the 31st Arkansas Confederate Infantry* (Conway AR: Arkansas Research, 1996) 75.

[7]*OR*, series I, vol. 38, ser. no. 74, 935.

be crossed."[8] The men of Dilworth's 3rd Brigade of Davis's Division moved slowly toward the creek, stopping frequently for skirmishers to look for a suitable crossing. At each short halt, "the men busied themselves gathering the fresh ripe blackberries that grew in great abundance by the roadside."[9] As the brigade got closer to Peach Tree Creek, they came across a conference being held along the road by generals Thomas, Palmer, and Davis, the unit's army, corps, and division commanders. It was clear to the men that they were about to embark on a mission of vital importance and that they would soon see action as they marched past the collection of "high brass." According to First Sergeant Henry J. Aten of the 85th Illinois, "There were occasional shots, and rifle balls fell about or whizzed harmlessly overhead.... As the 85th [Illinois] passed the group, a well-spent ball struck the boot of General Davis, making his foot sting for a moment, and his companions rallied him on getting the first hit."[10]

Davis's 2nd Division was on the extreme right of the Yankee armies, and it maintained its connection with the southern side of the Chattahoochee River while feeling its way forward in the woods and creek beds. In front of Davis's Division, Sears's Mississippi Brigade led by General Claudius Sears had been buying time, skirmishing, and falling back, which allowed the remainder of Stewart's Corps to slip down below Peach Tree Creek and establish a line of defense. Meanwhile, Ector's Texas and North Carolina Brigade prepared a substantial line of works on a protruding ridge, which forced Peach Tree Creek to circle it from the north at the mouth of Nancy Creek. Ector's men and Sears's Mississippians did such an effective job of blocking the Federal army's efforts to cross Peach Tree Creek between Moore's Mill and Peach Tree's confluence with the Chattahoochee River that it was Thursday, 21 July, before General James D. Morgan's 1st Brigade of Davis's 2nd Division could cross—and only after Sears's men had withdrawn the evening before. With Sears's determined fighters and the wide Peach Tree Creek in front of them, the Chattahoochee River to their right, or west of them, and a mill pond to their left, or east of them,

---

[8] Aten, *History of the Eighty-Fifth Regiment*, 196.
[9] Ibid., 196.
[10] Ibid., 197.

Morgan's Brigade was perfectly bottled up and held in check for three days.[11]

After reaching the mouth of Nancy Creek on the afternoon of 18 July, the 10th Illinois found themselves in a shoot out from several directions. With portions of the Regiment on both sides of Nancy Creek, the Illinois troops had inadvertently gotten pinned down below the commanding heights on the opposite side of Peach Tree Creek. From that position, Ector's Brigade kept it hot for the Illinois men. "Last night Companies I, H & D got so close to the Rebel works that our regiment could not be relieved today. So we have to remain until after dark," recorded John Hill Ferguson of the 10th Illinois. "After dinner, companies D, G, B, & C were ordered to advance and take possession of the creek at all hazzards. We advanced with caution feeling our way carefully, but no resistance was made. We got [to] the creek without any trouble." Ferguson explained, "We could see the Rebel work through the trees and under brush not over 30 yards from the creek in places. Their reason for not fireing on us was they wanted us to cross and advance towards their works, then they would make a dash on us and kill and capture the most of us."[12] Their brigade commander, General Morgan, feared such a strategy and according to one officer, "acted with caution."[13] The 10th Illinois remained pinned down by the Confederate fire from the bluffs opposite them along Peach Tree Creek until they were relieved by the 60th Illinois at dusk.[14]

In this area, a gristmill known as Moore's Mill, was located along Peach Tree Creek above the mouth of Nancy Creek and at the mouth of a small tributary known as Woodall Creek.[15] There, Morgan's Brigade was held up by the mill pond located there and the wild Texans and North Carolinians of Ector's Brigade on the heights overlooking the creek from the southern shore of Peach Tree Creek. Moore's Mill was a sash-saw mill and, closer to Nancy Creek, a gristmill "connected by a flume with the dam

---

[11]*OR*, series I, vol. 38, ser. no. 72, 670–71.

[12]Ibid., 659; Ferguson, *On to Atlanta*, 64.

[13]Ferguson, *On to Atlanta*, 64.

[14]Ibid.

[15]*OR*, series I, vol. 38, ser. no. 72, 670–71; Carol Proctor Scruggs, "Moore's Mill," *Georgia Historical Markers* (Valdosta GA: Bay Tree Grove Publishing, 1977) 221; Supplement to the *OR*, part II, vol. 31, ser. no. 43, 7.

which impounded the water of Peachtree and Woodall Creeks."[16] There was a ford across Peach Tree Creek below the dam.

During the afternoon of 19 July, the 10th Michigan deployed about thirty men as sharpshooters to occupy the attention of Ector's force while they figured out a way to get around the millpond. They also wanted to find a place to get across Peach Tree Creek without facing the entrenched Confederates on the heights while exposed to fire. According to Colonel Charles M. Lum of the 10th Michigan Infantry, "Several of our sharpshooters were hit by the rebels, who kept up a very hot fire, and 1 was killed before dark."[17] After dusk, three more companies from the 10th Michigan were sent forward to join the sharpshooters, and together they threw up some rifle pits to try to find protection from the vicious fire they were taking from the Rebels. One of the companies found protection in the gristmill. They climbed up to the loft and roof and were then as high or higher than the Rebel trenches on the opposite bank of the creek. They began exchanging fire with Sears's men from Moore's Mill where they were "only a few rods from the rebel works," or probably only about fifty to seventy-five yards.[18] During the night, some of the engineers of the 10th Michigan "destroyed the flume, letting out the water above the dam," according to General Morgan.[19] "When morning broke, a hot fire was opened on both sides and in our front," explained Colonel Charles M. Lum of the 10th Michigan; "Not a Johnnie was safe in showing a hand above his works; but from a flanking position they raked the ground, so that it was not safe for one of our men to leave his pit."[20]

As evening drew over the Moore's Mill fighting, Sears's Mississippi Brigade, which had been given a brief respite during the day from its fighting during the past two or three days north of Peach Tree Creek, replaced Ector's tired Texans and North Carolinians on the commanding heights south of Moore's Mill. Ector and his little brigade of just a thousand men held off four times their number for a day and a half, but at a cost of six killed, thirty-two wounded, and six missing, for a total loss of forty-four

---

[16]Scruggs, "Moore's Mill."
[17]*OR*, series I, vol. 38, ser. no. 72, 670.
[18]Ibid., 670–71. One rod was 16.5 feet, so 20 rods were 330 feet or 110 yards.
[19]Ibid., 649.
[20]Ibid., 671.

casualties. These casualties occurred chiefly during the sporadic rifle shooting throughout 19 July between Ector's Brigade and portions of Morgan's and Mitchell's brigades.[21] During the fighting along the Chattahoochee River and Peach Tree Creek (including both skirmish fire between 17 and 19 July north of the creek and defense of the Moore's Mill heights overlooking south of the creek on 20 July), Sears lost seven men killed, fifty-eight wounded, and fifty-one captured.[22]

Morgan's Brigade

The 10th Michigan lost twenty men killed and wounded, according to Colonel Lum, including Lieutenant Richard Teal, killed, and Lieutenant Dewitt C. Welling, wounded.[23] According to other sources, the 10th Michigan lost twenty-three killed and wounded.[24] Fighting alongside of the 10th Michigan were the 10th Illinois, the 16th Illinois, the 60th Illinois, and the 14th Michigan—all from Morgan's 1st Brigade.[25] Among the wounded were, on 18 July, Major Samuel J. Wilson, Captain Frank A. Munson, and a private in Company J, from the 10th Illinois.[26] On 19 July, the 10th Illinois lost one killed and six wounded, three mortally.[27] In the 16th Illinois, on 20 July, Sergeant Hamline, Corporal Hamline and Private J. M. Forrest of Company A were all captured.[28] In the action on 20 July,

---

[21]*OR*, series I, vol. 38, part I, ser. no. 74, pp. 908–9; part IV, ser. no. 76, 178–79.

[22]*OR*, series I, vol. 38, part III, ser. no. 74, 909.

[23]*OR*, series I, vol. 38, part I, ser. no. 72, 671; John Robertson, *Michigan in the War* (Lansing MI: W. S. George & Co., 1882) 308; Edwin Orin Wood, *History of Genesee County, Michigan: Her People, Industries and Institutions* (Charleston SC: Nabu Press, 2011) 387; Charles Lanman, *The Red Book of Michigan: A Civil, Military, and Biographical History* (Ann Arbor: University of Michigan Library, 2005) 348.

[24]Wood, *History of Genesee County*, 387; and Lanman, *Red Book of Michigan*, 348; but see Robertson, *Michigan in the War*, 308, which reported that in addition to the death of Lieutenant Teal and the wounding of Lieutenant "Willing," the 10th Michigan lost 17 men wounded, for a total of 19.

[25]William R. Scaife, *The Campaign for Atlanta* (Atlanta: self-published, 1993) 151.

[26]*OR*, series I, vol. 38, part I, ser. no. 72, 658–59.

[27]Ferguson, *On to Atlanta*, 62–66.

[28]*OR*, series I, vol. 38, part I, ser. no. 72, 662.

the 60th Illinois lost one officer killed, one enlisted man killed, and one enlisted man wounded.[29] Thus, Morgan's 1st Brigade lost, in three days of fighting, ten men killed, thirty-four men wounded (three mortally), and three men captured, for a total loss of forty-seven men. Portions of Mitchell's 2nd Brigade, particularly Colonel Henry B. Banning and his 121st Ohio Regiment (together with a couple of companies that had been detached from the 34th Illinois), also tangled with Ector's Brigade and Sears's Mississippians along Peach Tree Creek between the mouth of Nancy Creek and the Chattahoochee River.

The skirmishing and contested crossings of Peach Tree Creek by the Federal's Army of the Cumberland on Tuesday, 19 July, reached its climax in the action that has all but been lost from history. In what came to be called the Battle of Moore's Mill, Colonel Caleb J. Dilworth led his 3rd Brigade of Davis's 2nd Division in a hotly contested battle to secure a bridgehead over the creek near the mouth of Green Bone Creek. Before it was over, portions of two Confederate brigades and two Federal brigades would spill their blood and trade ground three times in fierce hand-to-hand combat. By dusk, the Yankees would hold the crossing, but they would pay dearly for their efforts.

Needing to secure a crossing over Peach Tree Creek, and with his other two brigades pinned down between the area around Moore's Mill and the Chattahoochee River to the west (because the Confederate positions on the heights south of the creek commanded all approaches in that area), General Jefferson C. Davis ordered Dilworth and his 3rd Brigade to find a place to cross and to take his brigade over to the south side of the creek east of the mill. Dilworth found what he thought was an opportunity on the low ground opposite the terminus of Green Bone Creek, a small tributary that flowed south into Peach Tree Creek. There, his men could cross the creek just out reach of the Confederate rifle pits located on a ridge on the south bank and overlooking the mill. Then, they could push into the interior of the wooded countryside. With this lodgment secured, reasoned Dilworth and Davis, a flanking movement could sweep the Confederates off of the heights opposite the mill.

To accomplish this task, at 1:00 PM Dilworth ordered Major J. T. Holmes to take five companies of the 52nd Ohio across a foot-log that had

---

[29]Ibid., 665.

been found to cross the creek. According to Sergeant Aten, "This was at a point near the mouth of Green Bone Creek, and a short distance beyond the crossing was a bluff some fifty feet in height, on which the enemy's skirmish line rested."[30] Taking half of the 52nd Ohio, "Major Holmes deployed his skirmishers in the bushes to the right and down the stream, and as soon as his reserve reached the south bank, all dashed forward with a shout and drove the enemy from the crest of the bluff and some four hundred yards beyond."[31] According to Sergeant Nixon B. Stewart, the regiment crossed

> on a log 28 feet from bank to bank. The water was about 8 feet deep and could not be forded. While we were laughing at an unlucky fellow in Co. H, who fell from the foot-log, the rebels opened fire on us from their skirmish line. As we reached the top of the hill, the enemy poured a galling fire on our right flank, and turned our left by a heavy reinforcement. The 98th Ohio had crossed above us, and came to our rescue, the enemy retreating into a dense pine thicket.[32]

With the rest of the regiment under the command of Lieutenant Colonel Charles W. Clancy across, the 52nd Ohio disappeared into the Georgia wilderness. "The left wing of our regiment, with Col. Clancy, was deployed in front and pushed down into the pines and lay down," remembered Sergeant Stewart. He continued, "The regiment worked like beavers completing a barricade of rails, behind which they lay. The advance sentinels came rushing back, shouting 'They are charging in front, four lines deep, with fixed bayonets.'"[33] Needing to support the bridgehead created by the Ohioans, Dilworth ordered the 85th Illinois to the south bank of Peach Tree Creek. "Crossing a stream in single file on a log takes time," remembered one veteran, "but as all realized the emergency the men passed rapidly over; ran eagerly up the bluff, and into line at the top. In front of the regiment as it formed on the crest, lay an open field, and beyond that was thick timber."[34] First Sergeant Henry J. Aten of Company G in the 85th

---

[30]Aten, *History of the Eighty-Fifth Regiment*, 197.

[31]Ibid.

[32]Nixon B. Stewart, *Dan McCook's Regiment, 52nd O.V.I.: A History of the Regiment, Its Campaigns and Battles from 1862 to 1865* (1900; repr., Huntington WV: Blue Acorn Press, 1999) 129–30.

[33]Stewart, *Dan McCook's Regiment*, 130.

[34]Aten, *History of the Eighty-Fifth Regiment*, 197.

Illinois explained, "the sharp, continuous firing gave notice that there was hot work on hand, and the 85th [Illinois] was hurried to the support of the 52nd [Ohio]."[35]

On the Confederate side, the veteran units of General A. P. Stewart's Army of Mississippi had been stretched thin trying to defend a stretch of territory from the Chattahoochee River crossings northwest of Atlanta to Peach Tree Creek from its mouth to near today's Northside Drive (roughly eight miles). At today's Northside Drive, which was also near the Howell Mill, Stewart's men connected with the left of Hardee's Corps, which was nearly twice as large as Stewart's corps-sized army. Stewart's army numbered fewer than 10,000 infantry with a total strength of about 12,400 men including artillery, staff, and escorts. While the remainder of Hood's army screened Atlanta from the probes of McPherson's and Schofield's Federal forces from the north and east, Stewart's men were charged with the task of trying to slow the majority of Thomas's Army of the Cumberland as its 60,000 man force probed for crossings over Peach Tree Creek.

During the course of the Georgia Campaign, the Southern army developed a fairly sound system of movement for its units as the men continually fell back from one position to another under the direction of General Joe Johnston. Most of Johnston's force was organized into groups of three brigades to a division. Ordinarily, one brigade guarded a position along the front of the line while a second brigade rested in its rear. This strategy served both to prepare a new line of entrenchments should they have to fall back to them and to be in supporting distance of the front should they need to be reinforced. Or, if the space being defended needed additional troops, two brigades were placed in the front line. The third brigade would then be free to move to one flank or another to strike an offensive blow, defend a flanking action by the Yankees, or fall further back behind the lines to rest and prepare yet a third line of defensive works. By rotating brigades in this manner, the outnumbered Confederates had been able both to thwart Federal probes and find some rest for their weary veterans. Because Sherman had numerical superiority with a force of 100,000–110,000 men to Johnston's 40,000–55,000 men (after receiving the reinforcements from the Army of Mississippi), this plan proved vital to keeping the army intact, relatively fresh, and confident.

---

[35]Ibid.

There were a couple of drawbacks to this arrangement, however. First, Southern brigades in both the Army of Tennessee and the Army of Mississippi ranged widely in terms of troop strength; some units were as small as 500 in Reynolds's Arkansas Brigade in the Army of Mississippi to 2,000 in Mercer's Georgia Brigade in Hardee's Corps. Typically, orders from corps and army commanders called for a brigade or a division to perform a certain task. On paper, most brigades in the Southern armies at this point in the war averaged 1,500 men while most divisions were fewer than 5,000 men. Therefore, when looking at defending a position or taking an offensive action, Confederate leaders were accustomed to using these figures when making tactical decisions and issuing orders.

For example, it was generally considered that a division front was about a mile in width, meaning that about 5,000 men could fill the space of 5,280 feet, assuming a double-file rank. Thus, when a Rebel commander asked a unit to move "a half of a division front," he meant for it to move a half a mile. Brigades should, therefore, naturally be able to cover about a third of a mile in width under this system. But, with the desire to group units by state (including adding newly arrived regiments to a brigade from the same state and with the inevitability of uneven fighting throughout a hard campaign), some units remained large in size if not experience, while others dwindled dramatically in troop strength but grew in moxie. To a lesser degree, the same inequity in unit size was found in Federal brigades, but as units were purposely mixed up with regiments from different states, and as division and corps commanders were able to transfer regiments freely from one brigade to another to keep relative balance among the brigades, it was much easier to manage and maintain relative equality in troop sizes among Federal brigades.

A second problem resulting from the Confederate system of rotating front line responsibility was that quite often, brigades from different divisions or even from different corps lined up next to each other. In many instances, they were compelled to work together during an engagement without a clear commander over the two brigades or with a leader from one unit or the other who tried unsuccessfully to impose his authority over the sister unit. This unintended circumstance created many examples of cooperation, but it also led to missed assignments and unnecessary risks of breaches to the Southern lines. While the Rebel breakdown in command structure could have been avoided by simply following the orders of the ranking officer on the field, all too often, soldiers responded only to their own commanders. Soldiers (usually from the same state or even from the same county or region of the state) understood and followed their unit's command style, so men usually followed their own leader, regardless of which officer was senior and particularly so when they faced conflicting orders.

These two problems created the perfect storm of danger for the Confederate forces defending the south bank of Peach Tree Creek around Moore's Mill on Tuesday, 19 July. First, General John Adams and his all-Mississippi Brigade from Loring's Division of Stewart's Army of Mississippi for two days had been successfully guarding the region around Peach Tree Creek above Moore's Mill. Second, to his left overlooking the mill and west of the mill was posted Ector's small Texas and North Carolina Brigade from French's Division. To the right, Reynolds's undersized Arkansas Brigade was assigned the space between Adams's right and the left of Hardee's Corps covered by Gist's Brigade. Thus, across a space of some three miles or so four Confederate brigades from four different divisions, including one from a different corps, were required to coordinate their efforts in shielding the south bank of Peach Tree Creek. At the same time, the army was adjusting to Johnston's removal from command.

The portion of the line overlooking the mouth of Green Bone Creek and the alluvial plain that formed on the south side of Peach Tree Creek (where the Federal crossing was about to be made) had been guarded by two companies of the 6th Mississippi and the 15th Mississippi Regiment led by Colonel Mike Farrell, a hard-fighting Irishman who had migrated to the South before the War.[36] This force numbered no more than 350 men out of the 1,500-man Mississippi Brigade of General Adams. During the past two days, these men had more or less picketed the half-mile space, but they had not received any significant threat from the slowly advancing Federals.

In the afternoon of 19 July, and immediately prior to the surprise crossing of Peach Tree Creek by the Federal forces, the Mississippians of the 15th and a part of the 6th Regiment were replaced by General Daniel Reynolds and his undersized Arkansas Brigade of General Walthall's Division. Reynolds's small brigade mustered only about six hundred rifles. Moreover, the 9th Arkansas (about eighty men) was compelled to remain in

---

[36]*OR*, series I, vol. 38, part III, ser. no. 74, 891.

its position east of the rest of Reynolds's Brigade. The 9th Arkansas served on picket detail with elements of General Gist's South Carolina and Georgia troops from Walker's Division of Hardee's Corps to cover the space just vacated by Reynolds's Brigade.

Thus, General Reynolds found himself trying to place his remaining force of about 520 Arkansans along a stretch of about a half a mile, which, if deployed in the manner the Mississippians had previously been compelled to do, would have been no more than a mere skirmish line of vedettes, a line of men roughly six feet apart. Unfortunately for Reynolds, however, before his men could get settled, an entire Federal brigade was forming to cross in his front, followed by a second Federal brigade from the north side of Peach Tree Creek, and yet a third brigade ready to cross and support a Federal bridgehead. Without support from the rear, and with a part of his own force detached and serving a mile or more away to the east with a brigade from a different division and corps, Reynolds turned to Colonel Farrell and his men, who had just moved from the position to take a new one a little further to the left and nearer Moore's Mill where they were to replace Ector's small brigade.[37]

At 1:00 PM, General Reynolds and his brigade was relieved by General Gist's Brigade except for the eighty men on the extreme left of Reynolds's line, and eighty men of the 9th Arkansas on the right of his line, who remained because they "could not be relieved from posts on the Pace's Ferry Road [today's Howell Mill Road] on account of the exposed position." Reynolds moved his small brigade to the left of the eighty men from the 7th Arkansas that remained on the left side of his original position. The space required to be covered was so large that when he redeployed, he placed the 25th Arkansas on a wide skirmish line between the right of General Adams's Mississippi Brigade, which was in front of and just east of Moore's Mill (near today's Moore's Mill Road and along the DeFoor's Ferry Road line as it faced Peach Tree Creek), and to the left of his eighty men from the 7th Arkansas that had remained (in the area near where Interstate 75 crosses Peach Tree Creek today). Reynolds did not have enough men to connect the points, and his left was several hundred yards away from the right of Adams's Brigade. He put the remainder of his brigade behind a skirmish line manned by the 9th Arkansas to give them a brief rest before he set out

---

[37] Ibid., 891, 893–94.

to examine his weak and exposed lines. Reynolds explained, "The men [the 25th Arkansas] were deployed at from five to ten paces apart." He then went to check the gap between his forces on the right when he discovered that "the enemy were passing to the left in front of our skirmishers, and had been doing so for some time; and anticipating an attack I proceeded at once to where my command was resting in the road, but before reaching the road I heard the shout of the enemy, who charged across the field in front of the gap and the right of the line just posted."[38]

The 25th Arkansas "was compelled to retire," explained Reynolds, "leaving two of their number prisoners." Reynolds then ordered Lieutenant Colonel Smith and the 2nd Arkansas "to move rapidly to support" the 25th Arkansas. He next ordered his remaining available force, the 1st Arkansas and the 4th Arkansas (which included the 31st Arkansas), "to deploy rapidly to fill up the gap, thinking it might only be a line of skirmishers," that his little brigade faced. He wrote, "The troops moved at a double-quick, but before they arrived at their designated positions I found the enemy were in force in line of battle and extending across and to the right and left of the gap, and were at the road in front of which [on each side of the gap] ran our picket line." This road generally followed the path of today's Defoors Ferry Road on the west side of the gap, but the road no longer exists east of the gap.[39]

To defend the breach, Reynolds would need a force of at least two full-strength brigades. Instead, he had available his undersized brigade of only 520 men (about a third of a brigade) to cover the Confederate right half of the breach in their line, Farrell's 15th Mississippi, and the two companies from the 6th Mississippi, a force of some 300 to 350 men, or roughly one-fifth of a brigade, to cover the Confederate left flank.[40] Clearly, Reynolds was going to either need a lot more men, or a super-ordinary effort by the ones at his disposal.

---

[38]Ibid., 935; Bass, *History of the 31st Arkansas Confederate Infantry*, 75.

[39]*OR*, series I, vol. 38, part III, ser. no. 74, 935–36.

[40]Dunbar Rowland, *Military History of Mississippi 1803–1898* (Jackson MS: Mississippi Dept. of Archives and History, 1908; repr. Spartanburg SC: The Reprint Co., 1988) 177.

Colonel Mike Farrell

Colonel Mike Farrell was no ordinary man, and his veteran 15th Mississippi Infantry Regiment were no ordinary soldiers. Veterans of three hard years of fighting, the 15th Mississippi had been galvanized into one of the South's finest fighting regiments. With an average age of twenty-three and with 75 percent of the men unmarried, the 15th Mississippi was the perfect balance of mature, healthy young men, most of whom didn't have wives and children at home. While more than two-thirds of the men were farmers, the others were a varied bunch, ranging from mechanics to merchants, carpenters to clerks, and blacksmiths to brick masons. One such brick mason was Mike Farrell, the son of Irish immigrants.[41]

Little is known of Farrell's personal background. It is unclear whether he was born in Ireland or in New York where his parents settled. By the time the Civil War broke out, Farrell had learned masonry while working at the Jefferson Barracks in St. Louis. He also had the skills of an infantry drillmaster, but whether he learned them while enlisted in the pre-war US Army or while laying bricks at the barracks is unknown. Regardless of how he learned, his ability to be an infantry drillmaster would earn him rapid promotion through the ranks after he enlisted as a private in the 15th Mississippi. A company of that regiment was being formed at Grenada, Mississippi, where he moved just before the war began. In the rural South, and especially north-central Mississippi, it was unusual to find an Irish-Catholic. While the overwhelming majority of immigrants to the South had come from Protestant parts of Ireland, England, and Scotland, most Irish-Catholic immigrants had settled in urban centers such as New York, Philadelphia, or Boston. Many Southerners had come to distrust "foreigners and Catholics," pronounced "furi'ners and cat-licks." With the prejudices of the day, it is remarkable that the thickly accented Irishman rose to lead this Mississippi regiment, but his strong character and sense of duty to his adopted Magnolia State had won the hearts of his men. Farrell stood six feet tall and wore his black hair straight, covering the brows above his blue eyes. Farrell had "the solid build of an athlete," and, surprisingly, had more than an average education as "he traveled with a copy of Shakespeare in his saddle

---

[41]Ed Gleeson, *New York Irish-Catholic Bricklayer in Gray: Colonel Mike Farrell Falls at Franklin*, courtesy Carter House Library and Archives, Franklin TN, 1–4, 9–10.

bags." He made the rank of colonel of the 15th Mississippi by 20 July 1862, just fourteen months after he had enlisted as a private. Colonel Farrell was not a rich man, either; the only horse he ever owned was one named Bullet, a gift from the officers and men of his beloved regiment.[42] Farrell was an extraordinary man, and his record was one of proud, bold service, replete with successes.

15th Mississippi

Baptized in battle at Mill Springs, Kentucky, in one of the first fights of the war on 19 January 1862, Farrell and the 15th Mississippi lost 44 men killed, 153 wounded, and 29 missing for a total of 226 men out of the 540 Confederates lost at that battle.[43] At the Battle of Shiloh, the 15th Mississippi again suffered staggering losses, with some 200 men falling out of the 500 that she brought into the fray.[44] In February 1864, Colonel Farrell led the 15th Mississippi in a drill contest against the 3rd Kentucky from the famous Kentucky Orphan Brigade while they were encamped at Canton, Mississippi. To settle a long dispute between the rival units, each regiment was given "an hour and a half to demonstrate their skills 'in the various movements in the manual of arms and other activities of military display.'" After a hotly contested contest witnessed by the entire town, the 15th Mississippi won both the admiration of the ladies of the village and the prize, a silk flag newly made by Mrs. Lattimore and other ladies of Canton.[45] The 15th Mississippi was no ordinary unit and included a number of officers and men who were fully capable of leading a regiment in battle, including Colonel Mike Farrell, Lieutenant Colonel James R. Binford, Captain Tom Gibson, Captain John L. Collins, and others who were often called upon to exercise independent commands. Earlier, the 15th Mississippi had given the Confederacy Major General E. C. Walthall, who had joined the 15th as a lieutenant in Company E, and Brigadier General William F. Brantley, who started as a captain in Company G.[46]

---

[42]Ibid., 1–10.

[43]Kenneth A. Hafendorfer, *Mill Springs: Campaign and Battle of Mill Springs, Kentucky* (Louisville KY: K H Press, 2001) 582–88.

[44]Ben Wynne, *A Hard Trip: A History of the 15th Mississippi Infantry, C. S. A.* (Macon GA: Mercer University Press, 2010) 77.

[45]Gleeson, *New York Irish-Catholic Bricklayer in Gray*, 7–10.

[46]Wynne, *A Hard Trip*, 3–33.

After just having moved to the left toward Moore's Mill, Colonel Farrell was approached by a dispatcher riding hard and requesting that Farrell and the Mississippians return to help him stop the Federal surge. The rider was none other than General Reynolds. The Irish colonel quickly summoned his troops to respond. The Mississippians rushed to recover the lost ground. Coming from the left or west of the Confederate position, Farrell's Mississippians came from a line located along today's Defoor Hills Road. Just northeast of there, across today's Defoor's Ferry Road and into a small gap in the ridge where today's Bohler Road switches back through it, was the 52nd Ohio Regiment, which had arrived only minutes before. The Ohioans had discarded their guns and knapsacks and busily began burrowing themselves into the ground as they began to erect breastworks. What happened next became legendary in homes across the Magnolia State.

According to Lieutenant Colonel James R. Binford of the 15th Mississippi, "General Reynolds had scarcely got his men on the line and before we could get our men together, when the enemy crossed the creek and charged him, driving his Brigade back from a line the 15th Miss. had successfully held for twenty-four hours." General Reynolds turned to Colonel Farrell for help. Binford witnessed the conversation:

> General Reynolds came dashing up to Colonel Farrell and requested him to return with the 15th [Mississippi] and help him retake the line. Notwithstanding his orders to return to camp as relieved, Col. Farrell was unwilling to leave our friends in distress, so he told General R. [Reynolds] to go back and recapture the right and he would take the left. By this time the Yanks had crossed in considerable force and had piled up their knapsacks and began throwing up breastworks.[47]

Farrell had directed his men into action so quickly that they had not yet had time to load their rifles. "Farrell advanced with the 15th [Mississippi] and soon came under the fire of the enemy. Exchanging a few shots with them, he ordered a charge and with that peculiar yell of the old 15th this Regiment went forward at a double quick...," explained Binford. "We drove the enemy back across the Creek capturing 193 prisoners, together with a number of guns, all their knapsacks, spades, picks, etc., but it cost us

---

[47]James R. Binford, "Recollections of the Fifteenth Regiment of Mississippi Infantry, C. S. A.," p. 50, vol. 5, box 2, Patrick Henry Papers, Mississippi Department of Archives and History (MDAH), Jackson MS, 75.

considerable, for in the charge we lost over 50 men and among them several officers," including Lt. Hugh Montgomery of Company I, who was killed. "It was in this charge that Lt. Richard N. Hall of Company G, also a brave and dashing officer," exclaimed Binford, "was the first to go over the Yankee works and as he leaped upon the top of the works, he saw a Yankee kneeling down loading his gun. Lt. Dick cried out 'Surrender!' and as the fellow was not as prompt in reply as Hall thought he ought to be," continued the Mississippian, "he brought his sword down with considerable force in his head cutting an ugly gash. It is unnecessary to say the Yank promptly surrendered." The Mississippians followed Hall's example. "Several of the Regiment had now scaled the works and finding the enemy engaged in the same business that Lt. Hall's man was, they were very promptly knocked down with their guns, as we had made the charge with empty guns."[48]

The surprised Yankees were quickly overwhelmed, and the 15th Mississippi bagged the majority of the 52nd Ohio in a matter of minutes. The rest of the shattered Ohio unit had fled to Peach Tree Creek and, discarding their knapsacks, rifles, and any other equipment that was slowing them down, waded, swam, and groped their way across the large creek to the safety of its northern banks. Sergeant Nixon B. Stewart of the 52nd Ohio recalled, "We must get out to let our men in the works open fire. 'Twas madness to defer. It was run the gauntlet or be taken to Andersonville prison, or death. They were upon us. The Colonel with 13 men went to prison, the rest filed to the right, down a small ravine, and started for liberty or death. It was the devil's own corner." The rout was on as Farrell's Mississippians chased the fleeing Ohioans. "We were but half way from the starting point to the brow of the hill," remembered Sgt. Stewart, "when the enemy poured a deadly volley into our ranks. Here 29 of the 154 fell, dead or wounded...."[49] Included among the Federal captured was Lieutenant Colonel Charles W. Clancy, commander of the 52nd Ohio. With some thirty-one men killed, wounded, or missing in his Ohio Regiment, in what must have seemed like a flash as the unarmed Mississippians had swarmed over them before they could respond, Clancy and some two hundred men surrendered, or more aptly put, were subdued.

---

[48]Ibid., 75–76.
[49]Stewart, *Dan McCook's Regiment*, 130.

Joining Farrell and the 15th Mississippi were Companies B and H of the 6th Mississippi, one of their sister units in Adams's Brigade. The 6th Mississippi had just moved back into a "zig-zag wooded defense line" where they had earlier been "to relieve Featherston's Brigade in the area adjacent to Moore's Mill."[50] According to the regiment's historian, Grady Howell, "the regiment had no sooner fallen into its new position than Capt. [William Candace] Thompson was ordered to take Companies B and H to another sector in support of Cowan's Battery."[51] As soon as they completed this task, the two companies were ordered to report to Colonel Farrell immediately. Farrell placed Thompson and his two companies on the left of his regiment and directed Thompson to command the left wing of his counter-assault.[52]

Thompson described the scene:

> We marched to the front, came to within twenty paces of a well-fortified regiment of Federals, who promptly opened fire on us. We dropped to the ground. With two of my men I crawled up near the red clay dirt of the enemy breastwork. In a quick judgement I signalled with my sword for my battalion to move forward with fixed bayonets. We rushed over the top and right down into the enemy trench. Not a shot was fired. There was a bloody struggle where, in hand-to-hand combat, men were thrusting bayonets through their fellow humans.[53]

Thompson's battalion were facing elements of the 22nd Indiana, which had come up in support of the 52nd Ohio and lengthened the right of the Federal line. He wrote, "Some of my men used both ends of their weapons, clubbing the Federals over the head with their gun butts. Suddenly forty-seven Federals threw down their guns, jumped up on the parapet near where I was standing, and raised their hands in surrender."[54]

The Mississippi captain and his little command had rushed into battle from their work detail so quickly that they, too, like their 15th Mississippi

---

[50]Rowland, *Military History of Mississippi 1803–1898*, 177; H. Grady Howell, Jr., *Going to Meet the Yankees: A History of the "Bloody Sixth" Mississippi Infantry, C. S. A.* (Jackson MS: Chickasaw Bayou Press, 1981) 225.

[51]Howell, *Going to Meet the Yankees*, 227; CSR Roll 155, Thompson, *Defenses of Atlanta*, 40.

[52]Howell, *Going to Meet the Yankees*, 227; Thompson, *Defenses of Atlanta*, 40–41.

[53]Ibid.

[54]Thompson, *Defenses of Atlanta*, 40–41.

counterparts, had not had time to load weapons before the charge. "While the prisoners were being assembled I signaled Needham McLendon, of my company, to come forward," explained Thompson; "I ordered him to take the captives off the field and report them back to brigade headquarters. As we were getting the Yankees formed they suddenly broke ranks and began running in the direction of their own lines." Thompson described the resulting chase. "We had no choice but to run after them, as our weapons had all been broken in the hand-to-hand fight. Nearly every one of us had a Federal to capture. They ran for the creek, jumped in, crossed, and kept on running. I was chasing a large, old Dutch captain," said Thompson. "This fellow slid down the bank and was standing in the water holding to a tree limb. He was puffing and blowing from the chase. He gave up and I helped him out of the creek. I asked him how he felt and his reply was, 'I am damned tired and ready to give up!'"[55]

Thompson and his band chased portions of Dilworth's Brigade all the way into Peach Tree Creek. "We were again rounding up most of the Federals on the bank of the creek and catching our breath. Just then a fresh enemy regiment moved up on the opposite bank and commenced throwing hot lead into us." This unit was the 16th Illinois of Morgan's Brigade, which was posted in the woods just west of Dilworth's imprudent crossing and north of Peach Tree Creek. "We could not return their fire on account of our broken muskets, so our only choice was to make a hasty retreat. We ran back to the fortifications where we had attacked the Federals. The pits were nearly full of dead and wounded and many other fallen were scattered on the surrounding grounds," remembered Thompson.[56]

"As we passed over these dead and wounded, one cowardly Federal who had been playing dead jumped up and shot one of my men in the arm. Since he was near his own forces, we had no chance of catching this man," said Thompson. He explained that as his men returned from the field and back into the wooded ridge that framed the plain, they were then relatively safe from the advancing Yankees, who were counterattacking to try to recapture the lost line at the edge of the field and recover their wounded men.

---

[569]Ibid.
[56]Ibid.

Thompson wrote, "Once the Federals had gathered their men they moved out and we in turn were able to rejoin our regiment safely."[57]

The survivors of the 52nd Ohio and 22nd Indiana were rescued by reinforcements from their brigade. The reinforcements had hurried across the log and made it to the old Confederate earthworks near the creek, which they quickly improved to use from the obverse direction. Sergeant Stewart of the 52nd Ohio happily recalled, "Over the works we went, to find the whole line with fixed bayonets, expecting a hand to hand conflict. Such firing as those comrades did do, as they cheered those who had escaped death. The rebel line falters—it stopped—it fled." The 52nd Ohio lost, according to Sergeant Stewart, with forty-seven wounded. Twenty-one were killed, including James J. Donaldson, Samuel M. Hanlin, Eli Gordon, and Elias Dimmit (all of Company E) and John F. Rightly mortally wounded. "Lt. Donaldson had drawn a new patent leather haversack that morning, remarking as he put it on, 'I will be a shining mark for the Johnnies.' He was shot through the haversack." Sergeant Stewart lamented, "Hanlin was shot through the thigh, severing an artery. Taking off his suspenders, he tied a knot in one of them, placing the knot over the artery, stopped the flow of blood. When dark came, we crawled to where he lay and found him dying from exhaustion."[58]

The Ohio veteran recalled that "many strange things occurred that morning. Elias Dimmit, of our company, said to me, 'I will be killed today, send my Bible and pictures to mother.' He fell in the recall of our skirmishers, shot through the knapsack, through 8 folds of a rubber blanket and 29 leaves of writing paper, out through his heart." Sergeant Stewart remembered that Captain Schneider, from Brooklyn Village (part of Cleveland), had fallen on the right of the line. "It was a hand-to-hand conflict on the right of the regiment," explained Stewart. "At the time of his death he [Schneider] was 28 and engaged to an excellent young lady of Cleveland. He received a letter from her the evening before the battle, urging him to resign and come home, as she had fears he would be killed in the next battle." Stewart overheard Schneider tell Major Holmes, "[I] have a dread presentiment of it myself, but my country is in peril. If I fall, let me fall in the van of the conquering host." Stewart explained, "When he was

---

[57]Ibid.
[58]Stewart, *Dan McCook's Regiment*, 130–31.

found his revolver was in his hand with one barrel empty. A rebel Major lay dead within a few feet of him. The hole in the Major's head was made by a 32 calibre, the same as the Captain's revolver, and the Major's bullet had struck the Captain in the temple. Both were dead."[59]

Stewart remembered the story of Frank Miser, of Company G, who had fallen, mortally wounded. "He was left on the battle field for a few hours, when his comrades returned he was dead. In his hand was a discharge paper from a hospital in Cincinnati, on the back of it was written these words, with a pencil:

> Dear father and mother,
> I am mortally wounded. I die like a soldier, and hope to meet you all in heaven.
> B. F. Miser."[60]

The new Northern force rapidly pursuing the receding Mississippians across the field was the 125th Illinois under Lieutenant Colonel James W. Langley. The 125th Illinois had crossed the creek third in the order of the brigade's crossings at the same point crossed by the 52nd Ohio and 85th Illinois before it but had been placed in a reserve position along the crest of the first slight hill in the field. When the 22nd Indiana (which had crossed fifth and moved to the right and formed on the right of the 52nd Ohio) and the Ohioans were sent flying back to the creek, word was sent to General Davis for help. Dilworth also called on the 125th Illinois, his only reserves south of the creek at the time, to respond. Lieutenant Colonel Langley, who had commanded the 125th Illinois since Colonel Oscar F. Harmon had been killed at Kennesaw Mountain on 27 June, ordered his regiment forward at the double-quick. They began to chase Thompson's little band across the western portion of the field south to the wooded heights beyond. Once the men of the 125th Illinois reached the original Federal line, they halted and went no further, choosing instead to improve these works and pull to safety the wounded men who had earlier fallen.[61]

---

[59]Ibid., 131–32.
[60]Ibid., 132.
[61]OR, series I, vol. 38, ser. no. 72, 712–13; Scaife, *Campaign for Atlanta*, 152.

Captain W. C. Thompson used his small battalion of companies B and H (no more than sixty men) with a portion of the 15th Mississippi that Farrell had detached to him to form the left wing of his little assault. While they were unable to keep all of their captured prize, they did succeed in picking up another sixty Yankees on their return to the woods before the 125th Illinois counter-thrust could reach them. They also succeeded in equipping themselves, for the most part, with Northern Springfield rifles, trading them for the broken Enfield and Austrian rifles they had used to club their way into routing most of the 22nd Indiana. To their right or east, Farrell and the rest of the 15th Mississippi finished putting the 22nd Indiana to flight along with Lieutenant Colonel Clancy's 52nd Ohio. During the fighting, companies B and H lost only ten to fifteen men.[62]

The terrain in this area prevented a line of sight between Farrell's Mississippians and Reynolds's Arkansans as each moved independently against Federal forces in their front. Unfortunately for Farrell and his men, the terrain also did not yield proper coordination in their counter-attacks. Lieutenant Colonel Binford described the scene as Farrell's Mississippians had seized and captured portions of one Federal regiment while routing another: "General Reynolds' Brigade, not having made their appearance on our right, Col. Farrell halted his men and rode to the right in search of the Arkansas Division [Brigade]; in doing so he rode about two hundred yards to the right and found himself in the rear of a Federal Regiment."[63] Farrell had unwittingly ridden upon the rear of the 85th Illinois, which had just crossed the creek. He moved his men moved at the double-quick across the flat field to the low range of hills that formed a bowl south of the creek and field. While still in column as it filed from the edge of the field near today's Bohler Road at its intersection with Chaumont Square, he deployed his men to cover the space to the left of the 52nd Ohio, which had disappeared over the ridge to the right. The 85th Illinois had only just come up to the woods along a low ridge and was partially separated by a small pond as it formed a line facing southeast in today's La Parc. Suddenly, the Irishman found himself in the rear of three hundred Yankees with only his horse, Bullet, to

---

[62]Thompson, *Defenses of Atlanta*, 40–41; Howell, *Going to Meet the Yankees*, 228; CSR Rolls 155–159; Rowland, *Military History of Mississippi 1803–1898*, 176.

[63]Binford, "Recollections of the Fifteenth Regiment of Mississippi Infantry, C. S. A.," p. 76.

console him. The rest of his Mississippi regiment was out of sight and out of reach in the wooded ridges and valleys just west of him.

Luck was with Mike Farrell and Bullet that day, or so it seemed, for the commander of the 85th Illinois, Major Robert G. Rider, and his Illinois troops had heard the fighting over the ridge to the right. Moreover, not taking the precaution of loading their rifles and then moving to the crest of the ridge either to support their embattled comrades or to take a stronger position for defense, the 85th Illinois Regiment became, Major Rider assumed, sitting ducks to the Mississippians behind them.[64] Binford described the scene:

> The Commanding Officer, seeing Col. F. [Farrell] in his rear, and having heard our charge, naturally supposed the entire command was in his rear and not waiting to see, but knowing Reynolds was in his front, he called out to Col. Farrell not to let his men fire, saying, "I surrender myself and Regiment." Col. F. asked him how many men he had. He replied, "About three hundred."

Still alone, the Mississippi colonel quickly plotted to bag the whole lot of them. "Farrell put on a bold front and said 'Order your men to stack arms and if you fire a single shot, I will kill every man you have got.' Col. F. at once put spurs to his horse and started after the Regiment to come up and take charge of his prisoners, but had not ridden very far when lo!" exclaimed Binford, "a straggling Yank [apparently from the 52nd Ohio] slipped out and throwing up his gun ordered him to surrender. Of course, as the Yank had the drop on him there was nothing else to do."[65]

Instead of panicking, however, the quick-thinking Farrell came up with another plan. Binford proudly explained, "But Farrell was full of schemes and resources, so he put his hand on his sword. When the Yank with his gun leveled on him said, 'Don't draw that sword; if you do I will kill you.' Farrell replied that he thought it was customary when an officer surrendered to give up his sword." The Northern captor listened. Binford continued,

> The thought of getting a fine metal scabbard and sword at once caught him and he said, "Why, yes, hand it to me," and walked up to Farrell's side, or

---

[64]*OR*, series I, vol. 38, ser. no. 72, 708–25.

[65]Binford, "Recollections of the Fifteenth Regiment of Mississippi Infantry, C. S. A.," p. 76.

rather front. Col. F. reached around and fastened his sword and taking it in his right hand and near the middle, handed it toward the Yankee, but instead of getting it in his hand, he got it on his head with all the force Col. F. could bring to bear, and with sufficient force to knock him down.[66]

Farrell was still in great danger. "Just at that time one of our men from Co. I, named Cox, came running up and ran his bayonet through the Yankee and in an instant another Yankee appeared and shot Cox through the head, killing him instantly. Farrell then put spurs to his horse and galloped back to the Regiment," said the relieved Binford, "but by this time the enemy had appeared again in our front in large force and we had to fall back." The 22nd Indiana had just arrived, threatening to flank the Mississippians on their left, and with Farrell's lost Yankee regiment looming in their right and rear, "so Col. F. did not get his 300 prisoners he had captured."[67]

According to Lieutenant Berryhill of the 43rd Mississippi, "The 15th [Mississippi] made a gallant charge driving the Yankees before them and in to the creek, capturing and bringing off 52 prisoners. Some 200 or more surrendered to them but not being supported by Reynolds [Arkansas Brigade] they all made their escape but the 52." Berryhill added, "We lost a good many men," including Eugene Harvey who was killed and Medy Oswalt, who was missing and presumed killed.[68] The 43rd Mississippi was a colorful bunch of characters. Earlier in the war they even had a camel for a mascot. He was called Douglas, but unfortunately he was killed during the siege of Vicksburg, shot by a Federal rifleman.[69]

Lieutenant Colonel Columbus Sykes of the 43rd Mississippi wrote his wife on 20 July about the fighting around Moore's Mill: "Yesterday evening we had a pretty little skirmish on our right, capturing about 150 prisoners, and killing and wounding a good many. A part of this brigade, the 15th Miss., was engaged; our loss in killed 8, wounded 27…and 2 missing." Sykes

---

[66]Ibid., 76–77.

[67]Ibid., 77.

[68]Berryhill, *Gentle Rebel*, 60.

[69]Columbus Sykes (lieutenant colonel, 43rd Mississippi Volunteer Infantry) to his wife, 29–31, Subject File, MI-4, 30A, Kennesaw Mountain National Battlefield Park Library, Kennesaw GA; Country Music Television's *CMT Magazine* (March-April 2004): 5; en.wikipedia.org/wiki/Douglas_the_camel (18 November 2014).

explained, "We are still on picket under a heavy picket fire. This Regt. Lost one man, killed yesterday."[70] Another veteran's story as recalled and retold around hearths in post-war Mississippi was that the 15th Mississippi Regiment "compelled the surrender of the 52nd Ohio Regiment which was liberated later."[71] Joel Watson recorded in his journal that the Yankees "crossed the creek and drove back our skirmishers and formed a line on our side of he creek," when the 15th Mississippi "charged and drove them to the creek and killed a great many of them."[72]

By the time the rest of the 85th Illinois reached the line they just established to the left of the 52nd Ohio, the Rebels met them with a furious counterattack. While the Mississippians under Colonel Farrell tangled with the Ohioans and other units that had come to their aid (the 125th Illinois and the 22nd Indiana), the men of the 85th Illinois were assaulted by Reynolds's Arkansas Brigade from their front and left. "It was the supreme moment," recalled Sergeant Aten, "—the crisis of the day, and Major Rider gave the order for the 85th to advance. The men rushed forward under a terrific fire, passed through the open field on the double quick, and struck the advancing enemy at the edge of the woods."[73] According to Aten, "this brought the 85th [Illinois] in line on the left of the 52nd [Ohio]. Two small regiments were now face to face with a rebel brigade of six regiments, and along the entire line the firing became fierce and deadly."[74]

Actually, the "rebel brigade of six regiments" that Aten's men faced numbered slightly fewer than four hundred Arkansans of Reynolds's Brigade available for the assault. The Ohio regiment faced about three hundred Mississippians of Farrell's 15th Mississippi plus another sixty or so men from companies B and H of the 6th Mississippi led by Captain Thompson. In contrast, the effective strength of the 22nd Indiana and the 52nd Ohio was about three hundred men each. Also, the 85th Illinois, supported by the 86th Illinois (also of Dilworth's Brigade) numbered about three hundred men along with another three hundred or so men in the 86th Illinois. Thus,

---

[70]Sykes to his wife, 31.

[71]J. C. Rietti, *Military Annals of Mississippi* (Jackson MS: John C. Rietti, c. 1896; repr. Spartanburg SC: The Reprint Co., 1988) 187.

[72]Joel Calvin Watson, Diary (Grenada MS: Grenada Public Library) 21; Wynne, *A Hard Trip*, 124.

[73]Aten, *History of the Eighty-Fifth Regiment*, 197–98.

[74]Ibid., 198.

some seven hundred Confederates were, in two separate and uncoordinated strikes, counterattacking about 1,200 Yankees in four regiments. Moreover, additional reinforcements were being rushed in from the Northern side; by the time the battle was over some 3,000 to 4,000 Yankees were on the field from two brigades, while the Rebels received no support.

Reynolds finally had his men deployed and ready to attack, but he could not find Farrell to coordinate the attacks. He had no idea that the Mississippians had already launched their attack, chased two regiments into Peach Tree Creek, and withdrew back to their original lines with as many prisoners and new Federal guns as they could carry. The relatively small amount of rifle fire had masked the sound of Farrell's assault. Frustrated at not finding Farrell, Reynolds sent Lieutenant Williams W. Dyer, his adjutant, to locate Farrell. Dyer was captured as Northern troops penetrated Reynolds's skirmish line and began erecting works along the edge of the wooded ridge. Reynolds continued to send dispatches to Farrell, and on the fourth one, he "found Colonel Farrell fortifying with rails, & c., at a distance from my left flank and at nearly right angles with it."[75]

After redeploying two companies of the 9th Arkansas to act as vedettes and protect the left flank, Reynolds ordered his brigade forward. The 85th Illinois, which had surrendered briefly to Colonel Mike Farrell when he appeared in their rear, now had another threat from their front. The spooked Illinois troops had seen enough of the southern shores of Peach Tree Creek. With little resistance the left and center of the regiment broke and fled for the creek. The right of the regiment was caught in the woods, fighting hand to hand with the Arkansans, who had come upon them so fast they didn't have time to run. Many of them were captured. Reynolds proudly reported in his memoirs, "The brigade advanced in fine style and drove the enemy back some distance capturing two flags and 80 or 90 prisoners." Actually, in Reynolds's official report of 23 July 1864 (four days after the battle), he said they captured eighty to one hundred Yankees during the engagement. It is likely that Reynolds included the Federals captured by both Farrell's Mississippians and his Arkansans. Federal casualty reports revealed forty-seven men missing from the 85th Illinois,

---

[75]OR, series I, vol. 38, part III, ser. no. 74, 936; James Willis, *Arkansas Confederates in the Western Theater* (Dayton OH: Press of Morningside Bookshop, 1998) 508.

thirty-five from the 22nd Indiana, twenty-six from the 52nd Ohio, one from 125th Illinois, and none missing from the 86th Illinois. Thus, Dilworth's 3rd Brigade lost 109 men and officers, including Lieutenant Colonel Clancy from the 52nd Ohio.[76]

Reynolds's men were prevented from sweeping the field as the 86th Illinois had just come up and protected the left and rear of the 85th Illinois, which had taken flight. Moreover, the majority of the five regiments of Mitchell's 2nd Brigade had crossed the creek and were deploying to the right of the Illinois troops and threatening to flank Reynolds's right, or breach his thin lines. Thus, Reynolds's men had to withdraw nearly two hundred yards, but in the center of the bulge, the 9th Arkansas boys were not ready to give up their hard-fought position. The brigade's historian recorded, "After intense fighting, the two wings of the Arkansas Brigade were driven in by the flanking movement of superior numbers. Despite the hand-to-hand fighting, the 9th Arkansas held its position in the center of the brigade, which was in a field protected by a fence." According to Private James Amason of the 9th Arkansas, "We wanted the fence and they wanted it, but we got the fence and forty of the blue boys and their guns." Reynolds ordered the remainder of his brigade to advance again and relieve the hitch on the 9th Arkansas. This was accomplished and the lost ground regained by these units, but increasing numbers of Federal units forced Reynolds and his brigade to retire. Reynolds explained that it was 7:30 PM and his brigade had been fighting for four hours since their skirmishers first lost the position sometime after 3:00 PM.[77]

Sergeant Aten of the 85th Illinois described the fighting: "On the right of the 85th it was a desperate hand-to-hand conflict, in which muskets were clubbed and the bayonet was freely used."[78] Concerning the plight of the Ohioans, Aten explained, "While engaged in this deadly struggle a large force of the enemy passed beyond the right of the 52nd [Ohio], then wheeling to the right it poured a wicked fire lengthwise of the line."[79] While

---

[76]*OR*, series I, vol. 38, part III, ser. no. 74, 936; Willis, *Arkansas Confederates in the Western Theater*, 508; *OR*, series I, vol. 38, part I, ser. no. 72, 712, 721, 724–26, 730–31; Aten, *History of the Eighty-Fifth Regiment*, 197–200.

[77]*OR*, series I, vol. 38, part III, ser. no. 74, 936; Willis, *Arkansas Confederates in the Western Theater*, 508–12.

[78]Aten, *History of the Eighty-Fifth Regiment*, 198.

[79]Ibid.

the Ohioans and Illinoisans were then routed and fled the field, Aten recalled the scene a bit more favorable to his fellow veterans:

> The advanced position of the two regiments was clearly untenable, but it was now a fight for time, in which the other regiments of the brigade might make the crossing and gain the crest of the bluff. No command was given, and if given, none could have been heard above the infernal din of battle. But the instinct of self-preservation was strong enough to tell experienced soldiers what to do, and when they saw the brigade formed and ready to receive the enemy on the bluff, the movement to the rear began at almost the same moment along the entire line. There was no panic—no rout, as the men retired by the right and left behind the brigade, but their ranks were sadly thinned, and along the line of fierce conflict windrows of dead were afterward found, in which the mingling of the blue and gray attested the stubborn nature of the fight. When darkness ended the struggle the entire brigade had been engaged. But we held the ground, and had secured for Sherman's army a safe footing on the south side of Peach Tree creek.[80]

In reality, the men of the 85th Illinois and the 52nd Ohio had skedaddled about a quarter of a mile back to the rest of their brigade, which had by this point formed a line of battle on the southern edge of the flood plain opposite the mouth of Green Bone Creek. Lieutenant Colonel Clancy had negligently sent his regiment too far forward in an effort to secure the high ground south of Peach Tree Creek before adequate support had reached the south bank of the creek. Following suit, the 85th Illinois had no choice but to support the movement of the Ohioans, and consequently, they shared in their fate, as did a number of men from the 125th Illinois and 22nd Indiana, which also went too far forward before the surprise Rebel counterattack.

In the aftermath of the day's fighting and the "no rout" as described by Sergeant Aten, the 9th Arkansas had possession the 85th Illinois's national colors and state flag. Aten described the scene as dusk mercifully closed on the day that had been so disastrous for the Illinois troops:

> After dark as the regiment [the 85th Illinois] gathered on the bank of the creek there was many a hearty handshake as comrades greeted those whom they feared had been killed or captured, and many anxious inquiries for those not in line.... Lt. Musselman of Company G, and others ran back

---

[80]Ibid.

into our line unhurt. At the end of the charge they found themselves close under the guns of the enemy, and under fire from both friend and foe. In this dilemma they dropped to the ground and remained between the lines until darkness afforded them an opportunity to escape from a very trying and perilous position. Their coming was a delightful surprise and produced a sensation not unlike that which the returning dead might be expected to create.[81]

Another Federal officer from a nearby unit observed the affair, noting that while Morgan's Brigade had acted with caution to the right, Dilworth's Brigade had advanced too far without adequate support: "But the 3 brigades on our left deployed 2 regiments, and crossed the creek, then charged on the Rebel skirmishers some 3 or 4 times, driveing them back each time until they got clear cross a large open field and formed their line along the adge of the timber, and went to building riffel pits." Of course, the "3 brigades" mentioned were Dilworth's and portions of Mitchell's and Morgan's Brigades, which later came to reinforce the lodgment. The Federal observer, 2nd Lieutenant John Hill Ferguson of the 16th Illinois, described the scene: "A great many had layen down their guns and knapsacks, to use the spads when they were surprised by a brigade of Rebs chargeing right unto them. Our skirmish line of corse ran back, but over half of the 2 regiments were killed wounded and captured."[82]

Ferguson, a native of Newton-Stewart, Scotland, explained, "These 2 regts. concisted of the 22ed Ind. and 52ed Ohio. The Rebs run right unto them and shot a great many in the creek as they were sweeming cross. Some jumped into the creek and got drownded." He witnessed the crumbling right of Dilworth's reconnaissance as Farrell's Mississippians chased them back to the creek. "This is rather a sad affair and badly managed as they ought to have been strongly supported at the creek. But they were like our regiment—had no support atall. But," added Ferguson, "the left of our regiment helped them out of it a great deal as they were in good range, and had a rakeing fire on the Rebs as they crossed the field, and killed and wounded a large number of them. But nothing compared with the loss these two regiments sustained."[83]

---

[81]Ibid., 198–99.
[82]Ferguson, *On to Atlanta*, 64.
[83]Ibid.

General Davis subsequently praised Colonel Dilworth and his brigade for their efforts, and he "was greatly pleased with the success gained."[84] Davis continued in his after-action report, "The loss was heavy on both sides considering the numbers engaged, and the day's work was exceedingly creditable to Colonel Dilworth and his command."[85] Major Holmes of the 52nd Ohio credited the 85th Illinois for saving his regiment from disaster. "Without the 85th Illinois, the 52nd Ohio would all have been killed or captured, and that movement would have failed," said the relieved major. "I mean by the statement to say, with emphasis, that if the part taken by your regiment in that day's work had been omitted, the crossing would have ended in disaster and failure."[86]

That night Dilworth's and Mitchell's Brigades dug in and secured their lodgment on the southern shore of Peach Tree Creek, using the timbers from a log house nearby to strengthen their lines. Opposing them, the Confederates who remained had constructed detached works manned by eight to ten men each, from which the Rebels could keep up a harassing fire on the Federals in the safety of their small works. In the evening, Mitchell's 2nd Brigade built a bridge over the creek and the division's artillery was sent across and put into action, keeping the Rebel sentries uncomfortable all night. Around 10:00 PM, the four Napoleons of Captain George Q. Gardner's 2nd Minnesota Battery opened up on the handful of Confederates who had the unfortunate duty to guard the picket line below the Federal's new bridgehead while their comrades withdrew to the Rebel earthworks encircling Atlanta. Together with the help of sharpshooters from Dilworth's Brigade, Gardner's guns quickly drove the remaining Southerners from sight. "In this action there were many fine shots," remembered one Illinois soldier who witnessed the Minnesota artillerists. "Captain Gardner never failed to plant a shell in one of these detached works, and when the shell burst those unhurt ran for the rear in the wildest confusion. But," added the appreciative Illinoisan, "the accurate aim of our men allowed but few of the enemy to escape."[87]

---

[84]Aten, *History of the Eighty-Fifth Regiment*, 199.
[85]*OR*, series I, vol. 38, ser. no. 72, 635.
[86]Aten, *History of the Eighty-Fifth Regiment*, 199.
[87]Aten, *History of the Eighty-Fifth Regiment*, 200.

While Mitchell's pioneers erected the bridge, they "observed the body of a beardless boy floating in the creek. He had been shot through the body and fallen unnoticed by his comrades into the stream." According to Sergeant Aten of Dilworth's Brigade, the boy "was clothed in the faded blue uniform of a private soldier of the Union, but beyond that nothing could be found to identify him in any way. So he was buried in a nameless grave, hero that he was, to lie among the unknown dead...."[88]

Among the casualties in Farrell's 15th Mississippi was John McKay of the Long Creek Rifles, which formed Company A.[89] Another death was that of Ben Hervey (Eugene Harvey) of Company F, who was killed from friendly fire by someone from the 9th Arkansas. One of his fellow Mississippians witnessed the sad scene, "'A soldier from the 9th Arkansas Regiment had followed up the 15th [Mississippi] and spied the prisoner in his blue suit and, not seeing his captor who was behind him, fired at the Yankee.'" The fellow Mississippian continued, "The bullet missed its intended target and instead passed through Hervey's right thigh."[90]

Farrell's 15th Mississippi had an effective strength of nearly three hundred men during the action; forty or fifty men were lost, including Lieutenant Hugh Montgomery of Co. I, who was killed. Companies B and H of the 6th Mississippi lost an additional ten to fifteen men out of its sixty-odd involved, for a total loss of fifty to sixty-five Mississippians (out of as many as 350 deployed during the engagement). Reynolds's Arkansas Brigade posted similar numbers. Losing eight killed, forty-eight wounded, and three missing for a total of fifty-nine men lost out of about four hundred present during the contest, Reynolds reported that he counted sixty dead Yankees in front of 2nd and 9th Arkansas lines. His men captured 102 rifles. Another veteran in front of the 9th Arkansas remembered counting eighty dead Yankees in front of his lines. Moreover, the Rebels had captured over a hundred Federals, wrecked three regiments, and re-supplied themselves with Springfield rifles.

---

[88]Ibid.

[89]F. M. Glass, "Long Creek Rifles: A Brief History," Pamphlet (Sallis MS: Long Creek Rifles Chapter, United Daughters of the Confederacy, August 1909).

[90]Wynne, *A Hard Trip*, 125; "History of the Water Valley Rifles, Company F, 15th Mississippi Infantry," p. 52–57, Supplement to the WPA Historical Research Project, Yalobusha County, 16 February 1937, Special Collections, J. D. Williams Library, University of Mississippi, Oxford MS.

The 9th Arkansas, which gained two Federal flags as trophies from the 85th Illinois, captured about forty Yankees. The Mississippians captured another sixty Federals. Taking Reynolds's and Farrell's losses together, the Confederates attacked with perhaps as many as 750 men; they lost 59 men in Reynolds's Brigade and a similar number from the Mississippi units, for a total loss of about 100 to 120 men. While there surely were some loses in the 6th Mississippi's two companies engaged, and Captain Thompson reported as such, remarkably, there were no casualties listed in the muster rolls of Company B (the New Guard from Rankin County) or Company H (the Simpson Fencibles from Simpson County) of the 6th Mississippi.[91]

Among the casualties in the 2nd Arkansas Mounted Rifles led by Colonel James A. Williamson, was twenty-seven-year-old Major James P. Eagle, who was wounded in the fight. The 2nd Arkansas suffered two killed, ten wounded, two mortally, and one captured for a total of thirteen men lost at Moore's Mill. Included in the losses of the 2nd Arkansas Mounted Rifles were John M. Bell, Leonidas Davis, and C. C. Robinson, who were killed; John E. Callahan and John M. Aston, who were fatally wounded; John R. Birmingham, James H. Selvidge, Samuel T. King, Mutt Beale, S. S. Brooks, C. Alfred, Robert N. Crank, J. Victor Green, John A. Kirkpatrick, and L. R. Muldrow, who were wounded; and Dennis Boultinghouse and Alexander Womack, who were captured. Boultinghouse subsequently died in prison.[92]

In the 4th Arkansas, Private Rufus W. May of Company F was killed, and Hospital Steward Private John P. Clark was wounded.[93] In the 1st Arkansas Mounted Rifles, twenty-three-year-old 1st Lieutenant Wiley Dyer was captured, and Private William Taylor was wounded. The 9th Arkansas lost twelve men at Moore's Mill with two killed, eight wounded (one mortally), and two who went out on skirmish line were captured.[94] The 31st

---

[91]"Company B—New Guard," 6th Mississippi Infantry Regiment, http://sixthmsinf.tripod.com/cob.htm (accessed 15 August 2014) and "Company H—Simpson Fencibles," 6th Mississippi Infantry Regiment, http://sixthmsinf.tripod.com/coh.htm (accessed 15 August 2014).

[92]Willis, *Arkansas Confederates in the Western Theater*, 508–512; Wesley Thurman Leeper, *Rebels Valiant: Second Arkansas Mounted Rifles* (Little Rock AR: Pioneer Press, 1964) 237–38, CSR Rolls 17–21.

[93]Willis, *Arkansas Confederates in the Western Theater*, 508–512.

[94]9th Arkansas Vertical Files, Chickamauga National Military Park Library.

Arkansas Regiment, which had merged with the 4th Arkansas but still maintained their unit designation within the regiments, lost two killed and two wounded.[95] Lieutenant Colonel Binford of the 15th Mississippi never did understand why Reynolds's brave Arkansans did not come to their aid. He could not know that at that moment they were busy with a brutal hand-to-hand struggle with the men of the 85th Illinois to their east. As Binford recollected, "We then returned to Brigade Headquarters with our 193 prisoners and all the captured property."[96]

On the Federal side, Dilworth's 3rd Brigade of Davis's 2nd Division in Palmer's XIV Corps, lost a total of 245 men, according to Official Reports[97]. The Brigade losses stated in the report were: 22nd Indiana, fifty-seven; 52nd Ohio, eighty-three; 85th Illinois, eighty-nine; 86th Illinois, ten; and 125th Illinois, six. Actually, the 85th Illinois sustained losses of fourteen men killed, forty-two wounded, and forty-seven captured or missing, of which twelve men were also wounded, for a total of ninety-one men.[98] In the 86th Illinois, one officer, Lieutenant William D. Faulkner of Company D was wounded; four men were killed, and five men were wounded for a total loss of ten officers and men.[99] The 125th Illinois lost one officer and one man killed, three men wounded and one man missing for a total of six officers and men. The dead officer was "Lt. Jones of Company D, commanding Company B, [who] died as he had lived—a true Christian soldier," according to Captain George W. Cook of the same unit.[100] In the 52nd Ohio, young John C. Brown, a native of Jefferson County, Ohio, born in 1844, lost his right leg and was thus incapacitated for further field duty. He later served the Buckeye State as its state treasurer from 1883 to 1891.[101] As for the rest of the Ohioans, the 52nd Ohio lost two officers and seventeen men killed, three officers and thirty-five men wounded, and one officer (Lieutenant Colonel Clancy) and twenty-five men missing or

---

[95]Bass, *History of the 31st Arkansas Confederate Infantry*, 75.

[96]Binford, "Recollections of the Fifteenth Regiment of Mississippi Infantry, C. S. A.," p. 77.

[97]*OR*, series I, vol. 38, part I, ser. No. 72, 721.

[98]Aten, *History of the Eighty-Fifth Regiment*, 204; Albert Castel, *Decision in the West* (Lawrence: University Press of Kansas, 1992) 367.

[99]*OR*, series I, vol. 38, part I, ser. no. 72, 721.

[100]Ibid., 725.

[101]http://www.heritagepursuit.com (3 April 2008).

captured, for a total of eighty-three officers and men according to the officer's report.[102] Sergeant Stewart of Company E reported that twenty-seven men were killed, forty-seven were wounded, and fourteen were captured for a total loss of eighty-eight men from the 52nd Ohio.[103] The 22nd Indiana reported losing five killed, seventeen wounded, and thirty-five missing, for a total loss of fifty-seven men. Among the wounded in the 22nd Indiana was Major Shea, who had his left arm amputated. Captain Taggart took command of the Hoosier regiment.[104] With the additional two losses in the 85th Illinois, the writer has confirmed a total of 247 losses in Dilworth's Brigade during the fighting at Moore's Mill.

The 1st Brigade, commanded by General James D. Morgan, continued to remain bottled up during this time between the Chattahoochee River and Nancy Creek, west of Colonel John G. Mitchell's 2nd Brigade. But, to help support the 3rd Brigade's crossing of Peach Tree Creek, which was being hard-pressed by the unexpected Confederate counterattack, Mitchell was ordered to send his brigade to the aid of Dilworth's men. Mitchell crossed his command on logs and rafts and threw the 34th Illinois forward to check the advance of the Arkansans and Mississippians, which had routed much of Dilworth's Brigade. Mitchell next placed the 78th Illinois and 98th Ohio to the left of Dilworth's lines and had them intrench.[105] The 98th Ohio "crossed [the creek] under a heavy fire of musketry" to come to the aid of the 3rd Brigade, which "was nearly surrounded."[106] There, "the regiment was formed in division column and marched across an open field to the rear of the 78th Illinois, which had taken position already on the bluff. In crossing the field, Sergeant Hindman, Company D, was killed."[107] Next, the 113th Ohio, crossed after the first three regiments of Mitchell's Brigade, the 34th Illinois, the 78th Illinois, and the 98th Ohio, had crossed and moved forward to the front and left. According to Captain Toland Jones of the 113th Ohio, "while the brigade was crossing we were ordered to form to the right, during which we suffered from a heavy flank fire, losing 2 killed and 2

---

[102]*OR*, series I, vol. 38, part I, ser. no. 72, 731.
[103]Stewart, *Dan McCook's Regiment*, 131–32.
[104]*OR*, series I, vol. 38, part I, ser. no. 72, 726.
[105]Ibid., 681.
[106]Ibid., 694.
[107]Ibid.

wounded."[108] The men were exposed on their left flank to fire from the Arkansans, which lasted until dark. The men then went to work improving their lines and erecting fortifications that were less than 200 yards from the Rebel lines.[109] In the action on 19 July, the 34th Illinois lost four men wounded.[110]

While the rest of Mitchell's Brigade had been sent east to support Dilworth's crossing of Peach Tree Creek at the mouth of Green Bone Creek, Colonel Henry B. Banning and his 121st Ohio Regiment was fighting his own little war against the left of Sears's Mississippi Brigade between the Chattahoochee River and Nancy Creek. During the evening of 18 July, Captain Robinson, with companies B and E, "erected a temporary bridge across the Peach Tree and built intrenchments on the south side."[111] Colonel Banning described the scene: "On the morning of the 19th the enemy opened early upon my line and made a vigorous effort to drive my companies back across the river. All day long and until late at night they kept up a heavy fire all along my line...."[112] During the fighting of 19 July, the 121st Ohio lost one man killed from Company E and two men wounded, one each from Companies E and K.[113] According to the busy commander, "A deserter, who swam the river and came to us under cover of the night, informed me that we had damaged the enemy very severely, killing and wounding, in addition to two commissioned officers, many of their men."[114]

Mitchell's 2nd Brigade lost during the action around Moore's Mill, four men wounded in the 34th Illinois. In the 78th Illinois, Private John Steen of Company A died from his wounds at a Federal field hospital at Vining Station, Georgia, on 22 July 1864; in Company B, Private John A. Edmonson died on 24 July 1864. There was one man killed, Sergeant Hindman of Company D in the 98th Ohio, and two men were killed and two men wounded from the 113th Ohio. In the 121st Ohio, one man was killed and two men were wounded during their fighting against the heights

---

[108]Ibid., 698.
[109]Ibid., 689.
[110]Ibid., 686.
[111]Ibid., 704–5.
[112]Ibid., 705.
[113]Ibid.
[114]Ibid.

below Moore's Mill. Colonel John Mitchell reported that the loss in his command was considerable, but the writer has confirmed that Mitchell's Brigade lost six men killed and eight men wounded for a total of fourteen casualties during its support of Dilworth's Brigade. Because the Federal regimental service records often failed to list those wounded or slightly wounded and only recorded those who were captured, or missing, it is likely that there were a number of additional casualties that failed to be documented.[115]

While the remainder of the Federal armies continued their encirclement of the Gate City, Morgan's Brigade and portions of Dilworth's and Mitchell's brigades remained pinned down by Sears's Mississippians atop the height below Moore's Mill. Some of the men found time for a bit of comfort. "Since we have got down to the creek, which is the line between us and the Rebs at the present. We have built good riffel pits close on the river bank. Black barries are plenty here and we have all gathered and eat what we wanted," explained John Ferguson of the 16th Illinois. "Some of the boys have got their cans and coffee pots full, although it was not altogether safe to be going around as the bullets whistled back and forth, some times comeing close enought to make a fellow dodge," he continued.[116]

During the evening of 19 July and in the morning of 20 July, Ferguson and his 16th Illinois were kept busy. Ferguson recorded in his diary on 20 July, "After being relieved from picket last night we marched back to where we left our knapsacks, a distance of about 1½ miles. The moon was just making hir appearance in the east so we concluded that we would remain there and eat supper, as our darkies had it partly cooked." Some freed black men who followed Sherman's lines had picked up odd jobs cooking, chopping wood, and performing other duties around camps for precious little pay, but for them it was a contribution to the effort to end slavery and a place to eat and lay their heads in relative safety. The 16th Illinois then sat and ate for the first time in thirty-six hours. "After all had dun eating we slung knapsacks and marched to finde and occupy the works lately occupied

---

[115.]http://civilwar.ilgenweb.org/reg_html/078_reg.html (18 November 2014); *OR*, series I, vol. 38, part I, ser. no. 72, 678–708.

[116]Ferguson, *On to Atlanta*, 64.

by the 60th Ills. The moon by this time was high enough to make our road nearly light as day," Ferguson recollected.[117]

"Haveing our suppors eat and been relieved and now marching in the rear out of range of Rebel bullets we all felt gay and mirry, although we had been on the skirmish line for two days and one night. We had to march about two miles. On reaching camp, or rather line of breastworks," explained Ferguson, where "we formed in the rear of them and stacked arms and received orders to draw two days rations. This deprived us of the pleasent night sleep we expected to have in the rear. It was after midnight when I lay down." The Scotland native would have a short night's sleep: "At 3 this morning orders came around to have breakfast eat, and all packed up, ready to move at day light. So I had to crawl out when just in the middle of my first sleep, and go around and awake the boys to get ready." Ferguson was relieved to discover that his orders to advance would be countermanded. "But day light came," he wrote, "and all were ready to comply with the order. But no move was made by our regiment, as we have remained here all day and expect to remain all night."[118]

Eventually, on 20 July, Colonel Banning would take the remainder of his command, the 121st Ohio, south of the creek, dislodge the remaining Rebels, and secure a lodge-head at the mouth of Peach Tree Creek and uncover the Rebel lines all the way down to the railroad bridge ruins, but he would be recalled by his brigade commander to re-cross Peach Tree Creek and join his command, by then well south of the creek along the DeFoor Ferry Road.[119] General Davis additionally ordered Captain George Q. Gardner and his 5th Wisconsin Battery to cross Peach Tree Creek and form with part of Dilworth's right in the plain along today's Hyde Manor Drive "to enfilade the Confederate positions on the high ground between Moore's Mill road and the Ridgewood road. Throughout the day, elements of Morgan's brigade, the right of Davis's Division, probed the defenses on the bluff overlooking Moore's Mill but without dislodging the defenders." Finally, after the Confederate assault at Peach Tree Creek failed, Sears's Mississippi Brigade was recalled, and the last Confederate hold on Peach

---

[117]Ibid., 65.
[118]Ibid.
[119]*OR*, series I, vol. 38, part I, ser. no. 72, 705.

Tree Creek and the Chattahoochee River was withdrawn.[120] According to 2nd Lieutenant Ferguson of the 16th Illinois, "The 10th Mich. and 60th Ills. crossed the creek where they relieved our regiment and drove the Rebels from their works and got posseasion of a large hill without much resistance, although we expected it would cost many precious lifes to take it."[121]

According to 2nd Lt. Ferguson, "On the morning of the 21st, men of the 10th Michigan Infantry, of Morgans brigade, who occupied Moore's Mill and the ground near it, discovered that the Confederates were abandoning the ground across the creek, including the stubborn bluff immediately in their front." For three days Sears's Mississippians had frustrated half of Davis's Division. "A reconnaissance quickly confirmed this impression and men of the 10th Michigan crossed the creek and occupied the works before the last of the defenders had fully withdrawn. With this final exchange of firing, the whole of Peachtree Creek passed to Union hands."[122] According to historian Colonel Allen P. Julian,

> Had not the Battle of Peachtree Creek taken place on the day on which these operations were reaching a climax, they would be well known today. But the eyes of history seem to see only the high drama along Collier Road, leaving it to a very few to remember that almost every foot of Peachtree Creek on down to its mouth was a battle ground, and that on the 17th, the 18th and the 19th of July, 1864, the most painstaking of the operations of both armies centered around the area [between the mouth of Peach Tree Creek and just east of Moore's Mill].[123]

Wrestling possession of the mouth of the creek away from the Confederates did not come without a price, however. According to Dr. Charles W. Jones, chief surgeon for the XIV Corps, about 125 men from Davis's 2nd Division were treated at the division field hospital for wounds received at the Moore's Mill fighting.[124]

---

[120]Allen P. Julian, *Operations through the Present Ridgewood Community*, p. 14, folder 4, box 4, mss 130, Wilbur G. Kurtz Collection, Keenan Research Center, Atlanta History Center, Atlanta GA.

[121]Ferguson, *On to Atlanta*, 65.

[122]Ibid.

[123]Julian, *Operations through the Present Ridgewood Community*, 14–15.

[124]*OR*, Supplement, part I, vol. 7, ser. no. 7, 12.

During the evening of Tuesday, 19 July, as Federal troops of General Palmer's XIV Corps crossed over to the southern side of Peach Tree Creek and effected a lodgment, Stewart's Army of Mississippi realigned their forces. Colonel William S. Barry of the 35th Mississippi Infantry in temporary command of Sears's Brigade, moved the Mississippi Brigade into the trenches held by Ector's Texas Brigade from below the railroad bridge crossing of the Chattahoochee River to just above the mouth of Peach Tree Creek. Ector's Texans were then moved to the left to cover the Marietta Road and the extreme left of the Confederate line.[125] Adams's Brigade supported this movement by covering the ground from Ector's right, near Bolton, to east of Moore's Mill, about a mile in length.[126]

From there, Reynolds's Arkansans, who had been hard-pressed all day, covered the area between just east of Moore's Mill, about seven hundred yards away, all the way to near Howell's Mill, a space of nearly two miles. There, Reynolds's right connected with Gist's Brigade and Hardee's Corps. To cover the two miles between Adams and Gist, Reynolds had only about six hundred men, eighty of whom were assisting General Gist. Thus, only the evening of 19 July, Reynolds's Brigade held the two miles between Moore's Mill and Howell's Mill, with just 520 men. The front door to Atlanta was wide open for Palmer's XIV Corps. To help Reynolds cover the ground, General Adams sent seven companies from the 20th Mississippi. Also, Adams left Bouanchard's Pointe Coupee Louisiana Battery, which had been previously placed on Reynolds's front. This battery consisted of four Napoleons under the command of the capable Captain Alcide Bouanchard. Because Reynolds was so thinly spread, his line covered the road behind the Peach Tree Creek between Howell's Mill and Moore's Mill, which connected them to Bolton to the west, instead of covering the banks and fords along the southern edge of the creek.[127]

With no Confederate cover along the banks of Peach Tree Creek from below Moore's Mill to near Howell's Mill, and with Reynolds's s mall brigade unable to provide the screen, General Adams sent one of his trusted Officers, Lt. Colonel James R. Binford, of the 15th Mississippi, to lead the

---

[125]David V. Stroud, *Ector's Texas Brigade and the Army of Tennessee, 1862–1865* (Longview TX: Ranger Publishing, 2004) 166; *OR* series I, vol. 38, ser. no. 74, 909.

[126]*OR*, vol. 38, part III, series 74, 891–92.

[127]Ibid., 891–94, Scaife, *Campaign for Atlanta*, 87, 186.

detached companies of the 20th Mississippi to do the job. Leaving three of the companies to cover a gap in the Confederate line in Reynolds's front near the Pointe Coupee Battery, Binford took four companies to the southern bank of Peach Tree Creek with orders to hold it until dark. The eloquent officer described his experience:

General Adams ordered me to take command of four companies from the Brigade (none from the 15th) and go down Peachtree Creek about one mile from where we had just had the fight and to hold the Creek and not allow the enemy to cross. He stated that the Brigade was going to fall back about four miles and it was absolutely necessary for me to hold my position until the Brigade had been gone one hour. To use common parlance, I thought that was a pretty "salty" order and especially to give a fellow who had been on the skirmish line all the previous night, but my duty was to obey, so I told me I would do it if possible. The enemy's pickets were just on the opposite bank of the creek and often not a hundred yards from my men, but not coming to show their beauty or fine shape, both sides stuck like lizards close to a tree. Had I not been a miserable sinner at that time, I think I would have offered up a devout prayer to the Lord to keep those fellows on their own side of the creek, for at least two hours or until I could get myself and men away from there. The question with me was how I could get my four companies away without being discovered. I soon settled upon the only plan I could devise and when the time came I put it into execution and it worked like a charm. The oft spoke of Arab that quietly folded his tent and stole away was not a circumstance to me stealing away from there. While I had no tent to fold, I had four companies of infantry which was far worse. But oh! That hour I was ordered to remain there. No two hours have ever been as long since. As a general thing I never feel lonely but though I sat very close behind a tree with the thought of no Confederate troops being no nearer than four miles of me and my four companies and just on the opposite bank of the creek was a large army of very unfriendly men and the probability of being at any moment attacked by them I must admit I felt *very* lonely. I suppose that is a very modest way to say I was badly frightened "all is well that ends well" and my getting-away scheme certainly worked like a charm, for I left there and Mr. Yank never did know or how I left, but I will say this—as soon as I got my command together and got them in the road the Brigade had gone, it would have taken pretty good cavalry to have overtaken us, for no grass grew under our feet. Both myself and men were that evening all terribly in love with the Brigade and were exceedingly anxious to be with it and about sundown we rejoined it.[128]

Stewart's Army of Mississippi subsequently fell back to the outer trenches that had been built in defense of the Gate City.

As portions of Palmer's XIV Corps and Geary's Division of Hooker's XX Corps crossed Peach Tree Creek east of Moore's Mill, between Howell Mill and today's Northside Drive, portions of several Southern brigades covered the creek, including Lieutenant Colonel Binford's small detachment. Early on the morning of 20 July, the 1st Division under General Robert W. Johnson got underway. McCook got his 1st Brigade underway at 3:00 AM, and by daylight, his men were in position to cross Peach Tree Creek and attack the Confederate positions,[129] but all they found were abandoned works as the Rebels in that area had already skedaddled.[130]

At the Howell Mill Road crossing, Johnson's 1st Division looked for an opportunity to cross. As the Yankees approached, "the Confederates held just long enough for artillery to be unlimbered on the south banks of the creek and for a detachment to prepare to burn the bridge."[131] The men of McCook's Brigade witnessed the action: "The bridge over Peachtree was aflame within moments of the last rebel crossing over; shortly after that, the Confederate batteries opened up on the Federal line."[132] With the crossing of Peach Tree Creek at the Buckhead Road by Howard's IV Corps on 19 July, the entire Peach Tree Creek front was open to the Yankees except for the mouth at the Chattahoochee River. It seemed to Sherman and his legions that the Confederates may be preparing to abandon Atlanta without a fight.

---

[128]Binford, "Recollections of the Fifteenth Regiment of Mississippi Infantry, C. S. A.," p. 77–78.

[129]*OR*, series I, vol. 38, part I, ser. no. 72, 524, 537, 540, 546, & 551.

[130]Ibid.

[131]Kirk C. Jenkins, *The Battle Rages Higher: The Union's Fifteenth Kentucky Infantry* (Lexington: University of Kentucky Press, 2003) 231.

[132]Jenkins, *Battle Rages Higher*, 231.

17

A HAMLET CALLED BUCKHEAD

We pressed on, and at two pm reached a place designated 'Buckhead,' a cross-roads, 6½ miles from Atlanta. One store-house and probably 2 or 3 other buildings, including dwelling houses, were all the town contained.[1]

When General Hood took command, the Confederate forces he inherited were deployed with Stewart's Corps, the Army of Mississippi, on the left, covering the northwest approaches to Atlanta, including the fords along the Chattahoochee River and Peach Tree Creek near its confluence with the river. Hardee's Corps was in the middle, facing north and guarding the Peach Tree Creek crossings from near Howell's Mill on the west to where the creek forks into two branches to the east. Hood's Corps, now temporarily commanded by General Cheatham, was posted to the east of Hardee, covering Atlanta from the roads northeast of town. To the right of Cheatham, Hood had just ordered General Wheeler with most of the Southern cavalry to cover Atlanta from the east and scout for Federal activity northeast and east of town. Over to the other side of Atlanta and linking up with General Stewart's Corps was General Jackson's Division of cavalry screening the Gate City from the west. Thus, Hood had a defensive front facing 180 degrees from west to east around Atlanta, and he had the Georgia militia inside the city's inner works as well.

While the Confederacy was experiencing the transfer of command on the evening of Sunday, 17 July, and throughout Monday, 18 July, the Federals were gearing up for the final push on Atlanta. A lull of a couple of weeks had provided a much needed respite. First Lieutenant Chesley A. Mosman of the 59th Illinois attended church services on Sunday where the chaplain of the 80th Illinois preached on the subject of "Let my son live" from Psalm 119. Afterward, the chaplain promised to provide a "funeral sermon for the men killed out of the Brigade during the campaign at an

---

[1]W. H. Newlin, D. F. Lawler, and J. W. Sherrick, eds., *A History of the Seventy-Third Regiment of Illinois Infantry Volunteers* (Decatur IL: Regimental Reunion Association of Survivors of the 73rd Illinois Infantry Volunteers, 1890)

early date." It was evident to the men of Howard's IV Corps (to which Mosman's regiment belonged) and to the remainder of Sherman's forces that heavy fighting was near. Mosman recorded in his diary on the evening of 17 July that companies A and B from the 59th Illinois "have served three full years today, and as their three years service is up the question is will the government seek to hold them by the phrase, 'or during the war.' Do those words extend the term of their enlistment beyond three years?" questioned the lieutenant. "Were [these words] not inserted so the government could discharge them before the expiration of three years? Quite an argument over it with Mennet [an outspoken captain of the regiment]."[2]

When Newton's Division reached Nancy Creek, they found the bridge partially burned and a brigade of Confederate cavalry together with a section of artillery waiting for them.[3] The 125th Ohio and the 3rd Kentucky were in front of Newton's Division; they were joined by skirmishers along with men from the 64th and 65th Ohio Regiments as part of a four-regiment demi-brigade commanded by Colonel Emerson Opdyke. "At 8:30 the rebels opened on us with one piece of artillery, and our Battery then went to the front, began work, and the rebel piece ceased firing," remembered veteran W. H. Newlin of the 73rd Illinois's Preacher Regiment.[4] First Lieutenant Ralsa C. Rice of the 125th Ohio recalled that "It was obvious that a determined resistance would be made, the place chosen being one of great natural strength. The road, after crossing the creek, climbed a hill, on the crest of which they had placed a Battery of two guns in a substantial earthwork."[5] With heavy timber flanking both sides and Nancy Creek in its front, the Confederate position was most formidable. According to General Howard, "On this account they were able to hold us in check some little time."[6] After placing a couple of batteries in position to respond, the Rebels gave way. "We extinguished the fire, saved a portion of the bridge, and

---

[2]Chesley A. Mosman, *The Rough Side of War: Civil War Journal of Chesley A. Mosman* (Garden City NY: Basin Publishing Co., 1987) 243.

[3]*OR*, series I, vol. 38, part I, ser. no. 72, 201.

[4]Newlin, Lawler, and Sherrick, eds., *A History of the Seventy-Third Regiment of Illinois Infantry Volunteers*, 322.

[5]Ralsa C. Rice, *Yankee Tigers: Through the Civil War with the 125th Ohio* (Huntington WV: Blue Acorn Press, 1992) 123.

[6]*OR*, series I, vol. 38, part V, ser. no. 76, 171.

reconstructed it," recorded Howard.[7] Captain Charles T. Clark of the 125th Ohio described the action as a "running fight for six miles to Buck Head."[8] "During the rest of the march...[to Buckhead] the rebel cavalry made quite stubborn resistance," added Howard.[9]

After flushing the Confederates out of their position along the heights at today's Chastain Park and the crossing over Nancy Creek at today's Powers Ferry Road, Opdycke's demi-brigade of four regiments pressed southward into the Georgia wilderness toward Buckhead. Captain Clark recalled,

> At a church farther on, the enemy made a second determined stand, and Opdyke sent the 65th Ohio also to the front line. A third stand was made on a hill from which they fired by volley but overshot. At Buck Head they rallied in and tried to hold their works, but were expelled before they had time to fairly form, and our own line advanced half a mile further and halted near Wheeler's late headquarters.

Confederate Cavalry leader General Joseph Wheeler had been based at Buckhead for the past two days awaiting developments of an expected Federal advance.[10]

Newton's men were being harassed by General John S. Williams's Kentucky Cavalry Brigade and elements of the Georgia state militia (dubbed Joe Brown's Pets after Georgia's governor). The militia had just been called up, and portions of it were stationed around Atlanta. For many of them, this was their first taste of combat. Nicknamed "Old Cero Gordo" for his fighting during the Mexican War, Williams and his Kentuckians were making quite a nuisance of themselves before Howard's IV Corps as they traveled across the rugged terrain between the Chattahoochee River and Buckhead (roughly along today's Powers Ferry Road where Nancy Creek intersects it in Chastain Park). "At one place regular barricades were

---

[7]Ibid.

[8]Charles T. Clark, *Opdycke Tigers: 125th Ohio Volunteer Infantry, A History of the Regiment and of the campaigns and Battles of the Army of the Cumberland* (Columbus OH: Spahr & Glenn, 1895; repr. Salem MA: Higginson Book Co., 1998) 287.

[9]*OR*, series I, vol. 38, part V, ser. no. 76, 171.

[10]Clark, *Opdyke Tigers*, 287.

constructed of logs and covered with boughs,"[11] explained the Federal corps commander. "When our men approached to within 150 yards they received a volley, but in this case as in several others the skirmishers cheered and charged them out."[12] Sergeant Newlin remembered, "At 11:30 it was discovered that the rebels had fallen back. Our loss was four men wounded. Col. Opdycke's horse [Old Barney] was shot."[13] The men gave Old Barney a full "burial of a soldier," burying him along the road under a tree where they posted a headboard that read "My Horse Barney."[14] Howard's skirmishers reported killing a Rebel colonel and wounding and capturing a Confederate captain.[15] Falling in the action were nineteen-year-old Private Amos Smith of Company A from the 65th Ohio and eighteen-year-old Private William J. Yeager of McLaughlin's Squadron of General Luther Bradley's 3rd Brigade. Both men were killed in the action near Buckhead.[16]

According to one Federal veteran of Kimball's Brigade, "Our brigade moved forward at 12 noon and crossed Nance's Creek [actually called Nancy Creek]. On the south bank of this stream the enemy had a Battery posted early in the day. It was ascertained that the forces engaged with us on this date were Williams's Cavalry." The Federal soldier explained,

> Skirmishing at the front continued. We pressed on, and at two PM reached a place designated "Buckhead," a cross-roads, 6½ miles from Atlanta. One store-house and probably 2 or 3 other buildings, including dwelling houses, were all the town contained. We met only slight resistance to our advance during the afternoon, the enemy yielding and falling back to within 6 miles of Atlanta.[17]

Lieutenant Mosman explained, "Report says that the men in our front are Georgia state militia and cavalry. They don't make very serious resistance to our advance. It seems that we are on their flanks, as our advance brought

---

[11]*OR*, series I, vol. 38, part V, ser. no. 76, 171.

[12]Ibid.

[13]Newlin, Lawler, and Sherrick, eds., *A History of the Seventy-Third Regiment of Illinois Infantry Volunteers*, 322.

[14]Rice, *Yankee Tigers*, 124.

[15]*OR*, series I, vol. 38, part V, ser. no. 76, 171.

[16]Wilbur F. Hinman, *The Story of the Sherman Brigade* (self-published, 1897) 1012, 1089.

[17]Newlin, Lawler, and Sherrick, eds., *A History of the Seventy-Third Regiment of Illinois Infantry Volunteers*, 322.

us to the end of a strong line of works. Didn't expect us from that direction, did you Johnny?" bragged Mosman. After camping at 3:00 PM, the men of Howard's IV Corps began to pillage the countryside surrounding Buckhead in search of food. According to Mosman, "Boys kill hogs and the squawk of the chicken is heard in the camp. Poor woman passes us going to visit her husband, a wounded prisoner in our hands." This was likely one of the middle-aged men from the Georgia state militia, which had just been sent out to slow Sherman's legions. Mosman recorded, "Report is that children are starving for want of something to eat in this region. Co. A secured a Rebel gun, a breech loader with a bayonet sheathed where the ramrod is in ordinary guns."[18]

Newton's men were ordered to bivouac for the night just south of the hamlet of Buckhead where their pioneers threw up works to protect them. "We could hear the noise of their axes being plied vigorously, as late as 10:30 PM," remembered one soldier.[19] With the remainder of Thomas's Army of the Cumberland still north and west of Nancy Creek and near the Chattahoochee River crossings, and with the remainder of Sherman's forces well to the east and southeast of Howard's men, the IV Corps was somewhat isolated from the remainder of the Federal armies. In fact, there was a gap of more than two miles from General Schofield's Army of the Ohio and Howard's men. Thus, the IV Corps were the only troops on the Buckhead Road as they neared Atlanta from the north. One of Newton's veterans remembered that on the evening of 18 July it "drizzled rain during the night."[20]

News of the action was reported in newspapers throughout the South. One such article, written by Harvey, on 19 July, appeared in the *Georgia Journal & Messenger* in Macon, Georgia, on Wednesday, 20 July. From "Peachtree Creek," Harvey wrote,

> The enemy advanced cautiously but steadily yesterday. Our cavalry dismounted and contested the ground obstinately. Williams's and Kelly's brigades were well handled, and displayed great coolness, but steady lines of infantry forced them finally to retire across the bridge over Peachtree creek,

---

[18]Mosman, *The Rough Side of War*, 244.
[19]Newlin, Lawler, and Sherrick, eds., *A History of the Seventy-Third Regiment of Illinois Infantry Volunteers*, 322–23.
[20]Ibid., 323.

but not until they had inflicted severe punishment upon the foe, with small loss to themselves. The loss of the enemy is thought to be about nine hundred. Our men fought from redoubts and ambuscades, hence they were not so exposed as the enemy.[21]

Only Williams's small Kentucky Brigade was posted in support of a battery behind a line of works just south of Nancy Creek along today's Powers Ferry Road corridor at Chastain Park. Kelly's Division of cavalry was actually east of Atlanta, fending off McPherson's advances toward Decatur.[22]

The *Georgia Journal & Messenger* writer was greatly exaggerating the Federal losses. According to their after-action reports, Colonel Emerson Opdycke led the detachment that opposed Williams's Kentucky Brigade in the van of Howard's IV Corps. Opdycke's 125th Ohio was deployed as skirmishers, and they were supported by the 64th and 65th Ohio, and the 3rd Kentucky when they "encountered Wheeler's cavalry, dismounted, supported by a 4-gun Battery." Lieutenant Colonel D. H. Moore explained that his 125th Ohio and the remaining Northern force "at 9 AM at Nancy's Creek charged him [Williams's Kentuckians] from his temporary intrenchments and drove him six miles, bivouacking early in the afternoon at Buck Head." According to Moore, the 125th Ohio lost one man killed and five men wounded, not nine hundred as reported by Harvey to the anxious Georgia readers.[23]

Captain Thomas J. Bryan of the 74th Illinois, which assisted Opdycke's advance across Nancy Creek, reported that the column "marched at 6 AM. At 8 AM skirmishing commenced, and for an hour was lively and continuous. Some shells were thrown from the Rebel batteries, but Spencer's guns getting into position soon silenced them. At 2 PM went into camp at Buck Head, and built works in the afternoon." "Spencer's guns" were Captain George W. Spencer's 1st Illinois Light Battery M, a Battery of four three-inch ordnance rifles. Later that afternoon, "a part of the regiment, in charge of Capt. Hobart H. Hatch [of the 125th Ohio] made a reconnaissance during the day, and found the enemy strongly posted on the

---

[21]*Georgia* (Macon GA) *Journal & Messenger*, 20 July 1864.

[22]*OR*, series I, vol. 38, part III, ser. no. 74, 951.

[23]*OR*, series I, vol. 38, part I, ser. no. 72, 296–97, 320, 355, 371–72; See also Clark, *Opdyke Tigers*, 287.

south bank of Peach Tree Creek."[24] Harvey with the *Georgia Journal &
Messenger* continued, "Fifty or twenty of the 1st Kentucky cavalry, including
the Lt. Colonel, adjutant and other officers, were captured by the enemy,
but our men rallied to the point, recaptured the prisoners, and took fifteen
Yankees."[25]

In addition to the 1st Kentucky Cavalry (known as John Russell
Butler's Regiment), led by Lieutenant Colonel Griffin; General John S.
Williams's Kentucky Brigade included the 2nd Kentucky Cavalry (called
Woodward's Regiment), under the direction of Major Thomas W. Lewis;
the 3rd Kentucky Cavalry, commanded by Colonel J. R. Butler; the 9th
Kentucky, under Colonel William C. P. Breckinridge; the 2nd Kentucky
Battalion, under Captain John B. Dortch; Allison's Tennessee Squadron,
led by Captain J. S. Reese; and Hamilton's Tennessee Battalion, directed by
Major Joseph Shaw.[26]

In the Thursday, 21 July edition of the Macon *Daily Telegraph*, in a
"Special Correspondence from the Memphis *Appeal*," more details
concerning the engagement were published: "The fight on Nance's Creek
yesterday between Williams's brigade and Hooker's entire corps, turns out to
have been of more importance than was at first supposed." Actually,
Williams's Kentuckians opposed Howard's IV Corps while other portions of
Kelley's Confederate Cavalry Division faced Hooker's XX Corps along
today's Paces Ferry Road as it crossed Nancy Creek and drove back the
Rebel cavalry to the vicinity of today's governor's mansion.[27] "Finding that
they were advancing in heavy force, Old Cerro Gordo [General John S.
Williams]," the article continued, "determined to impede their advance as
much as possible; until the commander-in-chief could be notified, and make
preparations to meet them." Williams's brigade had set a trap below Nancy
Creek at and near today's Chastain Park. The reporter explained,

---

[24]*OR*, series I, vol. 38, part I, ser. no. 72, 296–97, 320; William R. Scaife, *The
Campaign for Atlanta* (Atlanta: self-published, 1993) 148.

[25]*Georgia* (Macon GA) *Journal & Messenger*, 20 July 1864.

[26]Supplement to *OR*, part II, vol. 23, ser. no. 35, 3, 6–7, 37, 46; Scaife,
Campaign for Atlanta, 87.

[27]Albert Castel, *Decision in the West* (Lawrence: University Press of Kansas,
1992) 360; Scaife, *Campaign for Atlanta*, 86–87.

Dismounting their men, and concealing them in the dense undergrowth, he brought two pieces of artillery, and hastily constructed a masked Battery upon the opposite side of the road from the direction in which they were advancing, the woods opposite their position having been burned recently afforded them a fine view in their front. They had been in position but a short time, when the enemy's skirmishers were discovered, who pressed forward, closely followed by the main body, marching in column. Their skirmishers were allowed to approach within twenty paces. When the signal was given, and a murderous fire was poured into them at point blank range; the artillery opening at the same time with shell and canister upon the head of the column. The enemy broke and fled in wild confusion, but were again reformed, and advanced in line of battle.[28]

Colonel Opdycke, leading the van of Newton's Division for Howard's IV Corps, quickly formed flankers to advance and out-flank the Confederate position. With a rapid counter-attack across Nancy Creek, from three sides, Williams's Kentuckians quickly fled from the position, causing a portion of the 1st Kentucky to become overwhelmed and be captured. It was a part of Company A. According to its captain, the men "were attacked by the enemy, capturing several of the company." However, the Kentuckians did not have to wait long to be paroled: "Immediately afterward [they] were recaptured by the other portion of the company, which charged, and besides the [re-]capturing our own men, killed, wounded and captured twenty-five of the enemy."[29]

The article in the Macon *Daily Telegraph* continued:

General Williams then withdrew about one mile and formed another ambuscade, into which the enemy fell again; but after wavering some time, finally advanced again and tried to flank him upon the right. The 1st Kentucky, then in reserve, was ordered to charge them, in order to bring off the artillery and horses, which was done in gallant style, led by the gallant and intrepid McCawley, they closed upon the foe, and a hand to hand encounter took place, which has not been equaled during the war; our men using their butts of the guns and pistols, and the enemy their bayonets. Owing to the density of the thicket many of the officers were in advance of the line, and Lt. Colonel Griffin, commanding the regiment, came suddenly

---

[28]Macon (GA) *Daily Telegraph*, Thursday, 21 July 1864.
[29]Supplement to *OR*, part II, vol. 23, ser. no. 35, 3, 6–7.

upon the enemy, and boldly advancing demanded their surrender, telling them he had a regiment with him to which they replied that they had an army corps, and called upon him to surrender, which he and his adjutant and five of his captains, were very reluctantly compelled to do; but their captors had scarcely begun to rejoice over them, before the gallant 1st [Kentucky] was upon them, and driving them back in wild disorder, and yelling like so many incarnate devils, they recaptured all of them; also thereby saving the horses and artillery.

Five times during the day they were ambuscaded, and Gen. Williams estimates their loss at 500 killed and wounded, and twenty-two prisoners. Our loss was twenty-one, including Capt. McCawley, who General Williams says, was the best staff officer he ever saw in the army.[30]

According to General William B. Hazen, who commanded the 2nd Brigade of Wood's 3rd Division in the IV Corps, his men "marched about six miles to Buckhead, getting there at three PM. Formed on the right of Newton's Division and threw up works. 124th Ohio on picket. Hooker's corps joined us on the right at half-past five PM." After dark, Hazen adjusted his lines. He wrote, "Front line moved out about three hundred yards, to a ridge, at nine PM. Threw up new works and cut timber in front, working nearly all night. 23rd & 6th Kentucky on the left; 5th Kentucky and 6th Indiana in the centre; 1st & 41st Ohio on right of front line; 93rd Ohio in reserve." Hazen added, "No enemy in our front."[31]

Howard's IV Corps Secures a Bridgehead over Peach Tree Creek

On 19 July, General Stanley issued orders to his brigadiers to move out. As his division was second in line the day before, they would now be in the van. As Stanley's Division headed south from Buckhead, three roads emerged, two headed southeast toward Decatur (following along today's Roxboro Road) and one south to Atlanta (roughly following today's Lenox Road). Stanley and his 1st Division of Howard's IV Corps were ordered to proceed down these roads, feeling their way to the southeast to find a bridge over the north fork of Peach Tree Creek.

---

[30]Macon (GA) *Daily Telegraph*, Thursday, 21 July 1864.

[31]William B. Hazen, *A Narrative of Military Service* (Boston: Ticknor and Co., 1885) 271–72.

The 75th Illinois of General William Grose's 3rd Brigade was ordered to serve as a reconnoitering party on the Decatur Road all the way to Peach Tree Creek. Two companies of this regiment "were sent out in advance of the column," reaching the creek at 9:00 AM without any opposition.[32] Colonel John E. Bennett, leader of the 75th Illinois, sent sentinels over to the south side of the creek to search for signs of the enemy. The Illinoisans had reached the north fork of Peach Tree Creek without seeing any foe. Colonel Bennett described the next scene: "Two mounted men, wearing the uniform of U.S. soldiers, advanced within a few rods of these sentinels and refused to obey their orders. When ordered to halt, wheeled and rode off at a rapid rate. The sentinels discharged their pieces, wounding both of the men."[33] Lieutenant Mosman of the 59th Illinois recorded in his diary, "The 75th Illinois and 9th Indiana out on a chase."[34]

Mosman, who was in charge of the Pioneer Corps for the 59th Illinois, wrote, "About 12 we went out to a creek on the Decatur Road. The 59th [Illinois] pioneers build a bridge for the artillery. Came up with the 75th Illinois and 30th Indiana. We passed on over the creek that lay on the right of the road. It is quite a stream and we crossed on a log." This was the North Fork of Peach Tree Creek. The Pioneer commander recorded, "Companies B, D and F go out on skirmish line. Movement made cautiously and slow. Form a line of battle and move forward in thick underbrush. The 75th Illinois on our left, fronting south. Very little skirmishing and Co. B and F return to camp, leaving Co. D on the line." At that point General Stanley ordered the division to halt for the night and dig in. Mosman was responsible for the regiment's tools. "Lent tools to the Regiment to build works," he recorded in his journal. "Pioneers cut logs for Co. D as they are on picket and so can't build their part of the line." The Pioneers did not have to participate in the trench building once they felled the necessary logs. Mosman and one of his Pioneers, Gooding, decided to take advantage of the free time to "go to the creek for a wash but skirmishing becomes very heavy and we skedaddled to camp believing an attack about to occur," explained the dirty—but fleet-footed—lieutenant.[35]

---

[32] *OR*, series I, vol. 38, part I, series 72, 268.
[33] Ibid.
[34] Mosman, *The Rough Side of War*, 244.
[35] Ibid., 244–45.

General Howard recorded in his report, "Stanley meanwhile reconnoitered on the Decatur road. Driving the enemy's skirmishers, he seized the bridge, just burning, across the north fork of Peach Tree Creek and saved the most of it." There, Stanley's Division "repaired the old bridge and constructed a new one." After crossing the north fork of Peach Tree Creek, Stanley "encamped for the night."[36]

While Stanley's Division was busy to the east and southeast, Wood's Division was given the task of taking and securing a bridgehead over Peach Tree Creek at the Buckhead Road crossing. Following Stanley's Division in line of march on 19 July, Wood's 3rd Division "moved slowly with frequents halts, passing the little hamlet of Buckhead about one mile from our bivouac," recalled Adjutant Cope of the 15th Ohio.[37] The adjutant continued, "Here we found the head of our corps column [Stanley's Division] in camp."[38] It was customary for divisions and brigades to trade out positions each day while on the march so that the division or brigade in front on day one would rotate to end of the line for day two, and the division that had been second in line of march on day one would take the van on the second day. Therefore, the IV Corps, Wood's Division had been in the rear during the march on 18 July behind Stanley's Division, which was in rear of Newton's Division, and Wood's men were second in line on 19 July behind Stanley's Division, which was in the van. The assignment fell to Wood's Division to effect a crossing of Peach Tree Creek when they reached the Buckhead crossing. When they got there, they "found that the enemy had burned the bridge and were strongly intrenched on the opposite bank," according to Adjutant Cope.

Reporting from the south side of the creek, Harvey, in an article published in Macon on 20 July by the *Georgia Journal & Messenger*, explained that during the morning of 19 July, the Yankees began shelling the Southern defenses below Peach Tree Creek at the Buckhead Road site: "This morning the enemy opened a brisk shelling upon us from the opposite bank of the creek. They appear to be feeling for our position, and

---

[36]*OR*, series I, vol. 38, part I, series 72, 201.

[37]Alexis Cope, *The 15th Ohio Volunteers and Its Campaigns: War of 1861–5* (Charleston SC: Nabu Press, 2011) 523.

[38]Ibid.

endeavoring to elicit the fire of our batteries, but have not so far succeeded." Harvey added, "The sharpshooters are playing a lively hand this morning."[39]

Newton's 2nd Division followed Wood's and Stanley's Divisions to Peach Tree Creek and protected the left flank to the east toward Cross Keys and Decatur. The 3rd Brigade, led by General Luther P. Bradley, was assigned this task. "The 64th Ohio and 27th Illinois, under the command of Colonel Robert C. Brown, were ordered to make a reconnaissance along the Decatur road, if possible as far as Peachtree creek. About three miles out," remembered Lieutenant Colonel Wilbur F. Hinman of the 65th Ohio of the same brigade, "the column reached the creek and found the enemy's pickets in strong rifle-pits on the opposite bank, and the bridge burned. The situation was reported back to headquarters, and in a short time Colonel Brown's command was relieved by Stanley's division."[40] Meanwhile, Wood's Division prepared to make an assault on the Confederate works guarding the Buckhead Road crossing.

While Wood's officers reconnoitered the Rebel positions, Federal artillery poured a "hot fire" while Yankee skirmishers engaged the attention of the Confederates. Peach Tree Creek forms a peninsula around the southern shore; it contains a low ridge on which Confederates defending the Buckhead Road crossing were entrenched. There, the 2nd Tennessee, led by Colonel William D. Robison and Lt Colonel William J. Hale, and a battery of artillery, manned by Arkansans and commanded by Captain Thomas J. Key of Cleburne's Division, fired on any hostile movement coming from or across the Buckhead Road north of the creek.[41] Initially, Wood and his men were ordered to wait until General John Geary and his division of the XX Corps to the right arrived. When Geary's men came, they would press the Confederates from the right while Wood's Division launched an assault over the bridgehead. After several hours passed, it became evident that Geary's Division was held up and would not arrive. In fact, Geary's Division was busy effecting a crossing over the creek at today's Northside Drive, more than a mile to the west of Wood's position. With portions of Gist's Brigade

---

[39]*Georgia* (Macon GA) *Journal & Messenger*, 20 July 1864.

[40]Hinman, *Story of the Sherman Brigade*, 577.

[41]Thomas J. Key, *Two Soldiers: The Campaign Diaries of Thomas J. Key and Robert J. Campbell*, ed. Wirt Armistead Cate (Chapel Hill: University of North Carolina Press, 1938) 92; Scaife, *Campaign for Atlanta*, 184.

denying easy access to the southern side of the creek to Geary's White Star Division, it would be at least twenty-four hours before they would have been able to come to the aid of Wood's men at Buckhead Road. Consequently, after waiting from 1 PM until 4 PM with no sign of Geary, Wood and his two brigade commanders surveyed the Southern defenses and considered options on how to cross without any support.

Wood deployed his 1st Brigade under Colonel William H. Gibson to the left of the road while he sent the 3rd Brigade, led by Colonel Frederick Knefler, to the right. The Confederate positions commanded the approaches to the creek from the Buckhead Road corridor. Wood and Knefler quickly surmised that they would incur a substantial number of casualties should they attempt a forced crossing at that point. Noting that the creek itself posed a formidable obstacle with a width of "about thirty feet and the average depth about five feet," Wood determined to find a way across without drawing Rebel fire. To accomplish this task, he ordered one hundred hand-picked men, fifty from the 79th Indiana and fifty from the 9th Kentucky, to lead the assault. This detachment was led by Major George W. Parker of the 79th Indiana. Knefler's Brigade "was moved down the stream [to the west] some distance, to a point below the enemy's intrenchments on the opposite bank." These men moved west along today's Peachtree Battle Avenue, along the path of today's Nacoochee Drive and Woodward Way. They were shielded by a skirt of woods until they reached a flanking position from which they could cross the creek unmolested. "At this point a ravine leads down to the creek in such a way as to hide troops moving down it from the view of the opposite shore," explained General Wood.[42]

The remainder of Knefler's Brigade followed. Behind Parker's hundred hand-picked detachment, the remaining six regiments of Knefler's Brigade formed in support. He would send four regiments quickly across the creek behind his shock troops under Major Parker. The first line was led by Colonel George H. Cram of the 9th Kentucky and included the remainder of the 79th Indiana and 9th Kentucky regiments. The second line consisted of the 19th Ohio, commanded by Colonel Charles F. Manderson, while the third line, under Major Claggett, contained the 17th Kentucky. Knefler sent the 86th Indiana, under Colonel George F. Dick, to the right and into the

---

[42]*OR*, series I, vol. 38, part I, series 72, 381–82.

Georgia wilderness west of his brigade (along today's Peachtree Battle Avenue to Dellwood Drive) to guard his exposed right flank. Before sending the majority of his brigade to the right, Knefler moved the 59th Ohio, under the direction of Captain R. M. Higgins, forward along the north shores of Peach Tree Creek near the Buckhead Road to draw the attention—and fire—of the Confederate skirmishers away from Knefler's flanking movement. It worked. While Knefler's Brigade slipped to the right and into the woods along today's Peachtree Battle Avenue, the 59th Ohio exchanged fire with the Tennessee Confederates opposite them. When Knefler was ready to unleash his flank attack, he sent the Ohioans forward, again diverting the attention of the Rebels. According to Captain Higgins, "we skirmished until about 4 PM, when the regiment was ordered to charge. We did so, crossing the creek and entering the enemy's works, having 5 men wounded."[43] Around 4:00 PM the "pioneers were ordered to cut timbers for a temporary bridge across the creek" while plans were made for a forced crossing.[44]

The quick action by Yankees completely surprised the Rebel pickets. Lieutenant Colonel William J. Hale and forty men, two entire companies of the 2nd Tennessee Confederate Infantry Regiment, were captured. The brave 2nd Tennessee had sent 264 men into the Battle of Chickamauga and lost 159 in causalities. At Ringgold Gap the veteran regiment with just 133 men remaining helped to stave off the Federal advance, losing nine in the action under the command of Lieutenant Colonel William J. Hale. At Peach Tree Creek, Hale was wounded and captured on 19 July 1864, sent to Johnson's Island, Ohio, and paroled in August 1865. Also falling during the action around Peach Tree Creek on the previous day was Lieutenant Colonel Edwin L. Drake, a doctor, who was wounded in the right hip at Peach Tree Creek on 18 July 1864.[45]

According to Dr. W. J. McMurray of the 20th Tennessee Infantry Regiment of Smith's Brigade in Bate's Division, the 2nd Tennessee had been sent over to relieve the 20th Tennessee, which had been guarding the

---

[43]Ibid., 381–82, 450, 479.

[44]Cope, *15th Ohio Volunteers and Its Campaigns*, 523.

[45]Edwin L. Ferguson, "Sumner County, Tennessee, in the Civil War," ch. 2, ed. E. J. Keen, http://freepages.genealogy.rootsweb.ancestry.com/~providence/cw_chap2.htm (17 August 2014).

Buckhead Road for twenty-four hours. Thus, on the morning of 19 July, the 20th Tennessee was "withdrawn across the creek to get a little rest." McMurray continued, "The 2nd Tennessee had not been on duty but a short while until they were assaulted by a largely superior force, and about one half of the regiment were killed, wounded and captured. The 20th Tennessee was hastily aroused from sleep, thrown into line, and checked the enemy at the creek."[46]

The 2nd Tennessee Confederate was from Polk's Brigade in Cleburne's Division. They were ordered to guard the Buckhead Road bridgehead at Peach Tree Creek, but had failed to detect the flanking move and crossing by the Federals. According to one Tennessee soldier, "This regiment while on picket duty at Peach-tree Creek, near Atlanta, suffered a loss of two entire companies, under command of Lieut. Colonel Hale, by capture."[47] One of the veterans of the 15th Ohio remembered finding five dead Rebels in the trenches guarding Buckhead Road.[48]

Knefler described the surprise attack,

> General Wood ordered the advance to be made without further loss of time. The skirmishers advanced rapidly upon the enemy's position, followed closely by the first line of battle. The enemy opened with musketry and artillery, inflicting considerable loss, but he was driven from his position and the works taken, with a number of prisoners.

Major Parker was severely wounded while leading the initial wave. In addition to Parker, Knefler's shock troops lost a couple of men who were wounded in the 79th Indiana. Two men were killed and five were wounded in the 9th Kentucky. The second line, containing the 19th Kentucky, saw one man killed and four wounded. In the 17th Kentucky, forming the third line, one man was killed and two were wounded; the 13th Ohio saw three men wounded. With the five men wounded from the 59th Ohio, Knefler's Brigade lost four men killed and twenty-two men wounded, for a total of

---

[46]W. J. McMurray, *History of the 20th Tennessee Regiment Volunteer Infantry, C. S. A.* (Nashville, 1904; repr. Nashville: Elder's Bookstore, 1976) 319–20.

[47]J. B. Lindsley, ed., *Military Annals of Tennessee*, vol. 1 (Wilmington NC: Broadfoot Publishing, 1995) 134; Tennessee Historical Commission, *Tennesseans in the Civil War*, 2 vols. (Nashville: Civil War Centennial Commission, 1964) 1:178.

[48]Cope, *15th Ohio Volunteers and Its Campaigns*, 524.

twenty-six casualties sustained in taking and establishing a bridgehead over the creek at the Buckhead Road.[49]

To the east of the Buckhead Road, Gibson's 1st Brigade tangled with the Tennessee skirmishers. Deploying the 25th Illinois as a screen along the Buckhead Road and just east of the road, Gibson moved the balance of his brigade to the east behind and to the left of the men of the 25th Illinois. After Knefler's Brigade began his assault, Gibson's Brigade was ordered to attack and cross the creek, if possible, to form a double-envelopment of the Confederate position. While Knefler's surprise attack bagged two Rebel companies, Gibson's men were not able to flank or capture the Southerners in their front, the remaining Tennesseans choosing to flee to the safety of the high ridge (today called Cardiac Hill where Piedmont Hospital is located) to their rear. Moreover, the terrain in front of Gibson's Brigade was not favorable for such an envelopment or surprise movement. Gibson lost four men killed and nine men wounded in the action, most of which occurred during the subsequent skirmishing with Confederates on the ridge south of Gibson's newly won position. "This position was at once barricaded under a sharp fire from the enemy and held until dark," according to Gibson, "when we were relieved by General Hazen's Brigade and returned to our camp of the night previous at Buck Head." Among the wounded were Lieutenant Street of the 89th Illinois, who subsequently died of his wounds, and from the 15th Ohio, two men were slightly wounded by a stray ball. The 15th Ohio also saw Sergeant T. C. Cory wounded and two men killed on the morning of 20 July as the regiment proceeded to follow Stanley's Division to the east.[50]

Soon, the pioneers erected a footbridge beside the bridge that had been burned, and the remainder the 3rd Brigade and the 1st Brigade of Wood's Division crossed to the southern side. Wood then ordered General Hazen's 2nd Brigade to come down from Buckhead and begin constructing a permanent bridge at the Buckhead Road. Hazen sent Captain Zoller and his pioneers from the 5th Kentucky to perform the task and they "had the greater part done," according to Hazen, when they were relieved by Newton's Pioneers at about dark. Hazen noted that Major S. B. Eaton, his provost-marshal, "was severely wounded while assisting the work at the

---

[49]*OR*, series I, vol. 38, part I, series 72, 450–79.
[50]Ibid., 389–421.

bridge."[51] According to the Federal commander, Eaton "was wounded while we were repairing the bridge, the ball striking his belt, and, without perforating it, driving the belt into the abdomen, so that on withdrawing it, a very ugly and dangerous wound was left." Fearing that the disease-ridden Federal field hospitals and permanent hospitals in Chattanooga, Nashville, and Louisville would prevent Eaton's recovery, Hazen sent the young officer off "privately at night in an ambulance to the railroad, some distance to the rear, with orders to get on the train and make his way north as quickly as possible, exercising his own wits to avoid the doctors and hospitals." Eaton made it as far as Nashville, where he "was intercepted and taken to the hospital, where he at once became inoculated, and came near death's door with gangrene. Luckily," Hazen explained, "his perfect health and constitution saved him."[52] Hazen also reported that the 41st Ohio and the 6th Indiana each lost one man wounded for a total of three men wounded during the day. The 93rd Ohio also lost one man wounded; the 124th Ohio had one officer wounded on 19 July and one man wounded on 20 July.[53] Also on 20 July, the 41st Ohio lost two more men wounded, for a total of eight men wounded during the two days of fighting.[54]

Hazen's men dug into the ground to deepen and strengthen the small Federal foothold on the south bank of the creek. One veteran of the 41st Ohio described the scene:

Just at dusk the brigade crossed quickly and moved to the top of the steep bank. Here a line was formed to protect the crossing, and during the night it was strongly intrenched. The enemy was known to be in position not a thousand yards from the creek, and it was thought that when morning came he might attempt to crush any force that had crossed in the night. The 41st [Ohio] was in front, and built a good earthwork. The men had become expert in this work, intrenching tools were as much a part of the equipment as the rifle. After a regiment was halted in line, a few moments sufficed to produce a defense of no little value in case of attack, and a few hours would find it effectual against field artillery.

---

[51]Hazen, *A Narrative of Military Service*, 272.
[52]Ibid., 412.
[53]Ibid., 272.
[54]*OR*, series I, vol. 38, part I, ser. no. 72, 421–49.

Private Theodore Hawley of Company G, 41st Ohio, was proud of the newly created earthwork. "It was his first experience in this work," because he had been wounded in his two previous battles before even firing a shot. Hawley had just returned to the regiment on 19 July. "When the gray dawn [of 20 July] came, he was on the parapet, smoothing the surface and tamping it down. A sergeant called to him to come down, as the enemy's pickets would soon be firing. The warning was a moment too late...," remembered one witness. "For as the sergeant spoke, a rifle ball came whizzing by, and took off the fingers of one of Hawley's hands. He jumped down behind the works, and tears rolled down his cheeks as he exclaimed that he was ruined for the army at last, and had not fired a shot for the flag." Just to the south of the Ohioans stood silhouetted in the clear sky below them Rebel fortifications crowning the hill and commanding the entire field all the way to the creek. On this hill were elements of Hardee's Corps, which threatened any further Federal advance. "The regiment [41st Ohio] stood to arms before daybreak, but no attack came," much to the relief of Hazen's veterans.[55]

During the evening of 19 July, Wood Division was ordered to follow Stanley's Division to the southeast the next morning, and Newton's Division was ordered to replace Wood's men. Just before dusk, Hazen's 2nd Brigade of Wood's Division had been sent to the south side of the creek to defend the bridgehead created by Gibson's and Knefler's Brigades of Wood's Division. Meanwhile, these two brigades marched back to Buck Head to their camps to rest and retrieve their equipment. It would be morning before all of Newton's troops could be sent to the south side of the creek and Hazen's Brigade extracted. Newton's men continued work until the bridge was completed around midnight. According to Corporal John Raper of the 26th Ohio, "The crossing was made on the stringers of a partially destroyed bridge, other troops being engaged in tearing down some houses nearby to floor the bridges so the ammunition and the artillery would follow."[56]

---

[55]Robert L. Kimberly and Ephraim S. Holloway, *The 41st Ohio Veteran Volunteer Infantry in The War of the Rebellion 1861–1865* (Huntington WV: Blue Acorn Press, 1999) 92, 113.

[56]John T. Raper, "You may give it to them, Captain," in *Echoes of Battle: The Atlanta Campaign, An Illustrated Collection of Union and Confederate Narratives*, ed. Larry M. Strayer and Richard A. Baumgartner (Huntington WV: Blue Acorn Press, 1991) 213.

Maurice Marcoot of the 15th Missouri in Kimball's Brigade of Newton's Division, which followed Wood's Division to the south side of the creek, remembered, "By the time we had reached the opposite shore, it had become quite dark. The works of the enemy were but a short distance back from the river, and we had already captured a number of persons."[57] Once Hazen's Brigade was recovered, Wood's Division would proceed to the east behind Stanley's Division to Johnson Road (along today's Cheshire Bridge Road) in the morning. General Howard had been ordered by Sherman to take two of his three divisions to the east to help close the gap between his lines and the right flank of Schofield's XXIII Corps, which was closing in on Atlanta from the northeast (along today's Peachtree Road / North Druid Hills Road / Roxboro Road / Briarcliff Road corridor).[58]

Elsewhere, the men of Newton's Division, which had served in the lead of Howard's IV Corps the day before, followed Wood's and Stanley's divisions: "Orders were issued requiring the 73rd Illinois and 24th Wisconsin to move at 5 AM of July 19th, and make a reconnaissance up Peach Tree Creek."[59] According to one veteran from the 73rd Illinois, they

> got started by 6 AM, and moved eastward one and ½ miles, bearing southward, on road, when Co.'s B, G, & K of the 73rd [Illinois], were ordered out as skirmishers. When matters were properly adjusted, we pushed forward rapidly some two miles, through woods, striking the enemy in force, taking him by surprise. Some skirmishing took place, but none of the 73rd [Illinois] were killed or wounded, but quite a loss was inflicted on the enemy, as he was thoroughly surprised. After this little scout and skirmish, we returned to our bivouac, and remained there until 6:00 pm when our brigade and division marched southward on the Atlanta road [today's Peachtree Street], halting at Peach Tree Creek to get supper.[60]

---

[57]Donald Allendorf, *Long Road to Liberty: The Odyssey of a German Regiment in the Yankee Army: The 15th Missouri Volunteer Infantry* (Kent OH: Kent State University Press, 2006) 205.

[58]*OR*, series I, vol. 38, part I, ser. no. 72, 381–82; Scaife, *Campaign for Atlanta*, 92b.

[59]Newlin, Lawler, and Sherrick, eds., *A History of the Seventy-Third Regiment of Illinois Infantry Volunteers*, 323.

[60]Ibid.

During the evening of 19 July, as Newton's Division began to move to the south side of Peach Tree Creek to relieve Hazen's Brigade, Sergeant Newlin recalled,

> Some time after supper, at about 10:00 PM, we marched across Peach Tree Creek on a bridge which the pioneers had constructed at some point where the old bridge had been burned. We took position five miles from Atlanta, and ½ mile from the bridge, on the south bank of Peach Tree Creek. We relieved Wood's Division, occupying a line of works which it had erected on east side of the road. Cleburne's Division of Hardee's Corps was said to be to our front.[61]

In the midst of the Federal advances, parts of the Southern forces opposing them floundered trying to find a suitable position from which they could defend. Skirmishers from Cleburne's and Bate's divisions of Hardee's Corps were on the far right of the Southern lines facing Peach Tree Creek. They spent 19 July constructing earthworks along a line located about a mile south of Peach Tree Creek. In the middle of their work, they were halted and moved closer to the Creek where they heard firing. Too late to contest the crossing, they soon returned to their original position; they had done nothing but permit Sherman's forces to gain a foothold on the south side of Peach Tree Creek from which the Yankees could expand on and entrench their position during the night. Trailing Bate's infantry was the Washington Artillery, which "spent the whole time struggling along behind an entrenched line of battle of our men trying to get a position. We went for perhaps two miles, and then went back again. There was no road and it was through thick woods...."[62] One man in the battery noted, "Not a shot was fired along that whole line as I recall. Indeed, not even a sign of any enemy."[63] In Bullock's Florida Brigade, Sergeant Major Washington Ives remembered hearing "fierce fighting...going on to our east at the time," as the men marched and countermarched in the tangled underbrush below Peach Tree Creek.[64]

---

[61]Ibid.

[62]Nathaniel Cheairs Hughes, Jr., *The Pride of the Confederate Artillery: The Washington Artillery in the Army of Tennessee* (Baton Rouge: Louisiana State University Press, 1997) 196.

[63]Ibid.

[64]Washington Ives, *Civil War Journal and Letters of Sergeant Washington Ives*

Federal Corporal John T. Raper, of Blake's 2nd Brigade of Newton's 2nd Division in Howard's IV Corps remembered that Newton's Division did not advance any farther south past the bridgehead until after noon the following day, 20 July. In fact, Raper and at least part of Newton's Division did not cross Peach Tree Creek until the morning of 20 July. Raper wrote, "After noon on the 20th our division—Newton's—crossed and took position on top of the first range of hills south of the creek.... We gained the position on top of the hill almost without resistance and everything in front was quiet, and conspicuously so."[65] Newton's prudent action in taking this ridge, where the men instinctively began to entrench and improve their position in the couple of hours before they were attacked, proved to be key during the ensuing Confederate attack.

In another place along the Confederate line, the men of Gist's Brigade of Georgians and South Carolinians had been guarding the area near the railroad bridge along the Chattahoochee River at the time of the transfer of command from Johnston to Hood. Many of the citizens of Atlanta were still convinced that Sherman's main thrust for Atlanta would occur near the railroad bridge and the fords over the Chattahoochee River northwest of the Gate City. On Monday, W. H. T. Walker's Division, which included Gist's Brigade, was, according to Captain Charles M. Furman of the 16th South Carolina, "moved to the right crossed the Railroad & remained for the night bivouacked by the road side, Tuesday moved out a mile or more in advance of breast-works & relieved Reynolds Brigade—doing picket duty on Peach-Tree Creek."[66] The brigade that Gist's men relieved were General Daniel Reynolds's Arkansans, which had been ordered to slide to the west to connect with other Southern units in Stewart's Army of Mississippi near Moore's Mill.[67]

Approaching Peach Tree Creek from the north during the middle of Tuesday, 19 July, were the three brigades of General John Geary's 2nd Division of the XX Corps, with Colonel David Ireland's 3rd Brigade in the

---

4th Florida C. S. A.: First Hand Account Of Life On The Frontline During The American Civil War (Tallahassee FL: Jim R. Cabaniss, 1987) 14.

[65]Raper, "You may give it to them, Captain," in *Echoes of Battle*, 213–14.

[66]"Captain Charles Manning Furman, Company H, Sixteenth South Carolina," http://batsonsm.tripod.com/letters/letters9.html (accessed 15 August 2014).

[67]Supplement to *OR*, vol. 6, part II, ser. no. 18, 751, 759, 768.

van.[68] Geary put his twelve pieces of artillery into position and, at 3:00 PM, he opened fire on the hills occupied by the Rebels on the southern shore of Peach Tree Creek. Together with a "very heavy line [of infantry, he] poured in a furious musketry fire."[69] Colonel Ireland deployed the 137th New York under Lt. Colonel Koert S. Van Voorhis as skirmishers and ordered forward the 149th New York. Led by Colonel H. A. Barnum, the 149th New York filed across on the double-quick, formed on the other side into line, and charged and carried the hill. "All was done very quickly," according to division commander John Geary. "The enemy, completely surprised, fled, leaving 23 prisoners and their intrenching tools in our hands."[70]

In this area, the 16th South Carolina and the 46th Georgia of Gist's Brigade found themselves isolated from the rest of the Southern forces. Captain Furman explained, "Our Regt and part of the 46th Ga. were placed on the outer picket. In the evening the pickets on our right & left having given way we fell back and retired from the position."[71] While the 16th South Carolina managed to slip away, some of the 46th Georgia's soldiers were not so lucky. "Three-fourths of one company of the 46th were killed— wounded & missing," Furman continued. "Our Regt lost none and slept that night on the same ground it had occupied the preceding night."[72] The unlucky company from the 46th Georgia was Company E (known as the Harris Blues from Harris County); it lost twelve men in a matter of minutes. After 1st Sergeant F. A. Worrell was killed and 3rd Corporal Leander P. Hopkins was wounded, the company was enveloped on both sides by an onrushing and unnoticed foe. Captured were 2nd Sergeant Lorenzo D. Hutchinson, who had just been promoted to that rank the day before, along with privates William J. Bass, Henry S. Cash, Thomas Jefferson Daniel, Joseph D. Hart, Robert M. Moss (or Morris), Allen E. Richardson, Alfred A. Smith, Thomas B. Smith, and James Eugene C. Speer (or Spears). In addition to the twelve men from Company E who were put out of action, Company H, the Marion Volunteers from Marion County, lost 2nd Corporal George J. Barker when his left leg was permanently disabled.

---

[68]*OR*, series I, vol. 38, part II, ser. no. 73, 137.
[69]Ibid.
[70]Ibid., 137, 272.
[71]"Captain Charles Manning Furman."
[72]Ibid.

Private Jesse Benson was killed, and from Company K (Price Volunteers from Muscogee County), Private A. D. Dunnagan was killed. In all, there were fifteen casualties in the 46th Georgia: three men killed, two men wounded, and ten men captured.[73]

As sounds of the impending crisis neared Atlanta, eleven-year-old Joseph Manning Austin during "the night of July 5, 1864…lay awake and listened to the Yankees crossing the Chattahoochee River just a half mile down the hill from his home." Joseph's older sister Josephine recorded her father's Civil War stories, which were often repeated around the hearth of the family home. She wrote, "There had been fighting across the river for several days and the sound of the guns could be plainly heard." Josephine's father, Thomas Franklin Austin, and eldest brother, John Thomas Austin, fought for the Confederacy. John was in Virginia with Lee in Stonewall Jackson's old corps in the Army of Northern Virginia, and Thomas was serving as a sergeant in Company C, 2nd Georgia Infantry Reserve, which had only recently been called up to defend Atlanta. Thus, young Joseph had been left as the "man of the house."[74]

After the Yankees had swept through their Sandy Springs home, killing their cow, pigs and chickens, and taking their horse, young Joseph determined to join his father to fight the Yankees. While they were roasting and feasting on his family's livestock, the boy had stolen one of the Yankee's guns and hidden it in the hollow of a nearby tree. After inquiring among family and friends where his father's regiment was posted, Joseph discovered that his father was camped near Peach Tree Creek "where the defense of Atlanta was planned." He slipped from his family's home on Johnson Ferry Road and through the woods and jungles north of the creek to Peach Tree Creek. There, the boy "saw camp fires near the creek and, after he had determined they were not Yankees, he went up to the sentry and asked to be taken to his father." After a while, "one soldier came forth who knew his father…and the told the little boy that his father had been sent south to

---

[73]Lillian Henderson, *Roster of the Confederate Soldiers of Georgia*, vol. 4 (Hapeville GA: Longino and Porter, 1995) 924–1026.

[74]Josephine Manning Austin Dobbs, *Civil War Stories as told to her by her father, Joseph Manning Austin (1853–1931), Confederate Reminiscences and Letters 1861–1865*, vol. 3 (Atlanta: Georgia Division, United Daughters of the Confederacy, 1996–2000) 3–5; Chickamauga National Battlefield Park Library, Chickamauga TN.

Andersonville to serve as a guard at the Yankee prison." That soldier then sought and obtained permission to return the boy back through the Federal lines to his mother and home.

About a hundred years later a large, old tree was removed in Sandy Springs next door to the old family house. As the tree was being cut down, "an ancient rifle tumbled into the sunlight." It was an "old oak tree, some 75 feet high and 3½ feet in diameter," and "had a hollow which held the gun," according to a member of the Frankie Lyle chapter of the United Daughters of the Confederacy in Jonesboro, Georgia.[75]

As Tuesday, 19 July drew to a close, most of the veterans in the Southern Army knew that they were about to make an attack. It was no secret why Hood had replaced Johnston, and the closer Sherman's forces drew to Atlanta, the quicker the "ball would open" (a Civil War-era expression for starting the battle or main event). On the evening of 19 July, Martin Van Buren Oldham of the 9th Tennessee recorded in his diary, "We were not relieved last night as anticipated. All the other brigades were relieved. The Yankee raiders have succeeded in reaching the Georgia and the Montgomery and [Nashville] railroads doing some damage. In the evening cavalry came to relieve us." Concerning the forced crossing over Peach Tree Creek by Howard's IV Corps, Oldham added, "Fighting this evening on a part of the line. We will move out on our positions tonight and tomorrow the fight will open."[76]

On the Northern side of the lines, a different feeling prevailed. One newspaper report thus summed it up, "July 20, 4:30 AM. The army has lain perfectly quiet during the night. The rebels do not seem at all disposed to come out of Atlanta and throw down the gage of battle on open ground." The Northern journalist could not have been more wrong, but his opinion pervaded in the Federal camps along the banks of Peach Tree Creek as the men were lulled to sleep by its gentle passing. "Headquarters are agog, and the army will doubtless move early," added the reporter. "Another day's

---

[75]Ibid.

[76]Martin Van Buren Oldham, *Civil War Diaries of Van Buren Oldham, Company G, 9th Tennessee, 1863–1864*; http://www.utm.edu/departments/acadpro/library/departments/special_collections/ms.php (18 November 2014).

march will carry us across the second, if not the third of their three railroads."[77]

---

[77]*Rebellion Record 1862–69: A Diary of American Events*, vol. 11, comp. G. P. Putnam and D. Van Nostrand (New York: n.p.) 248, consisting of a series of newspaper accounts and articles in 12 volumes; ed., Frank Moore, vol. 11, 248 (courtesy Special Collections Department, Rome/Floyd County GA Library).

18

IF IT TAKES ALL SUMMER

You ole Yankees are the meanest folks I ever seed; you'uns don't fight we'uns fair; we'll throw up breastworks and fix a place to fight you'uns behind, and we'uns expect you'uns to fight us all before it; instead of that you'uns 'flink' around and pitch into we'uns eend. We fixed a place at Buzzard Roost for you'uns to fight us, and you'uns flinked us, and flinked us at Cartersville, and flinked us at Dallas, and you flinked us at Big Shanty, and you flinked us at Kenesaw; and it peers like you'uns are 'allus' pitchin' into we'uns eend. And 'tother day Capt. Hooker flinked around here with his critter company and throwed cannonades as big as my wash-kittle and jist knocked my ash-hopper all to pieces....[1]

Uncle Billy Sherman was confident of success. He never doubted that his veterans would drive Johnston's army through Georgia and capture Atlanta so long as the Washington politicians did not interfere with his plans and the Northern war correspondents stayed out of his way. The only question in the red-haired, fiery general's mind was how long it would take him. His counterpart in the eastern theater, General U. S. Grant, when questioned about whether his Army of the Potomac could continue to attack Lee's Army of Northern Virginia and maintain the pressure on the South after terrible losses were suffered in the Wilderness, replied "I propose to fight it out on this line if it takes all summer."[2] Sherman was well aware that the North's will to fight was a fickle thing and that public opinion could change like the direction of the wind. The winds of change were evident in the late spring 1864 as the war-torn nation grew weary. This despair led the Northern Democratic Party, which was desperate to regain control of the White House and Congress during this presidential election year, to espouse the position that the war could not be won without additional and

---

[1]B. F. McGee, *History of the 72nd Indiana Volunteer Infantry of the Mounted Lightning Brigade, 1882* (Lafayette IN: S. Vater & Co., Printers, 1882) 339.

[2]*OR*, series I, vol. 36, part II, ser. no. 73, 672; James M. McPherson, *Battle Cry of Freedom: The Civil War Era* (New York: Oxford University Press, 2003) 730.

unacceptable loss in men, money, and materials, and that the best outcome would be to sue for an honorable peace with the Southern states. Some Northern Democrats remarked that if the South wanted their "precious black pets, let them keep them." Some Northern Democratic newspapers wrote during this time that "Tens of thousands of white men must yet bite the dust to allay the Negro mania of the President."[3]

Another little-reported but very real reason beginning to shape the thought in the North was that by this point in the war, a number of freed slaves had made their way north to seek jobs in farms and factories. They were beginning to strain the North's economy, if not the comfort level of the Northern whites. By 1864, a number of freed blacks were joining the army and serving in various posts throughout the North and in the Ohio and Tennessee Valleys where the Federal army had gained and maintained control of vast portions of the South. The freed blacks were eager both to prove themselves equal to whites in the Northern Army (and in various jobs across the North) and to contribute their part to free all slaves and preserve the Union; however, many whites in the North were uncomfortable with having the freed blacks living among them or with giving them true equality and opportunities in their own communities.

By this time of the war, a number of people in the North supported *in theory* the idea that all men are created equal and that the South was wrong to continue slavery. This was the basis for the Republican Party's radical movement. However, most folks in the North had not yet reconciled themselves to the consequences of freeing an entire group of people and having them assimilate into their society. Most Northerners simply wanted to restore the Union, free the slaves, and permit the blacks either to return to Africa (a position President Lincoln espoused) or live in freedom chiefly in the rural South. Moreover, at first there was a reluctance in the North to permit freed blacks to serve in the army. When they were allowed to join, they were often placed in rear area posts guarding forts, railroads, bridges, or in various construction projects, which reminded many of the labors of their captive past. It is estimated that about 180,000 blacks joined the Federal army during the war. There is much speculation about why more blacks did not migrate North or join the army during the war; one possible explanation

---

[3]Columbus (GA) *Crisis*, 3 August 1864; McPherson, *Battle Cry of Freedom*, 769.

may be found in an old legend. One old slave advised a younger slave, who was contemplating running away, that the war was like two dogs fighting over a bone. The dogs were the North and the South, and the black people were the bone. "In both cases the bone had no part in the fight," therefore, they might as well just "wait and see" who wins, because they would likely still be the "bone" of one dog or the other, and it might not really change their fortunes anyway.[4]

This dilemma left many freed blacks without a home or place to go where they could get a fresh start. Many blacks thought that they were just as well off—or poorly off, as the case may be—to stay in the South where their families had been for several generations. This disparity in equality, in social opportunity, in class, in education, and in economic opportunity continued to keep blacks on the farm in the South until the post-World War II industrialization in the Northern cities. The civil rights movement finally alleviated some of that oppression and discriminatory policies as the United States continues to struggle to form a "more perfect Union." Suffice it to say that Sherman was feeling the pressure of an increasing angst among the Northern populace for many reasons, including the issue of slavery. He was made aware that Grant and Lincoln reasoned that they needed to try to wrap up this war—or at least make its successful conclusion obvious by the time that the Northern people went to the polls in November.

Another problem facing General Sherman was that many of his veteran soldiers were beginning to be mustered out of the army as their terms expired during summer 1864. Many Federal regiments were created during summer 1861 with three-year enlistments. Sherman was getting reinforcements, and new units (or units that heretofore had been guarding some post in the Tennessee Valley) were being sent to augment his force in front of Atlanta. They could not, though, replace the experience of these three-year veteran units, many of which had been with Sherman since Shiloh. One such regiment, the 6th Iowa, saw 160 men mustered out of the regiment on the evening of 16 July: "They were seasoned soldiers inured to the service, and their places could not be filled by raw recruits." While these brave veterans "had performed their contract with the government faithfully

---

[4]Emory M. Thomas, *The Confederate Nation: 1861–1865* (New York: Harper Perennial, 2011) 237.

and honorably and were justly entitled to their honorable discharges," their departure left the regiment with a fighting strength of just 214 men.[5]

The invasion of North Georgia by Sherman's legions provided an opportunity for different peoples to come face to face. One such experience was recorded by a veteran of the 72nd Indiana, a part of the Lightning Brigade, as they approached Cross Keys northeast of Atlanta:

> After going 12 miles we struck the rebels in force at Crosskeys, formed line of battle and skirmished with them for two or three hours, capturing a few prisoners without loss to ourselves. Near here we saw marks of ignorance that, up to this time, we had supposed were hardly possible in a free country. On our way we passed a log cabin; standing at the fence was a man whose looks indicated him to be four score years old. We asked how far it was to Atlanta. He said he had never been there but guessed it was about 16 miles. "How long have you lived here?" he was asked, "Ever since I kin ric'leck," he replied. "How far is it to Crosskeys?" "I don't know," he replied; and yet this man was not a fool. Soon after passing his house we saw by the side of the road a large chestnut tree. It had been peeled on the side next to the road and two large crossed keys cut in the wood, and under them were cut three notches; all of which we rightly interpreted, three miles to Crosskeys. Near the place we saw a large guide board with the letters Roswell painted upon it, and on the post under it were eight deeply cut notches, which, of course, meant eight miles to Roswell. We saw many such signs afterwards. Crosskeys is 13 miles from Atlanta, and our reconnaissance was a bold and risky one, as there was a large cavalry force of the enemy above McAfee's Bridge on the east side of the river, which might have easily cut off our retreat.[6]

On another occasion, the same Federal men found themselves confronted by a woman who was "blustering around" and in a "terrible rage" as she scolded the Yankee soldiers as they crossed by her home. When she was asked what was the matter, the woman "roared out":

> You ole Yankees are the meanest folks I ever seed; you'uns don't fight we'uns fair; we'll throw up breastworks and fix a place to fight you'uns behind, and we'uns expect you'uns to fight us all before it; instead of that you'uns 'flink'

---

[5]Henry H. Wright, *A History of the Sixth Iowa Infantry* (Iowa City: The State Historical Society of Iowa, 1923) 300–301.

[6]McGee, *History of the 72nd Indiana Volunteer Infantry*, 340–41.

around and pitch into we'uns eend. We fixed a place at Buzzard Roost for you'uns to fight us, and you'uns flinked us, and flinked us at Cartersville, and flinked us at Dallas, and you flinked us at Big Shanty, and you flinked us at Kenesaw; and it peers like you'uns are 'allus' pitchin' into we'uns eend. And 'tother day Capt. Hooker flinked around here with his critter company and throwed cannonades as big as my wash-kittle and jist knocked my ash-hopper all to pieces....[7]

After reaching Cross Keys, the Lightning Brigade and Minty's Brigade of Schofield's Army of the Ohio were ordered to Stone Mountain on 18 July to connect with McPherson's Army of the Tennessee. While en route, the men passed by a large plantation where scores of African Americans "came out 'to see dem Yankees.'"

Among the number was the funniest creature of the human species we ever saw. She was just about as thick as she was high, and the laughing surface of her face was simply extensive. She would weigh 300 pounds, and came waddling right out into the road, frightening our horses, and began immediately to talk and chatter like a parrot: "Where all you'uns gwine to?" We told her we were going down here to tear up the railroad. "What you'uns want to tar up de railroad fo'?" "To keep the rebels from using it." This puzzled her, and for a second she was silent, when some one told her we were Yankees. She was the very picture of astonishment, and said "No!" We told her we were, for a fact; when she raised her hands and said, "Dey dun tole us you all had horns!"[8]

At around 7:00 PM on 18 July, Sherman telegraphed Henry Halleck in Washington that he would make a "bold push for Atlanta" the next day, with McPherson's Army of Tennessee advancing on Decatur from the east, Schofield's Army of the Ohio moving on Decatur from the north, and Thomas and the Army of the Cumberland pressing Atlanta from the north. Sherman also ordered General Garrard's Federal Cavalry to continue to destroy the Georgia railroad to the east toward Augusta "as far as deemed prudent." From his headquarters at a house near Old Cross Keys, Sherman surveyed the situation. Unaware of Johnston's removal from command and surprised by the lack of Confederate activity, Sherman wrote to General Thomas on the afternoon of 18 July that "It is hard to realize that Johnston

---

[7]Ibid., 339.
[8]Ibid., 341.

will give up Atlanta without a fight, but it may be so. Let us develop the truth."[9]

---

[9]*OR*, series I, vol. 38, part V, ser. no. 76, 170.

19

THE LOSS OF ATLANTA

> I have seen an Atlanta paper of the 18th, containing Johnston's farewell
> order to his troops. From its tone and substance I infer he has been relieved
> by Jeff. Davis, who sent Bragg to Atlanta to bear the order. I also infer it is
> not for the purpose of getting another command. Hood succeeds.[1]

Sherman's belief that Johnston might give up Atlanta without a fight was
short-lived. The Federal commander went to bed on Monday, 18 July, after
a busy day of rapid advances toward Atlanta by all of his infantry with but
little resistance, seemingly confirming his suspicions that another Rebel
retreat was imminent. Tuesday morning, 19 July, brought news that drastic
changes were taking place on the Confederate side. After reading an Atlanta
newspaper brought to him by a Federal spy, Sherman discovered that his old
rival and pre-war friend, Joe Johnston, had been removed from command.
The news also revealed that a change of tactics would surely follow as
Johnston's replacement could only mean that his Fabian Policy was no
longer desired or tolerated by the Southern administration.

In a letter to Thomas written around 2:00 or 3:00 PM on 19 July,
General Sherman explained,

> I have seen an Atlanta paper of the 18th, containing Johnston's farewell
> order to his troops. From its tone and substance I infer he has been relieved
> by Jeff. Davis, who sent Bragg to Atlanta to bear the order. I also infer it is
> not for the purpose of getting another command. Hood succeeds.[2]

The Federal commander quickly sized up the news that Hood's
promotion could only mean that the Richmond administration would not
give up Atlanta without a fight. Realizing that his men were spread out and

---

[1]Ibid., 183. Sherman's dispatch does not provide the time it was sent, but it
includes a reference to some troop movements at 1:05 PM, and Thomas's reply letter
was sent at 4:45 PM.

[2]Ibid.

vulnerable to a counteroffensive, Sherman directed Thomas to hurry up his army to get across Peach Tree Creek to reach within supporting distance of the balance of his forces. "You must get across Peach Tree [Creek] either by moving direct on Atlanta, or, if necessary, leave a force to watch the [railroad] bridge [across the Chattahoochee] in possession of the enemy and move by the left. This is very important," Sherman added, "and at once as we may have to fight all of Hood' [Army] from east of Atlanta."[3] Sherman did correctly reason that if a Rebel assault were to be made, it would be after his army reached below Peach Tree Creek. He continued to believe that the threat of attack was to McPherson, east of the city, and not Thomas north of it. Hood, following Johnston's intended plan of attack, delivered a surprising assault on 20 July. Sherman's prophecy that McPherson's army was targeted would be realized in Hood's second sortie on 22 July after the Confederates failed to destroy Thomas along Peach Tree Creek. While Hood's offensive strategy failed, in Hood the South had a leader who was willing to take risks.

In 1862 during the Peninsular Campaign, Old Joe had allowed McClellan's Northern forces to reach within sight of Richmond, Virginia, before launching a partially successful counterstrike. In summer 1863, Johnston had failed to concentrate his forces quick enough to save Vicksburg from capture or Jackson from a fiery destruction. His lack of a plan, or timidity in executing one, assisted in the loss of a principal Confederate army of some 30,000 men. Now, during the Georgia Campaign of 1864, Johnston's plan, if he had one, was to defeat Sherman by not giving battle until he had the best opportunity to strike when his army was closer in size and strength to Sherman's legions. Johnston reasoned that as he drew into the interior of Georgia, and as he bled Sherman's men bit by bit, the Federal force grew weaker while his grew stronger through reinforcements and morale. A large body of contemporaneous letters and diaries support the feeling of many in his army that Johnston's strategy was understood and appreciated within his ranks as perhaps the better choice between headlong assaults and defending behind trenches.

Johnston was not without his flaws, however. Recent critical studies have analyzed the general's character flaws that help to explain his reluctance to give battle. One argument, which has been advanced by historians

---

[3]Ibid.

Stephen Davis, Steven Woodworth, and Richard McMurry, is that Johnston lacked the qualities to be an effective offensive commander. While other historians have praised Old Joe's reputation for defensive fighting, describing his skills as a "different valor," that is to say "the valor of the strategic and tactical defensive," a number of recent historians have begun to question whether Johnston really ever had a plan at all to defeat his foe.[4] Perhaps historian Steven Woodworth put it best when he said that "Johnston seemed to be skillful, but he lacked nerve."[5] Davis argues in his article, "A Reappraisal of the Generalship of John Bell Hood in the Battles for Atlanta," that Johnston's performance suggests "five major deficiencies as a military leader." Davis explains that: "(1) his lack of aggressiveness and repeated refusal to take the general offensive; (2) his failure to develop an overall plan to beat the enemy; (3) his pessimism and fear of defeat; (4) his conspicuous mistakes as tactician; and (5) his inability to retain the confidence and undivided support of his officers and men," all contributed to Johnston's failure to arrest Sherman's advance and each pointed to Johnston's inability to wage offensive strategy effectively.[6]

While this author strongly agrees that Davis's first three assertions contributed significantly to Johnston's failures, points four and five go too far. Repeated evidence of accounts written at the time of the events, particularly among the soldiers of the Gulf South, and of the Army of Mississippi revered "Ole Joe" much like the accounts of many who served under General Lee in the Army of Northern Virginia. The accounts Davis and McMurry point to as authority that Johnston did not have the confidence and support of his men come largely from men from parts of

---

[4]Grady McWhiney and Perry D. Jamieson, *Attack and Die: Civil War Military Tactics and the Southern Heritage* (Tuscaloosa: University of Alabama Press, 1984) 69; Gilbert E. Govan and James W. Livingood, *A Different Valor: The Story of General Joseph E. Johnston, C. S. A.* (Indianapolis: Bobbs Merrill, 1956) 87.

[5]Steven Woodworth, "A Reassessment of Confederate Command Options during the Winter of 1863–1864," in Theodore P. Savas and David A. Woodbury, eds., *The Campaign for Atlanta & Sherman's March to the Sea*, vol. 1, Essays of the American Civil War (Campbell CA: Savas Woodbury Publishing, 1994) 5.

[6]Stephen Davis, "A Reappraisal of the Generalship of John Bell Hood in the Battles for Atlanta," in Theodore P. Savas and David A. Woodbury, eds., *The Campaign for Atlanta & Sherman's March to the Sea*, vol. 1, Essays of the American Civil War (Campbell CA: Savas Woodbury Publishing, 1994) 54–55.

Tennessee and Georgia that had been overrun by the Northern armies during the last few months. These Southern accounts come from Rebel units that did see a number of desertions during the campaign because soldiers worried for their loved ones beyond the enemy's lines. The accounts are similar to other Southern records of men in Mississippi and Arkansas whose homes were overrun during the Vicksburg Campaign the year before. Desertion in the Army of Mississippi reached its zenith after the fall of Jackson and Vicksburg until the army moved away from the Magnolia State and into Alabama in February 1864. During the Georgia Campaign, there were relatively few desertions among these units as compared with men from regions that were then being lost to the advancing Yankee forces.

As for Johnston's tactical failures, to be sure, he had some, and Davis's article points to a few significant examples at Snake Creek Gap and Resaca; however, other evidence of Johnston's performance during the campaign point to his competency and skill in selecting fields of battle, or in utilizing the ground afforded him, such as at New Hope, Picket's Mill, and Kennesaw Mountain. As Lee did at the Wilderness, Johnston understood that he could strike Sherman's superior numbers in the wooded New Hope area with his undersized army and thus neutralize the Northern advantage. At Picket's Mill, and the corresponding lines at Lost Mountain, Pine Mountain, Noonday Creek, and Brushy Mountain, Johnston continued to stymie Sherman's probes and block his southeastward moves much like Lee did at Spotsylvania. Finally, after weeks of futile efforts to flank him, Sherman reluctantly launched a futile assault at Kennesaw Mountain just as Grant had done against Lee at Cold Harbor. The comparisons between the two campaigns, Grant vs. Lee in Virginia, and Sherman vs. Johnston in Georgia, are can be argued as similar.

One tactical failure that Johnston may have been guilty of is that during the weekend of 16 and 17 July, just prior to his removal from command, his men were deployed much too far to the west and northwest of Atlanta as they continued to guard river crossings and the southern side of the railroad bridgehead over the Chattahoochee River. Once Sherman's forces were across the river from Pace's Ferry to Roswell, a distance of more than six miles, Johnston's right flank had been exposed and he had to fall back below Peach Tree Creek as his next line of defense. Sherman's infantry continued to cross in force between 9 and 17 July, and all of it crossed north of Paces Ferry. Also, maintaining a foothold on the Chattahoochee River had no further military value for the Confederate army unless Johnston intended to either re-cross the stream and launch an attack on Sherman's rear. Perhaps Old Joe still believed a part of Sherman's infantry force continued to oppose his army on the north shore, and he believed that he needed to try and tie it down by offering a resistance. One could argue that Johnston was trying to block Sherman's approach from the west and inviting Sherman to cross the Chattahoochee north of Atlanta to set up his Peach Tree Creek counter-attack, but this is speculative.

In either event, the Southern commander risked exposing Atlanta to capture from the northeast; further, this was precisely the direction from which Sherman's force was bearing down on the Gate City. Johnston finally began to shift his army to the northeast during Sunday, 17 July, in preparation for a planned strike on a part of Sherman's force as it crossed Peach Tree Creek, but his men appear to have been moved too slowly to the anticipated attack position. His removal from command on the eve of his intended attack, coupled with the unchecked and rapid movement by McPherson far to the east of Atlanta, served to render another Johnston "offensive" undelivered. Moreover, General Joseph Wheeler failed to keep Johnston informed of the movements of McPherson and Schofield's armies to the east and northeast, a point of blame that can be placed at Old Joe's feet because he failed to order Wheeler to check their movements.

To General Hood's credit, once he took over command and considered his options, he quickly assessed the threat posed by McPherson's and Schofield's flanking maneuver and his need for intelligence on their exact locations prior to launching any counterstrike. Johnston seems to have kept the knowledge of Sherman's exact troop positions to himself (as Hood later opined), or he failed to think about the positions deeply enough to order Wheeler to handle, which is likely closer to the truth. There is no evidence that Johnston was keeping a close eye on the whereabouts of McPherson and Schofield during the weekend of 16–17 July; instead, it appears that he was focused on slowing Thomas's force between the Chattahoochee River and Peach Tree Creek in preparation to strike his Army of the Cumberland when it crossed the later stream. It seems that Johnston was content to remain under the impression that McPherson and Schofield were too far from Thomas to render support in the event of a strike on Old Pap and his force along the Peach Tree Creek line. Thus, while Johnston's plan of attack on Thomas was potentially sound, he appears to have failed to gather sufficient intelligence (or failed to have shared it with anyone) to ensure its success.

When Hood took command, a considerable portion of Wheeler's force remained far to the southwest, along the Chattahoochee River, as the Confederate cavalry extended Johnston's river defenses far beyond the reach of Sherman's. A modern-era comparison could be made to Hitler's determination to hold the German 15th Army at Calais while the Allied forces landed at the Normandy Beaches on D-Day. But this analysis stretches the point at bit, except to say that it is difficult for a commander who is on the tactical defensive to anticipate and redeploy his smaller, defensive force before the attacker can exploit his flanking movement. In fairness, Wheeler's cavalry had the task of guarding approximately forty miles of river crossings from today's Duluth to Six Flags over Georgia with only eleven small cavalry brigades. While Johnston is given great credit for his ability to anticipate and slide his men around to frustrate Sherman's movements during the Georgia Campaign, he did fail to anticipate or move rapidly enough to cover his flank or rear at Dalton during the Snake Creek Gap incident, at Resaca, and perhaps again just prior to Peach Tree Creek.

In military theory, there are typically two general strategic thoughts on how to win when leading a force against a vastly larger foe. First, strike early with quick, bold, and decisive offensive movements as early in the war as possible and before the numerically superior and richer enemy can organize and prepare, thereby removing its will to fight before it learns how or is prepared to fight. Second, lure the enemy into a long, costly, and seemingly endless war that drains its will to fight, thereby not risking a general, or all-out, fight to the death. In this strategy, the weaker side seeks to drag out the war as long as possible until the other side simply quits fighting, or until an intervening force such as an economic depression or a foreign power came to the rescue.

It is important to realize that for the Confederacy, both strategies—the defensive and the offensive—failed. As Lee eventually lost Richmond and Petersburg, so, too, Johnston would have lost Atlanta, and most likely, he would have given up Atlanta much earlier and long before the Northern presidential elections in November. Even if Johnston had demonstrated a desire to hold the Gate City, Sherman would have continued probing until he had compelled either Johnston's withdrawal or capitulation by encircling the city. Thus, it is likely that either strategy, Johnston's or Hood's, would have resulted in failure. It is also clear that trying each measure halfway, as the Confederacy did in summer 1864, was a recipe for disaster.

One veteran of Cleburne's Division lamented,

> from Peachtree Creek on to and through the battles of Nashville the best blood of the army was shed with a prodigality unsparing and unsurpassed in vain endeavors to accomplish the impossible, until there were left only a few at the surrender at High Point, N.C., to commemorate the deeds of daring of those who fell in the flame and forefront of battle.[7]

At Peach Tree Creek, the Confederacy began its series of reversals from which she would never recover. While doom of the Confederacy was perhaps inevitable, the new offensive strategy sped its end.

Sherman, who overstated the Rebel casualties, stated that some 3,240 Confederates had died at Peach Tree Creek, but he had lost 3,521 in casualties of all kinds.[8] Sherman probably wanted to justify his losses at the recent Battle of Kennesaw, where he had foolishly attacked against well-entrenched Southerners who were on the more desirable high ground. At Kennesaw, Sherman had lost some 3,000 men while the Confederates suffered only about 800 casualties. He was well aware that the re-election of President Lincoln that fall, and with it the fate of the war, rested on his shoulders and with the success or failure of his men. Since General U. S. Grant and the Army of the Potomac had stalled in front of Petersburg, Virginia, where General Lee and his men had forced Grant into a stalemate, it was up to Sherman to give the North a reason to continue the war. Any news that got back to Washington and the North about the Georgia Campaign had better be good news. In reality, the South had lost about 2,298 men at Peach Tree Creek while the North lost some 2,168 men—a virtual draw. The Confederates, however, could not afford to trade losses with their counterparts.

For his part, Sherman was caught unawares by Hood's assault at Peach Tree Creek even though General Schofield had warned him of Hood's rashness. In his post-war narrative, Sherman recorded that after his men began to converge on Atlanta on 19 July, he met "such feeble resistance that

---

[7] *Confederate Veteran* (August 1904): 391.

[8] James A. Connolly, *Three Years in the Army of the Cumberland* (Bloomington: Indiana University Press, 1996) 239.

I really thought the enemy intended to evacuate the place."[9] Describing the Confederate assault at Peach Tree Creek, the Sherman explained that "the enemy came pouring out of their trenches down upon them, they became commingled and fought in many places hand to hand."[10] Giving credit to General Thomas and remarking that he was in a fortuitous location during the battle, Sherman explained that "Thomas happened to be near the rear of Newton's position, and got some field-batteries in a good position, on the north side of Peach-Tree Creek, in which he directed a fire on a mass of the enemy, which was passing around Newton's left and exposed flank."[11]

Sherman wrote,

> After a couple of hours of hard and close conflict, the enemy retired slowly within his trenches, leaving his dead and many wounded on the field. Johnson's and Newton's losses were light for they had partially covered their fronts with light parapet; but Hooker's whole corps fought in open ground and lost about fifteen hundred men. He reported four hundred rebel dead left on the ground and that the rebel wounded would number four thousand; but, this was conjectural, for most of them got back within their own lines.

Sherman proudly concluded, "We had, however, met successfully a bold sally, had repelled it handsomely, and were also put on our guard; and the event illustrated the future tactics of our enemy."[12]

Undeterred by his failure to defeat Sherman at Peach Tree Creek, Hood attacked again just two days later east of Atlanta against General McPherson's Army of the Tennessee, as Sherman had feared. In what became known as the Battle of Atlanta, Hood lost about 5,500 men while Sherman lost 3,700 men—including General McPherson, who was killed early in the action. While both attacks slowed the Federal encirclement of Atlanta, neither battle stopped Sherman. A third battle in a week, at Ezra Church west of Atlanta, would further bleed Hood's battered army.

Much of the blame for the failures of the Confederacy in the loss of Atlanta has been laid at the feet of General John Bell Hood. As commander

---

[9]William T. Sherman, *Marching Through Georgia: William T. Sherman's Personal Narrative of His March Through Georgia*, ed. Mills Lane (Savannah GA: Beehive Press, 1978) 67.

[10]Ibid.

[11]Ibid., 67–69.

[12]Ibid., 69.

of the forces defending the Gate City, he was responsible for holding Atlanta, and he failed. Moreover, he heavily bled his little army with bold moves that produced no measurable gains and that led to and sped up the collapse of Atlanta. Hood lost in just eight days (20–28 July) as many or more men than Johnston had lost in more than three months of fighting. And, he had inflicted fewer casualties on Sherman's armies than his own army had received. Johnston's record revealed that for every man he lost, he was putting two to three of Sherman's men out of action; Hood was bleeding the South's second principal army dry. Any hope of defending Atlanta was lost when the Confederate army's life blood ran dry at Peach Tree Creek, Decatur, Ezra Church, and finally, at Jonesboro, where Hood's men failed to stop Sherman's legions from cutting off the last rail tie to Atlanta.[13] At least this has been the historical view of this tragic figure.

In fairness, however, Hood has been blamed for far more than he was responsible during the defense of Atlanta. A closer look at the battles for Atlanta reveals that Hood's plans for the battles of Peach Tree Creek, Atlanta (Decatur), and Lickskillet Road,[14] were reasonable. They arguably provided, by the time that Hood took over, the best chance for success for the beleaguered Confederate forces and the doomed city they defended. Historian and Johnston critic Stephen Davis provides an excellent diatribe in support of Hood's generalship during his defense of the Gate City in Davis's work "A Reappraisal of the Generalship of John Bell Hood in the Battles for Atlanta," in which Davis argues the point that Hood rather than Johnston provided a better chance for the defense of Atlanta with effective confutation.[15] It is reasonable to conclude that Hood's offensive actions

---

[13]Albert Castel, *Decision in the West* (Lawrence: University Press of Kansas, 1992) 380–83; James A. Connolly, *Three Years in the Army of the Cumberland* (Bloomington: Indiana University Press, 1996) 443; cf. Stanley F. Horn, *The Army of Tennessee* (Norman: University of Oklahoma Press, 1952) 352–54.

[14]A surprise attack to be delivered on 29 July on the Federal right flank, not the Ezra Church debacle on 28 July that resulted from S. D. Lee's excessive aggression.

[15]See Stephen Davis, "A Reappraisal of the Generalship of John Bell Hood in the Battles for Atlanta," 49–95, which provides an excellent discussion of Hood's unfair treatment concerning his conduct in the defense of Atlanta. Hood's horrendous performance at Franklin and Nashville and his subsequent bitter writings tarnish his previous performances during the war, including his reasonably

slowed Sherman, who had been permitted to more or less proceed unchecked for three months, and it is probable that Hood's efforts lengthened the Confederate hold on Atlanta for another forty days.

In his post-war writings, Johnston claims that he could have held the Gate City "forever," but he lacks any reasonable evidence to support his assertion.[16] While Johnston had tentatively planned an offensive operation along the Peach Tree Creek line, there is plenty of reason to believe that he might have abandoned it once he learned how close McPherson's forces were to Atlanta along the Decatur Road east of the city. Something had always come up to prevent his plans from being implemented in the past; it was reasonable to suspect it would happen again. In Hood, President Davis had found a general who would at least try to be the aggressor and take the fight to the enemy in hopes of better results.

Hood's plan at Peach Tree Creek, and to him must be given the credit of maturing Johnston's initial idea into a battle plan, was a sound one. A poor performance by Hardee and two of his divisions, Bate's and Maney's, sealed the defeat of his army at Peach Tree Creek, however. Further, Stewart's Corps lacked sufficient numbers to take advantage of their initial success. Finally, not enough credit has been given over the years to the quick and effective response by most of Thomas's Army of the Cumberland. Thomas's men acted with celerity and effectiveness to stop all Confederate gains and drive them back.

President Davis gave General Hood a directive: go on the offensive and try to hold Atlanta while reversing fortunes in Georgia. His tactical plans for battle were sound, and he was not a butcher as he has been labeled since the war—at least during the Atlanta Campaign. His plans for the Peach Tree Creek and Atlanta (Decatur) fights were well conceived and at least partially well delivered. Hood desired to catch a portion of Sherman's force while in motion and fight it in the open and on its flanks when and where it was most vulnerable. This was his strategy at the battles of Peach Tree Creek and Atlanta; his men did find the Federals in the open and in motion, surprised them, and to a degree, pushed them back until additional Northern forces stopped the Confederates.

---

sound efforts at Atlanta.

[16]Castel, *Decision in the West*, 538.

His tactical plan that led to the Ezra Church battle was also based on the same sound strategy: find a part of the Federal force in motion and out in the open west of Atlanta, send a part of the army out around and behind it, and strike it in the flank and rear. Unfortunately, S. D. Lee failed him completely as the Yankees "got there first with the most" (to quote Confederate General Nathan B. Forrest's famous strategy). Hood's role in the Ezra Church failure was in not getting his men moving west to attain the heights above the Lickskillet Road sooner. The Federal forces that participated at Ezra Church were on the move by 4:30 AM while the Confederates who would oppose them did not begin to leave Atlanta until around 10:00 AM. The Northerners got there first, and they secured for themselves the "high ground" and an easy victory, thanks to S. D. Lee's foolishly sending forth unsupported brigades of men in a series of disjointed and ill-fated attacks. Had he been on the scene, perhaps Hood could have stopped Lee from mindlessly continuing to send uncoordinated units into the Yankee meat-grinder; this is criticism he received on several fields of battle around Atlanta. But, like Lee at Richmond and Petersburg, Hood could not be expected to be on the scene at every point along a multi-mile front. He had to delegate tactical command for launching attacks during his defense of the Gate City to his subordinates and trust them to make adjustments as circumstances warranted. In all three battles, Peach Tree Creek, Atlanta, and Ezra Church, Hood employed a sound strategy, and in none of the three battles did Hood order or intend to strike Federals in prepared defenses or earthworks, an unfortunate mistake he would make three months later at the Battle of Franklin and that would haunt him for the rest of his life.

At Peach Tree Creek, Atlanta (Decatur), and at Ezra Church, the "fog of war" contributed to doom each of Hood's efforts. The term "fog of war" was first coined by the Prussian military analyst Carl von Clausewitz, who wrote, "The great uncertainty of all data in war is a peculiar difficulty, because all action must, to a certain extent, be planned in a mere twilight, which in addition not infrequently—like the effect of a fog or moonshine—gives to things exaggerated dimensions and unnatural appearance."[17] Military historians have used the term ever since "to describe the level of

---

[17]Karl von Clausewitz, *On War*, trans. J. J. Graham (London: N. Trübner 1873) 24; "Fog of war," http://en.wikipedia.org/wiki/Fog_of_war (17 August 2014).

ambiguity in situational awareness experienced by participants in military operations. The term seeks to capture the uncertainty regarding [a commander's] own capability, adversary capability and adversary intent during an engagement, operation or campaign."[18]

Hood's plans of battle for each of the three offensives were based on Sherman's forces being where he expected them to be. In all battle plans, a commander must make certain assumptions as to where and in what strength his foe is located before launching an attack against him; if the commander is blind as to his enemy's position or condition, his plans will be severely hindered. Part of the failures for each of these battles lies with General Joseph Wheeler's failure to inform Hood of Sherman's precise locations and failure to provide good intelligence on the time and direction of the Federal commander's next anticipated movement.

Because Joe Johnston had followed a policy of keeping his plans to himself, Wheeler and his cavalry were likely kept in the dark as to their purpose during the days leading up to the transfer of command. It was not until Tuesday, 19 July, that Hood began to take over leadership of the army, which had remained in a state of idleness (if not shock) throughout Monday, 18 July. If he planned to launch an attack against Thomas's force, Johnston should have had the bulk of Wheeler's cavalry far to the east, checking McPherson's movement and not slowing Thomas's advance on Peach Tree Creek. To his credit, one of Hood's first moves was to send Wheeler to the east and northeast of Atlanta to find Sherman's flank and to impede its progress toward the Gate City while he planned his strike against Thomas. Another factor created by the fog of war was that Thomas's Army of the Cumberland moved slower than expected, much to Sherman's continued disgust. But, the delays in Thomas's advance, perhaps in part caused by the resistance offered by Wheeler's horsemen between 17 and 19 July, served to permit the remainder of Sherman's force to swing around and threaten Atlanta from the east faster than expected.

It is likely that due to Hood's ignorance as to the whereabouts of Sherman's wings and his need to further assess his options, he delayed his attack until 20 July instead of 19 July, when the Johnston attack was supposed to take place, but Thomas's Army of the Cumberland did not

---

[18]Clausewitz, *On War*, 24; "Fog of War," http://en.wikipedia.org/wiki/Fog_of_war (17 August 2014).

begin crossing the creek until around 4:00 PM on 19 July. However, it is hard to criticize the new commander for taking a day or two to take in the situation, make a new plan, or adopt the one in place and make appropriate adjustments to it. Hood could be criticized, however, for determining to make the assault at 1:00 PM instead of earlier in the day. Had the attack occurred on the morning of 20 July, it appears likely that the Southerners would have achieved a much more successful result because Newton's Division would not yet have reached the heights known today as Cardiac Hill, or they would have only just arrived at the hill and would not have had Goodspeed's Battery in place or any defensive works erected. Moreover, Hooker's Corps would have been even less prepared to repel an attack than it was later in the day.

A combination of significant factors (McPherson's rapid movement to Decatur and the Augusta railroad east of Atlanta, the change in Southern commanders, the subsequent loss of time in getting ready to launch an assault, the natural suspicions and careful, if not timid, action by his chief subordinate, Hardee) proved to be disastrous to Hood's first offensive attempt. Additionally, the delay of the assault from 1:00 PM to 4:00 PM gave Thomas's Army of the Cumberland time to improve their circumstances. Finally, the rough wooded ridges and ravines that ran perpendicular to Hood's striking force served to splinter and isolate portions of his attackers, rending their assaults piecemeal. It is clear that the fog of war, if not bad luck, had bitten Hood at Peach Tree Creek.

At Decatur two days later, Hood's plans were thwarted by the unexpected presence of Dodge's Federal XVI Corps, which had only hours before been placed to the rear of and perpendicular to the left flank of the Northern line where Hood had planned to strike. But this surprise did not stop the young Southern commander from improvising and adjusting. Maintaining tactical command during the 22 July battle, Hood ordered Cheatham's Corps forward to support Hardee's attack, which very nearly helped to create a Confederate victory. Eventually, Sherman's shocked troops showed grit and determination in fending off and throwing back Hood's assault, and the outnumbered and exhausted Rebels reluctantly fell back to their trenches.

Finally, at Ezra Church just before his men could arrive, portions of Sherman's Federal forces reached the high ground overlooking the Lickskillet Road from which Hood planned to launch his third strike—this one against the Yankee right flank. The Rebel leader had correctly anticipated that Sherman would swing around to the west and try to cut his last rail link, which ran south of Atlanta, connected him to the rest of the South, and provided his only remaining line of supply. On 27 July, Hood ordered two of his corps, Lee's and Stewart's, to go out of the Atlanta trenches to the west via the Lickskillet Road on 28 July preparatory to a planned strike on the Federal flank north of that position on 29 July. Unfortunately for Hood and his men, the Federal army of the Tennessee had already reached the high ground needed in order to launch the following day's assault. Hood had been again a victim of bad timing. Further, to make matters worse, newly arrived corps commander General Stephen Dill Lee, acting on his own initiative, began a series of brutal and futile assaults against the recently procured Federal line with devastating results. At Ezra Church, Hood came up short again by bad luck, bad timing, and bad generalship by his field commander, all common threads in his three losses.

The numbers attributed as Hood's losses during the three battles around Atlanta by most historians (and virtually all general survey books on the Georgia Campaign) are totally unreliable and inflated. These estimates take casualty figures very loosely from one unit or portion of the battle and assume the same numbers for all units on the field, including estimating losses from units that were not participants or were barely engaged. Also, many accounts take Sherman's inflated estimates of Confederate losses at face value. Few serious studies have been undertaken to verify Southern losses during the battles for Atlanta. In the three battles during Hood's first ten days in command, Federal and Confederate losses were actually closer than has been widely known or recognized over the years. (The devastating piecemeal attacks at Ezra Church due to the fault of Corps commander Stephen D. Lee is the most notable exception.) The losses sustained by both sides during this period were:

Engagement	Estimated Federal Losses	Estimated Confederate Losses
Moore's Mill, Howell Mill & Buckhead Road, 19 July	270	302
Peach Tree Creek, 20 July	2,168	2,298
Atlanta (Decatur), 22 July[19]	3,722	5,500
Ezra Church, 28 July	632	2,657
Total	6,794	10,757

The difference, however, is that Sherman could afford to lose some men whereas the Confederate forces could not replace their losses.

In the years following the war, records became lost or destroyed, Southerners were soured, Yankees bragged, and few took serious account of battlefield losses. Moreover, in the wake of Hood's horrible decision to order a suicidal assault at Franklin, Tennessee, followed by an equally bad decision to pursue the Northern troops to Nashville where his army was virtually destroyed, Hood bashing became commonplace. His post-war writings where he bitterly and unfairly blamed his losses on these same troops and a number of his officers did not help Hood's reputation. It was difficult to find defenders of the man, his character, or of the decisions he made while in command of the Army of Tennessee. During this post-war period, many veterans of the Army of Tennessee and Army of Mississippi fondly

---

[19]The figures provided for the Atlanta battle of 22 July are based on the research of Stephen Davis and Albert Castel in Davis, "A Reappraisal of the Generalship of John Bell Hood in the Battles for Atlanta," in Theodore P. Savas and David A. Woodbury, eds., *The Campaign for Atlanta & Sherman's March to the Sea*, vol. 1, Essays of the American Civil War (Campbell CA: Savas Woodbury Publishing, 1994) 82–86; Castel, *Decision in the West*, 380–81, 411–12, 434. The remainder of the engagements' casualties are based upon research by the author.

remembered General Joe Johnston, but they began to call General John Bell Hood "The Butcher."

Another reason for the inaccurate and exorbitant figures attributed to Confederate losses comes from sincere efforts at counting known losses from units that left an after-action report attributing those losses to other Rebel units that did *not* leave a report or the report did not appear in print, such as in the *Official Records of the Union and Confederate Armies in the War of the Rebellion*, published by the US government between 1880 and 1900 under the direction of the Office of the Secretary of War and known by historians as the *Official Records*. The problem with this method of calculation, however, is that quite often, regiments and brigades that played a significant role in a battle would prepare a detailed report that included their casualties. But, units that did not perform as well or play a significant role in a particular battle might not have made serious mention or provided casualty lists. When the *Official Records* were created, the War Department had to decide which reports to include and which ones to omit; there wasn't enough room to include every record. (The *Official Records* comprises 129 volumes as it is). So, taking the casualty rates from one regiment or brigade and trying to extrapolate a similar ratio of casualties to the remaining units is unreliable.

Also, Confederate units varied greatly in size, so if one estimate was based on, for example, 600 lost in a brigade of 1,500 in a particular battle, these estimates then assume that all 10 brigades that participated had 600 casualties as well, when in some instances, a brigade only numbered 500 men. Quite often, during the uneven fighting at the Peach Tree Creek, Atlanta (Decatur), and Ezra Church battles, one unit might lose a third or half of its force, or 500 out of 1,000 or 1,500 men engaged, while other units lost between one and ten percent, or 10 to 100 men out of 1,000 engaged. Thus, bad math has also contributed to "Hood bashing" over the years.

Another reason that Hood's reputation has been tarnished over the years is the combination of the fondness with which the Southern soldiers remembered Old Joe Johnston and the cool, if not cold, feelings they had for Hood in the post-war years. Hood certainly did not help his cause when he wrote *Advance and Retreat*, which contained a number of negative and derogatory statements against the common soldier of the Army of Tennessee and several of its high ranking officers including Johnston and

Hardee.[20] Because the book was published after Hood's death, he didn't have an opportunity to edit the manuscript. Many of Hood's accusations against the officers and soldiers of the Army of Tennessee were false, distorted, or exaggerated. It will never be known whether Hood would have toned down the raw and hurtful claims in his manuscript if he had lived to edit his work. In any event, the book generated more ill will toward the unlucky Southern leader and solidified the hearts of veterans in defense of Johnston.

Ultimately, the responsibility for the defense of Atlanta rested with the president and Confederate cabinet. It was President Davis who believed that a change was needed. It was Davis who listened to the groaning of the Confederate Congress and his cabinet. It was Davis who placed his confidence in the discredited general, Braxton Bragg, whom he appointed his chief adviser. The Confederate president may have allowed his personal disdain for Joe Johnston to interfere with his decision. Nevertheless, Davis was responsible for deciding whether to continue to trust the fate of Atlanta to Johnston or to replace him with someone who would fight. The fall of Atlanta and the fate of the Confederacy would hang in the balance.

President Davis maintained an unreasonable expectation for the performance of General Joseph E. Johnston and his army. He believed that Johnston should be able to carry the battle to Sherman and drive him back into Tennessee and beyond. Davis either did not believe or did not appreciate the numerical superiority that Sherman enjoyed against the Southern forces during the Georgia Campaign. At all times, Sherman maintained a numerical superiority in men and a substantial superiority in both the number and quality of the artillery and supplies available to each army. The quality of the fighting men was, in the western theater, more or less even, with fine veteran units and a few green units found in both armies. The strength of both cavalries was more or less even, with the Federal forces maintaining a slight numerical superiority. One Southern veteran from Tennessee aptly put the situation in North Georgia during summer 1864:

> The authorities at Richmond had become impatient and dissatisfied because Johnston did not engage the enemy at Cassville, and especially because he had fallen back from his stronghold at Kenesaw Mountain. They could not

---

[20]John B. Hood, *Advance and Retreat* (New York: Da Capo Press, 1993) 161–65, 173.

realize the disparity of numbers and strength between the opposing armies. It was not to be expected that Johnston, with an army constantly on duty and worn out by a constant campaign without relief, could turn upon an army of double his numbers and superior equipments and drive it back from the country.[21]

The former soldier went on to explain that General Johnston was "wise and prudent" and knew what he was up against. Moreover, the veteran remembered Johnston "had confronted an enemy thus flushed with a series of brilliant successes and supplied with every convenience and appliance of modern warfare, and, with an inferior force and with inferior arms and ammunition, he had disputed every inch of his advance and checked his front daily."[22] Johnston bled Sherman's forces at every battle but kept his own army relatively protected and intact. The Confederate States of America simply could not survive a war where she traded man for man with a foe that outnumbered her by several times. After the first year or two, when it became apparent that the South could not maintain the offensive against the North, it was clear that a defensive strategy with timely counter-strikes would be the only way the South could win. By dragging out the conflict until a war-weary North relented, the Confederacy could perhaps win her independence. Every day that Johnston's army continued to survive, the Confederacy lived. Every time that Sherman failed to deliver a decisive blow or win a clear victory, the morale of the Northern people dropped and the Federal body count grew. Thus, "with a comparably small loss to his own army, [Johnston] had inflicted a severe loss to the enemy, to the extent of several thousand men."[23]

While Johnston's movements proved skillful in the face of the larger Federal forces opposing him, Hood is remembered for boldly trying to do the impossible: eradicate Sherman and the invading enemy armies threatening Atlanta and hold the city at all hazards. Despite Hood's best efforts, however, in a little more than a month Atlanta would fall to Sherman's armies, Hood would abandon middle Georgia, and his army would be severely weakened, with some 15,000 men left behind as

---

[21]Thomas A. Head, *Campaigns and Battles of the Sixteenth Regiment, Tennessee Volunteers* (McMinnville TN: Womack Printing Co., 1961) 136.

[22]Ibid.

[23]Ibid., 136–37.

casualties. Fully a third of Hood's men would be lost in a series of futile attempts to repel Sherman's legions from its clutches on the Gate City. The South would never know whether Lincoln's administration could survive the November election without the fall of Atlanta. Johnston's Fabian Policy would never be given the opportunity to be implemented fully because the Southern high command remained split on how to best to conduct its war strategy. The Confederacy's second independence would not be forthcoming. As the Georgia Campaign drew to a climax with Davis's decision to remove Johnston and replace him with Hood, the words of Sarah Huff waxed prophetic: "The clear-hearing statesmen of the Southland heard the doom bells ringing the death knell of the Southern Confederacy."[24]

The Battle of Peach Tree Creek would thus become the first nail in the coffin of the Confederacy. The fall of Atlanta that followed the Battle of Jonesboro forty days later sealed their fate.

---

[24]Sarah Huff, *My 80 Years in Atlanta*, http://www.artery.org/08_history/UpperArtery/CivilWar/SaraHuff/My80YearsInAtlanta_All.pdf, 1937 (18 November 2014) 11.

APPENDIX A

Confederate Order of Battle from the Chattahoochee River

ARMY OF TENNESSEE
General Joseph E. Johnston (removed 17 July 1864)
General John Bell Hood (from 18 July 1864)

Chief of Staff: Brigadier General William W. Mackall
Chief of Artillery: Brigadier General Francis A. Shoup
Chief Engineer: Lieutenant Colonel Stephen W. Presstman (until 20 July 1864)
Chief Engineer: Major General Martin L. Smith (from 20 July 1864)
Medial Director: Surgeon-Major A. J. Foard
Chief Ordnance Officer: Captain W. D. Humphries

HARDEE'S CORPS
Lieutenant General William J. Hardee

CHEATHAM'S TENNESSEE DIVISION
Brigadier General George E. Maney

Maney's Brigade
Colonel Francis M. Walker
1st and 27th Tennessee, Lt. Col. John L. House
4th Tennessee (Confederate), Lt. Col. Oliver A. Bradshaw
6th and 9th Tennessee, Col. George C. Porter, Lt. Col. John W. Buford
19th Tennessee, Maj. James G. Deaderick
50th Tennessee, Col. Stephen H. Colms

Strahl's Brigade
Brigadier General Otho F. Strahl
4th and 5th Tennessee, Major Henry Hampton
24th Tennessee, Col. John A. Wilson
31st Tennessee, Lt. Col. Fountain E. P. Stafford
33rd Tennessee, Lt. Col. Henry C. McNeill
41st Tennessee, Lt. Col. James D. Tillman

Carter's (Wright) Brigade
Colonel John C. Carter
   8th Tennessee, Col. John H. Anderson
16th Tennessee, Capt. Benjamin Randals
28th Tennessee, Lt. Col. David C. Crook
38th Tennessee, Lt. Col. Andrew D. Gwynne
51st and 52nd Tennessee, Lt. Col. John W. Estes

Magevney's (Vaughan) Brigade
Colonel Michael Magevney, Jr.
   11th Tennessee, Col. George W. Gordon
12th and 47th Tennessee, Col. William M. Watkins
29th Tennessee, Col. Horace Rice
13th and 154th Tennessee, Maj. William J. Crook.

CLEBURNE'S DIVISION
Major General Patrick R. Cleburne

Polk's Brigade
Brigadier General Lucius Polk
   1st and 15th Arkansas, Lt. Col. William H. Martin
5th Confederate, Col. James C. Cole
2nd Tennessee, William D. Robison
48th Tennessee (Nixon's Regiment), Capt. Henry G. Evans

Granbury's (Smith's) Texas Brigade
Brigadier General Hiram M. Granbury
Brigadier General James A. Smith (wounded July 22, 1864)
   6th Texas and 15th Texas Cavalry (dismounted), Col. Robert R. Garland
7th Texas, Capt. T. B. Camp
10th Texas, Col. Roger Q. Mills
17th and 18th Texas Cavalry (dismounted), Capt. George D. Manion
24th and 25th Texas Cavalry (dismounted), Lt. Col. William M. Neyland

Lowrey's Brigade
Brigadier General Mark P. Lowrey
   16th Alabama, Lt. Col. Frederick A. Ashford.
33rd Alabama, Col. Samuel Adams
45th Alabama, Col. Harris D. Lampley

32nd Mississippi, Col. William H. H. Tison
45th Mississippi, Maj. Elisha F. Nunn

Govan' s Arkansas Brigade
Brigadier General Daniel C. Govan
2nd and 24th Arkansas, Col. E. Warfield
5th and 13th Arkansas, Col. John E. Murray
6th and 7th Arkansas, Col. Samuel G. Smith
8th and 19th Arkansas, Col. George F. Baucum
3rd Confederate, Capt. M. H. Dixon

WALKER'S DIVISION
Major General William H. T. Walker

Mercer's Georgia Brigade
Brigadier General Hugh W. Mercer
1st Volunteer Georgia, Col. Charles H. Olmstead
54th Georgia, Lt. Col. Morgan Rawls.
57th Georgia, Lt. Col. Cincinnatus S. Guyton
63rd Georgia, Maj. Joseph V. H. Allen

Gist's Brigade
Brigadier General States Rights Gist
2nd Georgia Battalion Sharpshooters, Maj. Richard H. Whiteley
8th Georgia Battalion, Col. Zachariah L. Watters
46th Georgia, Maj. Samuel J. C. Dunlop
65th Georgia, Capt. William G. Foster
5th Mississippi, Lt. Col. John B. Herring
8th Mississippi, Col. John C. Wilkinson
16th South Carolina, Col. James McCullough
24th South Carolina, Col. Ellison Capers

Stevens's Georgia Brigade
Brigadier General Clement H. Stevens (killed)
1st Georgia Battalion Sharpshooters, Maj. Armur Shaaff
1st Georgia (Confederate), Col. George A. Smith
25th Georgia, Col. William J. Winn
29th Georgia, Capt. J. W. Turner

30th Georgia, Lt. Col. James S. Boynton
66th Georgia, Col. J. Cooper Nisbet

BATE'S DIVISION
Major General William B. Bate

    Tyler's Brigade
    Brigadier General R. C. Tyler
    Brigadier General Thomas B. Smith
    4th Georgia Battalion Sharpshooters, Maj. Theodore D. Caswell
    37th Georgia, Col. Joseph T. Smith
15th and 37th Tennessee, Lt. Col. R. Dudley Frayser
20th Tennessee, Lt. Col. William M. Shy
30th Tennessee, Lt. Col. James J. Turner

    Lewis's Kentucky "Orphan" Brigade
    Brigadier General Joseph H. Lewis
    2nd Kentucky, Col. James W. Moss
4th Kentucky, Lt. Col. Thomas W. Thompson
    5th Kentucky, Lt. Col. Hiram Hawkins
6th Kentucky, Col. Martin H. Corer
9th Kentucky, Col. John W. Caldwell

    Finley's Florida Brigade
    Brigadier General Jesse J. Finley
    1st and 4th Florida, Lt. Col. Edward Badger
    1st Florida Cavalry (dismounted), and 3rd Florida, Capt. Matthew H. Strain
6th Florida, Lt. Col. Daniel L. Kenan
7th Florida, Lt. Col. Robert Bullock

HOOD'S CORPS
Major General Benjamin F. Cheatham

HINDMAN'S DIVISION
Brigadier General John C. Brown

    Deas's Brigade
Colonel John G. Coltart
    17th Alabama Battalion Sharpshooters, Capt. James F. Nabers

19th Alabama, Lt. Col. George R. Kimbrough
22nd Alabama, Col. Benjamin R. Hart
25th Alabama, Col. George D. Johnston
39th Alabama, Lt. Col. William C. Clifton
50th Alabama, Capt. George W. Arnold

Tucker's Brigade
Colonel Jacob H. Sharp
9th Mississippi Battalion Sharpshooters, Maj. William C. Richards
7th Mississippi, Col. William H. Bishop
9th Mississippi, Lt. Col. Benjamin F. Johns
10th Mississippi, Lt. Col. George B. Myers
41st Mississippi, Col. J. Byrd Williams
44th Mississippi, Lt. Col. R. G. Kelsey

Manigault's Brigade
Brigadier General Arthur M. Manigault
24th Alabama, Col. Newton N. Davis
28th Alabama, Lt. Col. William L. Butler
34th Alabama, Col. Julius C. B. Mitchell
10th South Carolina, Col. James F. Pressley
19th South Carolina, Maj. James L. White

Walthall's Brigade
Colonel Samuel Benton
24th and 27th Mississippi, Col. Robert P. McKelvaine
29th and 30th Mississippi, Col. William F. Brantly
34th Mississippi, Capt. T. S. Hubbard

STEVENSON'S DIVISION.
Major General Carter L. Stevenson

Brown's Brigade
Colonel Joseph B. Palmer
3rd Tennessee, Lt. Col. Calvin J. Clack
18th Tennessee, Lt. Col. William R. Butler
26th Tennessee, Col. Richard M. Saffell
32nd Tennessee, Capt. Thomas D. Deavenport
23rd Tennessee Battalion and 45th Tennessee, Col. Anderson Searcy

Reynolds's Brigade
Brigadier General Alexander W. Reynolds
    58th North Carolina, Capt. Alfred T. Stewart
60th North Carolina, Col. Washington M. Hardy
54th Virginia, Lt. Col. John J. Wade
63rd Virginia, Capt. David O. Rush

Cumming's Brigade
Brigadier General Alfred Cumming
    2nd Georgia State Troops, Col. James Wilson
34th Georgia, Maj. John M. Jackson
36th Georgia, Maj. Charles E. Broyles
39th Georgia, Capt. J. W. Cureton
56th Georgia, Col. E. P. Watkins

Pettus's Brigade
Brigadier General Edmund W. Pettus
    20th Alabama, Col. James M. Dedman
23rd Alabama, Lt. Col. Joseph B. Bibb
30th Alabama, Col. Charles M. Shelley
31st Alabama, Capt. J. J. Nix
46th Alabama, Capt. George E. Brewer

CLAYTON'S DIVISION
Major General Henry D. Clayton

Stovall's Brigade
Brigadier General Marcellus A. Stovall
    1st Georgia State Troops, Col. E. M. Galt (wounded)
    40th Georgia, Capt. John F. Groover
41st Georgia, Maj. Mark S. Nall
42nd Georgia, Col. Robert J. Henderson
43rd Georgia, Maj. William C. Lester
52nd Georgia, Capt. Rufus R. Asbury

Baker's Brigade
Brigadier General Alpheus Baker

37th Alabama, Lt. Col. Alexander A. Greene
40th Alabama, Col, John H. Higley
42nd Alabama, Capt. R. K. Wells
54th Alabama, Lt. Col. John A. Minter

Gibson's Brigade
Brigadier General Randall L. Gibson
Austin's Louisiana Battalion Sharpshooters, Maj. John E. Austin
1st Louisiana (Regulars), Capt. W. H. Sparks
4th Louisiana Battalion, Maj. Duncan Buie
4th Louisiana (transferred from Quarles's Brigade 17 July 1864), Col. S. E. Hunter
30th Louisiana (transferred from Quarles's Brigade 17 July 1864), Lt. Col. Thomas Shields
13th Louisiana, Lt. Col. Francis L. Campbell
16th and 25th Louisiana, Lt. Col. Robert H. Lindsay
19th Louisiana, Col. Richard W. Turner
20th Louisiana, Col. Leon Von Zinken

Holtzclaw's Brigade
Brigadier General James T. Holtzclaw
18th Alabama, Lt. Col. Peter F. Hunley
32nd and 58th Alabama, Col. Bushrod Jones
36th Alabama, Lt. Col. Thomas H. Herndon
38th Alabama, Maj. Shep. Ruffin

CAVALRY CORPS
Major General Joseph Wheeler

MARTIN'S DIVISION
Major General William T. Martin

Allen's Alabama Brigade
Brigadier General William Wirt Allen
12th Alabama Battalion, Capt. Warren S. Reese
1st Alabama, Lt. Col. D. T. Blakey
3rd Alabama, Col. James Hagan
4th Alabama, Col. Alfred A. Russell
7th Alabama, Capt. George Mason

51st Alabama, Col. M. L. Kirkpatrick

Iverson's Georgia Brigade
Brigadier General Alfred Iverson
1st Georgia, Lt. Col. James H. Strickland
2nd Georgia, Maj. James W. Mayo
3rd Georgia, Col. Robert Thompson
4th Georgia, Maj. Augustus R. Stewart
6th Georgia, Col. John R. Hart

HUMES'S DIVISION
Brigadier General William Y. C. Humes

Ashby's Tennessee Brigade
Colonel Henry M. Ashby
1st (formerly the 6th) Tennessee, Col. James T. Wheeler
2nd Tennessee, Capt. William M. Smith
5th Tennessee, Col. George W. McKenzie
9th Tennessee Battalion, Maj. James H. Akin

Harrison's Brigade
Colonel Thomas H. Harrison
3rd Arkansas, Col. Amson W. Hobson
4th Tennessee, Lt. Col. Paul F. Anderson
8th Texas, Lt. Col. Gustave Cook
11th Texas, Col. George R. Reeves

KELLY'S DIVISION
Brigadier General John H. Kelly

Dibrell's Tennessee Brigade
Colonel George G. Dibrell
4th Tennessee, Col. William S. McLemore
8th Tennessee, Capt. Jefferson Leftwich
9th Tennessee, Capt. James M. Reynolds
10th Tennessee, Maj. John Minor
11th Tennessee (a portion was detached to East Tennessee 11 July 1864), Col.
Daniel W. Holman
Williams's Brigade

Confederate Order of Battle from the Chattahoochee River

Brigadier General John S. Williams
1st (Butler's, also called the 3rd) Kentucky, Col. John Russell Butler
2nd Kentucky Battalion, Capt. John Basket Dortch
2nd Kentucky (Woodward's Regiment), Maj. Thomas Wilson Lewis
9th Kentucky, Col. William Campbell Preston Breckinridge
Allison's (Tennessee) Squadron, Capt. J. S. Reese
Hamilton's (Tennessee) Battalion, Maj. Joseph Shaw

Anderson's Brigade
Brigadier General Robert H. Anderson
3rd Confederate, Lt. Col. John McCaskill
8th Confederate, Lt. Col. John S. Prather
10th Confederate, Capt, W. J. Vason
12th Confederate, Capt. Charles H. Conner
5th Georgia, Lt. Col. Edward Bird

Hannon's Alabama Brigade
Colonel Moses W. Hannon
53rdAlabama, Lt. Col. John F. Gaines
24th Alabama Battalion, Maj. Robert B. Snodgrass

ARTILLERY
HARDEE'S CORPS
Colonel Melancthon Smith

Hoxton's Battalion
8 Napoleons and 4 12-pounder Howitzers
Major Llewelyn Hoxton
Perry's (Florida) Battery, Capt. Thomas J. Perry
Phelan s (Alabama) Battery, Lieut. Nathaniel Venable
Turner's (Mississippi) Battery, Capt. William B. Turner

Martin's Battalion
6 Napoleons and 6 12-pounder Howitzers
Major Robert Martin
Bledsoe's (Missouri) Battery, Capt. Hiram M. Bledsoe
Ferguson's (South Carolina) Battery, Lt. John A. Alston; Lt. René Beauregard
Howell's (Georgia) Battery, Capt. Evan P. Howell

Hotchkiss's Battalion
8 Napoleons and 4 12-pounder Howitzers
Major Thomas R. Hotchkiss
Goldthwaite's (Alabama) Battery, Capt. Richard W. Goldthwaite
Key's (Arkansas) Battery, Capt. Thomas J. Key
Swett's (Mississippi) Battery, Lt. H. Shannon

Cobb's Battalion
8 Napoleons and 4 12-pounder howitzers
Major Robert Cobb
Gracey's (Kentucky) Battery, Lt. R. B. Matthews
Mebane's (Tennessee) Battery, Lt. J. W. Phillips
Slocomb's (Louisiana) Battery, Capt. Cuthbert H. Slocomb

HOOD'S CORPS
Colonel Robert F. Beckham

Courtney's Battalion
4 Napoleons, 4 12-pounder Howitzers, and 4 3-inch ordnance rifles
Major Alfred R. Courtney
Dent's (Alabama) Battery, Capt. Staunton H. Dent
Douglas's(Texas) Battery, Capt. James P. Douglas
Garrity's (Alabama) Battery, Lt. Philip Bond

Eldridge's Battalion
6 Napoleons, 2 12-pounder Howitzers, and 4 3-inch ordnance rifles
Major John W. Eldridge
Eufaula (Alabama) Battery, Capt. McDonald Oliver
Fenner's (Louisiana) Battery, Capt. Charles E. Fenner
Stanford's (Mississippi) Battery, Lt. James S. McCall

Johnston's Battalion
12 Napoleons
Captain Maximillian Van Den Corput
Corput's (Cherokee Georgia) Battery, Lt. William S. Hoge
Marshall's (Tennessee) Battery, Capt. Lucius G. Marshall
Rowan's (Georgia) Battery, Capt. John B. Rowan

WHEELER'S HORSE ARTILLERY

8 12-pounder Howitzers, and 8 3-inch ordnance rifles
Lieutenant Colonel Felix H. Robertson
  Ferrell's (Georgia) Battery (one section), Lt. Nathan Davis
Huggins's (Tennessee)Battery, Lt. Nat. Baxter
Ramsey's (Tennessee) Battery, Lt. D. Breck. Ramsey
White's (Tennessee) Battery, Lt. Arthur Pue, Jr.
Wiggins's (Arkansas) Battery, Lt. J. Wylie Calloway

ARTILLERY RESERVE
Lieutenant Colonel James H. Hallonquist

  Williams's Battalion
  4 Napoleons, 4 12-pounder Howitzers, and 4 3-inch ordnance rifles
  Lieutenant Colonel Samuel C. Williams
    Barbour (Alabama) Battery, Capt. Reuben F. Kolb
Jefferson (Mississippi) Battery, Capt. Putnam Darden
Jeffress's(Virginia) Battery, Capt. William C. Jeffress

  Palmer's Battalion
  8 Napoleons and 4 3-inch ordnance rifles
  Major Joseph Palmer
    Lumsden's (Alabama) Battery, Capt. Charles L. Lumsden
Anderson's (Georgia) Battery, Capt. Ruel W. Anderson
Havis's(Georgia) Battery, Capt. Minor W. Havis

  Waddell's Battalion
  10 12-pounder Howitzers, and 2 12-pounder Blakely rifles
  Major James F. Waddell
    Barret's (Missouri) Battery, Capt. Overton W. Barret
Bellamy's (Alabama) Battery, Capt. Richard H. Bellamy
    Emery's (Alabama) Battery, Capt. Winslow D. Emery

FIRST DIVISION GEORGIA MILITIA
Major General Gustavus W. Smith

  1st Brigade
  Brigadier General Reuben W. Carswell
  1st Regiment, Col. Edward H. Pottle
  2nd Regiment, Col. James Stapleton

3rd Regiment, Col. Q. M. Hill

2nd Brigade
Brigadier General Pleasant J. Phillips
4th Regiment, Col. James N. Mann
5th Regiment, Col. S. S. Stafford
6th Regiment, Col. J. W. Burney

3rd Brigade
Brigadier General Charles D. Anderson
7th Regiment, Col. Abner Redding
8th Regiment, Col. William B. Scott
9th Regiment, Col. J. M. Hill

4th Brigade
Brigadier General Henry Kent McCay
10th Regiment, Col. C. M. Davis
11th Regiment, Col. William t. Toole
12th Regiment, Col. Richard Sims

ARMY OF MISSISSIPPI
Lieutenant General Alexander P. Stewart

LORING'S DIVISION
Major General William Wing Loring

Adams's Mississippi Brigade
Brigadier General John Adams
6th Mississippi, Col. Robert Lowry
14th Mississippi, Lt. Col. Washington L. Doss
15th Mississippi, Col. Michael Farrell
20th Mississippi, Col. William N. Brown
23rd Mississippi, Col. Joseph M. Wells
43rd Mississippi, Col. Richard Harrison

Featherston's Mississippi Brigade
Brigadier General Winfield S. Featherston
1st Mississippi Battalion Sharpshooters, Maj. James M. Stigler
3rd Mississippi, Col. Thomas A. Mellon (wounded)

22nd Mississippi, Maj. Martin A. Oatis (wounded)
31st Mississippi, Col. Marcus D. L. Stephens (absent sick), Lt. Col. James Drane (wounded)
33rd Mississippi, Col. Jabez L. Drake (killed)
40th Mississippi, Lt. Col. George P. Wallace (wounded)

Scott's Brigade
Brigadier General Thomas M. Scott
27th, 35th, and 49th Alabama, Col. Samuel S. Ives
55th Alabama, Col. John Snodgrass
57th Alabama, Lt. Col. W. C. Bethune (wounded)
12th Louisiana, Col. Noel L. Nelson

FRENCH'S DIVISION
Major General Samuel G. French
Colonel William H. Young

Ector's Brigade
Brigadier General Mathew D. Ector
29th North Carolina, Lt. Col. Bacchus S. Proffitt
39th North Carolina, Col. David Coleman
9th Texas Cavalry (dismounted), Col. William H. Young
10th Texas Cavalry (dismounted), Col. C. R. Earp
14th Texas Cavalry (dismounted), Col. John L. Camp
32nd Texas Cavalry (dismounted), Col. Julius A. Andrews

Cockrell's Missouri Brigade
Brigadier General Francis M. Cockrell
Colonel Elijah Gates
1st Missouri Cavalry and 3rd Missouri Battalion Cavalry (dismounted), Lt. Col. D. Todd Samuel
1st and 4th Missouri, Lt. Col. Hugh A. Garland
2nd and 6th Missouri, Col. Peter C. Flournoy
3rd and 5th Missouri, Col. James McCown

Sears's Mississippi Brigade
Brigadier General Claudius W. Sears
Colonel William S. Barry
7th Mississippi Battalion, Lt. A. J. Farmer

4th Mississippi, Col. Thomas N. Adaire
35th Mississippi, Lt. Col. Reuben H. Shotwell
36th Mississippi, Col. William W. Witherspoon
39th Mississippi, Maj. R. J. Durr
46th Mississippi, Col. William H. Clark

WALTHALL'S DIVISION
Major General Edward C. Walthall

Quarles's Brigade
Brigadier General William A. Quarles
1st Alabama, Maj. Samuel L. Knox
42nd Tennessee, Col. Isaac N. Hulme
46th and 55th Tennessee, Col. Robert A. Owens
48th Tennessee, Lt. Col. Aaron S. Godwin
49th Tennessee, Col. William F. Young
53rd Tennessee, Col. John R. White

Cantey's Brigade
Colonel Edward Asbury O' Neal
17th Alabama, Col. Virgil S. Murphey
26th Alabama, Maj. David F. Bryan
29th Alabama, Col. John F. Conoley
37th Mississippi, Col. Orlando S. Holland

Reynolds's Arkansas Brigade
Brigadier General Daniel H. Reynolds
1st Arkansas, Col. Lee M. Ramsaur
2nd Arkansas, Col. James A. Williamson
4th and 31st Arkansas, Col. Henry G. Bunn
9th Arkansas, Col. Isaac L. Dunlop
25th Arkansas, Col. Charles J. Turnbull

ARMY OF MISSISSIPPI (STEWART'S) CAVALRY CORPS
Brigadier General William H. (Red) Jackson

Armstrong's Mississippi Brigade
Brigadier General Frank C. Armstrong

Confederate Order of Battle from the Chattahoochee River

1st Mississippi, Col. R. A. Pinson
2nd Mississippi, Maj. John J. Perry
28th Mississippi, Col. Peter B. Starke
Ballentine's Mississippi Regiment, Lt. Col. William L. Maxwell

Ross's Texas Brigade
Brigadier General Lawrence S. Ross
1st Texas Legion, Col. Edwin R. Hawkins
3rd Texas, Lt. Col. Jiles S. Boggess
6th Texas, Lt. Col. Peter F. Ross
9th Texas, Col. Dudley W. Jones

Ferguson's Brigade
Brigadier General Samuel W. Ferguson
2nd Alabama, Lt. Col. John N. Carpenter
56th Alabama, Col. William Boyles
12th Mississippi Battalion, Col. William M. Inge
Miller's (Mississippi) Regiment, Col. Horace H. Miller
Perrin's (Mississippi) Regiment, Col. Robert O. Perrin
Scout Company (Mississippi Cavalry), Capt. Thomas C. Flournoy

ARMY OF MISSISSIPPI (STEWART'S) ARTILLERY
Lieutenant Colonel Samuel C. Williams

Myrick's Battalion
12 Napoleons
Major John D. Myrick
Barry's (Tennessee) Battery, Capt. Robert L. Barry
Bouanchaud's (Louisiana) Battery, Capt. Alcide Bouanchaud
Cowan's (Mississippi) Battery, Capt. James J. Cowan

Preston's Battalion
12 Napoleons
Major William C. Preston (killed)
Selden's (Alabama) Battery, Lt. Charles W. Lovelace (wounded)
Tarrant's (Alabama) Battery, Lt. Seth Shepard
Yates's (Mississippi) Battery, Capt. James H. Yates

Storrs's Battalion

10 Napoleons and 2 3-inch ordnance rifles
Major George S. Storrs
Guibor's (Missouri) Battery, Lt. Aaron W. Harris
Hoskins's (Mississippi) Battery, Capt. James A. Hoskins
Ward's (Alabama) Battery, Capt. John J. Ward

JACKSON'S HORSE ARTILLERY
Waties's Battalion
8 3-inch ordnance rifles
Captain John Waties
Croft's (Georgia) Battery, Capt. Edward Croft
King's Missouri) Battery, Capt. Houston King
Waties's(South Carolina) Battery, Lt. R. B. Waddell

APPENDIX B

FEDERAL ORDER OF BATTLE FROM THE
CHATTAHOOCHEE RIVER

Major General William T. Sherman, Commanding
Headquarters Guard: 7th Company Ohio Sharpshooters, Lt. William Mc Crory
Artillery: Brigadier General William F. Barry, Chief of Artillery

ARMY OF THE CUMBERLAND
Major General George H. Thomas
Escort: Company I, 1st Ohio Cavalry, Lt. Henry C. Reppert
Artillery: Brigadier General John M. Brannan, Chief of Artillery

IV ARMY CORPS
Major General Oliver O. Howard

FIRST DIVISION
Major General David S. Stanley

First Brigade
Colonel Isaac M. Kirby
21st Illinois, Maj. James E. Calloway, Capt. William H. Jamison
38th Illinois, Lt. Col. William T. Chapman
31st Indiana, Col. John T. Smith
81st Indiana, Lt. Col. William C. Wheeler
1st Kentucky, Col. David A. Enyart
2d Kentucky, Lt. Col. John R. Hurd
90th Ohio, Lt. Col. Samuel N. Yeoman
101st Ohio, Col. Isaac M. Kirby, Lt. Col. Bedan B. Mc Danald

2nd Brigade
Colonel Jacob E. Taylor
59th Illinois, Col. P. Sidney Post
96th Illinois, Col. Thomas E. Champion, Maj. George Hicks
115th Illinois, Col. Jesse H. Moore
35th Indiana, Maj. John P. Dufficy, Capt. James A. Gavisk, Lt. Col. Augustus G.
Tassin

84th Indiana, Lt. Col. Andrew J. Neff, Capt. John C. Taylor
21st Kentucky, Col. Samuel W. Price, Lt. Col. James C. Evans
23d Kentucky, Lt. Col. George W. Northup
40th Ohio, Col. Jacob E. Taylor, Capt. Charles G. Matchett, Capt. Milton Kemper
45th Ohio, Col. Benjamin P. Runkle, Lt. Col. Charles H. Butterfield, Capt. John H. Humphrey
51st Ohio, Lt. Col. Charles H. Wood, Col. Richard W. McClain
99th Ohio, Lt. Col. John E. Cummins, Capt. James A. Bope

3rd Brigade
Colonel P. Sidney Post
59th Illinois, Col. P. Sidney Post, Lt. Col. Clayton Hale
75th Illinois, Col. John E. Bennett, Lt. Col. William M. Kilgour
80th Illinois, Lt. Col. William M. Kilgour, Maj. James M. Stookey
84th Illinois, Col. Louis H. Waters
9th Indiana, Col. Isaac C. B. Suman
30th Indiana, Lt. Col. Orrin D. Hurd, Capt. William Dawson
36th Indiana, Lt. Col. Oliver H. P. Carey
84th Indiana, Capt. John C. Taylor, Capt. Martin B. Miller
77th Pennsylvania, Capt. Joseph J. Lawson, Col. Thomas E. Rose

Artillery
Captain Theodore S. Thomasson
Indiana Light. 5th Battery, Capt. Alfred Morrison
Pennsylvania Light, Battery B, Capt. Samuel M. McDowell, Capt. Jacob Ziegler

SECOND DIVISION
Brigadier General John Newton

First Brigade
Brigadier General Nathan Kimball
36th Illinois, Col. Silas Miller, Capt. James B. Mc Neal, Lt. Col. Porter C. Olson
44th Illinois, Col. Wallace W. Barrett, Lt. Col. John Russell, Maj. Luther M. Sabin, Lt. Col. John Russell
73d Illinois, Maj. Thomas W. Motherspaw
74th Illinois, Col. Jason Marsh, Lt. Col. James B. Kerr, Capt. Thomas J. Bryan
88th Illinois, Lt. Col. George W. Smith
28th Kentucky, Lt. Col. J. Rowan Boone
2d Missouri, Lt. Col. Arnold Beck, Col. Bernard Laiboldt (stationed at Dalton GA)
5th Missouri, Col. Joseph Conrad
24th Wisconsin, Maj. Arthur MacArthur, Jr.

2nd Brigade
Brigadier General George D. Wagner (sick 10–25 July)
Colonel John W. Blake
100th Illinois, Maj. Charles M. Hammond
40th Indiana, Col. John W. Blake,
57th Indiana, Lt. Col. Willis Blanch
28th Kentucky, Lt. Col. J. Rowan Boone, Maj. George W. Barth
26th Ohio, Lt. Col. William H. Squires
97th Ohio, Col. John Q. Lane

3rd Brigade
Brigadier General Luther P. Bradley
27th Illinois, Lt. Col. William A. Schmitt
42d Illinois, Lt. Col. Edgar D. Swain, Capt. Jared W. Richards, Maj, Frederick A. Atwater
51st Illinois, Capt. Theodore F. Brown, Capt. Albert M. Tilton
79th Illinois, Lt. Col. Henry E. Rives, Maj. Terrence Clark, Capt. Oliver O. Bagley
3d Kentucky, Col. Henry C. Dunlap, Capt. John W. Tuttle
64th Ohio, Lt. Col. Robert C. Brown, Maj. Samuel L. Coulter
65th Ohio, Lt. Col. Horatio N. Whirbeck, Capt. Charles O. Tannehill, Maj. Orlow Smith
125th Ohio, Col. Emerson Opdycke, Lt. Col. David H. Moore

Artillery
Captain Wilbur F. Goodspeed
1st Illinois Light, Battery M, Capt. George W. Spencer
1st Ohio Light, Battery A, Lt. Charles W. Scovill

THIRD DIVISION
Brigadier General Thomas J. Wood

First Brigade
Colonel William Gibson
Colonel Richard H. Nodine
25th Illinois, Col. Richard H. Nodine
35th Illinois, Lt. Col. William P. Chandler
89th Illinois, Col. Charles T. Hotchkiss, Lt. Col. William D. Williams
32d Indiana, Col. Frank Erdelmeyer
8th Kansas, Col. John A. Martin, Lt. Col. James M. Graham
15th Ohio, Col. William Wallace, Lt. Col. Frank Askew
49th Ohio, Col. William H. Gibson, Lt. Col. Samuel F. Gray
15th Wisconsin, Maj. George Wilson, Lt. Col. Ole C. Johnson

2nd Brigade
Brigadier General William B. Hazen
59th Illinois, Capt. Samuel West
6th Indiana, Lt. Col. Calvin D. Campbell
5th Kentucky, Col. William W. Berry
6th Kentucky, Maj. Richard T. Whitaker, Capt. Isaac N. Johnston
23d Kentucky, Lt. Col. James C. Foy, Maj. George W. Northup
1st Ohio, Maj. Joab A. Stafford (Guarding Western & Atlantic Railroad)
6th Ohio, Col. Nicholas L. Anderson (Guarding Western & Atlantic Railroad)
41st Ohio, Lt. Col. Robert L. Kimberly
71st Ohio, Col. Henry K. McConnell
93d Ohio, Lt. Col. Daniel Bowman
124th Ohio, Col. Oliver H. Payne, Lt. Col. James Pickands

3rd Brigade
Colonel Frederick Knefler
79th Indiana, Col. Frederick Knefler, Lt. Col. Samuel P. Oyler, Maj. George W. Parker
86th Indiana, Col. George F. Dick
9th Kentucky, Col. George H. Cram
17th Kentucky, Col. Alexander M. Stout
13th Ohio, Col. Dwight Jarvis, Jr., Maj. Joseph T. Snider
19th Ohio, Col. Charles F. Manderson, Lt. Col. Henry G. Stratton
59th Ohio, Capt. Charles A. Sheafe, Capt. John L. Watson, Capt. Robert H. Higgins

Artillery
Captain Cullen Bradley
Illinois Light, Bridges's Battery, Capt. Lyman Bridges, Lt. Morris D. Temple, Lt. Lyman A. White
Ohio Light, 6th Battery, Lt. Oliver H. P. Ayres, Lt. Lorenzo D. Immell

ARTILLERY BRIGADE
Major Thomas W. Osborn
Captain Lyman Bridges

XIV ARMY CORPS.
Major General John M. Palmer

FIRST DIVISION.
Brigadier General Richard W. Johnson
Provost Guard: 16th United States, Company D, 1st Battalion, Capt. Charles F. Trowbridge

First Brigade
Colonel Anson G. Mc Cook
104th Illinois, Lt. Col. Douglas Hapeman
42nd Indiana, Capt. James H. Masters, Capt. Gideon R. Kellams
88th Indiana, Lt. Col. Cyrus E. Briant
15th Kentucky, Col. Marion C. Taylor, Lt. Col. William G. Halpin.
2nd Ohio, Capt. James F. Sarratt
33d Ohio, Lt. Col. James H. M. Montgomery, Capt. Thaddeus A. Minshall.
94th Ohio, Lt. Col. Rue P. Hutchins
10th Wisconsin Capt. Jacob W. Roby
21st Wisconsin, Lt. Col. Harrison C. Hobart, Maj. Michael H. Fitch

2nd Brigade
Brigadier General John H. King
11th Michigan, Col. William L. Stoughton, Capt. Patrick H. Keegan
69th Ohio, Col. Marshall F. Moore, Lt. Col. Joseph H. Brigham, Capt. Lewis E. Hicks
15th United States (9 Companies 1st and 3rd Battalions), Maj. Albert Tracy, Capt. Albert B. Dod
15th United States (6 Companies 2nd Battalion), Maj. John R. Edie, Capt. William S. Mc Manus
16th United States (4 Companies 1st Battalion), Capt. Alexander H. Stanton, Capt. Ebenezer Gay.
16th United States (4 Companies 2nd Battalion), Capt. Robert P. Barry
8th United States (8 Companies 1st and 3rd Battalions), Capt. George W. Smith, Capt. Lyman M. Kellogg
18th United States (2nd Battalion), Capt. William J. Fetterman
19th United States (1st Battalion and A, 2nd Battalion), Capt. James Mooney, Capt. Lewis Wilson

3rd Brigade
Colonel Marshall F. Moore
37th Indiana, Lt. Col. William D. Ward, Maj. Thomas V. Kimble
38th Indiana, Lt. Col. Daniel F. Griffin
21st Ohio, Col. James M. Neibling, Lt. Col. Arnold McMahan.
74 th Ohio, Col. Josiah Given, Maj. Joseph Fisher
78th Pennsylvania, Col. William Sirwell
79th Pennsylvania, Maj. Michael H. Locher, Capt. John S. McBride
1st Wisconsin, Lt. Col. George B. Bingham

Artillery
Capt. Lucius H. Drury

1st Illinois Light, Battery C, Capt. Mark H. Prescott
1st Ohio Light, Battery I, Capt. Hubert Dilger

SECOND DIVISION
Brigadier General Jefferson C. Davis

First Brigade
Brigadier General James D. Morgan
10th Illinois, Col. John Tillson
16th Illinois, Col. Robert F. Smith, Lt. Col. James B. Cahill
60th Illinois, Col. William B. Anderson
10th Michigan, Col. Charles M. Lure, Maj. Henry S. Burnett, Capt. William H. Dunphy
14th Michigan, Col. Henry R. Mizner
17th New York, Col. William T. C. Grower, Maj. Joel O. Martin (regiment joined 21 August)

2nd Brigade
Colonel John G. Mitchell
34th Illinois, Lt. Col. Oscar Van Tassell
78th Illinois, Col. Carter Van Vleck, Lt. Col. Maris R. Vernon
98th Ohio, Lt. Col. John S. Pearce, Capt. John A. Norris, Capt. David E. Roatch
108th Ohio, Lt. Col. Joseph Good (Guarding Western & Atlantic Railroad)
113th Ohio, Lt. Col. Darius B. Warner, Maj. Lyne S. Sullivant, Capt. Toland Jones
121st Ohio, Col. Henry B. Banning.

3rd Brigade
Col. Caleb J. Dilworth
85th Illinois, Maj. Robert G. Rider, Capt. James R. Griffith
86th Illinois, Lt. Col. Allen L. Fahnestock, Maj. Joseph F. Thomas
110th Illinois, Lt. Col. E. Hibbard Topping
125th Illinois, Lt. Col. James W. Langley
22nd Indiana, Maj. Thomas Shea, Capt. William H. Taggart, Capt. William H. Snodgrass.
52nd Ohio, Lt. Col. Charles W. Clancy (captured 19 July at Moore's Mill), Maj. James T. Holmes

Artillery
Captain Charles M. Barnett
2nd Illinois Light, Battery I, Lt. Alonzo W. Coe
Wisconsin Light, 5th Battery, Capt. George Q. Gardner, Lt. Joseph McKnight

THIRD DIVISION
Brigadier General Absalom Baird

First Brigade
Brigadier General John B. Turchin (sick from 15 July)
Colonel Moses B. Walker
19th Illinois, Lt. Col. Alexander W. Raffen (regiment mustered out of service 9 June)
24th Illinois, Capt. August Mauff (regiment mustered out of service 28 June)
82nd Indiana, Col. Morton C. Hunter
23nd Missouri, Col. William P. Robinson
11th Ohio, Lt. Col. Ogden Street (regiment mustered out of service 10 June)
17th Ohio, Col. Durbin Ward
31st Ohio, Col. Moses B. Walker, Lt. Col. Frederick W. Lister
89th Ohio, Maj. John H. Jolly, Col. Caleb H. Carlton
92nd Ohio, Col. Benjamin D. Fearing

2nd Brigade
Colonel Newell Gleason
75th Indiana, Lt. Col. William O'Brien (wounded 20 July at Peach Tree), Maj. Cyrus J. Mc Cole
87th Indiana, Lt. Col. Edwin P. Hammond
101st Indiana, Lt. Col. Thomas Doan
2d Minnesota, Col. James George, Lt. Col. Judson W. Bishop
9th Ohio, Col. Gustave Kammerling (regiment mustered out of service 22 May)
35th Ohio, Maj. Joseph L. Budd.
105th Ohio, Lt. Col. George T. Perkins

3rd Brigade
Colonel George P. Este
10th Indiana, Lt. Col. Marsh B. Taylor
74th Indiana, Lt. Col. Myron Baker (killed 5 August at Utoy Creek), Maj. Thomas Morgan
10th Kentucky, Col. William H. Hays
18th Kentucky, Lt. Col. Hubbard K. Milward (stationed at Ringgold, Ga.)
14th Ohio, Maj. John W. Wilson (wounded 1 September at Jonesboro), Capt. George W. Kirk
38th Ohio, Col. William A. Choate, Capt. Joseph Wagstaff

Artillery
Captain George Estep
Indiana Light, 7th Battery, Capt. Otho H. Morgan

Indiana Light, 19th Battery, Lt. William P. Stackhouse

Artillery Brigade
Major Charles Houghtaling
Reserve Artillery: Indiana Light, 20th Battery, Capt. Milton A. Osborne

XX ARMY CORPS
Major General Joseph Hooker
Escort: 15th Illinois Cavalry, Company K, Capt. William Duncan

FIRST DIVISION
Brigadier General Alpheus S. Williams

First Brigade
Brigadier General Joseph F. Knipe
Colonel Warren W. Packer (commanded from 3–17 July and 28 July 28–28 August)
5th Connecticut, Col. Warren W. Packer, Lt. Col. Henry W. Daboll, Maj. William S. Cogswell
3d Maryland (detachment), Lt. David Gove (Gore?), Lt. Donald Reid
123d New York, Lt. Col. James C. Rogers
141st New York, Col. William K. Logie (killed 20 July at Peach Tree), Lt. Col. Andrew J. McNett
46th Pennsylvania, Col. James L. Selfridge

2nd Brigade
Brigadier General Thomas H. Ruger
27th Indiana, Col. Silas Colgrove (wounded 20 July at Peach Tree), Lt. Col. John R. Fesler
2d Massachusetts, Col. William Cogswell, Lt. Col. Charles F. Morse
13th New Jersey, Col. Ezra A. Carman
107th New York, Col. Nirom M. Crane
150th New York, Col. John H. Ketcham
3d Wisconsin, Col. William Hawley

3rd Brigade
Colonel James S. Robinson (sick from 24 July)
Colonel Horace Boughton
82d Illinois, Lt. Col. Edward S. Salomon
101st Illinois, Lt. Col. John B. LeSage
45th New York, Col. Adolphus Dobke (sent to Nashville 6 July)
143d New York, Col. Horace Boughton, Lt. Col. Hezekiah Watkins, Maj. John Higgins

61st Ohio, Col. Stephen J. McGroarty (wounded 20 July at Peach Tree), Capt. John Garrett
82d Ohio, Lt. Col. David Thomson
31st Wisconsin, Col. Francis H. West (regiment joined brigade 21 July)

Artillery
Captain John D. Woodbury
1st New York Light, Battery I, Lt. Charles E. Winegar
1st New York Light, Battery M, Capt. John D. Woodbury

SECOND DIVISION
Brigadier General John W. Geary

First Brigade
Colonel Charles Candy
5th Ohio, Lt. Col. Robert L. Kilpatrick, Maj. Henry E. Symmes, Capt. Robert Kirkup
7th Ohio, Lt. Col. Samuel McClelland (mustered out 11 June)
29th Ohio, Col. William T. Fitch, Capt. Myron T. Wright, Capt. Wilbur F. Stevens
66th Ohio, Lt. Col. Eugene Powell, Capt. Thomas McConnell
28th Pennsylvania, Lt. Col. John Flynn
147th Pennsylvania, Col. Ario Pardee, Jr., Lt. Col. John Craig

2nd Brigade
Colonel Patrick H. Jones
33d New Jersey, Col. George W. Mindil, Lt. Col. Enos Fourat, Capt. Thomas O'Connor
119th New York, Col. John T. Lockman, Capt. Charles H. Odell, Capt. Chester H. Southworth
134th New York, Lt. Col. Allan H. Jackson (wounded 20 July Peachtree), Capt. Clinton C. Brown
154th New York, Lt. Col. Daniel B. Allen, Maj. Lewis D. Warner
27th Pennsylvania, Lt. Col. August Riedt (mustered out 23 May)
73d Pennsylvania, Maj. Charles C. Cresson (wounded 15 June at Pine Mountain)
109th Pennsylvania, Capt. Frederick L. Gimber (wounded 15 June at Pine Mountain), Capt. Walter G. Dunn, Capt. Hugh Alexander, Capt. William Geary

3rd Brigade
Colonel David Ireland
(wounded 15 May at Resaca, returned to command 2 June)
60th New York, Col. Abel Godard. Capt. Thomas Elliott.
78th New York, Lt. Col. Harvey S. Chatfield, Col. Herbert von Hammerstein

102d New York, Col. James C. Lane, Maj. Lewis R. Stegman, Capt. Barent Van Buren
137th New York, Lt. Col. Koert S. Van Voorhis
149th New York, Col. Henry A Barnum
29th Pennsylvania, Lt. Col. Thomas M. Walker, Maj. Jesse R. Millison
111th Pennsylvania, Col. George A. Cobham, Jr. (killed 20 July), Lt. Col. Thomas M. Walker

Artillery
Captain Charles C. Aleshire
13th New York Light Battery, Lt. Henry Bundy
Pennsylvania Light, Battery E, Capt. James D. McGill (resigned 8 July), Lt. Thomas S. Sloan

THIRD DIVISION
Brigadier General William T. Ward

First Brigade
Colonel Benjamin Harrison
102d Illinois, Col. Franklin C. Smith (wounded 16 June, Gilgal Church), Lt. Col. James M. Mannon
105th Illinois, Col. Daniel Dustin, Lt. Col. Everell F. Dutton
129th Illinois, Col. Henry Case
70th Indiana, Lt. Col. Samuel Merrill
79th Ohio, Col. Henry G. Kennett, Lt. Col. Azariah W. Doan, Capt. Samuel A. West

2nd Brigade
Colonel John Coburn
33rd Indiana, Maj. Levin T. Miller (wounded 2 June at Mars Hill Church) Capt. Edward T. McCrea
85th Indiana, Col. John P. Baird (replaced 17 July), Lt. Col. Alexander B. Crane
19th Michigan, Maj. Eli A. Griffin, Capt. John J. Baker, Capt. David Anderson
22d Wisconsin, Col. William L. Utley, Lt. Col. Edward Bloodgood

3rd Brigade
Colonel James Wood, Jr.
20th Connecticut, Col. Samuel Ross (replaced 16 July), Lt. Col. Philo B. Buckingham
33d Massachusetts, Lt. Col. Godfrey Rider, Jr.
136th New York, Lt. Col. Lester B. Faulkner, Maj. Henry L. Arnold
55th Ohio, Lt. Col. Edwin H. Powers, Capt. Charles P. Wickham

73d Ohio, Maj. Samuel H. Hurst (wounded 15 May at Resaca)
26th Wisconsin, Lt. Col. Frederick C. Winkler

Artillery
Captain Marco B. Gary
1st Michigan Light, Battery I, Capt. Luther R. Smith
1st Ohio Light, Battery C, Lt. Jerome B. Stephens

Reserve Artillery Brigade
Major John A. Reynolds
5th United States, Battery K, Capt. Edmund C. Bainbridge

Reserve Brigade
Colonel Heber Le Favour
10th Ohio, Col. Joseph W. Burke (mustered out 27 May)
9th Michigan, Lt. Col. William Wilkinson
22d Michigan Lt. Col. Henry S. Dean (joined 31 May)

Pontoniers
Colonel George P. Buell
58th Indiana, Lt. Col. Joseph Moore
Pontoon Battalion, Capt. Patrick O'Connell (battalion sent to Chattanooga 17 June)

Siege Artillery
11th Indiana Battery, Capt. Arnold Sutermeister

Ammunition Train Guard
1st Battalion Ohio Sharpshooters, Capt. Gershom M. Barber

ARMY OF THE TENNESSEE
Major General James B. McPherson (killed 22 July at Atlanta)
Escort: 4th Company Ohio Cavalry, Capt. John S. Foster, Capt. John L. King
1st Ohio Cavalry, Company B, Capt. George F. Conn

XV ARMY CORPS
Major General John A. Logan

FIRST DIVISION
Brig. Gen. Peter J. Osterhaus (sick 15 July–15 August)
Brigadier General Charles R. Woods

First Brigade

Brigadier General Charles R. Woods
Colonel Milo Smith [who is this?]
26th Iowa, Col. Milo Smith, Lt. Col. Thomas G. Ferreby
30th Iowa, Lt. Col. Aurelius Roberts
27th Missouri, Col. Thomas Curly, Maj. Dennis O'Connor
76th Ohio, Col. William B. Woods

2nd Brigade
Colonel James A. Williamson
4th Iowa, Lt. Col. Samuel D. Nichols, Capt. Randolph Sry
9th Iowa, Col. David Carskaddon, Maj. George Granger
25th Iowa, Col. George A. Stone
31st Iowa, Col. William Smyth

3rd Brigade
Colonel Hugo Wangelin
3d Missouri, Col. Theodore Meumann
12th Missouri, Lt. Col. Jacob Kaercher, Maj. Frederick T. Ledergerber
17th Missouri, Maj. Francis Romer
29th Missouri, Lt. Col. Joseph S. Gage, Maj. Philip H. Murphy
31st Missouri, Lt. Col. Samuel P. Simpson, Maj. Frederick Jaensch
32d Missouri, Capt. Charles C. Bland, Maj. Abraham J. Seay

Artillery
Major Clemens Landgraeber
2d Missouri Light, Battery F, Capt. Louis Voelkner, Lt. Lewis A. Winn
Ohio Light, 4th Battery, Capt. George Froehlich, Lt. Louis Zimmerer

SECOND DIVISION
Brigadier General Morgan L. Smith

First Brigade
Brigadier General Giles A. Smith (transferred to XVII Corps 20 July)
Colonel James S. Martin
55th Illinois, Lt. Col. Theodore C. Chandler, Capt. Jacob M. Augustin, Capt. Francis H. Shaw
111th Illinois, Col. James S. Martin, Maj. William M. Mabry
116th Illinois, Capt. John S. Windsor
127th Illinois, Lt. Col Frank S. Curtiss, Capt. Alexander C. Little, Capt. Charles Schryver
6th Missouri, Lt. Col. Delos Van Deusen
8th Missouri, Lt. Col. David C. Coleman (mustered out 16 and 25 June)
30th Ohio, Lt. Col. George H. Hildt

57th Ohio, Lt. Col. Samuel R. Mott

2nd Brigade
Brigadier General Joseph A. J. Lightburn
111th Illinois, Col. James S. Martin
83d Indiana, Col. Benjamin J. Spooner (wounded 27 June at Kennesaw), Capt. George H. Scott
30th Ohio, Col. Theodore Jones
37th Ohio, Lt. Col. Louis von Blessingh (sick from 23 May), Maj. Charles Hipp, Capt. Carl Moritz
47th Ohio, Col. Augustus C. Parry (wounded 27 June at Kennesaw), Lt. Col. John Wallace (wounded 22 July at Atlanta), Maj. Thomas T. Taylor
53d Ohio, Col. Wells S. Jones, Lt. Col. Robert A. Fulton
54th Ohio, Lt. Col. Robert Williams, Jr., Maj. Israel T. Moore

Artillery
Captain Francis De Gress (commanded from 12 July)
1st Illinois Light, Battery A, Capt. Peter P. Wood, Lt. George McCagg, Jr., Lt. Samuel S. Smyth
1st Illinois Light, Battery B, Capt. Israel P. Rumsey (consolidated with Battery A, 12 July)
1st Illinois Light, Battery H, Capt. Francis De Gress

THIRD DIVISION
(Guarding Railroad at Cartersville)
Brigadier General John E. Smith
Escort: 4th Missouri Cavalry, Company F, Lt. Alexander Mueller

First Brigade
Colonel Jesse I. Alexander
Colonel Joseph B. Mc Cown
63d Illinois, Col. Joseph B. Mc Cown, Lt. Col. James Isaminger
48th Indiana, Lt. Col. Edward J. Wood
59th Indiana, Lt. Col. Jefferson K. Scott
4th Minnesota, Lt. Col. John E. Tourtellotte, Maj. James C. Edson
18th Wisconsin, Lt. Col. Charles H. Jackson

2nd Brigade
Colonel Green B. Raum
13th Illinois (detachment), Lt. Mark M. Evans
56th Illinois, Lt. Col. John P. Hall
17th Iowa, Col. Clark R. Wever
10th Missouri, Col. Francis C. Deimling, Capt. Joel W. Strong

24th Missouri, Company E, Lt. Daniel Driscoll
80th Ohio, Lt. Col. Pren Metham

3rd Brigade
Brigadier General Charles L. Mattheis
Colonel Benjamin D. Dean
Colonel Jabez Banbury
93d Illinois, Lt. Col. Nicholas C. Buswell, Maj. James M. Fisher
5th Iowa, Col. Jabez Banbury, Lt. Col. Ezekiel S. Sampson
10th Iowa, Lt. Col. Paris P. Henderson, Lt. David H. Emry
26th Missouri, Lt. Col. John McFall, Col. Benjamin D. Dean

Artillery
Captain Henry Dillon
Wisconsin Light, 6th Battery, Lt. Samuel F. Clark, Lt. James G. Simpson
Wisconsin Light, 12th Battery, Capt. William Zickerick

Cavalry: 5th Ohio, Col. Thomas T. Heath

FOURTH DIVISION
Brigadier General William Harrow

First Brigade
Colonel Reuben Williams
26th Illinois, Lt. Col. Robert A. Gillmore
90th Illinois, Lt. Col. Owen Stuart, Capt. Daniel O'Connor
12th Indiana, Lt. Col. James Goodnow, Col. Reuben Williams
100th Indiana, Lt. Col. Albert Heath

2nd Brigade
Brigadier General Charles C. Walcutt
40th Illinois, Maj. Hiram W. Hall, (regiment joined 3 June)
103d Illinois, Lt. Col. George W. Wright (wounded 27 June Kennesaw), Capt. Franklin C. Post
97th Indiana, Col. Robert F. Catterson (sick from 25 June), Lt. Col. Aden G. Cavins
6th Iowa, Lt. Col. Alexander J. Miller (wounded 28 May, Dallas), Maj. Thomas J. Ennis
46th Ohio, Capt. Joshua W. Heath (killed 22 July, Atlanta), Lt. Col. Isaac N. Alexander

3rd Brigade
Colonel John M. Oliver

48th Illinois, Col. Lucien Greathouse (killed 22 July at Atlanta), Maj. Edward Adams

99th Indiana, Col. Alexander Fowler (on leave from 26 July), Lt. Col. John M. Berkey

15th Michigan, Lt. Col. Austin E. Jaquith (disabled 5 June) Lt. Col. Frederick S. Hutchinson

70th Ohio, Maj. William B. Brown (killed 3 August), Capt. Louis Love, Capt. Henry L. Philips

Artillery
Major John T. Cheney
Captain Henry H. Griffiths
Captain Josiah H. Burton
1st Illinois Light, Battery F, Capt. Josiah H. Burton, Lt. Jefferson F. Whaley, Lt. George P. Cunningham
Iowa Light, 1st Battery, Lt. William H. Gay, Capt. Henry H. Griffiths, Lt. William H. Gay

XVI ARMY CORPS (LEFT WING)
Major General Grenville M. Dodge
Brigadier General Thomas E.G. Ransom
Escort: 1st Alabama Cavalry, Lt. Col. George L. Godfrey., Col. George E. Spencer
52d Illinois, Company A, Capt. George E. Young

SECOND DIVISION
Brigadier General Thomas W. Sweeny (relieved 25 July)
Brigadier General John M. Corse

First Brigade
Brigadier General Elliott W. Rice
52d Illinois, Lt. Col. Edwin A. Bowen
66th Indiana, Lt. Col. Roger Martin (sick 23 July), Maj. Thomas G. Morrison, Capt. Alfred Morris
2d Iowa, Lt. Col. Noel B. Howard (wounded 22 July), Maj. Mathew G. Hamill
7th Iowa, Lt. Col. James C. Parrott, Maj. James W. McMullin, Capt. Samuel Mahon

2nd Brigade
Colonel Patrick E. Burke (wounded 16 May, Rome)
Lieutenant Colonel Robert N. Adams (commanded 16–23 May)
Colonel August Mersy (commanded 23 May–24 July)
Colonel Robert N. Adams (commanded from 24 July)

9th Illinois (mounted), Lt. Col. Jesse J. Phillips (wounded 9 May, Snake Creek Gap), Maj. John H. Kuhn (mustered out 26 July), Capt. Samuel T. Hughes
12th Illinois, Maj. James R. Hugunin, Lt. Col. Henry Van Sellar
66th Illinois, Maj. Andrew K. Campbell, Capt. William S. Boyd
81st Ohio, Lt. Col. Robert N. Adams, Maj. Frank Evans, Capt. Noah Stoker, Capt. William Clay Henry

3rd Brigade (stationed at Rome from 22 May)
Colonel Moses M. Bane
7th Illinois, Col. Richard Rowett, Lt. Col. Hector Perrin
50th Illinois, Maj. William Hanna
57th Illinois, Lt. Col. Frederick J. Hurlbut
89th Iowa, Col. Henry J. B. Cummings, Lt. Col. James Redfield, Maj. Joseph M. Griffiths

Artillery
Captain Frederick Welker
1st Michigan Light, Battery B, Capt. Albert F. R. Arndt
1st Missouri Light, Battery H, Lt. Andrew T. Blodgett
1st Missouri Light, Battery I, Lt. John F. Brunner

FOURTH DIVISION
Brigadier General James C. Veatch (sick from 17 July)
Brigadier General John W. Fuller (commanded 17 July–4 August and after 20 August)
Brigadier General Thomas E. G. Ransom

First Brigade
Brigadier General John W. Fuller (commanded division 17 July–4 August and after 20 August)
Colonel John Morrill (wounded 22 July, Atlanta)
Lieutenant Colonel Henry T. McDowell
64th Illinois, Col. John Morrill, Lt. Col. Michael W. Manning
18th Missouri, Lt. Col. Charles S. Sheldon, Maj. William H. Minter
27th Ohio, Lt. Col. Mendal Churchill
39th Ohio, Col. Edward F. Noyes, Lt. Col. Henry T. McDowell, Maj. John S. Jenkins

2nd Brigade
Brigadier General John W. Sprague
35th New Jersey, Col. John J. Cladek, Lt. Col. William A. Henry, Capt. Charles A. Angel
43d Ohio, Col. Wager Swayne

63d Ohio, Lt. Col. Charles E. Brown (wounded 22 July, Atlanta), Maj. John W. Fouts

25th Wisconsin, Col. Milton Montgomery (wounded July, Atlanta), Lt. Col. Jeremiah M. Rusk

3rd Brigade (joined 7 August from Decatur AL)
Colonel James H. Howe
Colonel William T. C. Grower
Colonel John Tillson
10th Illinois, Capt. George C. Lusk (regiment joined 20 August)
25th Indiana, Lt. Col. John Rheinlander, Capt. James S. Wright
17th New York, Maj. Joel O. Martin
32d Wisconsin, Col. Charles H. De Groat

Artillery
Captain Jerome B. Burrows
Captain George Robinson
1st Michigan Light, Battery C, Capt. George Robinson, Lt. Henry Shier
Ohio Light, 14th Battery, Capt. Jerome B. Burrows, Lt. Seth M. Laird, Lt. George Hurlbut
2d United States, Battery F, Lt. Albert M. Murray, Lt. Joseph C. Breckinridge, Lt. Lemuel Smith, Lt. Rezin G. Howell

XII ARMY CORPS
Major General Frank P. Blair, Jr.
Escort: 1st Ohio Cavalry, Company M, Lt. Charles H. Shultz,
9th Illinois (mounted infantry), Company G, Capt. Isaac Clements,
11th Illinois Cavalry, Company G, Capt. Stephen S. Tripp

THIRD DIVISION
Brigadier General Mortimer D. Leggett
Escort: 1st Ohio Cavalry, Company D, Lt. James W. Kirkendall

First Brigade
Brigadier General Manning F. Force (wounded 22 July, Atlanta)
Colonel George E. Bryant
20th Illinois, Lt. Col. Daniel Bradley, Maj. George W. Kennard, Capt. John H. Austin
30th Illinois, Col. Warren Shedd (captured 22 July, Atlanta), Lt. Col. William C. Rhoads, Capt. John L. Nichols
31st Illinois, Col. Edwin S. Mc Cook (sick from 27 June), Lt. Col. Robert N. Pearson, Capt. Simpson S. Stricklin

45th Illinois, Lt. Col. Robert P. Sealy (guarding Western Atlantic Railroad at Etowah)
12th Wisconsin, Col. George E. Bryant, Lt. Col. James K. Proudfit
16th Wisconsin, Col. Cassius Fairchild, Maj. William F. Dawes

2nd Brigade
Colonel Robert K. Scott (captured 22 July, Atlanta)
Lieutenant Colonel Greenberry F. Wiles
20th Ohio, Lt. Col. John C. Fry (wounded 22 July, Atlanta), Maj. Francis M. Shaklee
32d Ohio, Col. Benjamin F. Potts
68th Ohio, Lt. Col. George E. Welles (wounded 22 July, Atlanta)
78th Ohio, Lt. Col. Greenberry F. Wiles, Maj. John T. Rainey

3rd Brigade
Colonel Adam G. Malloy
17th Wisconsin, Lt. Col. Thomas McMahon, Maj Donald D. Scott
Worden's Battalion, Maj. Asa Worden

Artillery
Capt. William S. Williams
1st Illinois Light, Battery D, Capt. Edgar H. Cooper
1st Michigan Light, Battery H, Capt. Marcus D. Elliott, Lt. William Justin
Ohio Light, 3d Battery, Lt. John Sullivan

FOURTH DIVISION
Brigadier General Walter Q. Gresham (wounded 20 July, Bald Hill)
Brigadier General Giles A. Smith
Escort: 11th Illinois Cavalry, Company G, Capt. Stephen S. Tripp

First Brigade
Colonel William L. Sanderson (commanded until 18 July)
Colonel Benjamin F. Potts
53d Illinois, Lt. Col. John W. McClanahan (transferred from 2nd Brigade 18 July)
23d Indiana, Lt. Col. William P. Davis, Lt. Col. George S. Babbitt
53d Indiana, Lt. Col. William Jones (killed 22 July, Atlanta), Maj. Warner L. Vestal (wounded 22 July, Atlanta), Capt. George H. Beers
3d Iowa (three companies), Capt. Daniel McLennan, Capt. Pleasant T. Mathes, Lt. Lewis T. Linnell, Lt. D. W. Wilson
32d Ohio, Capt. William M. Morris, Lt. Col. Jeff. J. Hibbets (transferred from 3rd Division 18 July)

2nd Brigade (Guarding Western & Atlantic Railroad)

Colonel George C. Rogers
Colonel Isaac C. Pugh (commanded 5–19 July)
14th Illinois, Capt. Carlos C. Cox
15th Illinois, Maj. Rufus C. McEathron
32d Illinois, Col. John Logan (transferred from 1st Brigade 18 July), Lt. Col. George H. English
41st Illinois, Maj. Robert H. McFadden
53d Illinois, Lt. Col. John W. Mc-Clanahan

3rd Brigade
Colonel William Hall
Brigadier General William W. Belknap
11th Iowa, Lt. Col. John C. Abercrombie
13th Iowa, Col. John Shane, Maj. William A. Walker
15th Iowa, Col. William W. Belknap, Maj. George Pomutz
16th Iowa, Lt. Col. Addison H. Sanders (captured 22 July 22 at Atlanta with most of regiment), Capt. Crandall W. Williams

Artillery
Captain Edward Spear, Jr.
Captain William Z. Clayton
2d Illinois Light, Battery F, Lt. Walter H. Powell (Battery and Powell captured 22 July at Atlanta)
Minnesota Light, 1st Battery, Capt. William Z. Clayton, Lt. Henry Hurter
1st Missouri Light Battery C, Capt. John L. Matthaei (Posted at Allatoona and Big Shanty)
Ohio Light, 10th Battery, Capt. Francis Seaman (Posted at Big Shanty from 11 July)
Ohio Light, 15th Battery, Lt. James Burdick

ARMY OF THE OHIO
(XXIII ARMY CORPS)
Major General John M. Schofield
Escort: 7th Ohio Cavalry, Company G, Capt. John A. Ashbury

Engineer Battalion
Captain Charles E. Mc Alester
Captain Oliver S. Mc Clure (commanded from 23 June)

FIRST DIVISION (disbanded and dispersed among 2nd and 3rd Divisions 9 June)
Brigadier General Alvin P. Hovey (on leave from 9 June)

First Brigade

Colonel Richard F. Barter
120th Indiana, Lt. Col. Allen W. Prather
124th Indiana, Col. James Burgess (sick from 10 June), Col. John M. Orr
128th Indiana, Col. Richard P. De Hart (wounded 7 June, Lost Mtn.), Lt. Col. Jasper Packard

2nd Brigade
Colonel John C. Mc Quiston
Colonel Peter T. Swaine (commanded from 23 June)
123d Indiana, Lt. Col. William A. Cullen, Col. John C. Mc Quiston
129th Indiana, Col. Charles Case (resigned 15 June), Col. Charles A. Zollinger
130th Indiana, Col. Charles S. Parrish
99th Ohio, Lt. Col. John E. Cummins

Artillery
Indiana Light, 23d Battery, Lt. Luther S. Houghton, Lt. Aaron A. Wilber
Indiana Light, 24th Battery (transferred to Stoneman's Cavalry Division 6 July and captured 31 July at Sunshine Creek), Capt. Alexander Hardy

SECOND DIVISION
Brigadier General Henry M. Judah (dismissed 18 May for incompetency at Resaca)
Brigadier General Milo S. Hascall

First Brigade
Brigadier General Nathaniel C. Mc Lean
Brigadier General Joseph A. Cooper (commanded from 4 June)
91st Indiana, Lt. Col. Charles H. Butterfield, Col. John Mehringer
25th Michigan, Lt. Col. Benjamin F. Orcutt (sick from 10 July), Capt. Samuel L. Demarest, Capt. Edwin Childs
3d Tennessee, Col. William Cross, Maj. R. H. Dunn
6th Tennessee, Col. Joseph A. Cooper, Lt. Col. Edward Maynard, Capt. Marcus D. Bearden, Capt. William Ausmus

2nd Brigade
Colonel William E. Hobson
107th Illinois, Maj. Uriah M. Laurance, Lt. Col. Francis H. Lowry
80th Indiana, Lt. Col. Alfred D. Owen, Maj. John W. Tucker, Capt. Jacob Ragle
13th Kentucky, Col. William E. Hobson, Lt. Col. Benjamin P. Estes
23d Michigan, Lt. Col. Oliver L. Spaulding, Maj. William W. Wheeler
111th Ohio, Col. John R. Bond, Lt. Col. Isaac R. Sherwood
118th Ohio, Lt. Col. Thomas L. Young (sick from 18 June), Capt. Edgar Sowers, Capt. William Kennedy, Capt. Rudolph Reul

3rd Brigade
Colonel Silas A. Strickland
14th Kentucky, Col. George W. Gallup
20th Kentucky, Lt. Col. Thomas B. Waller
27th Kentucky, Lt. Col. John H. Ward, Capt. Andrew J. Bailey
50th Ohio, Lt. Col. George R. Elstner (killed 8 August, East Point), Maj. Hamilton S. Gillespie

Artillery
Captain Joseph C. Shields
Indiana Light, 29d Battery, Capt. Benjamin F. Denning (mortally wounded July near Kennesaw Mtn.), Lt. Edward W. Nicholson
1st Michigan Light. Battery F, Capt. Byron D. Paddock, Lt. Marshall M. Miller
Ohio Light, 19th Battery, Capt. Joseph C. Shields

THIRD DIVISION
Brigadier General Jacob D. Cox

First Brigade
Colonel James W. Reilly
112th Illinois, Col. Thomas J. Henderson (wounded 14 May at Resaca), Lt. Col. Emery S. Bond, Maj. Tristram T. Dow
16th Kentucky, Col. James W. Gault (sick from 29 May), Maj. John S. White, Capt. Jacob Miller
100th Ohio, Col. Patrick S. Slevin (wounded 6 August at Utoy Creek), Capt. Frank Rundell
104th Ohio: Col. Oscar W. Sterl
8th Tennessee, Col. Felix A. Reeve, Maj. William J. Jordan, Capt. Robert A. Ragan, Capt. James W. Berry

2nd Brigade
Brigadier General Mahlon D. Manson (wounded 14 May at Resaca)
Colonel John S. Casement (commanded 14 May–June 4)
Colonel Daniel Cameron
65th Illinois, Lt. Col. William S. Stewart
63d Indiana, Col. Israel N. Stiles, Lt. Col Daniel Morris
65th Indiana, Lt. Col. Thomas Johnson, Capt. Walter G. Hodge, Capt. William F. Stillwell, Capt. Edward A. Baker
24th Kentucky, Col. John S. Hurt, Lt. Col. Lafayette North
103d Ohio, Col. John S. Casement
5th Tennessee, Col. James T.. Shelley, Maj. David G. Bowers

3rd Brigade (organized 5 June)

Brigadier General Nathaniel C. McLean (sent to Kentucky 17 June)
Colonel Robert K. Byrd (commanded 17 June–14 July)
Colonel Israel N. Stiles
11th Kentucky, Col. S. Palace Love, Lt. Col. Erasmus L. Mottley
12th Kentucky, Lt. Col. Laurence H. Rousseau
1st Tennessee, Col. Robert K. Byrd, Lt. Col. John Ellis
5th Tennessee, Col. James T. Shelley (resigned 22 July), Maj. David G. Bowers

Dismounted Cavalry Brigade
Colonel Eugene W. Crittenden
16th Illinois, Capt. Hiram S. Hanchett
12th Kentucky, Lt. Col. James T. Bramlette, Maj. James B. Harrison

Artillery
Major Henry W. Wells
Indiana Light, 15th Battery, Capt. Alonzo D. Harvey
1st Ohio Light, Battery D, Capt. Giles J. Cockerill

CAVALRY CORPS
Brigadier General Washington L. Elliott
Escort: 4th Ohio, Company D, Capt. Philip H. Warner

FIRST DIVISION
Brigadier General Edward M. McCook

First Brigade
Colonel Joseph B. Dorr (captured 30 July at Brown's Mill)
Lieutenant Colonel James P. Brownlow (commanded 20 July–12 August)
Brigadier General John T. Croxton (commanded from 12 August)
8th Iowa, Lt. Col. Horatio G. Barrier, Col. Joseph B. Dorr, Maj. Richard Root, Maj. John H. Isett
4th Kentucky (mounted infantry), Col. John T. Croxton, Lt. Col. Robert M. Kelly, Capt. James H. West, Lt. Granville C. West, Capt. James I. Hudnall
2d Mich., Maj. Leonidas S. Scranton, Lt. Col. Benjamin Smith (regt. sent Franklin TN 29 June)
1st Tennessee, Col. James P. Brownlow

2nd Brigade
Colonel Oscar H. La Grange (captured 9 May at Varnell Station)
Lieutenant Colonel James W. Stewart (captured 26 May at Acworth)
Lieutenant Colonel Horace P. Lamson (commanded from 26 May)
Lieutenant Colonel William H. Torrey (captured 30 July at Brown's Mill)

Appendix B
Federal Order of Battle from the Chattahoochee River

2d Indiana, Lt. Col. James W. Stewart, Maj. David A. Briggs
4th Indiana, Lt. Col. Horace P. Lamson, Maj. George H. Purdy, Capt. Albert J. Morley
1st Wisconsin, Maj. Nathan Paine (killed 28 July at Palmetto), Capt. Henry Harnden, Capt. Lewis M. B. Smith, Lt. Col. William H. Torrey

3rd Brigade (stationed at Wauhatchie TN)
Colonel Louis D. Watkins
Colonel John K. Faulkner (commanded 5 July–10 August)
4th Kentucky, Col. Wickliffe Cooper
6th Kentucky, Maj. William H. Fidler
7th Kentucky, Col. John K. Faulkner, Maj. Robert Collier

Artillery
18th Indiana Battery, Lt. William B. Rippetoe, Capt. Moses M. Beck

SECOND DIVISION
Brigadier General Kenner Garrard

First Brigade
Colonel Robert H. G. Minty
4th Michigan, Lt. Col. Josiah B. Park, Maj. Frank W. Mix, Capt. L. Briggs Eldridge
7th Pennsylvania, Col. William B. Sipes, Maj. James F. Andreas, Maj. William H. Jennings
4th United States, Capt. James B. McIntyre

2nd Brigade (in North Alabama until 6 June)
Colonel Eli Long (wounded 20 August at Lovejoy Station)
Colonel Beroth B. Eggleston
1st Ohio, Col. Beroth B. Eggleston, Lt. Col. Thomas J. Patten
3d Ohio, Col. Charles B. Seidel
4th Ohio, Lt. Col. Oliver P. Robie

3rd Brigade (mounted infantry) "Lightning Brigade"
Colonel John T. Wilder (sick from June 14)
Colonel Abram O. Miller
98th Illinois, Lt. Col. Edward Kitchell
123d Illinois, Lt. Col. Jonathan Biggs
17th Indiana, Lt. Col. Henry Jordan, Maj. Jacob G. Vail
72d Indiana, Col. Abram O. Miller, Maj. Henry M. Carr, Capt. Adam Pinkerton, Lt. Col. Samuel C. Kirkpatrick

Artillery
Chicago (Illinois) Board of Trade Battery, Lt. George I. Robinson

THIRD DIVISION
Brigadier General Judson Kilpatrick (wounded 13 May at Resaca, resumed 28 July)
Colonel Eli H. Murray (commanded 12–21 May)
Colonel William W. Lowe (commanded 21 May–23 July)

First Brigade
Lieutenant Colonel Robert Klien
Lieutenant Colonel Matthewson T. Patrick
Major J. Morris Young
3d Indiana (four companies), Maj. Alfred Gaddis
5th Iowa, Maj. Harlon Baird, Maj. J. Morris Young, Capt. Martin Choumee (in pursuit of Wheeler's Cavalry into Tennessee from 27 July)

2nd Brigade
Colonel Charles C. Smith
Major Thomas W. Sanderson (commanded 2 July–6 August)
Lieutenant Colonel Fielder A. Jones
8th Indiana, Lt. Col. Fielder A. Jones, Maj. Thomas Herring, Maj. Thomas Graham (in pursuit of Wheeler's Cavalry into Tennessee from 27 July)
2d Kentucky, Maj. William H. Effort (killed 4 August at Triune TN), Maj. Owen Star (in pursuit of Wheeler's Cavalry into Tennessee from 27 July)
10th Ohio, Maj. Thomas W. Sanderson, Maj. William Thayer

3rd Brigade
Colonel Eli H. Murray
Colonel Smith D. Atkins
92d Illinois (mounted infantry), Col. Smith D. Atkins, Capt. Matthew Van Buskirk, Maj. Albert Woodcock
3d Kentucky, Maj. Lewis Wolfley, Lt. Col. Robert H. King
5th Kentucky, Col. Oliver L. Baldwin, Maj. Christopher T. Cheek

Artillery
10th Wisconsin Battery, Capt. Yates V. Beebe

STONEMAN'S CAVALRY DIVISION (destroyed 31 July at Sunshine Church)
Major General George Stoneman (captured 31 July at Sunshine Church)
Colonel Horace Capron
Escort: 7th Ohio, Company D, Lt. Samuel Murphy, Lt. Washington W. Manning

Appendix B
Federal Order of Battle from the Chattahoochee River

First Brigade (in pursuit of Wheeler's Cavalry into Tennessee from 27 July)
Colonel Israel Garrard
9th Michigan, Col. George S. Acker
7th Ohio, Lt. Col. George G. Miner

2nd Brigade
Colonel James Biddle (captured July 31 at Sunshine Church)
Colonel Thomas H. Butler
5th Indiana, Col. Thomas H. Butler (captured 31 July at Sunshine Church), Maj. Moses D. Leeson
6th Indiana, Lt. Col. Courtland C. Matson, Maj. William W. Carter (captured 3 August at King's Tanyard)

3rd Brigade
Colonel Horace Capron
14th Illinois, Lt. Col. David P. Jenkins
8th Michigan, Lt. Col. Elisha Mix (captured 31 July at Sunshine Church), Maj. William L. Buck (captured 3 August at King's Tanyard), Maj. Edward Coates
 McLaughlin's Ohio Squadron, Maj. Richard Rice

Independent Brigade
Colonel Alexander W. Holeman
Lieutenant Colonel Silas Adams (commanded from 27 July)
1st Kentucky, Lt. Col. Silas Adams
11th Kentucky, Lt. Col. Archibald J. Alexander

Artillery
24th Indiana Battery, Capt. Alexander Hardy (captured with Battery 31 July at Sunshine Church)[1]

---

[1]Official Records of the War of the Rebellion, series I, vol. 38, part I, serial no. 72, 89–114; William R. Scaife, *The Campaign for Atlanta* (Atlanta: self-published, 1993) 145–73.

APPENDIX C

ESTIMATED STRENGTH OF HOOD'S ARMY*

Hardee's Corps
1st Division, Cheatham's

Maney's Brigade	1,200
Strahl's Brigade	1,000
Wright's Brigade	1,400
Vaughan's Brigade	1,200
Total	4,800

2nd Division, Cleburne's

Polk's Brigade	1,000
Govan's Brigade	1,200
Lowrey's Brigade	1,500
Granbury's Brigade	1,200
Total	4,900

3rd Division, Walker's

Mercer's Brigade	2,000
Stevens's Brigade	1,500
Jackson's Brigade	1,000**
Gist's Brigade	1,200
Total	5,700

4th Division, Bate's

Lewis's Brigade	700
Finley's Brigade	1,000
Tyler's Brigade	1,300
Total	3,000
Total Hardee's Corps	18,400

Hood's Corps
1st Division, Hindman's

Deas's Brigade	1,200
Manigault's Brigade	1,200

Tucker's Brigade	1,000
Walthall's Brigade	1,200
Total	4,600
2nd Division, Stevenson's	
Cummings's Brigade	1,500
Brown's Brigade	800
Baker's Brigade	1,000
Reynolds's Brigade	1,200
Total	4,500
3rd Division, Stewart's:	
Gibson's Brigade	800
Stovall's Brigade	1,200
Clayton's Brigade	1,500
Moore's Brigade	1,000
Total	4,500
Total Hood's Corps	13,600
Stewart's Corps	
1st Division, Loring's:	
Featherston's Brigade	1,500
Adams's Brigade	1,500
Scott's Brigade	1,200
Total	4,200
2nd Division, French's:	
Cockrell's Brigade	2,000
McNair's Brigade	1,000
Sears's Brigade	1,200
Total	4,200
3rd Division, Walthall's:	
Cantey's Brigade	2,000
Ector's Brigade	1,000***
Quarles's Brigade	1,000
Total	4,000
Total Stewart's Corps	12,400
Grand Total	44,400

*OR, series I, vol. 38, part V, serial 76, pp. 178–89.

**Jackson's Brigade was broken up and the majority of its regiments were temporarily attached to Gist's Brigade.

***Should have said "Reynolds's Arkansas Brigade."

BIBLIOGRAPHY

Primary Sources
Treatises and Official Records

Atlas to Accompany the Official Records of the Union and Confederate Armies in the War of the Rebellion. Washington, DC: Government Printing Office, 1891.

"Capture of Colors of 31st Miss.at Peachtree Creek, The Army of The Cumberland," National Archives, Washington, DC.

"Cockrell's Brigade Casualties at Peach Tree Creek," National Archives, microfilm 1045, roll 1 (old microfilm roll 22, box 15), Tennessee State Library and Archives, Nashville.

"Compiled Service Records of Confederate Soldiers Who Served in Organizations from the Union and Confederate States of America during the War of the Rebellion," record group 269, National Archives, Washington, DC.

Congress of the Confederate States of America. *Journal of the Congress of the Confederate States of America*. 1861–1865. 7 volumes. Washington, DC: US Government Printing Office, 1904–1905.

Featherston, Winfield Scott. "Official Report of the Tennessee Campaign," subject file, Manuscript Division, Tennessee State Library and Archives, Nashville.

"Featherson's Brigade Casualties at Peach Tree Creek," microfilm 1045, roll 2, Tennessee State Library and Archives, Nashville.

"Inspection Reports and Related Records Received by the Inspection Branch in the Confederate Adjutant and Inspector General's Office, Featherston's Brigade, Loring's Division, Stewart's Corps, Army of Tennessee." 20 August 1864 and 22 September 1864, microfilm M935, roll 1, National Archives, Washington, DC. Courtesy of James Odgen, Historian, Chickamauga and Chattanooga National Military Park, US Department of the Interior.

John Bell Hood Letters. Record group 9, volume 33, record 151, box 15–16, Mississippi Department of Archives and History, Jackson, Mississippi.

Johnston, Henry Phelps, compiler. *Record of Service of Connecticut Men in the Army and Navy of the United States during the War of the Rebellion*. Hartford CT: Case, Lockwood & Brainard, 1889.

Medical & Surgical History of the War of the Rebellion, Part 3, Surgical Volume 2. Washington, DC: US Government Printing Office, 1870.

Power, J. L., compiler. Army of Mississippi recently organized regiments and battalions under requisition of 7,000, 8 May 1862, record group 9, volume 33, record 151, box 15–16, Mississippi Department of Archives and History, Jackson, Mississippi.

———, compiler. J. L. Power 1864 Scrapbook, file z 742v, record group 9, volume 33, record 151, box 8, Mississippi Department of Archives and History, Jackson, Mississippi.

———, compiler. J. L. Power and Family Papers, file z 0100.000s, record group 9, volume 33, record 151, box 8, Mississippi Department of Archives and History, Jackson, Mississippi.

———, compiler. List of engagements in Mississippi, record group 9, volume 33, record 151, box 15–16, Mississippi Department of Archives and History, Jackson, Mississippi.

————, compiler. Mississippi Casualties at Gettysburg, & letter dated March 9, 1907 presumably by Power; record group 9, volume 33, record 151, box 15–16, Mississippi Department of Archives and History, Jackson, Mississippi.

————, compiler. Return of Breckinridge's division, 21 July 1862, record group 9, volume 33, record 151, box 15–16, Mississippi Department of Archives and History, Jackson, Mississippi.

"Quarterly Report of Deceased Soldiers of 31st Regt. Miss. Volume for the 3rd Quarter of the year 1862," Compiled Service Records, RG 269, roll 341, Mississippi Department of Archives and History, Jackson, Mississippi.

"Record of Union Battlefield Burials, Atlanta Campaign," Marietta National Cemetery, Marietta, Georgia.

Rice, F. "Grand Summary of Casualties in Cheatham's Division," Benjamin F. Cheatham Papers, Tennessee State Library and Archives, Nashville.

Roster of Confederate cemetery in Chattanooga, Tennessee, National Park Service, Chattanooga.

"Scott's Brigade Casualties at Peach Tree Creek," microfilm 1045, roll 2, Tennessee State Library and Archives, Nashville.

Supplement to the Official Records of the Union and Confederate Armies. Wilmington NC: Broadfoot Publishing Company, 1995–2001.

Thackery, David T. *A Light and Uncertain Hold, A History of the 66th Ohio Volunteer Infantry.*

Thomas, J. D. and L. F. Burks, *Chairman His. Comm. Camp Rodes*, 22 February 1897, Roll of the Tuscaloosa Plow Boys, Company G, 38th Tennessee Infantry Regiment.

United States Department of the Interior. "Atlanta Campaign." Kennesaw Mountain National Battlefield Park, Kennesaw, Georgia.

United States National Archives and Records Administration. "Sixth Census of the United States, 1840." Microfilm M704.

————. "Seventh Census of the United States, 1850." Microfilm M432.

————. "Eighth Census of the United States, 1860." Microfilm M653.

United States Naval observatory records and vertical files, US Naval Academy, Nimitz Library, Annapolis, Maryland.

United States War Department, compiler. *The Official Military Atlas of the Civil War.* Washington, DC: Government Printing Office, 1891.

————, compiler. *Official Records of the Union and Confederate Armies in the War of the Rebellion.* 128 volumes. Washington, DC: Government Printing Office, 1880–1901.

Diaries, Journals, Personal Accounts, and Letters

"Appomattox." Untitled article, *Richmond Dispatch*, quoted in the *Macon Daily Telegraph*, 4 August 1864, Washington Library, Macon, Georgia.

Bainbury, Chester. *Bainbury's Civil War Diary.* Edited by Charles Wesley Lawrence. Cleveland OH: Cleveland Plain Dealer, 1960.

T. Otis Baker Papers, Company B, 10th Mississippi Infantry, Subject files, Mississippi Department of Archives and History, Jackson, Mississippi.

Robert W. Banks Letters. Carter House Library and Museum, Franklin, Tennessee.

Banks, Robert Webb. *The Battle of Franklin, November 30, 1864. The Bloodiest Engagement of the War Between the States.* New York: The Neale Publishing Company, 1908.

Belknap, Colonel William W. *History of the Fifteenth Regiment, Iowa Veteran Volunteer Infantry.* Keokuk IA: R. B. Odgen and Son, 1887.

Bell, Rachael. Letter to Mrs. Mollie J. Bell, 8 July 1862. Thornton Collection, Special Collections, Mitchell Memorial Library, Mississippi State University, Starkville, Mississippi.

Berryhill, S. Newton. "Fresh Tidings from the Battlefield." In Ernestine Clayton Deavors, editor, *The Mississippi Poets.* Memphis: E. H. Clarke & Brother, 1922.

Berryhill, William Harvey. *The Gentle Rebel: The Civil War Letters of William Harvey Berryhill, 1st Lt., Co. D, 43rd Regt., Miss. Vols.* Edited by Mary Miles Jones and Leslie Jones Martin. Yazoo City MS: The Sassafras Press, 1982.

Bevens, William E. *Reminiscences of a Private: William E. Bevens of the First Arkansas Infantry, C.S.A.* Edited by Daniel E. Sutherland. Fayetteville: University of Arkansas Press, 1992.

Biddle, James. Diary. Burton Historical Collection, Detroit Public Library.

Biggers, J. A. Diary. 2nd Mississippi Cavalry, Subject Files, Mississippi Department of Archives and History, Jackson, Mississippi.

Binford, James R. Recollections of the 15th Regiment of Mississippi Infantry, CSA, Chickamauga and Chattanooga National Military Park Library, Subject Files.

Black, S. L. Letter to Thomas Benton Roy, 31 May 1880. In Thomas Benton Roy, "General Hardee and the Military Operations around Atlanta," *Southern Historical Society Papers* 8 (August/September 1880): 347–50.

Brown, W. C. Diary. Special Collections, Chattanooga-Hamilton County Bicentenial Library, Tennessee.

Bryan, Marquis L. Letter to wife, 16 April 1864, Coffee County Historical Society, vertical file box 13, Coffee County, Tennessee.

Captain I. A. Buck Subject File, PW-5, Cleburne's Division at Atlanta, Kennesaw National Battlefield Park, Kennesaw, Georgia.

Burnett, Major Thomas J. Letter to wife, 18 June 1864, *Georgia Journal*, 13 November 1924, Pearce Civil War Collection, Navarro College, Corsicana, Texas.

Caldwell, Frank Hollis. Reminiscences, Special Collections, Chattanooga-Hamilton County Bicentenial Library, Tennessee.

Campbell, Henry. "Three Years in the Saddle" (diary), Special Collections, Wabash College, Crawfordsville, Indiana.

Cannon, J. P. *A History of the 27th Regiment Alabama Infantry. "Bloody Banners and Barefoot Boys."* Edited by Noel Crowson and John V. Brogden. Shippensburg PA: Burd Street Press, 1997.

———. *Inside of Rebeldom: The Daily Life of a Private in the Confederate Army.* Washington, DC: National Tribune, 1900.

Carpenter, Arthur B. *Letters, Civil War Miscellaneous and Manuscripts Collection.* New Haven: Yale University Press.

Chambers, William Pitt. *Blood and Sacrifice, The Civil War Journal of a Confederate Soldier.* Edited by Richard Baumgartner Huntington WV: Blue Acorn Press, 1994.

Clark, Walter A. *Under the Stars and Bars, Or, Memories of Four Years Service with the Oglethorpes, of Augusta, Georgia.* Jonesboro GA: Freedom Hill Press, Inc., 1987.

Cline, William. Diary. Special Collections, University of Notre Dame Library.

Conner, W. H. Letter to Dunbar Rowland (state historian), 20 October 1927, 33rd Mississippi vertical files, record group 9, box 8, Mississippi Department of Archives and History, Jackson, Mississippi.

Cooper, R. C. Letters, Confederate file 37, Carter House, Franklin, Tennessee.

Sylvester, Lorna Lutes, editor. "'Gone for a Soldier': The Civil War Letters of Charles Harding Cox," *Indiana Magazine of History* 68/3 (September 1972): 181–239.

Craig, R. A. B. Letters, Confederate file 35, Carter House, Franklin, Tennessee.

Crenshaw, R. F. Letter to Ella Austin, 13 December 1860, Archives and Special Collections, J. D. Williams Library, University of Mississippi, Oxford, Mississippi.

Crittenden, John. Letters, Center for American History, box 2, file 2 Q 491, University of Texas, (copy also available at Auburn University Library).

Crumpton, Washington Bryan. *A Book of Memories*. Montgomery AL: Baptist Mission Board, 1921.

Cutter, George H. Diary, in author's personal papers, Dalton, Georgia.

Davis, Jefferson. The Rise and Fall of the Confederate Government. 2 volumes. New York: D. Appleton & Company, 1881.

Day, D. L. *My Diary of Rambles with the 25th Massachusetts Volunteer Infantry*. Milford MA: King and Billings, 1884.

Dickinson, Charles H. Diary, Wisconsin State Historical Society, call number RSI, N 168-volume I; F 587.C48, Madison, Wisconsin.

Dillworth, Colonel W. S. Letter to editor, *Macon Daily Telegraph*, 20 June 1864, Geneological and History Department, section 100-104 N, Washington Memorial Library, Macon, Georgia.

Dixon, Mumford H. Diary. David M. Rubenstein Library, Duke University, Durham, North Carolina.

Dobbs, Josephine Manning Austin. Civil War stories as told to her by her father, Joseph Manning Austin (1853–1931). In *Confederate Reminiscences and Letters, 1861–1865*, 3–5. Volume 3. Atlanta: United Daughters of the Confederacy, 1996.

Drake, Edwin L. *The Annals of the Army of Tennessee and Early Western History*. Volume 1. Jackson TN: The Guild Bindery Press, 1878.

Dunn, Matthew A. Letters, Special Collections, section Z-1792.00f, Mississippi Department of Archives and History, Jackson, Mississippi (also available at Kennesaw Mountain National Battlefield Park, vertical files Mississippi-11, Kennesaw, Georgia).

Early, Jubal A. and Ruth H. Early. *Lieutenant General Jubal Anderson Early, C.S.A.: Autobiographical Sketch and Narrative of the War Between the States*. Philadelphia: J.B. Lippincott Company, 1912.

Elmore, Bruce. Letter to wife, 29 July 1864, MSS 673 F, Manuscript Collection, Kenan Research Center, Atlanta History Center.

Faulkinbury, Henry Newton. Diary. Mississippi Department of Archives and History, Jackson, Mississippi. Special permission by Bob Lurate.

Featherston Collection, Archives and Special Collections, J. D. Williams Library, University of Mississippi, Oxford.

Fitch, Michael H. *Echoes of the Civil War as I Hear Them*. New York: RF Fenno and Company, 1905.

Fleming, L. H., letter to Lou. 3 July 3 1864. Moseley Family Letters. Z0545.000. Manuscript Collection. Mississippi Department of Archives and History, Jackson MS.

French, Samuel G. *Two Wars*. 1901; reprinted, Huntington WV: Blue Acorn Press, 1999.

Gates, Arnold, editor. *The Rough Side of War: The Civil War Journal of Chesley A. Mosman*. Garden City NY: Basin Publishing Company, 1987.

Gill, Maynard. Letters to President Davis and General Bragg, June 1864, Compiled Service Records of Confederate Soldiers Who Served in Organizations from the Union and Confederate States of America during the War of the Rebellion, record groups 269, R 342, Mississippi Department of Archives and History, Jackson, Mississippi.

Gleeson, Ed. "New York Irish-Catholic Bricklayer in Gray. Colonel Mike Farrell Falls at Franklin," Carter House, Franklin, Tennessee.

Grant, Ulysses S. *The Civil War Memoirs of Ulysses S. Grant*. New York: C.L. Webster & Company, 1885.

Hampton, Thomas B. Letters, file 2R30, Center for American History, University of Texas at Austin.

Hapeman, Douglas, war diary.

Hazen, William B. *A Narrative of Military Service*. Boston: Ticknor and Sons, 1885.

Howard, O. O. *Autobiography of Oliver Otis Howard*. Volumes 1 and 2. New York: The Baker & Taylor Company, 1907.

Hudson, Weldon I., editor. *The Civil War Diary of William Spencer Hudson*. St. Louis: Micro-Records Publishing Co., 1973. Mississippi Department of Archives and History, Jackson, Mississippi.

Huff, Sarah, "My 80 Years in Atlanta," subject files, Atlanta History Center, Atlanta, Georgia.

Hurst, Samuel H. *Journal-History of the Seventy-Third Ohio Volunteer Infantry*.

Ives, Washington. *Civil War Journal and Letters of Serg. Washington Ives, 4th Florida C.S.A.* Transcribed and edited by Jim R. Cabaniss. Tallahassee: self-pubished, 1987. Unpublished copy of journal at vertical files, Chickamauga National Battlefield Park Library, Chickamauga, Georgia.

J. B. Sanders Subject File (Company H, 37th Mississippi), Mississippi Department of Archives and History, Jackson, Mississippi.

James W. Drane, Jr. personal papers. Crossville, Tennessee.

James M. Wilcox subject file. Folder 7, Mississippi Collection, Kennesaw Mountain National Battlefield Park, Kennesaw, Georgia.

Jennings, James Madison. Letters to Martha Kimbriel Jennings, in *The History of Webster Co., Miss.* Dallas TX: Curtis Media Corp., 1985.

Johnson____. Letter to General Johnson, 13 August 1863, Special Collections, Thornton Collection, Mitchell Memorial Library, Mississippi State University, Starkville, Mississippi.

Johnson, J. N. Reminiscences. *Confederate Reminiscences and Letters, 1861–1865*, 83–85. Volume 15. Atlanta: United Daughters of the Confederacy, 2000.

Johnson, R. W. *A Soldier's Reminiscences in Peace and War*. Philadelphia: J. B. Lippincott Company, 1886.

Johnson, Willa Davis. "Reminiscences of the Sixties." *Confederate Reminiscences and Letters, 1861–1865*: Georgia Division, United Daughters of the Confederacy, 1996–2000.

Johnston, Joseph E. *Narrative of Military Operations during the Late War Between the States*. New York: D. Appleton & Company, 1874.

Kellogg, Edgar Romeyn. Diary. Manuscript Collection. US Army Military History Institute, Carlisle Barracks PA.

Kennerly, James A. Letter to sister, 8 August 1864, vertical files, James Kennerly Papers, Wilson's Creek National Park Library, Republic, Missouri.

Kern, John, diary, Old Courthouse Museum, Vicksburg, Mississippi.

King, Green. Letters. Confederate file 102, Carter House, Franklin, Tennessee.

King, Jack. Letter to wife, 19 July 1864. In Mills Lane, editor, *"Dear Mother: Don't Grieve about Me. If I Get Killed, I'll Only Be Dead": Letters from Georgia Soldiers in the Civil War.* Savannah GA: Beehive Press, 1977.

Kirwan, A. D., editor. *Johnny Green of the Orphan Brigade.* Lexington: University of Kentucky Press, 1956.

Kollock, Frederick N. Diary during the war, 1864, Company B, 29th Pennsylvania, Ireland's 3rd Brigade, Geary's 2nd (White Star) Division, transcribed by Charles S. Harris, subject files, Chickamauga National Military Park Library, Chickamauga, Georgia.

Landingham, Irenus Watson. Letter to mother, 14 July 1864, folder 5, Special Collections, Auburn University Library, Auburn, Alabama.

Longacre, Glenn V., and John E. Haas, editors. *"To Battle for God & the Right": The Civil War Letters of Emerson Opdycke.* Champaign: University of Illinois Press, 2007.

Maddox, R. F. Letter, *Confederate Veteran* 8 (June 1900): 257.

Markam, Rev. Dr. Thomas R. "Tribute to the Confederate Dead," *Southern Historical Society Papers,* volume 10 (April 1882): 175.

McCall, Phil, editor. "Private Isaiah Crook Diary, 37th Ga., Smith's Brigade, Bate's Division, Hardee's Corps," vertical files, Kennesaw Mountain Battlefield Park Library, Kennesaw, Georgia.

McCuistion, Mitchell Henderson. Diary, Special Collections, University of Texas at Austin Library.

McDermid, Angus. "Letters from a Confederate Soldier," edited by Benjamin Rountree, *Georgia Review* (1964).

McElroy, Cyrus Decatur. *The Diary of a Confederate Volunteer.* San Antonio: Southern Literary Institute, 1935.

McNeilly, James H. "A Day in the Life of a Confederate Chaplain," *Confederate Veteran,* volume 26 (1918): 471.

Mannis, Jedediah and Galen R. Wilson, editors. *Bound to Be a Soldier: The Letters of Private James T. Miller, 111th Pennsylvania Infantry, 1861–1864.* Knoxville: University of Tennessee Press, 2001.

Miller, J. M. *Recollections of "A Pine Knot" in the Lost Cause.* Greenwood MS: Greenwood Publishing Company, n.d.

Montgomery, Frank Alexander. *Reminiscences of a Mississippian in Peace and War.* The Robert Clarke Company Press, 1901. Available online at docsouth.unc.edu/fpn/montgomery/montgom.html.

Mothershead, W. I. Letter, folder 5, location SG024896, Alabama Archives, Montgomery, Alabama.

Murphy, Virgil S. Letter to cousin, 21 June 1864, vertical files, Kennesaw Mountain National Battlefield Park Library, Kennesaw, Georgia.

Neal, A. J. Letter to father, 20 July 1864, pp. 28–29, vertical files, Kennesaw Mountain National Battlefield Park Library, Kennesaw, Georgia.

Nisbet, James Cooper. *4 Years on the Firing Line*. Edited by Bell Irvin Wiley. Jackson TN: McCowat-Mercer Press, 1963.

Norton, Reuben S. Journal 1861, Special Collections, Rome/Floyd County Library, Rome, Georgia.

Oldham, Martin Van Buren. *Civil War Diaries of Van Buren Oldham, Company G, 9th Tennessee, 1863–1864*. Edited and introduction by Dieter C. Ullrich. Martin: University of Tennessee at Martin Library, 1998.

Otto, John Henry. *Memoirs of a Dutch Mudsill*. Edited by David Gould and James B. Kennedy. Kent OH: Kent State University Press, 2004.

P. C. Key Family Letters. Hargrett Rare Book and Manuscript Library, University of Georgia.

Palmer, Solomon. Diary, subject file PW-51, Kennesaw National Battlefield Park, Kennesaw, Georgia.

Park, Horace. Letters, file Ms 2386, Hargrett Rare Book and Manuscript Library, University of Georgia, Athens, Georiga.

Phisterer, Frederick. Manuscript. Larew-Phisterer Family Papers, US Army Military History Institute, Carlisle Barracks PA.

Pierson, Stephen. "From Chattanooga to Atlanta in 1864–A Personal Reminiscence (1907)," *Proceedings New Jersey Historical Society*, volume 16 (1931): 506–43.

Porter, Albert Quincy. Diary. Z0565.000. Manuscript Collection. MDAH.

Power, J. L. 1864 scrapbook, Mississippi Department of Archives and History, Jackson, Mississippi.

Pressnall, James S. Memoirs, subject files, Carter House, Franklin, Tennessee.

Priest, John Michael editor. *John T. McMahon's Diary of the 136th New York, 1861–1864*. Shippensburg PA: White Mane Publishing Company, 1993.

Rice, Ralsa C. *Yankee Tigers, through the Civil War with the 125th Ohio*. Edited by Richard A. Baumgartner and Larry M. Strayer. Huntington WV: Blue Acorn Press, 1992.

Rorer, Walter A. Letters. Transcribed by T. Glover Roberts. Carter House, Franklin, Tennessee.

Roundtree, Benjamin, editor. "Letters from a Confederate Soldier," *Georgia Review*, volume 28 (Fall 1964): 267.

Roy, T. B. "General Hardee and the Military Operations Around Atlanta," *Southern Historical Society Papers*, volume 8 (January 1880): 382.

Sherman, William T. *Marching through Georgia, William T. Sherman's Personal Narrative of His March through Georgia*. Edited by Mills Lane. New York: Behive Press/Arno Press, 1978.

Shoup, F. A. "Works at the Chattahoochee River," *Confederate Veteran*, volume 3 (January 1895): 262–65.

Smith, Benjamin L., Jr. Autobiography, Confederate vertical files, Carnton Archives, Franklin, Tennessee (copy also available in author's personal papers, Dalton, Georgia).

Smith, Elias. Letter to Sydney Howard Gay, 31 May 1864, MS 0475, Sydney Howard Gay Papers, Columbia University, Butlery Library, New York, New York.

Smith, Robert Davis. Diary. Special Collections, Chattanooga-Hamilton County Bicentenial Library, Tennessee.

Stephens, M. D. L. "Recollections of 31st Mississippi," Special Collections, record group 9, volume 136, record group 151, box 20, section 3-289, Mississippi Department of Archives and History, Jackson, Mississippi.

———. A Brief History of the Stephens Family, 14 February 1911, copy in author's personal papers, Dalton, Georgia.

———. *A History of Calhoun County.* Transcribed by Ken Nail. Pittsboro MS: Calhoun County School District, 1975.

Stevenson, Carter L., to T. A. Stevenson, 28 August 1885, Special Collections, David M. Rubenstein Rare Books and Manuscript Library, Duke University, Durham, North Carolina.

Stewart, Alexander P. "Address to his Corps," *Macon Daily Telegraph*, 2 August 1864, Washington Memorial Library, Macon, Georgia.

Sykes, Columbus. Letters to wife, Columbus Sykes subject file MI-4, p. 30A, Kennesaw National Battlefield Park Library, Kennesaw, Georgia.

Thomas, Jim. "Soldiers of Florida," vertical files, Chickamauga National Military Park Library, Chickamauga, Georgia.

Thompson, J. C. Letter to A. P. Stewart, 8 December 1867, box 1, folder 5, Joseph E. Johnston Collection, Earl Gregg Swem Library, College of William & Mary, Williamsburg, Virginia.

Thompson, W. C. "From the Defenses of Atlanta to a Federal Prison Camp," *Civil War Times Illustrated* 3/10 (February 1965): 40–44.

Thornton, Solomon M. Letters, Special Collections, Thornton Collection, Mitchell Memorial Library, Mississippi State University, Starkville, Mississippi.

Tower, Lockwood, editor. *A Carolinian Goes to War: The Civil War Narrative of Arthur Middleton Manigault, Brigadier General.* Columbia: University of South Carolina Press, 1964.

Tuttle, Miletus. Letters, Hargrett Rare Book and Manuscript Library, University of Georgia, Athens, Georgia.

Walthall Collection, Archives and Special Collections, J. D. Williams Library, University of Mississippi, Oxford, Mississippi.

Warren, George. Diary.

Watkins, Sam R. *Co. Aytch.* Chattanooga TN: Times Printing Company, 1900.

Watson, James. "Private Watson Writes Home," *The Webster Progress* (Bellfontane MS), 15 July 1937, James Watson subject file (private, Company B, 31st Mississippi Infantry), Kennesaw Mountain National Military Park Library, Kennesaw, Georgia.

Watson, Joel Calvin. Diary. Special Collections, Grenada Public Library, Grenada, Mississippi.

Wiggins, Sarah Woolfolk, editor. *The Journals of Josiah Gorgas, 1857–1878.* Tuscaloosa and London: University of Alabama Press, 1995.

Wilkes, Abner James. "A Short History of My Life in the Late War between the North and the South, 46th Mississippi, Sears' Brigade," Wilson's Creek National Battlefield Park Library, Republic, Missouri.

William A. Drennan Papers. File Z-131, Special Collections, Mississippi Department of Archives and History, Jackson, Mississippi.

Winkler, Frederick C. Civil War letters, American Civil War Collection, Dakota State University, Madison, South Dakota.

Womack, William A. Diary. Author's personal papers, Dalton, Georgia.

Wood, James. "Report of the Operations of the 3rd Brigade, 3rd Division of the XX Army Corps," in *The Atlanta Campaign of 1864*. Albany NY: Weed, Parsons & Company, Printers, 1889.

Wood, J. B. Letters to Sarah Wood. Author's personal papers, Dalton, Georgia.

Worsham, J. W. Reminiscences of the battle around Atlanta. In *Confederate Reminiscences and Letters, 1861–1865*. Volume 3. Atlanta: United Daughters of the Confederacy, 1996. Courtesy of Chickamauga National Battlefield Park Library.

Wyatt, J. N. Letter to J. B. Cunningham, 10 August 1864. *Confederate Veteran*, volume 5 (1897): 521.

Younger, Edward, editor. *The Diary of Robert Garlick Hill Kean*. New York: Oxford University Press, 1957.

Racine Boy Letter to Friend T., 21 July 1864, subject file PW-4, Kennesaw Mountain National Battlefield Park, Georgia.

A. J. Neal Papers, Emory University Archives, Atlanta, Georgia.

Secondary Sources
Newspapers and Periodicals
The Atlanta Journal
Atlanta Appeal
Augusta Daily Chronicle and Sentinel
Binghamton Standard
The Chattanooga Daily Rebel
Tribune
Daily Commercial
Cincinnati Daily Gazette
Clarion-Ledger Jackson Daily News
Columbus Crisis
Columbus Sentential
Confederate Veteran Magazine
Daily Southern Crisis
Georgia Journal & Messenger
Harper's Weekly
Ithaca Journal
National Tribune
New York Herald
New York Times
New York Tribune
New York Weekly Tribune
Daily Intelligencer
Macon Daily Telegraph
Meridian Star
The Ottawa Illinois Republican
Savannah Republican
Southern Historical Society Papers
The Pantagraph
Tri-Weekly Citizen

Walker County Messenger
Wyoming Mirror
Yalobusha Pioneer

Published Books and Articles

Adamson, A. P. *Brief History of the 30th Georgia Regiment.* Jonesboro GA: Freedom Hill Press, 1987.

Adolphson, Steven J. "An Incident of Valor in the Battle of Peach Tree Creek, 1864, (The 104th Illinois)," *Georgia Historical Quarterly*, volume 57 (1973): 406–20.

Allendorf, Donald. *Long Road to Liberty, The Odyssey of a German Regiment in the Yankee Army: The 15th Missouri Volunteer Infantry.* Kent OH: Kent State University Press, 2006.

Anders, Leslie. *The Eighteenth Missouri.* Indianapolis, Bobbs-Merrill, 1968.

Andrews, J. Cutler. *The North Reports the Civil War.* Pittsburgh: University of Pittsburgh Press, 1955.

Aten, Henry J. *History of the Eighty-Fifth Regiment, Illinois Volunteer Infantry.* Hiawatha KS: Regimental Association, 1901.

Bailey, Ronald H. *The Civil War: Battles for Atlanta, Sherman Moves East.* Alexandria VA: Time-Life Books, 1985.

Banning, Leroy F. *Regimental History of the 35th Alabama Infantry, 1862–1865.* Bowie MD: Heritage Books, 1999.

Barnard, George N. *Photographic Views of Sherman's Campaign.* New York: Dover Press, 1977.

Barnard, Harry V. *Tattered Volunteers: The Twenty-Seventh Alabama Regiment, C.S.A.* Northport AL: Hermitage Press, 1965.

Bass, Ronald R. *History of the 31st Arkansas Confederate Infantry.* Conway: Arkansas Research Press, 1996.

Bates, Samuel Penniman. *History of Pennsylvania Volunteers, 1861–1865.* 5 volumes. Philadelphia: T.H. Davis & Company, 1875.

Bearss, Edwin C. *The Campaign for Vicksburg.* 3 volumes. Dayton OH: Morningside Press, 1985.

Bearss, Margie Riddle. *Sherman's Forgotten Campaign: The Meridian Expedition.* Baltimore: Gateway Press, 1987.

Beaudot, William J. K. *The 24th Wisconsin Infantry in the Civil War: The Biography of a Regiment.* Mechanicsburg PA: Stackpole Books, 2003.

Bennett, Lyman G., and William M. Haigh. *History of the 36th Regiment Illinois Volunteers during the War of the Rebellion.* Aurora IL: Knickerbocker & Hodder, 1876.

Bergeron, Arthur W., Jr., and Clement Hoffman Stevens, "The Confederate General." In William C. Davis, editor, *The End of an Era.* Six volumes. (Garden City NY: Doubleday, 1984)Bettersworth, John K., editor. *Mississippi in the Confederacy as They Saw It.* 2 volumes. Baton Rouge: Brepolis Publishers, 1961

Bevier, R. S. *History of the First and Second Missouri Confederate Brigades, 1861–1865, and from Wakarusa to Appomattox, a Military Anagraph.* St. Louis: Bryan, Brand & Company, 1879.

Blackburn, Theodore W. *Letters from the Front: A Union "Preacher" Regiment (74th Ohio) in the Civil War.* Dayton OH: Press of Morningside House, 1981.

Bollet, Alfred J. "The Truth About Civil War Surgery," *Civil War Times* 43/4 (October 2004): 34–41.

Bonds, Russell S. *War Like the Thunderbolt*. Yardley PA: Westholme Publishing, 2009.

Bowen, Oscar du Bose. *Gospel Ministry of Forty Years*. Handsboro MS.

Bowers, John. *Chickamauga and Chattanooga: The Battles that Doomed the Confederacy*. New York: Harper Collins, 1994.

Bowman, John S. editor. *The Civil War Day by Day*. New York: Dorset Press, 1989.

Boyle, John Richards. *Soldiers True: The Story of the One Hundred and Eleventh Regiment Pennsylvania Veteran Volunteers and of Its Campaigns in the War for the Union, 1861–1885*. New York: Eaton & Mains; Cincinnati: Jennings & Pye, 1903.

Bradford, Ned, editor. *Battles and Leaders of the Civil War*. New York: The Fairfax Press, 1979.

Bradley, G. S. *The Star Corps, 22nd Wisconsin*.

Bradley, James. *The Confederate Mail Carrier*. Mexico MO: James Bradley, 1894.

Bradley, Mark L., editor. "The Battle of Bentonville. As Described by Another Eye-Witness–A Native of North Carolina–Now a Distinguished Citizen of Arkansas." *Civil War Regiments: A Journal of the American Civil War* 6/1 (1998): 93–106.

Brant, J. E. *History of the Eighty-Fifth Indiana Volunteer Infantry, Its Organization, Campaigns and Battles*. Bloomington IN: Indiana University Press, 1902.

Brewer, Willis. *Alabama: Her History, Resources, War Record, and Public Men, from 1540 to 1872*. Montgomery AL: Barrett & Brown, 1872.

Brown, Edmund R. *A History of the 27th Indiana*. Monticello IN: Edmund R. Brown, 1899.

Brown, Thaddeus C. S., Samuel J. Murphy, and William G. Putney. *Behind the Guns: The History of Battery I, 2nd Regiment, Illinois Light Artillery*. Carbondale: Southern Illinois University Press, 1965.

Bryant, Edwin E. *Third Wisconsin Veterans, 1861–1865*. Madison WI: Democrat Printing Company, 1891.

Buell, Thomas B. *The Warrior Generals, Combat Leadership in the Civil War*. Pittsburgh: Three Rivers Press 1997.

Busey, John W., and Martin, David G. *Regimental Strengths and Losses at Gettysburg*. 4th edition. Hightstown NJ: Longstreet House, 2005.

Calkins, William Wirt. *The History of the One Hundred and Fourth Regiment of Illinois Volunteer Infantry, War of the Great Rebellion, 1862–1865*. Chicago: Donohue & Henneberry, 1895.

Cannan, John. *The Atlanta Campaign, May–November, 1864*. Conshohocken PA: Combined Publishing, 1991.

Carlock, Chuck. *History of The Tenth Texas Cavalry (Dismounted) Regiment, 1861–1865*. North Richland Hills TX: Bibal Press, 2001.

Carroon, Robert G., editor. *From Freeman's Ford to Bentonville, The 61st Ohio Volunteer Infantry*. Shippensburg PA: Burd Street Press, 1998.

Carter, Samuel, III. *The Siege of Atlanta, 1864*. New York: St. Martin's Press, 1973.

Carter, W. R. *History of the First Regiment of Tennessee Volunteer Cavalry in the Great War of the Rebellion, With the Armies of the Ohio and Cumberland, under Generals Morgan, Rosecrans, Thomas, Stanley and Wilson, 1862–1865*. Knoxville: Gaut-Ogden Company Printers, 1902.

Castel, Albert. *Decision in the West: The Atlanta Campaign of 1864*. Lawrence: University Press of Kansas, 1992.

Cate, Jean M., editor. *"If I Live to Come Home": The Civil War Letters of Sergeant John March Cate*. Pittsburgh: Dorrance Publishing Company, 1995.

Cate, Wirt Armistead, editor. *Two Soldiers: The Campaign Diaries of Thomas J. Key, C.S.A. and Robert J. Campbell, U.S.A.* Chapel Hill: University of North Carolina Press, 1938.

Catton, Bruce. *The American Heritage New History of the Civil War*. Edited by James M. McPherson. New York: Penguin, 1996.

———. *A Stillness at Appomattox*. Garden City NY: Doubleday, 1954.

Charnley, Jeffrey. "Neglected Honor: The Life of General A. S. Williams of Michigan (1810–1878)." Ph.D. dissertation, Michigan State University, 1983.

Cisco, Walter Brian. *States Rights Gist: A South Carolina General of the Civil War*. Shippensburg PA: White Mane Publishing Company, 1991.

Clark, Charles T. *Opdycke Tigers, 125th O. V. I.: A History of the Regiment and of the Campaigns and Battles of the Army of the Cumberland.*

von Clausewitz, Karl. *On War*. Translated by James John Graham. London: N. Trübner, 1873.

Clemmer, Gregg S. *Valor in Gray: Confederates who Received the Medal of Honor.*

Coffey, David. *John Bell Hood and the Struggle for Atlanta*. Abilene TX: McWhiney Foundation Press and McMurry University, 1998.

Coggins, Jack. *Arms & Equipment of the Civil War*. Garden City NY: Doubleday, 1962.

Coleman, Kenneth. *A History of Georgia*. Athens: University of Georgia Press, 1977.

Collins, John L. "Gallant Mike Farrell," *Confederate Veteran* 34/10 (1926): 372.

Commager, Henry Steele, editor. *The Blue & the Gray*. New York: The Fairfax Press, 1982.

Connecticut Adjutant General's Office. *Record of Service of Connecticut Men in the Army and Navy of the United States during the War of the Rebellion*. Hartford CT: Press of the Case, Lockwood & Braintwood Co., 1889.

Connelly, Thomas L. *Army of the Heartland, The Army of Tennessee, 1861–1862*. Baton Rouge: Louisiana State Press, 1967.

———. *Autumn of Glory, The Army of Tennessee, 1862–1865*. Baton Rouge: Louisiana State Press, 1971.

———. *The Marble Man: Robert E. Lee and his Image in American Society*. Baton Rouge: Louisiana State Press, 1977.

Connolly, James A. *Three Years in the Army of the Cumberland*. Bloomington: Indiana University Press, 1959.

Cope, Alexis. *The 15th Ohio and Its Campaigns, War of 1861–5*. Columbus OH: Alexis Cope, 1916.

Cox, Jacob D. *Atlanta*. 1903; reprinted, Dayton OH: Morningside Press, 1987.

Cozzens, Peter. *The Battle of Chickamauga: This Terrible Sound*. Champaign: University of Illinois Press, 1996.

———. *The Battles for Chattanooga, The Shipwreck of Their Hopes*. Champaign: University of Illinois Press, 1994.

Crabb, Martha L. *All Afire to Fight: The Untold Tale of the Civil War's Ninth Texas Cavalry*. New York: First Post Road Press, 2000.

Cram, George F. *Soldiering with Sherman, The Civil War Letters of George F. Cram*. Edited by Jennifer Cain Bornstedt. DeKalb: Northern Illinois University Press, 2000.

Crute, Joseph H. Jr. *Units of the Confederate States Army*. Midlothian VA: Derwent Books, 1987.

Cubbison, Douglas R. "'A Hard Nut To Crack': The Siege of Decatur, Alabama, October 26–29, 1864," *Columbiad: A Quarterly Review of the War Between the States* 2/1 (Spring 1998): 97–115.

Cunningham, H. H. *Doctors in Gray: The Confederate Medical Service.* Baton Rouge: Louisiana State Press, 1958.

Cunningham, O. Edward. *Shiloh and the Western Campaign of 1862.* New York: Savas Beatie, 2007.

Daniel, Larry J. *Shiloh, The Battle that Changed the War.* New York: Simon & Schuster, 1997.

Daniel, Larry J. *Cannoneers in Gray: The Field Artillery of the Army of Tennessee.* Tuscaloosa: University of Alabama Press, 2005.

Davis, Burke. *The Civil War, Strange and Fascinating Facts.* New York: Fairfax Press, 1982.

Davis, Stephen. *Atlanta Will Fall: Sherman, Joe Johnston, and the Yankee Heavy Battalions.* Wilmington DE: Rowman &Littlefield, 2001.

———. "A Reappraisal of the Generalship of John Bell Hood in the Battles for Atlanta." In Theodore P. Savas and David A. Woodbury, editors, The Campaign for Atlanta & Sherman's March to the Sea, Volumes I & II, Essays of the American Civil War. Campbell CA: Savas Woobury Publishers, 1994.

———. "How Many Civilians Died in Sherman's Bombardment of Atlanta?," *Atlanta History: A Journal of Georgia and the South* 45/4 (2003): 4–23.

———. "So Much for Historical Accuracy: The Misplacement of the Howell Battery Marker," 27 July 1997, author's personal papers, Dalton, Georgia.

Davis, William C. *The Commanders of the Civil War.* New York: Smithmark, 1991.

———. *The Orphan Brigade: The Kentucky Confederates Who Couldn't Go Home.*

———, and Bell I. Wiley. *The Image of War, 1861–65.* 6 volumes. New York: Doubleday, 1981–1983. (Reprint in 2 vols: New York: Black Dog and Leventhal, 1994.)

Dodge, Grenville. *The Battle of Atlanta and Other Campaigns.* Council Bluffs IA: The Monarch Printing Company, 1911.

Dodge, Grenville M. "The Late Gen. J. M. Schofield," *Confederate Veteran*, volume 14 (October 1907).

Dodson, William Carey. *Campaigns of Wheeler and His Cavalry, 1862–1865.* 1899; reprint, Jackson TN: The Guild Bindery Press, 1980.

DuBose, John Witherspoon. *General Joseph Wheeler and the Army of Tennessee.* New York: The Neale Publishing Company, 1912.

Dwight, Captain Henry. "How We Fight at Atlanta," *Harper's New Monthly Magazine*, volume 29 (October 1864): 939–43.

Dyer, John P. *The Gallant Hood.* Indianapolis: Bobbs-Merrill Company, Inc., 1950.

Eddy, Thomas Mears. *The Patriotism of Illinois.* 2 volumes. Chicago: Clark & Co., 1865–1866.

Elliott, Sam Davis. *Soldier of Tennessee, General Alexander P. Stewart and the Civil War in the West.* Baton Rouge: Louisiana State Press, 1999.

Evans, Clement Anselm, editor. *Confederate Military History.* 19 volumes. 1899; reprint, Wilmington NC: Broadfoot Publishing Company, 1987.

Evans, David. *Sherman's Horsemen: Union Cavalry Operations in the Atlanta Campaign.* Bloomington: Indiana University Press, 1996.

Fellman, Michael. *The Making of Robert E. Lee.* New York: Random House, 2000.

Fenton, E. B. "From the Rapidan to Atlanta. Leaves from the Diary of Commpanion E. B. Fenton, Late Twentieth Connecticut Volunteer Infantry. Read before the Commandery of the State of Michigan MOLLUS, Detroit, April 6th, 1893." In Sydney C. Kerksis, editor, *The Atlanta Papers*, 213–34. Dayton OH: Morningside Books, 1980.

Ferguson, Edwin L. *Sumner County, Tennessee in the Civil War*. Edited by Diane Payne. Tompkinsville KY: Monroe County Press, 1972.

Ferguson, John Hill. *On to Atlanta, The Civil War Diaries of John Hill Ferguson, 10th Illinois Regiment of Volunteers*. Lincoln: University of Nebraska Press, 2001.

Fitch, John. *Annals of the Army of the Cumberland*. Philadelphia: J. B. Lippincott & Company, 1864.

Fleharty, S. F. *A History of the 102nd Illinois Infantry Volunteers*. Chicago: 1865.

Fleming, James R. *Band of Brothers: A History of Company C, 9th Tennessee Regiment*.

———. *The Confederate Ninth Tennessee Infantry*. Gretna LA: Pelican Publishing Company, 2006.

Foner, Eric. *Free Soil, Free Labor, Free Men: The Ideology of the Republican Party before the Civil War*. New York: Oxford University Press, 1995.

Foote, Shelby. *Fort Sumter to Perryville*. Volume 1 of *The Civil War: A Narrative*. New York: Vintage Books. 1958.

Foster, John Y. *New Jersey and the Rebellion*. Newark NJ: 1868.

Foster, Samuel T. *One of Cleburne's Command, The Civil War Reminiscences and Diary of Captain Samuel T. Foster, Granbury's Texas Brigade, C.S.A.* Edited by Norman D. Brown. Austin: University of Texas Press, 1980.

Fowler, John D. *Mountaineers in Gray: The Nineteenth Tennessee Volunteer Infantry Regiment, C.S.A.* Knoxville: University of Tennessee Press, 2004.

Fox, William F. *Regimental Losses in the American Civil War, 1861–1865*. Albany NY: Albany Publishing Company, 1889.

Fryman, Robert J. "Fortifying the Landscape, An Archaeological Study of Military Engineering and the Atlanta Campaign." In Clarence R. Geier and Stephen R. Potter, editors, *Archaeological Perspectives on the American Civil War*, 43–55. Gainesville: University Press of Florida, 2002.

Garrett, Franklin. *Atlanta and Its Environs*. 2 volumes. Athens: University of Georgia Press, 1954.

Garrison, Web. *Atlanta and the War*. Nashville: Rutledge Hill Press, 1995.

Gillum, Jamie. *An Eyewitness History of the 16th Regiment Tennessee Volunteers, May 1861–May 1865*. Self-published, 2005.

Glass, F. M. "Long Creek Rifles: A Brief History." Sallis MS: Long Creek Rifles Chapter, United Daughters of the Confederacy, 1909.

Govan, Gilbert Eaton, and James W. Livingood. *A Different Valor: The Story of General Joseph E. Johnston, C.S.A.* New York: Bobbs-Merrill, 1956.

Goodson, Gary Ray, Sr. *Georgia Confederate 7,000, Army of Tennessee, Part II: Letters and Diaries*. Shawnee CO: Goodson Enterprises, 2000.

Goodspeed, Wilbur. *Biographical and Historical Memoirs of Mississippi*. Chicago: Goodspeed Publishing Co., 1891.

Gottschalk, Phil. *In Deadly Earnest*. Columbia MO: Missouri River Press, 1991.

Gresham, Matilda McGrain. *Life of Walter Quintin Gresham, 1832–1895*. 2 volumes. Chicago: Rand, McNally & Company, 1919.

Groom, Winston. *Shrouds of Glory: From Atlanta to Nashville: The Last Great Campaign of the Civil War*. New York: Atlantic Monthly, 1995.

Haas, Garland A. *To the Mountain of Fired and Beyond, The Fifty-Third Indiana Regiment from Corinth to Glory*. Carmel IN: Guild Press of Indiana, 1997.

Hafendorfer, Kenneth A. *Mill Springs, Campaign and Battle of Mill Springs, Kentucky*. Louisville KY: KH Press, 2001.

Hall, Richard. *Patriots in Disguise*. New York: Marlowe & Company, 1994.

Hart, B. H. Liddell. *Sherman*. New York: Frederick A. Praeger, Inc., 1958.

Head, Thomas A. *Campaigns and Battles of the Sixteenth Regiment, Tennessee Volunteers, 1861–1865*. Nashville: Cumberland Presbyterian Publishing House, 1885.

———. *Sumner County, Tennessee in the Civil War*. Edited by Diane Payne (self-published, 1972.

Hebert, Walter H. *Fighting Joe Hooker*. Lincoln: University of Nebraska Press, 1999.

Henderson, Lillian, editor. *Georgia Confederate Pension and Record Office. Roster of the Confederate Soldiers of Georgia, 1861–1865*. 7 volumes. Hapeville GA: Longino & Porter, 1955–1958.

Henry, Robert Selph. *"First with the Most": Forrest*. Indianapolis: Bobbs-Merrill Company, 1944.

Hewett, Janet B., editor. *The Roster of Confederate Soldiers, 1861–1865*. 16 volumes. Wilmington NC: Broadfoot Publishing Company, 1995.

Hinde, Paul. "Benj. Harrison, 23rd President, in Battle of Peachtree Creek," *Inn Dixie Magazine* (January 1937).

Hinman, Wilbur F. *The Story of the Sherman Brigade*. Alliance OH: Press of Daily Review, 1897.

Hoehling, A. A. *Last Train from Atlanta*. New York: Thomas Yoseloff, Printer, 1958.

Hood, John Bell. *Advance & Retreat*. 1880; reprinted, New York: Da Capo Press, 1993.

Horn, Stanley F. *The Army of Tennessee*. Norman: University of Oklahoma Press, 1953.

Hornady, John R. *Atlanta: Yesterday, Today and Tomorrow*. Atlanta: American Cities Book Company, 1922.

Howell, H. Grady, Jr. *For Dixie Land I'll Take My Stand: A Muster Listing of All Known Mississippi Confederate Soldiers, Sailors and Marines*. 5 volumes. Madison MS: Chickasaw Bayou Press, 1998.

———. *Going to Meet the Yankees, A History of the "Bloody Sixth" Mississippi, C.S.A.* Jackson MS: Chickasaw Bayou Press, 1981.

———. *To Live and Die in Dixie, A History of the Third Mississippi Infantry, C.S.A.* Jackson MS: Chickasaw Bayou Press, 1991.

Hoyt, Bessie Willis, *Come When the Timber Turns*. Banner Elk NC: Pudding Stone Press, Lees-McRae College, 1983.

Hughes, Nathaniel Cheairs, Jr. *General William J. Hardee: Old Reliable*.

———. *The Pride of the Confederate Artillery, The Washington Artillery in the Army of Tennessee*. Baton Rouge: Louisiana State Press, 1997.

Hughes, Robert M. *General Johnston*. Great Commanders series. New York: D. Appleton and Company, 1893.

Jenkins, Kirk C. *The Battle Rages Higher: The Union's Fifteenth Kentucky Infantry*. Lexington: University Press of Kentucky, 2003.

Johnson, Mark W. *That Body of Brave Men, The US Regular Infantry and the Civil War in the West*. Cambridge: Da Capo Press, 2003.

Johnson, Robert Underwood, and Clarence Clough Buell, editors. *Battles and Leaders of the Civil War*. 4 volumes. New York: The Century Company, 1887–1888.

Jones, Terry L. "'The Flash of Their Guns Was a Sure Guide': The 19th Michigan Infantry in the Atlanta Campaign." In Theodore P. Savas and David A. Woodbury, editors, *The Campaign for Atlanta & Sherman's March to the Sea*, 157–95. 2 volumes. Savas Campbell CA: Woodbury Publishers, 1994.

Jordan, Weymouth T., Jr., editor. *North Carolina Troops, 1861–1865: A Roster*. 15 volumes. Raleigh NC: University Graphics, 1966–1999.

Kellogg, Mary E., editor. *Army Life of an Illinois Soldier, Including a Day by Day Record of Sherman's March to the Sea: Letters and Diary of the Late Charles W. Willis*. Washington, DC: Globe Printing Company, 1906.

Kennett, Lee. *Marching through Georgia: The Story of Soldiers & Civilians during Sherman's Campaign*. New York: Harper-Collins Publishers, 1995.

Key, William. *The Battle of Atlanta and the Georgia Campaign*. New York: Twayne Publishers, 1958.

Kimberly, Robert L., and Ephraim S. Holloway. *The 41st Ohio Veteran Volunteer Infantry in the War of the Rebellion, 1861–1865*. Huntington WV: Blue Acorn Press, 1999.

Krick, Robert K. *The Gettysburg Death Roster, The Confederate Dead at Gettysburg*. 3rd edition. Dayton OH: Morningside Press, 1981.

Lanman, Charles. *The Red Book of Michigan: A Civil, Military, and Biographical History*. Detroit: E.B. Smith & Company, 1871.

Leeper, Wesley Thurman. *Rebels Valiant: Second Arkansas Mounted Rifles*. Little Rock AR: Pioneer Press, 1964.

Lewis, Lloyd. *Sherman, Fighting Prophet*. Lincoln: University of Nebraska Press, 1993.

Lindsley, John Berrien, editor. *Military Annals of Tennessee, Confederate*. 2 volumes. Wilmington NC: Broadfoot Publishing Company, 1995.

Little, George, and James R. Maxwell. *A History of Lumsden's Battery, C.S.A.* Tuscaloosa AL: R. E. Rhodes Chapter, United Daughters of the Confederacy, 2002.

Livermore, Thomas L. *Numbers and Losses in the Civil War in America, 1861–65*, Boston: Houghton, Mifflim and Company, 1900.

Longacre, Edward G. *Cavalry of the Heartland: The Mounted Forces of the Army of Tennessee*. Yardley PA: Westholme Publishing, 2009.

Madaus, Howard Michael, and Robert D. Needham. *The Battle Flags of the Confederate Army of Tennessee*. Milwaukee Public Museum, 1976.

Marcoot, Maurice. *Five Years in the Sunny South*. St. Louis: Missouri Historical Society, 1890.

Marvin, Edwin E. *The Fifth Regiment Connecticut Volunteers, A History*. Hartford CT: Press of Wiley, Waterman & Eaton, 1889.

Mauck, Elaine C. *The Mountain Campaigns in Georgia, or War Scenes on the Western & Atlantic Railroad*. Camden SC: North Mountain Press, 1995.

McBride, John R. *History of the 33rd Indiana Veteran Volunteer Infantry*. Indianapolis: Wm. B. Burford, Printer, 1900.

McCarley, J. Britt. *The Atlanta Campaign: A Civil War Driving Tour of Atlanta-Area Battlefields*. Atlanta: Cherokee Publishing Compan, ND.

McDonough, James Lee. *Shiloh, in Hell before Night*. Knoxville: University of Tennessee Press.

————, and Thomas Connelly. *Five Tragic Hours, The Battle of Franklin.* Knoxville: University of Tennessee Press, 1983.

————, and James Pickett Jones. *War So Terrible, Sherman and Atlanta*, New York: W. W. Norton & Company, 1987.

McGee, Benjamin F. *History of the 72nd Indiana Volunteer Infantry of the Mounted Lightning Brigade.* Lafayette: S. Vater & Co., 1882.

McMorries, Edward Young. *History of the First Regiment Alabama Volunteer Infantry, C.S.A.* Montgomery: Brown Printing Company, 1904.

McMurray, W. J. *History of the Twentieth Tennessee Regiment Volunteer Infantry, C.S.A.* Nashville: Elder's Bookstore, 1976.

McMurry, Richard. *Atlanta 1864: Last Chance for the Confederacy.* Lincoln: University of Nebraska, 2000.

McMurry, Richard M. *John Bell Hood and the War for Southern Independence.* Lexington: University Press of Kentucky, 1982.

McPherson, James M. *Battle Cry of Freedom: The Civil War Era.* New York: Ballantine, 1988.

McWhiney, Grady, and Perry D. Jamieson. *Attack and Die: Civil War Military Tactics and the Southern Heritage.* Chicago: University of Alabama Press, 1982.

Meinhard, Robert W. "The First Minnesota at Gettysburg," *Gettysburg Historical Articles of Lasting Interest*, 1 July 1991, 83.

Merrill, Catharine. *The Soldier of Indiana in the War for the Union.* Indianapolis: Merrill & Company, 1869.

Merrill, C. E. "Fearful Franklin," *Nashville World*, [ca. December 1884]. Reprinted in "Save the Franklin Battlefield" (newsletter), April 2002, pp. 3–4.

Merrill, Samuel. *The Seventieth Indiana Volunteer Infantry in the War of the Rebellion.* Indianapolis: The Bowen-Merrill Company, 1900.

Miles, Jim. *Fields of Glory.* Nashville: Rutledge Hill Press, 1995.

Miller, John A. "A Memoir of the Days of '61," H. B. Simpson History Complex, Hillsboro, Texas.

Miller, Rex. *The Forgotten Regiment: A Day-by-day Account of the 55th Alabama Infantry Regiment, C.S.A., 1861–1865.* Williamsville NY: Patrex Press, 1984.

Mitchell, Joseph B. *The Badge of Gallantry.* New York: 1968.

Moe, Richard. "Narrative of the First Regiment." In *Minnesota in the Civil and Indian Wars, 1861–1865*, 1–66. Volume 1. St. Paul: Pioneer Press Company, 1891.

————. *The Last Full Measure, The Life and Death of the First Minnesota Volunteers.* New York: Henry Holt & Company Inc., 1993.

Moore, J. J. "Jackson, Mississippi, Camp Douglas," *Confederate Veteran* (June 1903).

Morris, Roy, Jr. *Sheridan: The Life and Wars of General Phil Sheridan.* New York: Crown Publishing, 1992.

Neal, Diane and Thomas Kremm. *The Lion of the South: General Thomas C. Hindman.* Macon GA: Mercer University Press, 1993.

Newlin, William H. *The Preacher Regiment, 1862–65, History of the 73rd Illinois Volunteer Infantry.* Springfield: Regimental Reunion Association of Survivors of the 73rd Illinois Infantry Volunteers, 1890.

O'Connor, Richard. *Thomas: Rock of Chickamauga.* New York: Prentice-Hall, 1948.

Obreiter, John. *The Seventy-Seventh Pennsylvania at Shiloh, History of the Regiment.* Harrison PA: Harrisburg Publishing Company, 1908.

Overmyer, Jack K. *A Stupendous Effort: The 87th Indiana in the War of the Rebellion.* Bloomington: Indiana University Press, 1997.

Owen, Thomas McAdory. *History of Alabama and Dictionary of Alabama Biography.* Volume 3. Chicago: S. J. Clarke Publishing Company, 1921.

Parks, Joseph H. *General Leonidas Polk, C.S.A.: The Fighting Bishop.* Baton Rouge: Louisiana State University Press, 1962.

Perry, Henry F. *History of the 38th Indiana Volunteer Infantry.* Palo Alto CA: F.A. Stuart, Printer, 1906.

Poole, John Randolph. *Cracker Cavaliers: The 2nd Georgia Cavalry under Wheeler and Forrest.* Macon GA: Mercer University Press, 2000.

Pula, James S. *The Sigel Regiment: A History of the 26th Wisconsin Volunteer Infantry, 1862–1865.*

Purdue, Howell and Elizabeth. *Patrick Cleburne Confederate General.* Hillsboro TX: Hill Junior College Press,1973.

Quiner, E. B. *The Military History of Wisconsin: A Record of the Civil and Military Patriotism of the State, in the War for the Union.* Chicago: Clark & Co. Publishers, 1866.

Rabb, James. *W. W. Loring. Florida's Forgotten General.* Manhattan KS: Sunflower University Press, 1996.

Reed, Wallace Putnam. *History of Atlanta.* Syracuse NY: D. Mason & Company, 1889.

Reid, Harvey. *Uncommon Soldiers: Harvey Reid and the 22nd Wisconsin March with Sherman.* Edited by Frank L. Byrne. Knoxville: University of Tennessee Press, 2001.

Rennolds, Edwin H. *A History of the Henry County Commands which Served in the Confederate States Army.* Jacksonville FL: Sun Publishing Company, 1904.

Ridley, Bromfield L. *Battles and Sketches of the Army of the Tennessee.* Mexico MO: Missouri Printing & Publishing Company, 1906.

Rietti, J. C. *Military Annals of Mississippi.* 1893; reprint, Spartanburg SC: The Reprint Company, 1976.

Robertson, John. *Michigan in the War.* Lansing MI: W. S. George & Company, 1882.

Roddy, Ray. *The Georgia Volunteer Infantry, 1861–1865.* Kearney NE: Morris Publishing, 1998.

Rollins, Richard, editor. *The Returned Battle Flags.* Redondo Beach CA: Rank & File Publications, 1995.

Rowell, John W. *Yankee Artillerymen: Through the Civil War With Eli Lilly's Indiana Battery.* Knoxville: University of Tennessee Press, 1975.

Rowland, Dunbar. *Military History of Mississippi, 1803–1898.* Edited by H. Grady Howell, Jr. Spartanburg SC: The Reprint Company, Publishers, 1978.

Roy, Thomas Benton,"General Hardee and the Military Operations Around Atlanta," *Southern Historical Society Papers*, volume 8 (August and September 1880): 347–50.

Russell, D. W. *Confederate Veteran* (February 1899).

Russell, James Michael. *Atlanta 1847–1890: City Building in the Old South and the New.* Baton Rouge: Louisiana State Press, 1988.

Sandburg, Carl. *Abraham Lincoln, The Prairie Years & The War Years.* New York: Harcourt Brace & Company, 1954.

Scaife, William R. *The Campaign for Atlanta.* Atlanta: self-published, 1993.

Schuyler, Hartley and Graham. *Illustrated Catalog of Civil War Military Goods.* New York: Dover Publications, 1985.

Bibliography

Secrest, Philip. "Resaca: For Sherman a Moment of Truth," Atlanta Historical Journal 22/1 (Spring 1978): 9–41.

Secrist, Philip L. *Sherman's 1864 Trail of Battle to Atlanta*. Macon GA: Mercer University Press, 2006.

Siegel, Alan A. *Beneath the Starry Flag, New Jersey's Civil War Experience*. New Brunswick NJ: Rutgers University Press, 2001.

Sifakis, Stewart. *Compendium of the Confederate Armies*. 10 volumes. New York: Facts on File, Inc., 1992–1995.

Smith, Timothy B. *Champion Hill, Decisive Battle for Vicksburg*. New York: Savas Beatie LLC, 2004.

———. *This Great Battlefield of Shiloh, History, Memory, and the Establishment of a Civil War National Military Park*. Knoxville: University of Tennessee Press, 2004.

Stephens, Larry D. *Bound for Glory, A History of the 30th Alabama Infantry Regiment, Confederate States of America*. Ann Arbor MI: Sheridan Books, 2005.

Stewart, Bruce H., Jr. *Invisible Hero: Patrick R. Cleburne*. Macon GA: Mercer University Press, 2009.

Stewart, Nixon B. *Dan McCook's Regiment, 52nd Ohio Volunteer Infantry, a History of the Regiment, Its Campaigns and Battles from 1862–1865*. 1900; reprint, Huntington WV: Blue Acorn Press, 1999.

Stone, Henry. "1st Wisconsin Volume Inf." In Sydney C. Kerksis, editor, *The Atlanta Papers*. Dayton OH: Morningside Press, 1980.

———. "From the Oostanaula to the Chattahoochee." In *The Mississippi Valley, Tennessee, Georgia, Alabama, 1861–1864*, edited by Military Historical Society of Massachusetts, 419. Volume 8 of *Military Historical Society of Massachusetts Papers*. Wilmington NC: Broadfoot Press, 1990.

Strayer, Larry M., and Richard A. Baumgartner, eds. *Echoes of Battle: The Atlanta Campaign*. Huntington WV: Blue Acorn Press, 1991.

Stroud, David V. *Ector's Texas Brigade and the Army of Tennessee, 1862–1865*. Longview TX: Ranger Publishing, 2004.

Sullivan, James R. *Chickamauga and Chattanooga Battlefields*. National Park Service Historical Handbook, series 25, Washington, DC: National Park Service, 1956. Chickamauga and Chattanooga National Military Park, Chickamauga, Georgia.

Sunderland, Glenn W. *Five Days to Glory: A. S. Barnes and Company*. Cranbury NJ: 1970.

Sword, Wiley. *The Confederacy's Last Hurrah*. Lawrence: University Press of Kansas, 1992.

Symonds, Craig L. *Joseph E. Johnston, a Civil War Biography*. New York: W. W. Norton & Company, 1992.

———. *Stonewall of the West, Patrick Cleburne and the Civil War*. Lawrence: University of Kansas Press, 1997.

Tennesseans in the Civil War, A Military History of Confederate and Union Units with Available Rosters of Personnel. 2 volumes. Nashville: Civil War Centennial Commission, 1964–1965.

Thatcher, M. P. *A Hundred Battles in the West*. Detroit: L. F. Kilroy, Printer, 1884.

Thomas, Emory M. *The Confederate Nation: 1861–1865*. New York: Harper Collins Publishers, 1979.

Thomas, Wilbur D. *General George H. Thomas, The Indomitable Warrior*. New York: Exposition Press, 1964.

Thompson, Ed Porter. *History of the Orphan Brigade 1861–65*. Cincinnati: Caxton Publishing House, 1868.

Thompson, Illene D. and Wilbur E. *The Seventeenth Alabama Infantry: A Regimental History and Roster*. Bowie MD: Heritage Books, Inc., 2001.

Tower, R. Lockwood, editor. *A Carolinian Goes to War, The Civil War Narrative of Arthur Middleton Manigault, Brigadier General, C. S. A*. Columbia: University of South Carolina Press, 1983.

Tucker, Glenn. *Chickamauga, Bloody Battle in the West*. Dayton OH: Bobbs-Merrill Company, 1961.

Tucker, Phillip Thomas. "The First Missouri Brigade at the Battle of Franklin," vertical files, Wilson's Creek National Park Library, Republic, Missouri.

Underwood, Adin B. *33rd Massachusetts*.

Upson, Theodore F. *With Sherman to the Sea, The Civil War Letters, Diaries and Reminisces of Theodore F. Upson*. Bloomington: Indiana University Press, 1958. Copy at Zack Henderson Library, Georgia Southern University, Statesboro, Georgia.

Van Horne, Thomas B. *History of the Army of the Cumberland*. 2 volumes. Cincinnati: Robert Clarke & Company, 1876.

Vaughan, Alfred J. *Personal Record of the Thirteenth Regiment, Tennessee Infantry, C.S.A*. Memphis: S. C. Toof & Company, 1897.

Walker, Cornelius Irvine. *Rolls and Historical Sketch of the Tenth Regiment So. Ca. Volunteers in the Army of the Confederate States*. Charleston SC: Walker, Evans, & Cogswell, 1881.

Walker, Scott. *Hell's Broke Loose in Georgia, A History of the 57th Georgia*. Athens: University of Georgia Press, 2005.

Wallace, Frederick Stephen. ["At Peachtree Creek"], *National Tribune*, 10 June 1909, Library of Congress, Washington, DC.

Warner, Ezra J. *Generals in Gray*. Baton Rouge: LSU Press, 1959–1988.

Welcher, Frank J., and Larry Liggett. *Coburn's Brigade: 85th Indiana, 33rd Indiana, 19th Michigan & 22nd Wisconsin in the Western Civil War*. Carmel IN: Carmel Press, 1999.

Wert, Jeffry D. *General James Longstreet, The Confederacy's Most Controversial Soldier*. New York: Simon & Schuster, 1993.

White, William Lee and Charles Denny Runion, editors. *Great Things Are Expected of Us: The Letters of Colonel C. Irvine Walker, 10th South Carolina Infantry, C. S. A*. Knoxville: University of Tennessee Press, 2009.

Wiley, Bell Irvin. *Embattled Confederates, An illustrated History of Southerners at War*. Illustrated and compiled by Hirst D. Milhollen. New York: Harper & Row, 1964.

———. *The Life of Johnny Reb, The Common Soldier of the Confederacy*. Baton Rouge: Louisiana State University Press, 1943.

Willett, Elbert Decatur. *History of Company B (originally Pickens Planters), 40th Alabama Regiment, Confederate States Army, 1862 to 1865*. Anniston AL: Norwood, 1902.

Williamson, David. *The Third Battalion and the 45th Mississippi Regiment*. Jefferson NC: McFarland & Company, Inc., 2004.

Williams, Alpheus Starkey. *From the Cannon's Mouth, The Civil War Letters of General Apheus S. Williams*. Edited by Milo M. Quaife. Detroit: Wayne State University Press, 1959.

Williams, T. Harry. *Lincoln and His Generals*. New York: Alfred A. Knoff, 1952.

Willis, James. *Arkansas Confederates in the Western Theater*. Dayton OH: Morningside House, 1998.

Wills, Charles Wright. *Army Life of an Illinois Soldier: One Hundred and Third Illinois*. Washington, DC: Globe Printing Company, 1906.

Wood, Edwin Orin. *History of Genesee County, Michigan, Her People, Industries and Institutions*. Indianapolis: Federal Pub. Company, 1916.

Woodhead, Henry, editor. *Voices of the Civil War—Atlanta*. Richmond: Time Life Books, 1997.

Woodworth, Steven. "A Reassessment of Confederate Command Options during the Winter of 1863–1864." In Theodore P. Savas and David A. Woodbury, *The Campaign for Atlanta & Sherman's March to the Sea, Volumes I & II, Essays of the American Civil War*. Campbell CA: Savas Woobury Publishers, 1994.

Woodworth, Steven E. *Nothing but Victory, The Army of the Tennessee*. New York: Alfred A. Knopf, 2005

Wright, George W. "Sgt. James E. Wright," *Confederate Veteran* (March–April 1993): 30–38.

Wright, Henry H. *A History of the Sixth Iowa Infantry*. Iowa City IA: State Historical Society of Iowa, 1923.

Wynne, Ben. *A Hard Trip, A History of the 15th Mississippi Infantry, CSA*. Macon GA: Mercer University Press, 2003.

Wynne, Lewis N. and Robert A. Taylor, editors. *This War So Horrible: The Civil War Diary of Hiram Smith Williams, 40th Alabama Confederate Pioneer*. Tuscaloosa AL: University of Alabama Press, 1993.

Young, Callie B. *From These Hills: A History of Pontotoc County*.

Young, L. D. *Reminiscences of a Soldier of the Orphan Brigade, June 26, 1916*. Paris KY: Louisville Courier-Journal Job Printing Company, 1918.

Zinn, John G. *The 33rd New Jersey in the Civil War, The Mutinous Regiment*. Jefferson NC: McFarland & Company, 2005.

Roster of the 2nd Ga. Battl., S.S., G.G.M. 35/1–2 (Winter/Spring 1995), vertical files, Chickamauga National Battlefield Park Library.

Internet

www.civilwararchive.com/CORPS/20thhook.htm (7 May 2006).

"128th New York Infantry Regt.," http://www.28thga.org/123ny_pictures_hq.html (4 April 2008).

"134th New York Infantry," http://www.dmna.state.ny.us/historic/reghist/civil/infantry-/134thInf/134thInfHistSketch.htm (7 May 2006).

"26th Alabama," http://www.rootsweb.ancestry.com/~alcw26/26thala.htm (20 March 2008).

www.dmna.state.ny.us/historic/reghist/civil/artillery/13thIndBat/13thIndBatTable.htm (13 April 2008).

"26th Wisconsin," http://www.russscott.com/~rscott/26thwis/26pgwk64.htm (10 November 2008).

"2nd Alabama Cavalry," http://www.archives.state.al.us/referenc/alamilor/2ndcav.html (21 December 2008).

"37th Mississippi Infantry," http://www.reynolds-genealogy.com/research/37th_mississippi_regiment.htm (15 October 2008).

"43rd Mississippi Infantry," http://43rdms.homestead.com/camel.html (27 August 2008).

"57th Alabama Flag," http://www.archives.state.al.us/referenc/flags/072.html (22 November 2008).

"57th Alabama Infantry,"
http://www.managementaides.com/my_interests/hispanic_america.htm (22 November 2008).

"6th Mississippi Infantry," http://sixthmsinf.tripod.com/index.htm (2 January 2009).

"78th Illinois Infantry," http://civilwar.ilgenweb.net/reg_html/078_reg.html (2 January 2009).

"Brookwood Hills Subdivision," http://www.buckhead.net/brookwood-hills/ (31 December 2008).

"Dahlonega Gold Ruch," www.dahlonegagagold.com/dghist.html (1 August 2008).

Davis, Burke. "The Civil War, Strange and Fascinating Facts," www.civilwarhome.com/casualties.htm (15 May 2008).

"Franklin, Tn." http://www.heritagepursuit.com/Franklin.htm (3 April 2008).

"Georgia Militia at Turner's Ferry, July 5, 1864," http://www.hmdb.org/marker.asp?marker=17022 (29 November 2009).

"History of the 28th Regiment, Pennsylvania Volunteers, Goldstream Regiment," http://www.pa-roots.com/~pacw/infantry/28th/28thorg.html. (7 May 2006).

"Indiana Regiments in the Civil War," http://www.indiana.edu/~liblilly/wpa/wpa_info.html. (16 June 2008).

"Kennesaw Mtn.," http://ourgeorgiahistory.com/ogh/Kennesaw_Mountain_National_Battlefield_Park (16 June 2008).

"Kennesaw Mtn.," http://www.nps.gov/kemo/index.htm (15 June 2008).

"The Letters and Papers of Charles Manning Furman," http://batsonsm.tripod.com/letters/letters9.html. (1 March 2008).

"McCarty, Bettie Louise, A History of Edward McCarty and His Descendants," http://www.peachtreebattlealliance.org/id52.html (10 January 2009).

Moore, Isaac V. "Our Confederate Ancestors, Co. E. 37th Ga." Edited by Ronald E. Jones, http://www.tennessee-scv.org/camp87/csa.htm (4 April 2002).

"O'Neal's Brigade, Col. Edward Asbury O'Neal," http://aotw.org/officers.php?officer_id=643; 26th Alabama Infantry, Flag (25 September 2006).

Overby, Charles A. "Georgia Gold," article in Gems and Minerals; www.goldmaps.com/east/georgia_gold_mines.htm (1 August 2008).

"Sumner Co., Tennessee in the Civil War," http://www.rootsweb.com/~tnsumner/sumnfg15.htm (1 March 2008).

Taylor, Samuel. "The Battle of Peachtree Creek." http://ngeorgia.com/history/peachtreecreek.html, (6 June 2003).

"Taylors's Rosters and Notes, Co. D, 16th South Carolina," http://www.geocities.com/BourbonStreet/Square/3873/franklin7d.html (27 August 2008).

"Texas in the Civil War," http://history-sites.com/mb/cw/txcwmb/index.cgi?noframes;read=8412 (10 February 2008).

"Timekeeping at the US Naval Observatory," http://tycho.usno.navy.mil/history.html (27 July 2008).

"Union Regimental Histories." http://www.civilwararchive.com/Unreghst/unnyinf9.htm (7 May 2006).

von Clausewitz, Carl. "On War," book 2, chapter 2, paragraph 24,
     http://en.wikipedia.org/wiki/Fog_of_war (19 April 2009).
"Weather,"
     http://www.as.ysu.edu/~wbuckler/Weather/Readings/z_time_on_weather_maps.htm
     (27 July 2008).
Williams, David. "The Georgia Gold Rush, Twenty-Niners, Cherokees, and Gold Fever,
     Colombia, S.C.," www.goldrushgallery.com/dahlmint/show_men_pic15.html, (1
     August 2008).
http://bioguide.congress.gov/scripts/biodisplay.pl?index'W000145.

Other

22nd Wisconsin, subject file PW-4, Kennesaw National Battlefield Park, Kennesaw,
     Georgia.
A. H. "A Memorial," 17 September 1896, The Drane House, French Camp, Mississippi.
Adjutant general, State of Illinois. "Report of the Adjutant General of the State of Illinois."
     In Jasper N. Reece and Isaac Hughes Elliot, editors, *History of One Hundred and Fifth
     Infantry*, 5:686–88. 5 volumes. Springfield IL: Phillips Bros., [1900].
Atlanta History Center, "Turning Point: The American Civil War" (exhibit).
Biggs, Greg. E-mail to author, 2, 7–8, 29–31 December 2008, in author's personal papers,
     Dalton, Georgia.
———. "The 'Shoupade' Redoubts: Joseph E. Johnston's Chattahoochee River Line," *Civil
     War Regiments, A Journal of the American Civil War* 1/3 (1990): 77–108.
Bird, Frank. Interview with author, May 2008.
"Brief History of Tupelo," *Clarion-Ledger/Jackson Daily News*, 22 Febraury 1987, 7–9.
Brown, Chuck. "The Atlanta Campaign, May 7 through September 3, 1864, with a Focus on
     the Dallas Line in Relation to Pickett's Mill" (map and time line).
Bunker, Robert M. Interview with author, July 2009.
Carlisle, Virginia Patterson, *Ye Olde Scrapbook: A Portrait of Choctaw County Before the World
     Changed*. Ackerman MS: Choctaw County Historical and Genealogical Society, Inc.,
     [1987].
Clauss, Erol. "The Atlanta Campaign, July 18, 1864." Ph.D. dissertation, Emory University,
     1965. Special Collections, Zack Henderson Library, Georgia Southern University,
     Statesboro, Georgia.
Cole, Steve. "Texas Confederate Cemetery in Clarke County, Miss.," *Our Heritage* 29/3
     (April 1988): 1–5.
Covington, Tommy, compiler and editor. *Tippah County Heritage*. Volume 2. Ripley MS:
     Tippah County Historical Genealogical Society, 1994.
Cubbison, Douglas R. "Fireworks Were Plenty, The XV and XVI Army Corps at the Battle
     of Ruff's Mill, Georgia, July 3–5, 1864," Kenan Research Center, Atlanta History
     Center, Atlanta, Georgia.
Foote, Shelby. Interview. *The Civil War: A Film by Ken Burns*. Episode 2, "A Very Bloody
     Affair" (1990).
Georgia Historical Markers. Valdosta GA: Bay Tree Grove Publishers, 1973.
Harrrison, Patrick Morgan. "Confederate Dead at Canton, MS."
     Http://msgw.org/madison/Canton/index.htm.
Heery, George and Betty. Interview by author, 27 March 2008, tape recording, in author's
     personal papers, Dalton, Georgia.

"History of the Water Valley Rifles, Company F, 15th Mississippi Infantry." Supplement to the WPA Historical Research Project, Yalobusha County, 16 February 1937, Special Collections, J. D. Williams Library, University of Mississippi, Oxford.

Jones, Eugene W., Jr. *Enlisted for the War: The Struggles of the Gallant 24th Regiment, South Carolina Volunteers, Infantry, 1861–1865.* Highstown NJ: Longstreet House, 1997.

Jones, Joseph. "Roster of the Medical Officers of the Army of Tennessee, Volume XXII, Richmond, Va. Jan.–Dec. 1894," pp. 165–274. In *Southern Historical Society Papers.* Volume 24. Richmond VA: Southern Historical Society, 1876–1943.

Julian, Allen P. "Operations through the Present Ridgewood Community, July 1864," MSS 130, box 4, folder 4, Wilbur G. Kurtz Collection, Kenan Research Center, Atlanta History Center.

Kaufman, Dave. "Riverchat," *Upper Chattahoochee Riverkeeper* (Fall 2002): 6–7.

Kaufman, David R. *Peachtree Creek: A Natural and Unnatural History of Atlanta's Watershed.* Athens: University of Georgia/Atlanta History Center, 2007.

Kincaid, Gerald Allen, Jr. "The Confederate Army: An Analysis of the Forty-Eighth Tennessee Volunteer Infantry Regiment, 1861–1865." Ph.D. dissertation, Ohio State University, 1980. Www.dtic.mil/cgi-bin/GetTRDoc?AD=ADA299772, 4 April 2013.

Kurtz, Wilbur G. "Atlanta in the Summer of 1864," *Inn Dixie Magazine* (January 1936).

———. "Battles of Atlanta," September 1895, MS 130, box 11, folder 6, Wilbur G. Kurtz Papers, Kenan Research Center, Atlanta History Center.

———. "Embattled Atlanta" (map), March 1930, MS 130, Wilbur G. Kurtz Papers, Kenan Research Center, Atlanta History Center.

———. "French's Division Hood's Left Flank," MS 15, Wilbur G. Kurtz Papers, Kenan Research Center, Atlanta History Center.

———. Typescript of markers, MS 130, box 38, Wilbur G. Kurtz Papers, Kenan Research Center, Atlanta History Center.

———. "Loring's Hill," box 55, folder 5, Wilbur G. Kurtz Papers, Kenan Research Center, Atlanta History Center.

———. "Peach Tree Dead," box 32, folder18, Wilbur G. Kurtz Papers, Kenan Research Center, Atlanta History Center.

———. "What James Bell Told Me about the Siege of Atlanta," 15 July 1935, MS 130, Wilbur G. Kurtz Papers, Kenan Research Center, Atlanta History Center.

Kurtz, Wilbur G., Sr. "Captain Thomas J. Key's Battery which was at the Battle of Peachtree Creek, July 20, 1864" (letter to members of the Atlanta Civil War Roundtable, 19 May 1955), MS 130, scrapbook 28, Wilbur G. Kurtz Papers, Kenan Research Center, Atlanta History Center.

Livingston, Melinda Burford, and Charles A. Rich. "A Treasure on the Trace—The French Camp Story." The Drane House, French Camp, Mississippi.

Long, Robert R. "A Brief History of the Battle of Peachtree Creek, July 20, 1864," in author's personal papers, Dalton, Georgia.

McCall, Phil, Private Isaiah Crook, 37th Ga. Smith's Brigade, prepared for 1998 Crook Reunion, courtesy Kennesaw Mountain Battlefield Park Library, vertical files.

McGavok Home and Cemetery records, subject files, Carnton Plantation Museum and Archives, Franklin, Tennessee.

McIntire, Carl. "Stories Reveal Old Greensboro's Bloody Legacy," *Mid-South Magazine*, 13 July 1975, 7–9.

McMurry, Richard M. "The Atlanta Campaign, December 23, 1863 to July 18, 1864." Ph.D. dissertation, Emory University, 1967, Zack Henderson Library, Georgia Southern University, Statesboro, Georgia.

Madry, Mrs. John Gray. "Battle of Peachtree Creek, July 20, 1864," MS 130, Wilbur G. Kurtz Collection, Kenan Research Center, Atlanta History Center, Atlanta, Georgia.

Mitchell, Margaret. *Gone With the Wind.* New York: Macmillan Company, 1936.

Morris, Roy, Jr., and Phil Noblitt. "The History of a Failure, Spring 1864: A Federal Army Tries to Slip through Georgia's Snake Creek Gap," vertical files, Crown Gardens and Archives, Dalton, Georgia.

Murphree, T. M. "History of Calhoun County," Special Collections, Calhoun County Library, Bruce, Mississippi.

Newspaper clipping of list of staff officers, Mississippi Department of Archives and History, Jackson, Mississippi, record group 9, vertical file 136.

Noblitt, Phil. "The Battle of Peachtree Creek," *America's Civil War* (September 1998): 39–43.

Van Nostrand, D. "How We Fight in Atlanta," 248. In Frank Moore, editor, *The Rebellion Record. A Diary of American Events.* Volume 11. New York: NP.

Orr, J. L. Proposed Senate bill on use of African Americans in Confederate military service, 30 January 1864. *Southern Historical Society Papers, New Series, No. XII, Volume L, First Congress, 4th Session.* Richmond VA: Southern Historical Society, 1953.

Osborne, Seward, Jr. "George Young: Forgotten Hero of Peach Tree Creek; North South Trader, Mar.–Apr. 1980; & Poem of The 143rd New York Vols.," Atlanta History Center, MS 612–F.

Papers of the Military Historical Society of Massachusetts, Vol VIII, The Mississippi Valley, Tennessee, Georgia, Alabama, 1861–1864. Wilmington NC: Broadfoot Publishing Company, 1989.

Popowski, Howard. "Battle of Dug Gap, May 8, 1864, Georgia Gilbraltar," Crown Gardens and Archives, Dalton, Georgia.

"Resaca Confederate Cemetery." United Daughters of the Confederacy, Georgia, 1993. Crown Gardens and Archives, Dalton, Georgia.

Rose, Kenny R. *Calhoun County, Mississippi: A Pictorial History.* Special Collections, Calhoun County Library, Bruce, Mississippi.

Simmons, Hugh. Letters to author, 20 and 22 August 2007, author's personal papers, Dalton, Georgia.

Stone, Larry. "Snake Creek Gap—Resaca," Crown Gardens and Archives, Dalton, Georgia.
———. "The Battle of Resaca (& Nance Springs)," Crown Gardens and Archives, Dalton, Georgia.

Stribbling Jimmy, compiler. "Roster of Members of the 31st Miss. Inf. Volume, Company D." In author's personal papers, Dalton, Georgia.

Thomas, Diane C. "City-Scape, Atlanta," The Magazine of the Urban South 22/4 (October 1982): 11–16.

Trammell, Randy. *Tilton. Georgia and the Civil War.* Dalton GA: self-published, 1998.

Twain, Mark, and Charles Dudley Warner. *The Gilded Age.* Chicago: American Publishing Company, 1873.

Warwick, Rick. "The Horrors of Battle of Franklin," Heritage Foundation of Franklin and Williamson County, July 2006, vertical files, The Carter House and Museum, Franklin, Tennessee.

Wetzel, C. Robert, "Mudheads," *Envoy* (newsletter), April 1999. Indianapolis: Emmanuel Christian Seminary.

William N. Nokes biographical information, Confederate file 134, Carter House and Museum, Franklin, Tennessee.

William Wing Loring subject file, Mississippi Department of Archives and History, Jackson, Mississippi.

WPA, "Records for Calhoun Co. Miss.," Mississippi Department of Archives and History, Jackson, Mississippi, record group 139, box 11, section 4, file 10654.

———. "Records for Choctaw Co. Miss.," Mississippi Department of Archives and History, Jackson, Mississippi, record 139, box 11, section 5, file 10661.

INDEX